ســ

India's New Right

*Powering the Current
Wave of Nationalism
and Civilisational Revival*

Abhijit Majumder

Copyright © 2024 Abhijit Majumder

Abhijit Majumder has asserted his rights under the Indian Copyright Act to be identified as the author of this work.

All rights reserved under the copyright conventions. No part of this publication may be reproduced or transmitted in any form or by any means, electronic or mechanical, including photocopying, recording or any information storage or retrieval system, without the prior permission in writing from the publisher.

This book is solely the responsibility of the author(s) and the publisher has had no role in the creation of the content and does not have responsibility for anything defamatory or libellous or objectionable.

BluOne Ink Pvt. Ltd does not have any control over, or responsibility for, any third-party websites referred to in this book. All internet addresses given in this book were correct at the time of going to press. The author and publisher regret any inconvenience caused if addresses have changed or sites have ceased to exist, but can accept no responsibility for any such changes.

ISBN: 978-81-968471-7-3

First published in India 2024
This edition published 2024

BluOne Ink Pvt. Ltd
A-76, 2nd Floor, Sector 136, Noida
Uttar Pradesh 201301
www.bluone.ink
publisher@bluone.ink

Kali, Occam and BluPrint are all trademarks of BluOne Ink Pvt. Ltd.

Contents

Acknowledgements	vii
Introduction: Civilisational Cyclone Alert	1
Chapter 1: New Species of 'Sanghi'	25
Chapter 2: Making Constitution Meet Civilisation	55
Chapter 3: History: The New Kurukshetra	91
Chapter 4: Whoosh of an Economic Tide	138
Chapter 5: Narrative War: Mainstream Media vs Social Media	176
Chapter 6: Reviving Hinduness in Popular Culture	229
Chapter 7: Nationalism and Mission Northeast	261
Chapter 8: Bharat's Queer and Conservative	297
Chapter 9: Our Minorities, Their Minorities	327
Chapter 10: Bharat's Giant, Waking Diaspora	374
Chapter 11: Cow, Caste, Conflict, and Conversions	399
Notes	467
About the Author	471

Acknowledgements

No book is created by the author alone. Much inspiration and perspiration go into it. Many people play a role in its birth. For *India's New Right*, I thank BluOne Ink's publishing director, Praveen Tiwari, at the outset. Without his patience and persistence, it would not have been easy for me to write the book. I also thank the excellent editing team led by Thanglenhao Haokip.

Credit to journalists Debdutta Bhattacharjee and Geetika Mishra for helping me with reams of high-quality transcription.

I am deeply grateful to RSS sah sarkaryawah Arun Kumar for making me see Bharat from a perspective I had not before. Many Sangh pracharaks, vicharaks, purna kaliks working in the remotest and most challenging zones of this nation have facelessly contributed to the book. I shall be in their debt.

I thank friends who kept prodding me to tie myself to the writing desk and finish the book.

And finally, I thank my family for always being there.

I dedicate this book to my baba, whose political views often clash with mine and from whom I have learnt to respect differences and converse across ideological chasms.

Introduction: Civilisational Cyclone Alert

Walking with bloodied feet through centuries of invasions and colonial rule, its tale twisted and retold by its oppressors, a civilisation has decided to write its own story again. This is the story of that story.

This book is about this slice of time in Bharat's life. Standing at the vanishing river-island of this moment, it is hard to count exactly how many ways it is exceptional. Since the turn of this millennium, a series of events have unfolded and conditions have unrolled leading up to it. It is a simultaneous revolt and revival that this land, known for centuries as Bharat or Hind long before India, has not witnessed since its freedom from British colonial rule in 1947. If one were to keep aside the epochal political goal of independence, the force of this civilisational resurgence could be the strongest in centuries. There is also a collective desire to move forward from the colonisation of the Indian mind.

The book's title is inaccurate, one must admit upfront. Bharat does not have a Right Wing in the Western sense. Many nationalists (or 'Indics' or 'dharmics', as many call themselves) do not endorse a pure laissez-faire economy without any protection for local industry or the poor. They have no problem with alternative sexuality, fluid gender, or abortion in the early stages if it is the mother's choice. They are all anti-Left, but one cannot define such a large and strong movement by what it is not. Many even have a problem with being narrowly defined as nationalists, as Bharat's ancient wisdom and traditions transgress the nation's boundaries into universalism. The word 'dharmic' is too morally loaded for the comfort of some. 'Indic' may not immediately connect with an international reader. So, we have used 'Right' as a convenient, portable shorthand in *India's New Right*, strictly to be understood in Bharat's context.

The new nationalists do not carry an emblem tattooed into their flesh. They are not an elite club or secret society. They are every person, everywhere—quietly wiping your floor in the morning, poring over a newspaper on the local train, teaching your child, sending forwards in your family WhatsApp group, giving you change back at a toll plaza, driving your cab, talking on TV or YouTube, playing PUBG with friends at a sleepover, ordering whisky sour at the bar, or making love to you. Say something snide about India, and they may snap at you or give you a cold glare. The awakening has been infectious, the shift in attitude palpable.

But the eddies of change are not always pretty or poetic. They can be murky, ugly, thick with bile. Alongside sophisticated intellectual combat, disruptive economic thought, and a determined cultural revival, there is vigilante justice, street lynching, and resistance of swords with swords on the frontline of religious or demographic skirmishes.

The scorching rise of India's new nationalism coincides with Narendra Modi's ascent to power. The country's small but disproportionately influential intellectual elite, which has weaponised and wielded Nehruvian secularism, abhors the movement's Hindu overtones. This mainly English-speaking class of writers, journalists, academicians, actors, Left-leaning historians, and activists calls this new nationalism an assault on minorities and the country's secular institutions.

Modi: Man in the Middle

The time this book is about cannot be captured without mentioning the man standing at the centre of this cyclonic shift—Prime Minister Narendra Damodardas Modi. He is the protagonist looming in every page, every act of this ever-unfolding story.

Some argue that his politics and persona have set off this dramatic transformation. But it is more likely the other way around. The churn of time has thrown up Narendra Modi. No individual inspires the new Right or enjoys its trust more than Prime Minister Modi.

Even from his own words, the desire to effect profound and millennial changes, to set Bharat toward a distant, gilded future, and to brush with immortality is clear.

Here are excerpts from his recent speeches, including the one delivered after the pran pratistha of the Ayodhya Ram Mandir on 22 January 2024:[1]

> 'The government's third term will lay the foundations of India for the next 1000 years.'
>
> 'January 22nd, 2024, is not a mere date on the calendar, it is the origin of a new kaal chakra [long era].'
>
> 'We have to expand our consciousness from Dev to Desh, Ram to Rashtra—from deity to nation'
>
> 'This is Bharat's time, and Bharat is now going to move forward. After centuries of anticipation, we have reached here.'

Whether it is replacing King George's Cross on the Indian Navy with an image of Chhatrapati Shivaji; renaming Aurangzeb Road, Allahabad, and Aurangabad; or installing the sengol from Tamil Nadu (the Hindu spiritual symbol of justice, transfer of power, and good governance) in the new Parliament, Modi displays an irrepressible intent to decolonise.

In a speech, he said that whenever we get a glimpse of colonial slavery, even in the tiniest of things, within us or around us, we have to liberate ourselves from it.[2]

In another speech, he mentioned:

> For India and the many nations around the world, for countless generations, living in the shackles of colonialism had been a compulsion. Since the time of India's independence, a post-colonial era started around the world. Many nations got freedom. Today, there is no country which exists ostensibly as a colony of another country. But that does not mean that the colonial mindset has ended.[3]

He also made digs at his main political opponent, the Congress, 'Who was inspired by the British? [...] If you were not influenced by the British, then why did Bharat's budget come at 5 o'clock in the evening, because the British Parliament started in the morning?'[4]

This urge to decolonise and revitalise a wounded civilisation is leaving a long, concrete trail of actions. The Modi government has spent nearly Rs 7,000 crore on 122 projects to revive civilisational places of pilgrimage. From opening the Ram Mandir to the BAPS Hindu Mandir in Abu Dhabi to the Shrinathji Temple in Bahrain, he is personally spearheading a civilisational revival. Part of that is the restoration of the

Somnath Temple in Gujarat, Char Dham, Kedarnath Temple in Uttarakhand, Kalika Temple in Delhi, Gyanvapi corridor in Kashi, Mahakal corridor in Ujjain, and the Martand Sun Temple, as well as the 700-year-old Mangaleshwar Bhairav Temple among fifteen temples in Kashmir.

Modi steers his actions along the path of Sri Aurobindo and Swami Vivekananda, who believed that 'aatma bismriti' or self-amnesia leads to 'aatma ninda' or self-abuse, 'aatma heenata' or low self-esteem, and destroys 'aatma biswas' or self-confidence.

Besides the civilisational revival, Modi's highway of self-sufficiency and national pride branches out to every sector, from yoga to millets, from patents to Make in India in defence and other sectors.

Modi has convinced this generation that the freedom struggle, which was incomplete in 1947, is now being completed.

The nationalists (Indics or dharmics) assert that their target is not minorities but the abiding and destructive minoritism of an intelligentsia fattened by seven decades of state patronage from the dynastic Centre–Left Congress party. They say their resistance is against the British and communist distortions of history, which cover up the genocide of Hindus by Islamists for centuries on a globally unparalleled scale, just for the sake of secularism. Their anger is directed against the media and academia for subverting rich pre-colonial, pre-Islamic Indian knowledge, heritage, and achievements, while unquestioningly playing the minority victimisation trope.

In modern India, the majority of Hindus have borne the brunt of partition on the basis of religion, religious violence, and discrimination as part of state policy, the dharmics argue. Their revolt has been against endemic corruption and the cornering of the nation's resources by tiny but all-powerful 'liberal', elitist networks. Perhaps for the first time, ordinary Indians are waking up and vocalising their angst about a losing 1,000-year demographic war, which has taken away Afghanistan, Pakistan, and Bangladesh from Bharat and threatens to sever more limbs.

But above all, the insurrection of India's faceless millions has been against the constant attacks on their simple day-to-day traditions, their festivals, their way of life, and the core of their spiritual existence through punishing policies, judicial whiplash, op-ed pieces, and what they view as Leftist, often foreign-funded, anti-Hindu and anti-India activism. While all this may seem like a response solely directed *against* an enemy, the new nationalism has a happy quirk. It also stands *for* something. There is a cross-disciplinary revival of pride in one's self, one's nation, one's traditions, one's civilisation, and one's place in the world.

This pride is invested in the uniquely Indian philosophical sense of 'swa-' or the self as a cultural and spiritual collective. This self is not a narrow, individual being in the Western sense, who rows through life like a forlorn boatman in the ocean. Down the ages, 'swa-' has manifested itself in swa-shiksha (own education), swa-bhasha (own language), swa-bhiman (self-respect), swa-bhoomi (own land), swa-dharma (own duties and virtues), and swa-raj (self-rule). Even during the most savage persecution, the Bhartiya civilisation has shown extraordinary resilience to keep alive and reestablish that spirit of swa-.

To understand today's resurgence, a brief journey across events and conditions that led up to this moment is necessary. It is important to trace the extensive wounding and gritty recoveries of Bharat's sense of 'swa-'. When Muslim invaders like Bakhtiyar Khilji destroyed entire universities like Nalanda, smaller educational spots came up locally. Temples, for instance, were the hubs of social, cultural, educational, and economic activity. Social structures were built around temples. Every zone had a big mandir. So, when temples were being attacked, pillaged, and destroyed, worship shifted to the home and neighbourhood or mohalla. Ramlila, Krishna raas lila, Devi puja, and other community religious functions sprung up.

Indian saints like Ramdas, Tulsidas, Chaitanya Mahaprabhu, Narsi Mehta, Guru Nanak, Namdev, and Sant Gyaneshwar were contemporaneous with the rule of Islamic dynasties like the Mughals, yet they upheld tradition, devotion, and the essence of 'swa-' undaunted.

The Islamic invasions of Bharat were among the world's most significant holocausts. In his book *Growth of Muslim Population in Medieval India*, historian K.S. Lal estimates—detailing events and studying the population of India between 1000 CE and 1500 CE—that 60 million to 80 million Hindus were slaughtered by the invaders.

Scholar Koenraad Elst writes in his book *Negation in India*:

> The Muslim conquests, down to the 16th century, were for the Hindus a pure struggle of life and death. Entire cities were burnt down and the populations massacred, with hundreds of thousands killed in every campaign, and similar numbers deported as slaves. Every new invader made (often literally) his hills of Hindu skulls. Thus, the conquest of Afghanistan

in the year 1000 was followed by the annihilation of the Hindu population; the region is still called the Hindu Kush, i.e. Hindu slaughter.

Bloodied but resilient, Bharat walked on, but one stroke of the pen did more damage to it than the slashes from a million swords.

If there was a single biggest assault on the sense of 'swa-', it was the creation of the English Education Act of 1835. Thomas Babington Macaulay was its architect. Education in Sanskrit, Arabic, and Persian was drastically defunded and relegated to the cobwebbed back shelves. English now occupied their space.

Macaulay averred:

> I have conversed, both here and at home, with men distinguished by their proficiency in the Eastern tongues.… I have never found one among them who could deny that a single shelf of a good European library was worth the whole native literature of India and Arabia.

And then he eloquently stated the purpose of the new act, which still resonates prophetically to this day:

> We must at present do our best to form a class who may be interpreters between us and the millions whom we govern; a class of persons, Indian in blood and colour, but English in taste, in opinions, in morals, and in intellect.

Nearly 200 years later, Bharat's English-speaking elite remains the most vocal opponents of decolonising the nation's mind. Even after Independence, India under its first prime minister, Jawaharlal Nehru, chose a colonial continuity in education and outsourced history and humanities to entrenched Leftist academic syndicates. History was distorted to underplay the immense achievements of pre-British, pre-Islamic Bharat, and to whitewash the flagrant genocide of Hindus, Sikhs, Jains, and Buddhists thereafter. Postulates, like the Aryan Invasion Theory, which have been thoroughly discredited later, were invented to belittle India's indigenous achievements and suggest that Aryans were actually East European people who came on horseback, defeated the inferior people of this land, settled here, and triggered a great intellectual leap by composing the Vedas, Upanishads, and other defining texts. The Saraswati, a now dried-up river on the banks of which swathes of this civilisation flourished, was rendered mythical. The existence of a destroyed Ram Mandir at Ayodhya, over which Babri Masjid was built, was denied till the masjid was destroyed 463 years after it was built; an archaeological survey team with a Muslim on it, K.K. Muhammed, found pillars of the razed temple, and Hindus won the case after seventy years of litigation.

While Independence could have been the occasion to earnestly begin the process of breaking away from the traumatic immediate past, decolonise society and education, and consciously acknowledge and initiate reconciliation with the truth of a 1,000-year holocaust, the brown sahibs from Macaulay's laboratory stopped any of that from happening.

In the name of positive discrimination towards minorities, the Indian State turned Hindus into perpetually gaslighted, second-class citizens and Muslims into an ever-regressive, incendiary vote bank, never to be integrated with the national mainstream or accorded real benefits.

The Hindu personal laws were changed under the Hindu Code Bills in 1955 and 1956. These included the Hindu Marriage Act, Hindu Succession Act, Hindu Minority and Guardianship Act, and the Hindu Adoptions and Maintenance Act. Curiously, Muslim personal laws were left untouched, despite the fact that they allow deeply problematic practices like polygamy, instant triple talaq (divorce on the spot by simply uttering 'talaq, talaq, talaq'), and nikah halala (if a divorced couple wants to get back together, the wife has to marry and have sex with a third man, leave him, and only then return to her ex-husband).

While at the individual level, legislation and state policy began to discriminate between communities, a grand geopolitical appeasement of Islamists was afoot in Jammu and Kashmir. Nehru was adamant about giving it special status under Article 370, which for decades would work as a bulwark against the integration of the Muslim-majority state with India and encourage separatist impulses. The chief author of the Constitution, B.R. Ambedkar, and Bhartiya Jana Sangh leader Syama Prasad Mookerjee were openly opposed to the special status, and according to some accounts, the then home minister Sardar Vallabhbhai Patel privately expressed his reservations to his close friend and colleague Jawaharlal. Nevertheless, Nehru ensured that Article 370 was passed by the Constituent Assembly in 1949.

Not satisfied, Nehru then brought in Article 35A in J&K, bypassing Parliament through a Presidential Order. Together with Article 370, it severely impinged on the rights of women, lower castes, migrant workers, and LGBTQ+ individuals, until the current BJP government struck both articles down on 5 August 2019, and made J&K a union territory governed directly by the Centre.

Besides Ram Mandir and Kashmir, the two most potent issues that shook the Hindu collective consciousness in the 1980s were the Shah Bano case and the ban on *The Satanic Verses* in India.

In 1978, Shah Bano Begum of Indore, then sixty-two years old, was divorced by her husband. She filed a case in the Supreme Court and won the right to alimony. All hell broke loose. Muslim politicians launched a vicious campaign, and Islamist mobs hit the streets demanding that the verdict be scrapped because it was against Quranic laws. The Congress government of Rajiv Gandhi, in power with the most staggering majority in India's electoral history—404 out of 514 seats—capitulated. It passed the Muslim Women (Protection of Rights on Divorce) Act, 1986, diluting the Supreme Court order and limiting the right of Muslim divorcées to alimony from their ex-husbands to a period of just 90 days following the divorce. A nation watched aghast as a polity buckled under threat from Islamist mobs. Little did Indians realise that a similar spectacle was to happen again shortly.

On 14 February 1989, the ailing Ayatollah Khomeini of Iran issued a fatwa calling for writer Salman Rushdie's head over his book, *The Satanic Verses*, which he claimed had slighted Islam. Under the prime ministership of Rajiv Gandhi, the Indian government acted with alacrity upon receiving a petition from parliamentarian Syed Shahabuddin. India banned the book on 5 October, before all others, even the Islamic world, leaving a permanent blot on its record in matters of freedom of expression.

Around the time these events were unfolding, many of the children of history, who would drive the biggest wave of Indic resurgence so far, were being born—millennials, followed by Gen Z. They were born in an economically liberalised India, unencumbered by the baggage of Nehruvian socialism, permit raj, and the identity crisis of desperate Indians who went to the West to escape poverty and stagnation. In 1991, a new India came into existence.

It was 24 July 1991. Prime Minister P.V. Narasimha Rao, a man with a permanent pout and very few words, announced the abolition of the Industries (Development and Regulation) Act, 1951. All licensing of new industries, except for a few sectors, was removed. It was the beginning of tectonic economic reforms, and Rao did it without fanfare, without even a press conference. It was as if a 'happy bomb' had been dropped on the Indian economy. The impact was deafening.

Buoyed by the openness of globalisation, a confident India began to emerge. Indians were no longer diffidently holding out their passport at immigration. A self-assured generation, which knew it could compete against anybody in the world, was slowly taking shape.

This was one of the most profound turning points in modern Indian life. The opening up of the economy, the advent of the internet, and the arrival of social media (Facebook and Twitter both launched in India in 2006) were directly responsible for the political change we are witnessing today. These events started shaping a citizenry that would not accept chicanery and corruption and was armed with very powerful tools to fight against them.

While liberalisation brought a certain confidence and prosperity among a large section of the population which had remained untouched by these changes, the internet and social media revolutionised information and democratised opinion on an unprecedented scale. Earlier, the only way to counter an op-ed writer's view was to write a letter to the editor, who would most likely promptly trash it. Now, star journalists, anchors, and intellectuals were being challenged with facts right under their posts, prompting an alarmed intelligentsia to label every challenger as a 'troll'. But there was no escape. It became hard to hide in a digitised world; even more difficult to hide incompetence with bluster, snobbery, or fake victimhood.

But even this wired generation did not get weaponised overnight. Like their predecessors, they helplessly watched dark events unfold, lies proffered, hypocrisy rage for over a decade before they started organising themselves and rising in defiance.

They watched the selective vilification of Hindus over the 2002 Gujarat riots. Since Narendra Modi was then the chief minister of Gujarat, the media and intelligentsia kept branding the communal violence as a genocide of Muslims by Hindus. They would often conveniently black out the fact that fifty-nine Hindus were burned to death in a train near Godhra station by a Muslim mob on 27 February 2002, which led to the Hindu retaliation. Official figures put the death toll at 1,044, with 223 missing and 2,500 injured. Of the dead, 790 were Muslim and 254 Hindu. In which 'genocide' do so many supposed 'perpetrators' die? But TV and newspaper coverage was relentlessly one-sided. The Left and 'liberal' lobby of editors, who had near-total control over media, would edit and manipulate copy or footage sent from the ground by local reporters to suit the Congress establishment's narrative.

The nation also silently watched Sonia Gandhi, the Italian-born wife of Rajiv Gandhi, nearly become prime minister and later run the nation with an invisible remote. People started asking themselves if a nation of over a billion was unable to produce an Indian-born leader to lead the country. Resurfacing in public memory was the fact that although Sonia married Rajiv in 1968, she acquired Indian citizenship only in 1983. In between, her name mysteriously appeared on the voting list in 1980, although she was not an Indian citizen at the time.

Delhi lawyer P.N. Lekhi even filed a public interest petition before the Delhi High Court, arguing that Sonia did not meet the definition of an Indian citizen as outlined in Article 5 of the Constitution. But all this did not stop Sonia Gandhi from running the country as the super-PM, often overturning decisions by the soft-spoken Prime Minister Manmohan Singh. Images of Singh or other senior members of the Union cabinet genuflecting before her deepened the dismay of millions of Indians about her extra-constitutional authority. She reinforced the tyranny of the unelected by creating the National Advisory Council (NAC) to 'advice' the prime minister. The NAC was a motley group of Left-minded activists, economists, former bureaucrats, and suchlike. It was Sonia's tool to go above the head of PM Singh and his council of ministers.

Bibek Debroy, now the chairman of the PM's Economic Advisory Council, wrote in 2013:

> NAC is neither fish nor fowl. NAC is not answerable to the executive or legislature. Incidentally, the Planning Commission isn't accountable to Parliament either. It was set up through an executive order.
>
> De jure, any advisory body's role is to make recommendations. NAC's role has been much beyond that. In multiple instances, it has dictated to the government. It, thus, owes its power to the clout of the chairperson. When

the chairperson's clout diminishes, so does NAC's. This has been evident since 2006. The modifications in the Food Security Bill are a case in point.

A nominated, not elected, oligarchy determines the fates of millions. That this is done in the name of the poor is beside the point. Most damage to the poor has been done in the name of the poor. Borrowing from George Orwell's evocative descriptions in 1984, there are the Proles (Indian poor), and NAC represents the 'Inner Party'—this is crony socialism at its worst.

While crony socialists were dictating policy, the United Progressive Alliance (UPA) government, run by the Congress with other friendly 'secular' parties, was not disappointing the crony capitalists either. Scam after scam started getting exposed, mainly by the comptroller and auditor general's office. In the ten years the UPA was in office, more than ten major economic offences were carried out. From the allocation of 2G mobile spectrum to coal blocks, from the purchase of AgustaWestland choppers to Czech Tatra trucks for the defence forces, from siphoning off funds for the Commonwealth Games to cricket spot-fixing in the Indian Premier League, from B. Ramalinga Raju cooking Satyam's books to politicians and bureaucrats grabbing army land to build a high-rise called Adarsh on the Mumbai seafront … very few areas were left untouched. During those years, 'phone banking' came to mean wealthy industrialists could simply call public sector banks and get bad loans worth hundreds of crores using political clout.

This wanton corruption was to prove the UPA regime's undoing. As the nation appeared like a moving ATM van for all to loot but none to steer, citizens' anger was slowly building up for a tornado-like anti-corruption movement. The landfall was in 2011.

The India Against Corruption (IAC) movement, with Anna Hazare at its helm, exuding a village simpleton aura, marked the beginning of the end for the UPA. Massive crowds from all walks of life and diverse ideologies spontaneously gathered at the Ramlila Maidan, where Anna and his aides like Arvind Kejriwal (who later founded the Aam Aadmi Party and is now the chief minister of Delhi), Prashant Bhushan, Kiran Bedi, and Kumar Vishwas, led the charge.

Social media hissed with outrage; television went live with daylong coverage every day. A haughty government first tried to steamroll the protests by making high-profile arrests of yoga guru Ramdev and then of Hazare himself, but eventually agreed to the protesters' terms in Parliament after a long and tumultuous debate.

For the mobile phone-wielding, social media-savvy generation, that was the first taste of collective success against what they euphemistically called the 'system'.

Even before the popular resistance against corruption had started, something else was gnawing on the nation's mind. It was the naked minoritism by the political parties that called themselves secular. Selectively blaming Hindus for Gujarat, Assam, or UP's Muzaffarnagar riots was one aspect of it. A lot more was unfolding.

The biggest of them was the 26/11 Mumbai terror attack. It was the world's most notorious terror attack after 9/11. Armed Lashkar-e-Toiba jihadis trained and dispatched from Pakistan stormed crowded places in Mumbai and started indiscriminately killing people. After massacres at the Chhatrapati Shivaji Terminus, Taj Mahal Hotel, Chabad House, and Leopold bar, 175 people were dead.

What stupefied and angered the nation was the Congress-led government's unpreparedness despite dozens of terror attacks earlier, its nonchalance (the home minister was busy changing suits for TV cameras while the attack was on), and ultimately, the initial attempts to somehow blame 'Hindu terror' for the carnage. If one of the terrorists, Ajmal Kasab, had not been caught alive because of the incredibly brave, life-sacrificing effort by low-ranked police officer Tukaram Omble, the entire attack could have been passed off as a Hindu plot. So sure was the Pakistani spy agency Inter-Services Intelligence (ISI) of the Indian establishment's political need to blame such violence on Hindus and please Muslims that the terrorists were sent wearing the Hindu sacred thread, 'kalava', on the wrists and had Hindu names on their identity cards. Kasab's assumed name was Samir Dinesh Chaudhari.

Predictably, Congress politicians like Digvijaya Singh had started blaming the Rashtriya Swayamsevak Sangh (RSS)—an overarching Hindu socio-cultural-political organisation and perhaps the largest NGO in the world—before the truth emerged.

Even after such a massacre and one of the Pakistani perpetrators caught alive, the Indian government of the day did not attack Pakistan despite considerable air, ground, and naval superiority. It practically did nothing other than sending dossier after dossier to Islamabad, which mockingly dismissed each of those. Zakiur Rehman Lakhvi, one of the chief masterminds of 26/11, was put under such farcical detention that he sired a child with one of his wives while in jail.

While the 26/11 perpetrators were roaming freely in Pakistan, making babies, and raising funds to escalate jihad against India, the Congress government was busy inventing

'Hindu terror'. It had a sinister political motive. It wanted to draw a false equivalence with Islamist terror, as it felt Islam was being singled out as the single largest source of terror in the world and in India. To save Muslims from embarrassment, the party was willing to concoct evidence and completely disregard facts. From the 2007 Samjhauta Express blasts to the 2008 Malegaon explosion, every single case of 'Hindu terror' started falling flat in courts. Witnesses told the court that Congress leaders had been forcing them to name RSS functionaries in terror cases. One after the other, Hindus accused of terror started to get acquitted.[5] The people of India had been watching it all. Only this time, the walls of silence were beginning to break.

In the midst of all this, Prime Minister Manmohan Singh said something that the nation would not forget, and it has now been proven, is unwilling to forgive.

Speaking at the National Development Council on 9 December 2006, he said, 'We will have to devise innovative plans to ensure that minorities, particularly the Muslim minority, are empowered to share equitably the fruits of development. These must have the first claim on resources.'[6]

Coming from a genteel and measured man, it was recklessly opportunistic. It mocked the principles of equality, secularism, fairness, and justice. The majority knew that day that they were on their own, that they would have to stand up for themselves. They cannot rely even on the holder of the nation's highest office.

Then came the Communal Violence Bill of 2011 or the Prevention of Communal and Targeted Violence (Access to Justice and Reparations) Bill, 2011. For sheer gall, it deserved a medal. It was the audacious handiwork of Sonia Gandhi's handpicked and unelected NAC. This project was led by activist Harsh Mander.

The document was an exposition of the Congress establishment's anti-Hindu fantasy. It sought to permanently portray Hindus as the perpetrator of any communal violence anywhere in India, and minorities as perpetual victims. Its scope encompassed the 'whole of India', undermining federalism since law and order is a state subject.

This is how it defined communal violence (pay attention to the word 'group', because therein lies the devil):

> Communal and targeted violence means and includes any act or series of acts, whether spontaneous or planned, resulting in injury or harm to the person and or property, knowingly directed against any person by virtue of his or her membership of any group, which destroys the secular fabric of the nation.

And what is a 'group'?

> Group means a religious or linguistic minority in any State in the Union of India, or Scheduled Castes and Scheduled Tribes within the meaning of clauses (24) and (25) of Article 366 of the Constitution of India. [emphasis added]

So, upper-caste Hindus would always be deemed perpetrators and not victims, even if they were torn apart by violence. Which they repeatedly have been, from the Moplah riots to the pogrom of Brahmins after Gandhi's assassination to the Kashmiri Pandit exodus. The bill clearly defined 'victims' as only minorities.

> 'Victim' means any person belonging to a group as defined under this Act, who has suffered physical, mental, psychological or monetary harm or harm to his or her property as a result of the commission of any offence under

this Act, and includes his or her relatives, legal guardian and legal heirs, wherever appropriate.

And according to the bill, only the majority community was capable of hate propaganda. Not minorities or lower castes:

> Hate propaganda – Notwithstanding anything contained in any other law for the time being in force, whoever publishes, communicates or disseminates by words, either spoken or written, or by signs or by visible representation or otherwise acts inciting hatred causing clear and present danger of violence against a group or persons belonging to that group.

The communal agenda of the bill was so blatant and dangerous that even Digvijaya Singh, in a rare moment of reason, rejected it.

Senior journalist R. Jagannathan wrote:

> First, it is surprising why an unelected body like the National Advisory Council (NAC), which is home to Sonia Gandhi groupies, was allowed to draft a Bill that is so crucial to communal harmony. This is a Bill that requires a national consensus, and getting a bunch of Congress-leaning activists to masquerade as the voice of civil society is nonsense. Second, the Bill is itself communal in nature. According to a key definition of the people who are presumably the focus of targeted violence, 'group' means a religious or linguistic minority, in any state in the Union of India, or Scheduled Castes and Scheduled Tribes (SC/ST). If you take away the fact that religious minorities and the SC/STs between them account for over 40% of the total population, the Bill cleverly posits that the other 60%

(which may include upper castes Hindus, other backward castes and some miscellaneous groups) are the only people capable of targeted violence. Are we saying 40% can never target 60%, given that these numbers are distributed all over the country?

But the Congress was unstoppable. It brought the well-meaning Right to Education (RTE) for underprivileged children to get quality education through reservation in school seats. However, the burden of conscience was only placed on secular and Hindu educational bodies. Minority institutions were summarily exempt. Why? Must minorities bear no responsibility for nation-building? There are obviously no satisfactory answers.

And finally, one of the biggest reasons for dissent of the new generation is the public display of anti-nationalism and anarchy in their own habitat—campuses. There has been brazen communist and Islamist radicalisation in institutions like Jawaharlal Nehru University (JNU), Jadavpur University, Jamia Millia Islamia, Aligarh Muslim University, and the Film and Television Institute of India, often led by their Left-leaning or Islamist-minded faculty. These cabals actively persecute nationalist or Hindu voices.

In May 2000, two army officers were mercilessly beaten up in JNU for objecting to a couple of Pakistani poets bad-mouthing India at a programme. Sixteen years later, a programme was organised in JNU to honour the terrorist mastermind of the 2001 Parliament attack, Afzal Guru, who was hanged later. Chants of '*Bharat tere tukde tukde/ Inshallah inshallah*' and 'Azaadi' filled the air. Then in 2020, Jamia turned into a battlefield with students attacking the police with stones over the Citizenship Amendment Act.

Professors like G.N. Saibaba were arrested for furthering Maoist terrorism, which has killed thousands in India.

Students across the nation have silently watched radical, anti-India forces take over their space. They have seen their values trampled on, their traditions mocked. Thousands of them quietly started organising themselves and have become committed foot soldiers of the new nationalist movement.

A hundred grievances have been adding up over the years. Hindu temples, for instance, are still placed under government control, while every other religion is free to run their trusts and institutions without any interference.

Entry of women of reproductive age at the Aiyappa Temple at Sabarimala becomes a big feminist legal issue. The petitioners do not realise that the tradition was created because only the celibate form of Aiyappa is worshipped at that temple. In temples that depict other life phases of Aiyappa, women are not barred. Rehana Fathima, a Muslim activist, reportedly tried to enter the Sabarimala Temple carrying sanitary pads. Interestingly, India has at least nine or ten temples like Kamakhya in Assam, Attukal Bhagavathy Temple in Kerala, Brahma Temple at Rajasthan's Pushkar, Devi Kanya Kumari Temple in Tamil Nadu, and Durga Mata Temple in Bihar's Muzaffarpur where men are not allowed to enter year-round or during certain days. Also, the near-total absence of women in mosques was never raised.

Strong Hindu mobilisation has also happened over conversions, whether forcible or through inducements. More and more youngsters have become aware of the demographic war across centuries that has taken away Afghanistan, Pakistan, and Bangladesh from India.

Cases of love jihad, where Muslim youth convert and marry Hindu women often under false names and pretexts, have also galvanised young Hindu men and women.

While the new nationalism surged, the ranks of one of its chief drivers, the RSS, swelled. In March 2023, the Sangh stated it had 72,000 shakhas or centres in the country, and the target was to increase it to a lakh by 2025, the centenary year of the RSS.

This marks a significant increase from 57,000 shakhas in 2019, with the Sangh having added 19,584 shakhas since 2010, representing the highest growth in the organisation's history. Specifically, between 2010 and 2014, when the BJP was still out of power, the RSS added approximately 6,000 new shakhas. The organisation has intensified its efforts in certain states where politics and demography present greater challenges. For instance, in Bengal, the Sangh aims to incorporate 700 new shakhas by 2024, supplementing its existing 1,900.

The age profile of RSS members has also decreased sharply. About 60 per cent of RSS shakhas are composed of school and college students, while nearly 29 per cent consist of young businessmen and traders. Interest in the RSS has surged. The 'Join RSS' section of the official RSS website received 28,843 requests in 2013. By September-end 2019 alone, that section had received 1.03 lakh requests.

The RSS-run ekal vidyalayas, or one-teacher schools, have proliferated rapidly, just like water hyacinths. There were 27,000 ekal vidyalayas in 2010, 34,000 in 2011, and 51,717 in 2013. By August 2020, the number had surpassed 1,03,000, with 2,100 schools located in the remotest corners of the Northeast. Recently, there has been significant growth in ekal vidyalayas in Kashmir. The RSS anticipates that there will be over 2,00,000 single-teacher schools by 2030.

"RSS is building a society, not an organisation. Change is the exhibition of the power of Sangh," says a top RSS leader.

But the RSS is just one crucial piece in the Indic resurgence. It is undoubtedly one of the main thought enablers. However, there are millions outside the formal Sangh fold who are quietly doing their bit for the civilisational cause.

This book tells the story of India's new nationalism, portrayed through the lives and worldviews of both well-known and lesser-known individuals driving it. You'll encounter protagonists ranging from those in the power corridors of Delhi to those on the frontlines of violent resistance in Bengal and Kerala. You'll journey through the hills and rainlands of the Northeast, witnessing the slow reawakening of converted indigenous peoples, to Rajasthan's deserts where refugees have arrived from Pakistan. From influential policymakers to bestselling authors, star lawyers, Muslims challenging orthodoxy, and those facilitating ghar wapsi to bring back the converted to the Hindu fold, this book provides glimpses into their lives, work, and viewpoints.

The new nationalists are an astonishingly diverse group of people. Some have left well-paying jobs abroad to return to India and pursue something meaningful. Many are tantalisingly enigmatic—anonymous historians, scientists-turned-media personalities, Christian or Muslim swayamsevaks, conservative queers. Without meeting and listening to them, understanding the resurgence is impossible.

India's new Right is an incredible mix, much like India itself.

CHAPTER I

New Species of 'Sanghi'

India's Left-minded individuals and liberals had typecast nationalists as provincial and regressive, not quite exposed to Western modernity. They were seen as solid in their mother tongue but sputtering when challenged in English because they had not attended English medium schools. Unfashionable. Never heard of Burberry or Prada. They would be derisively called 'vernac' or 'Chutney Mary'. They came pre-cancelled. In this aspect, India is unique. Worldwide, the class wall between the rich and poor usually drives such prejudice. But in India, elitists block out a staggering mass of talented individuals with the invisible wall of a colonial language, even seventy-five years after independence.

The rise of Narendra Modi has dramatically changed that. Or rather, the prime minister owes his rise partly to the revolt of this massive, muted mass. A liberalised economy has lifted millions of Indians out of poverty and created a neo-middle class that is confident in its traditional identity and aspires to do better in life. Access to cheap mobile phones and the internet has empowered them with information and armed them with opinions.

Alongside this neo-middle-class phenomenon, something else has started happening. A part of the small but influential urban, English-speaking young population has started waking up from the deep slumber induced by colonial, convent, or Leftist education. With the explosion of everyday information and technology, they can see through fake narratives and combat the high and mighty commentariat with facts. These commentators had previously gone unchallenged due to the one-way communication in legacy media.

In this chapter, we will meet some of them. They are an abomination to India's Left and 'liberal' ecosystem. They come from the same privileged families, speak, dress, and party in the same way, and have had the same education, but they sting very differently. They are like fellow creatures who have broken away from prison and now mock those with whom they once shared a cell. It was easier for India's English-speaking gentry to dismiss the old 'Sanghi' (a disparaging term for those from or sympathetic to the RSS) as the great unwashed. The new 'Sanghi' is a perplexing mix, with people ostensibly from the urban-liberal ranks.

Ajit Datta

The white walls of the Sri Aurobindo Society beach office in Puducherry vibrated with Vedic chants by more than fifty young boys in white dhotis. A festive buzz hung in the air. It was August 2018, and the first Pondy Lit Fest had just started. This festival was one of the initial platforms for the new nationalists. However, even a simple literary festival did not come easy for them. Alliance Française, which was supposed to host the event, backed out at the last moment due to pressure from powerful Left-leaning groups who wanted the 'Right Wing' LitFest cancelled, despite the participation of vocally liberal celebrities like Kalki Koechlin and the fact that there were only two or three political sessions in the entire event.

Undismayed by the bullying, organisers Partha Hariharan and Alo Pal managed to shift the event from the Alliance Française Auditorium and Maison Colombani to the Sri Aurobindo Society beach office premises. The book readings were moved to the Aurodhan Art Gallery. By then, guests had arrived, and the sessions of 'Bharat Shakti' began rolling.

Darting to every corner of the venue filled with acclaimed writers, journalists, economists, and historians was a twenty-one-year-old young man with a ponytail, Ajit Datta. He was one of the main organisers, coordinating with every participant, ensuring sessions began and ended on time, food and accommodations were well taken care of, and celebrity tantrums were calmly managed. In between, he also conducted a couple of sessions in crisp English. (Speaking English or living an urban, Westernised life cannot be the measure of someone's worth. However, it is important to mention this in the context of some of the young individuals driving the new Indic resurgence.)

Born in 1996 to parents who were both Aurobindo followers, Ajit grew up in the Aurobindo ashram. When his parents moved to the Philippines and eventually to Singapore, Ajit was fifteen. He insisted on continuing his education at the Sri Aurobindo International Centre of Education in Puducherry.

> Congress was in power, and reports of its corruption had started bothering me. Along came Modi. I started supporting him when I was sixteen. It was entirely because of the individual and the hope that he represented for India. I was

quite ignorant about history or ideology. I was not very sensitive to the hypocrisies of journalists and opinion makers the way I am now.

Ajit soon became a supporter of the BJP. His journey on the path of Hindutva had begun.

In 2012, he began following the highly popular nationalist social media handle, The Frustrated Indian (TFI), managed by Atul Mishra. He joined the group of young writers and contributors assembled by TFI to challenge the Left-liberal narrative. When TFI launched a website in 2015, Ajit began writing for it.

After graduating in 2017, he decided to take a year-and-a-half off from studies or any professional pursuit. He began working full-time for the 2019 elections. He mentions that some of the groundwork he did is confidential. However, part of his work was with the Bluekraft Digital Foundation, run by Akhilesh Mishra. This work involved writing online opinions, running pro-Modi pages, and countering the opponent's narrative.

> To my mind, 2019 was the most important election. Maybe even more than 2014. In the past, non-Congress governments had come and gone. They could not build a firm ground and were not durable, they could not make deep and long-term changes. It was absolutely critical for Modi to win in 2019.

Ajit says the preconceived notions he had about the RSS have also been shattered along the way. The Sangh has shown remarkable flexibility on contemporary issues like multiculturalism or Section 377 of the Indian Penal Code, a British-era legislation that criminalised acts of homosexuality.

He says, 'Here is a sarsangchalak [RSS chief] who is a professor of physics and can speak on Yuval Noah Harari's *Sapiens* for an hour. And still, they try to project the RSS as intellectually backward.'

Ajit has recently written a book on BJP's firebrand Assam chief minister, Himanta Biswa Sarma, who has redefined saffron politics in the Northeast, playing a pivotal role in bringing the entire region under the party's control.

Writing the book, watching Himantada at work, was quite an eye-opening experience. I realised I am not cut out for full-time politics. It's relentless. 24/7. You always have to be alert, responsive. You cannot let your guard down for a moment.

Ajit is currently pursuing his master's in global diplomacy at the School of Oriental and African Studies (SOAS), University of London. He is working on a dissertation focussing on the Quad, the emerging global alliance of the US, India, Japan, and Australia aimed at countering China's maritime aggression in the Indian Ocean.

Think India

Just as a tornado draws unsuspecting leaves and twigs into its vortex, a generation raised on Jay Z and the Marvel multiverse is suddenly finding itself being swept into the revival storm of a very ancient civilisation. Youngsters are becoming vocal on social media, forming secret shakhas and clandestine groups in Westernised institutions, and creating and sharing toolkits to counter the Left and Islamist narrative.

Words are the daisy cutters of this war, they realise. Their toolkit advises keyboard troops to refrain from using 'Muslims' or 'Christians' to evade detection by social media algorithms and avoid quick accusations of bigotry by their opponents, who they say are skilled at labelling anybody with a different opinion as 'fascist' and playing the victim. Instead, a toolkit advises using terms like 'monotheistic Abrahamic religions'. Additionally, it suggests using 'pagans' instead of 'Hindus' to unite native religions across countries and faiths. The young nationalists advocate playing the victim card because, unlike their opponents, they claim that Hindu victimhood is genuine.

One of the primary drivers of this movement has been the student union of the Sangh Parivar, the ABVP. Its growth has been remarkable in recent years, characterised by a nuanced and strategic approach, with a long-term vision in sight.

ABVP's membership has surged, particularly since the 2016 JNU controversy surrounding an event honouring Parliament attack mastermind Afzal Guru.

In 2014–15, ABVP had 13,27,924 members across 7,126 college units. By 2019–20, this number had risen to 33,39,693 members across 21,408 college units. In 2021–22, the membership has reached 31,45,180 with three months to spare. In just six years, ABVP has expanded to nearly three times its original size and reach.

It has fostered numerous interest-based groups catering to students' diverse interests. For addressing environmental concerns, there is Students for Development. For engaging in social work, there is Students for Seva, a unit that has excelled throughout the COVID-19 pandemic. For artists, there is Rashtriya Kala Manch. Foreign students studying in India can join ABVP's World Organisation for Students and Youth

(WOSY). Indian students studying in foreign universities can become members of ABVP Overseas, while for research scholars, there is Students for Holistic Development of Humanity (SHODH).

One of its central projects, which targets middle- and upper-middle-class, English-speaking, urban Indian students at national institutes, is Think India. The idea to create something like Think India began to take shape around 2003–04, during the tenure of the BJP under Atal Behari Vajpayee. The almost complete absence of nationalistic student bodies in premier institutes such as the Indian Institutes of Technology (IITs), Indian Institutes of Management (IIMs), Indian Institute of Science, and the National Law University necessitated this initiative.

Think India was launched in 2007 with a small event on the Art of Living campus in Bengaluru. Today, it has expanded to over eighteen NLUs, all the National Institute of Technology campuses, approximately thirteen IITs, Indian Institutes of Science Education and Research, Indian Institutes of Information Technology, National Institutes of Fashion Technology, and the IIMs. Think India offers internship programmes in law, policymaking, social work, journalism, and parliamentary affairs. For example, the legal internship, Vidhi, serves as a link between top lawyers and students. Sansadiya, the parliamentary internship, connects students with parliamentarians.

Think India quickly collected over 1,000 student signatures within twenty-four hours against the anti-CAA protests. It also coordinated a Tiranga Yatra at IIT Bombay. Furthermore, over 500 students and employees of the Indian Institute of Engineering Science and Technology, Shibpur, rallied under its banner to protest the recent anti-Hindu violence in

Bangladesh. Its most vocal campaigns have targeted the Left's cancel culture.

Shivam Raghuvanshi

Shivam Raghuvanshi joined Think India in 2016 while studying at the National Law University, Patiala. He quickly rose to the position of national co-convener. The twenty-five-year-old is now based in Bengal, heading Think India's east zone operations, maintaining contact with both students and victims of the state's violent post-election incidents in 2021. Shivam says:

> To gain acceptance among urban youngsters, ABVP had to reinvent its image. The Left has portrayed it as a student union of toughies. Think India was conceptualised to educate youngsters about their responsibilities towards the nation while pursuing their careers.
>
> I noticed that many of my seniors were nationalists, but they never spoke up. With Think India, the fear of being cancelled started to dissipate. As things became increasingly polarised, we realised that if we did not speak up now, we might never get another chance later.
>
> One of my seniors, a Kashmiri Pandit girl, used to be very 'woke' at the university. A few months ago, I noticed her social media posts. She has suddenly become a vocal nationalist!

Shivam and others who work closely with youngsters say that today's teenagers are emerging as mutants when it comes to unabashed identity politics and aggressive nationalism. This is the Instagram generation. They have had access to Instagram since around Class VIII or IX. They consume information through short videos and graphics. Unsurprisingly, given their age, they are the most rebellious and ideologically aggressive, often resembling a burst of loose cannons. But there is another fascinating dynamic at play within this group. Their behaviour is often based on the desire to be noticed or admired by the opposite sex. 'The boys often post shrill or outrageous comments just to get noticed by girls,' says Shivam.

Armed with nuggets of information from WhatsApp forwards and Instagram reels, many of them feel empowered enough to challenge the 'pseudos' and 'liberandus' on social media.

Interestingly, non-Left students observe that one of the biggest challenges to spreading their views on campus is that the Left has effectively marketed themselves to girls, portraying communism and socialism as compassionate, artistic, and progressive ideologies. Many girls on national university campuses still believe that the Left advocates for justice for the underdog. Left-controlled academia has carefully avoided mentioning that Joseph Stalin and Mao Zedong each killed more than double the number of people massacred in Nazi Germany. They also overlooked the fact that the Left has produced a succession of violent dictators like Lenin, Castro, Pol Pot, the Kim family, Ceausescu, Chavez, and others. Furthermore, they fail to acknowledge that Che Guevara was more of a sadistic executioner and misogynist than the intrepid revolutionary he is often depicted as on T-shirts.

Nevertheless, those who work with students on Indian campuses note that one of the primary reasons most boys join Left politics or conceal their nationalistic views is because they fear being looked down upon by the majority of girls.

Though it may seem trivial, it is a significant factor. Gain the support of the girls, and the boys will likely follow suit.

Somya Luthra

There are exceptions, and these exceptions are growing rapidly enough to potentially become the norm. Somya Luthra is one such exception. At twenty-one, she is studying law at Nirma University, Ahmedabad. The Delhi girl already boasts about 21,000 Twitter followers, including prominent BJP and RSS functionaries. She is one of the more prominent social media warriors.

When she was fourteen, she began tweeting about the hypocrisy of Indian liberals on matters of religion, society, and the economy. She also expressed on social media the hope that Modi held out for her generation. By the time she was seventeen, a well-known minister in Modi's cabinet noticed her and invited her to a couple of meetings.

As the 2019 general elections approached, Somya was already becoming quite a bit of a ninja on social media, handling Instagram pages, hunting in packs on Twitter, and being added to large pro-Modi WhatsApp groups.

> I have never been a member of the BJP. However, my social media savvy led me to contribute to election strategy and fight social media battles. One thing led to another. I won't name names, but I received messages from a few important people who wanted the opinion of a young BJP supporter for first-time voters. One of my suggestions to them was that since people in my age group hardly use Twitter, one should try capturing Instagram, Snapchat, and other such applications.

One had to compete with all the anti-Modi comedy pages, and it had to be subtle. Because most youngsters are no longer interested in facts; they want entertainment along with the political message.

Somya, however, was a rare teenager who preferred Twitter over Instagram.

> Although my generation is more hooked to Instagram, and I can navigate it well, I would say no app is better for making friends and networking than Twitter. On Instagram, you only see their photos. There is a limit to what photos can tell you about a person. People obviously will post about the best moments of their lives, so it's all fake. Whereas on Twitter, you get to know what a person feels about certain issues. It's often very raw. You tend to at least have a glimpse of that person.

Her political views began to take shape early. Around the age of thirteen, she started reading S.L. Bhyrappa's iconic book, *Aavarana*. Then she moved on to Mulk Raj Anand's *Untouchable*.

> Slowly, my political opinion started to form. As a kid, you don't realise what Left or Right is, but you know that you have certain beliefs. Then the 2014 general election came, so I just started tweeting randomly. People of my age group weren't very interested in politics at that time. They were mostly on Instagram. So, when I started tweeting randomly, I got noticed.

Somya comes from an Arya Samaj family, a Hindu sect that opposes elaborate rituals, the caste system, and even idol worship. She prays and is not an atheist. Her father works in a multinational corporation, and her mother is a chartered accountant.

At this point, one common experience that every young 'Sanghi' mentions is extreme stigmatisation by peers and, in many cases, teachers.

> It's not cool to be a 'Sanghi' or to talk about Hindutva. Law schools still have a very anti-BJP, anti-RSS environment. When people first speak to me and learn about my background, they assume I am the typical Left-liberal. When they speak with me for a little longer, they are unable to digest it. They are like, 'Oh shit, *ye kya bol gayi* [what is she saying].' Then they check out my Twitter profile and realise *ki ye ladki kya hai* [what this girl is about]. But I think people like us can make a change because we can show them that we are not the fanatics they think we are. Just because we press a different button on election day doesn't make us different or uncool. We do the same things as they do.

She mentions a conference where strategic affairs expert Abhijit Iyer-Mitra and others were discussing gay rights.

> The Left doesn't expect such discussions. They try hard to prove that the Indian Right does not accept the LGBTQ+ community. But I personally know many on the Right who are more compassionate about LGBTQ+ issues than those on the Left.

Somya remembers being shouted at by a college professor for her viral tweet when the Goods and Services Tax (GST) was passed. Additionally, after reading some of her social media posts, the school friends she had for years, who had travelled together on the school bus from nursery to Class XII, stopped talking to her. She says, 'They not only blocked me, but they also blocked my best friend. They were so intolerant of any counter-opinion.'

She explains that perception has started to change now. More and more people are being vocal about opinions they would never have voiced earlier.

> We created this WhatsApp group of Right-leaning law students. Think India is enabling a fair bit of change. It makes sure that its members feel they are part of a greater organtion, family, and cause. When I faced trolling, I received calls from my Think India seniors. People aren't shy to come forward anymore. The perception that if you come from a big city, if you are 'cool', you have to be a liberal is changing. Earlier, just to fit into the cool circles, one would pretend to be liberal. That perception is really changing now.

Somya is from a generation born long after the Ram Janmabhoomi movement. Even the 2008 Mumbai attacks are hazy in their memory, as they were pre-teens at the time. But Congress and India's powerful Left-liberal media establishment failed to realise that their words and deeds would come to haunt them for generations.

> 26/11 changed the fundamental perception of how evil people can become just to gain attention. For instance, how some journalists compromised the safety of hostages and troops trying to rescue them by showing live images. Or Congress leader Digvijaya Singh trying to blame the RSS for the terror attack. I remember it faintly, and I have read about what was done.

She says what sets this wave of nationalists apart from earlier ones is technology.

> I think with changing times, the way we express our ideology has also changed. During the Ram Mandir movement, the focus was on street protests. We now think, 'Get a PhD, get into a university, become a professor, influence others with your ideology.' This is a more intellectual movement, with the added advantage of technology. Look at how wonderfully technology is used in elections, or how MyGov issues certificates on national quizzes related to COVID-19 online.

Somya's social media time has shrunk; studies have taken over. However, she still goes online to debunk Left-liberal propaganda.

> I'm not an extremist. But there are some issues that require common sense. When 2.5 crore people got vaccinated on the prime minister's birthday, some people were still unhappy. I tweeted that even if I agree with your conspiracy story that they waited until his birthday to do it, what's better than a PM who wants to vaccinate his countrymen on his birthday?

Women's issues bring out Somya's most combative self. Her Twitter bio describes her as 'Your friendly neighbourhood feminist', an unlikely moniker India's new nationalists give themselves. She couldn't fathom why, for instance, instead of rejoicing, some were distraught when instant triple talaq (Islamic divorce by the husband merely uttering 'talaq, talaq, talaq) got outlawed.

> The Hindu family laws were amended in the 1950s. But why such a reaction, even from some Hindus, when oppressive Muslim personal laws are being touched? Swami Vivekananda said, 'The way we treat our women is the thermometer of society.'

Her angry posts touch on a range of women's issues, such as when the minister of women and child development Smriti Irani was being slut-shamed, for instance, or when the Congress government of Rajasthan passed a bill legitimising child marriage.

Going against her ideological allies, she lashed out when a Twitter user made a sexually loaded remark about journalist Rana Ayyub, known for her anti-Hindutva views, while she was helping with COVID-19 relief. '*Doodh ki thaili bahar reh gayi* [the milk bags have been left out],' a Twitter user posted with a photo of Ayyub standing next to a packed relief truck. Somya fiercely criticised the post and faced trolling for it.

Typical of her generation, she does not uncritically accept things. While she acknowledges that the BJP's dreaded IT cell was needed to break down the one-sided and manufactured narrative of India's elitist Left-liberal ecosystem, she believes it should work on its flaws.

> Lately, the IT cell is being filled up with North Indian boys who lack understanding of certain issues and the nuance of expression. They sometimes make more enemies than friends by harping on the vegetarian vs non-vegetarian debate or drinking, or emphasising the need for girls to cover themselves fully while going to temples. They have botched up on the Tamil–Hindi issue and have not been critical enough of Muslim women being mock-auctioned on websites like Sulli Deals and Bulli Bai. Even with people who tweet in favour of the BJP nine times out of ten, they pounce on that one time.

These days, Somya writes occasional pieces for well-known websites and newspapers like Firstpost, New Indian Express, and Live Law. Her law degree helps her analyse bills and policies better. She argues that nationalists, not the Left and self-proclaimed liberals, are the real progressives who are bringing about change in marriageable age, making sanitary pads available for the poor, or ensuring COVID-19 vaccination for the young.

Optimism lights up her large eyes when you ask her about India's future. She hopes the country will be a safer place for women, health will receive a higher percentage of the GDP, smaller cities will prosper, and the process of ending the Northeast's isolation, which PM Modi has initiated, will make the region flourish.

Razual Purewal

The new wave is not just shattering the stereotype that the 'Sanghi' comes from a certain provincial background; it is breaking a trope within that stereotype—that the Indic resurgence is exclusively Hindu nationalism. Many youngsters like twenty-two-year-old Razual Purewal prove it is not.

She comes from an affluent, landed Jat Sikh family in Punjab. In the state's current political whirlpool, it is certainly not the kind of profile that would automatically support the BJP or RSS's idea of nationalism.

Razual has always studied in an upscale, English-medium school and loves her Shakespeare, especially *Hamlet*. Some of her friends have been at the forefront of the protests and the social media war against the new farm laws that the Modi government introduced and then withdrew in the face of sustained demonstrations, almost solely in Punjab. Wealthy, upper-caste Sikh 'arthiyas' or agricultural middlemen were the engine behind the agitation. They sensed their income from assured buying by the government at minimum support prices would drastically fall if the agricultural reforms went through. Sensing anger against Modi, Khalistani separatists backed by Pakistan's ISI in Canada, the UK, the US, and Germany came to fish.

In the middle of all this, risking the wrath of her family, friends, and the community at large, Razual joined the ABVP's Think India at the National Law University in Chandigarh.

> I don't come from a family with a history of being part of the RSS or the Parishad [ABVP]. I come from a very liberal background. My current work and activism clash with that. The best part of being in this milieu in Think India is that I have become very patient. I used to be really impulsive. Like … oh my god, this needs to be done. Why isn't it happening? I have now started taking everyone's opinions into consideration and bonding with people from diverse backgrounds. That is what is taught. They teach you to be more open and receptive. I am amazed at how devoted they are to the idea of a nation.

The farm protests made Razual's life a little difficult. Her community was up in arms, her friends were vehemently fighting the BJP-led central government.

> I received a lot of backlash. I lost a lot of friends that way. Well, you know, people were not ready to listen rationally. They were not ready to accept that they could be wrong. People in Punjab have always been privileged. A steady flow of wealth has always come their way. They are not ready to give it up.

Meanwhile, Razual's talent was being recognised in ABVP. Despite her unconventional background, she had started making strides.

With ABVP, it was extremely challenging. There were people from every background. Some were middle-aged, and some were hardcore Hindi speakers who weren't very liberal. So, when I got the responsibility of being the nagar mantri, I was taken aback.

We started initiatives that made a difference. In Mohali, which is my zone, we have a lot of private and national institutions like the National Institute of Fashion Technology, the Indian Institute of Science Education and Research, the National Institute of Pharmaceutical Education and Research, and the Indian School of Business. I told the ABVP that we can only attract that crowd not by slogan-shouting but through intellectually stimulating activities and fresh perspectives.

She, for instance, organised a discussion on Neha Dwivedi's book on Captain V.N. Thapar, *Vijyant at Kargil*. Students from the many army schools in and around Mohali and the Army Institute of Law started attending ABVP events and meetings.

The Parishad also invited people to write articles on the farmers' protests. Those pieces often caught the attention of ABVP, RSS, and eventually, the BJP, highlighting where the government or party was falling short and what needed to be done.

The ABVP also initiated an anti-COVID-19 drive, distributing PPE kits and thermometers, while urging government hospitals to handle the epidemic load. Razual believes these efforts attracted more people to the ABVP than mere slogans could have. 'People are going to embrace your ideology if you cater to their needs and give them what they want,' she asserts.

For Razual, Think India offers a socially less diverse but intellectually more vibrant environment. She has been tasked with managing the debating forum.

> We voice our opinion on everything under the sun. We organise debates and group discussions on issues of national importance. Our last event was a group discussion on the appointment of women to the higher judiciary. This was in July 2001, before three women judges were appointed to the Supreme Court. I'm quite impressed with the progress we have made. In Think India, I estimate that 50 per cent of us are raw, not having any sort of ideological affiliation. If we bring about a change, it can really make a difference. They bring these [ideas] back to their colleges, and it just creates a huge network.

Razual is very optimistic about the new National Education Policy (NEP). She believes it will accomplish much more than just instilling patriotism and decolonising the mind.

> Education is the road that can actually connect India and make it a world leader. Once the NEP is implemented, no matter what background people come from, no matter what their privilege, whether they are going to a good school or a bad school, public school or a private school … they will all be on a level playing field. They will have the same resources, the same education facilities, and the same exposure. For example, under the NEP, one can choose their subjects. A student in a government institution may end up with similar tools and facilities as those in an International Board school.

She says her state, Punjab, has a lot of pent-up anger that needs to be addressed.

I read three books on Punjab over the last year after the farmers' protests started. These books are written by ideologically neutral people. I realised that Punjabis, deep inside, are very angry about what happened during Partition and the bifurcation of Punjab and Haryana under the Punjab Reorganisation Act of 1966. They are also very angry about the Sikh riots in 1984 and what happened with the Rajiv–Longowal Accord between the then PM Rajiv Gandhi and Akali leader Harchand Singh Longowal. Since Punjab lost Lahore during Partition, Nehru came up with the idea of Chandigarh. But, Chandigarh was made a union territory, and Punjab was made to share it as its capital with Haryana.

Razual says Punjabis are also angry about issues related to irrigation. They are upset with Rahul Gandhi for singling out Punjab regarding the drug menace and claiming that 70 per cent of Punjabi youth are addicts. She feels Punjab has been politically shortchanged because it has only seven Lok Sabha seats.

She warns against tarring the entire Sikh community with the Khalistani brush. The handful with separatist or terrorist instincts are mostly abroad, trying to foment trouble. Although the terms sound similar, Khalistan should not be confused with Khalsa, the pure and awakened community of Sikhs founded by Guru Gobind Singh. The community needs strong leadership and deeper political engagement, she says.

Razual has actively supported the Sangh's stand on Akhand Bharat, which led to the abrogation of Article 370 and the full integration of Jammu and Kashmir with the Union of India.

> The choice was between the right to self-determination and territorial integrity, one of the oldest and most false dilemmas

in international law. With the abrogation of Article 370 from Jammu and Kashmir on 5 August 2019, neither was India's territorial integrity put at stake, nor was the intent of the separatists, who have been promulgating terrorism in the region, fulfilled.

Adjusting her glasses, she ends with a plea for a more inclusive India, where diverse options are respected and varied energies are channelled into building a strong nation.

Bharat Suryaprakash

Bengaluru, the Indian city of tech startups and unicorns often compared to Silicon Valley, has two doors. Through one door, the city steps into the technologically wired world of the future. The Indian Institute of Science develops smartphone-turn-malaria-detectors, nanoscale water purifiers, and a revolutionary molecule inhibitor, while hundreds of startups sell everything from micro-mobility to new-age grocery delivery, easy tax computation, and smart investments. A 2021 Klynveld Peat Marwick Goerdeler (KPMG) report ranked Bengaluru 8th among global tech innovation hubs. Through the other door, the city travels through the glorious miles of tradition, delves into India's civilisational reserves, and strives to preserve them. It has been central to the Indic revival and the rise of Hindutva in South India.

Bengaluru's demography makes it a fertile ground for technological innovation and cultural resurgence. It has been ranked as the most millennial-friendly city in the country, with 37 per cent of the population in the age group of fifteen to thirty-five. The city has more than a hundred engineering colleges, producing over 90,000 engineering graduates each year.

With an eye on this, the RSS started its IT Milan shakhas, or camps for techies, in Bengaluru in 2012. By 2019, 7,000–8,000 techies were attending the city's 150-odd shakhas. The programme has since spread to other IT hubs like Hyderabad, Pune, Delhi, Gurugram, and Noida.

A big controversy broke out when reports started emerging that two of India's top techie executives, Zoho co-founder and CEO Sridhar Vembu and Accenture's managing director and head of Chennai operations Rama S. Ramachandran, were to attend the RSS's 'Resurgent Bharath' event in Chennai in February 2020. Ramachandran denied knowledge of it, while Vembu asked trolls to take a walk. It had no effect on the growing alliance between Hindutva, nationalism, and techies. If anything, such outrage and attempts to ideologically censor hardworking professionals only bolstered their popularity and led to more enrolments.

The story of Bharat Suryaprakash, an SAP consultant in Bengaluru, exemplifies how young techies have become a formidable and committed intellectual force for the movement.

He hails from Hassan in Karnataka, the hometown of former PM and Janata Dal (Secular) chief H.D. Deve Gowda. A local RSS pracharak spotted him very early when he was in Class VIII. Despite his initial inhibition to wear the khaki shorts, he eventually came around and started attending the shakhas.

While in high school at a convent, he was approached again, this time by his private tutor, who introduced him to people in the ABVP. Thus, the journey down the Hindutva Road began for the grandson of a well-known local tailor and freedom fighter and the son of an ardent Deve Gowda supporter.

He began holding protest rallies and marches, opposing the activities of the Left-wing student union organisation, Students' Federation of India (SFI). He became vocal about why the Ram Mandir should be rebuilt at the site of the demolished Babri Masjid.

> Then the Bajrang Dal contacted me. At that time, the Bajrang Dal movement was at its peak, with Pramod Muthalik heading it. He later founded Sri Ram Sena. I joined the Bajrang Dal and was also part of some conversions they were doing. But I did not approve of the way Bajrang Dal was raiding clubs or nightclubs, threatening couples, and beating them up. When I drink, it is my choice. Being a Hindu doesn't mean that I can't drink or hang out with friends. I want to support the Hindu cause, but I don't want to be that kind of a hardcore Hindutva activist.

Bharat has collaborated with prominent Hindutva activists like Kiran Kumar S. on mass tree-planting drives and the rejuvenation and rebuilding of old Hoysala temples. He has worked against conversions by missionaries, occasionally interrupting prayer meetings where people were being coaxed or coerced into converting and sometimes reporting zealot colleagues hell-bent on evangelising in the workplace. He has also been part of teams that stopped trucks laden with cows from being taken to Kerala from Alur in Karnataka for slaughter.

When Bharat came to Bengaluru, he was not in touch with the Sangh for a long time. It was 2013. Before the Karnataka Assembly elections, he started creating and sharing pro-BJP memes, some of which mocked Manmohan Singh or the Nehru–Gandhi family. He also shared news about the Congress's scams.

Around this time, he met a software engineer named Kulkarni, who was working with a global software giant as an engineer. Kulkarni contacted the twenty-six-year-old Bharat after the election results and introduced him to a young man named Chetan Azad. Chetan expressed his desire to start a voluntary outfit to work for Modi's 2014 campaign. He clarifies that neither Kulkarni nor Azad was part of Modi's official team. Buoyed by the BJP's victory in Karnataka, a spontaneous movement was gaining steam among the young.

One of the less-discussed features of this movement, he says, is how caste boundaries started to dissolve. While he is a Brahmin, Chetan is from a backward caste. Modi himself, being from a backward caste, helped break many barriers.

> I came to know about Modi after the 2002 Gujarat riots. I knew that fifty-nine kar sevaks were burnt alive on the Godhra train. After that, the Gujarat riots happened. Yeah, the killings should not have happened, but you can't do anything about it. If my son or someone close had died, I would have definitely sought revenge. It's a spontaneous reaction. If your family has been burnt alive, you would seek revenge. But it is amazing how he developed Gujarat after that. It is more developed than Karnataka. His skills, the way he speaks, the way he leads attracted me to follow Narendra Modi. For me, he stands for development, job creation, and Hindutva.

In 2013, he teamed up with Chetan Azad to form the Namo Army on social media and campaigned to get Modi elected as PM. He says one of the powerful triggers was the Congress's proposed Prevention of Communal and Targeted Violence (Access to Justice and Reparations) Bill, 2011, which sought to portray the majority community as the sole villains in cases of communal violence, and minorities as perennial victims, even if the reality was often the opposite.

Transitioning from an intense offensive on social media, the new team also started working on the ground, meeting people, and influencing their opinions.

> We never knew we would receive such massive support from the general public. We had provided them with a number to give us a missed call. We received lakhs of missed calls. But we did not have the funds to renew it. We were never funded by any political party. So, we all volunteered to contribute Rs 2,000 per head from our own pockets.

By then, Bharat had left his job at Infosys and joined Thomson Reuters. His new workplace offered flexible timings. He would arrive at the office at 10 a.m. and leave at 4 p.m. After that, his political work would commence.

> Those in the Sangh would often tell us, 'Why are you running behind a person? You should not be person-oriented, you should be ideology-oriented.' RSS does not encourage vyakti pujan or the worship of individuals. So, I said, 'Let's not listen to the Sangh at this point,' because I was neither a party member nor with the Sangh. None of us wanted to meet Modi or get his appreciation. Our only aim was to see him as the PM.

His involvement was limited in the 2019 general elections, running an online campaign called Namo Bharat. He says the relentless selective coverage, selective bashing of Hinduness, and disregard of one's traditions—such as what happened in Sabarimala—still drive him to act.

Bharat turned down foreign work trips and even marriage proposals while working for Modi's 2014 campaign. 'I wanted to marry only after seeing Modi as the prime minister,' he mentions.

Chetan Azad and some of his other friends resigned from their jobs to work for the campaign.

> Chetan's family is not well-to-do. He resigned from his job and worked for the mission. He was in an accounts job, getting around Rs 15,000–20,000 at that time as a fresher. If you have a gap of one year, I know how you have to struggle to get a job. It is not easy if you have a career gap of one year. After Modi became PM, Chetan struggled for approximately seven months to get another job. Nobody helped him. He is such a selfless volunteer.

Chetan, like Bharat, campaigned for Modi again in 2019.

Disha Satra

Idling on the quaint, stony bridges over the green waters of the Ljubljanica River, one least expects to hear about India and its prime minister from local residents. Disha Satra, then twenty-three, was astonished to see instant recognition of Modi in unexpected corners of Slovenia's Ljubljana or Croatia's Dubrovnik while on a holiday with friends in 2018.

The Mumbaikar, or rather Thanekar, was already popular as a young nationalist influencer on Twitter under the handle 'Sabudana Khichadi'. She was convinced by the changes she saw around her after Modi's ascent to power. However, the international respect she witnessed on that leisure trip overwhelmed her.

> Yeah! I swear I am not lying. I have travelled to a lot of countries. Earlier, I found them looking down on us. India was not a brand. Now, India has actually become a brand, thanks to Modi. He is going everywhere, making these efforts. Earlier, people only knew the President of the US or Russia. That's it. But now, everyone knows Modi. The Croatian President is also a Modi fan, apparently.

A big-city girl from an affluent Jain family, her posts take on the self-proclaimed liberals' daily dose of doublespeak. Unlike others, her chosen battleground is Twitter, regardless of her age. 'Whatever is on Twitter eventually makes its way to Facebook. I feel like I am two steps ahead of them. When they see a meme today, I can tell them I saw it two months ago. And on Twitter, I gain a lot of knowledge,' says the economics graduate from Ruia College, Mumbai.

But she says platforms like Buzzfeed and ScoopWhoop, along with their Facebook and Instagram pages, have great sway over youngsters. The non-Left is often outmatched by the sophistication and insidiousness of their content.

> When I was on Facebook, I used to follow all these 'cool' pages called Buzzfeed, ScoopWhoop, and Huffington Post. Even when Modi was popularising yoga, they were making fun of it. I realised they were not being neutral. On Twitter, everything was completely different. But ScoopWhoop, Buzzfeed, and others are also influencing a lot of neutral people, college students who don't have much knowledge about politics. They see these posts and think supporting Modi is mediocre. They think Shashi Tharoor has such

command over English. He is so cool. Being liberal is so cool. Why is the BJP doing Hindu–Muslim? But they don't see that Tharoor does north–south. He is racist, sexist, casteist … whatever.

Spunky, young influencers usually do not escape the BJP's incredibly sharp talent spotters. So, she had a meeting with cabinet minister Piyush Goyal and blurted out, 'Sir, please leave everything aside right now and change the image of the BJP. Do something about it.'

He apparently asked her for ideas. She suggested reaching out to and persuading some content creators from the Left to collaborate, as well as creating platforms that counter Buzzfeeds and ScoopWhoops with equally sleek content.

Like many other young Indians, Disha admired Arvind Kejriwal and his brand of politics, which arrived with the India Against Corruption (IAC) movement. However, she became disillusioned when Kejriwal's Aam Aadmi Party went right ahead and formed a coalition government with the same Congress, which was the embodiment of corruption that IAC fought against. Her admiration ended there.

Disha faces the same social ostracism from her peers that almost every young nationalist is subjected to.

> Today, there is an event in Khar. Many of my Twitter friends are meeting there. I am not invited because I am not a Leftist. They have even tweeted stuff like 'Sabudana Khichadi is very pretty, but she supports Modi'. There are guys who won't follow me on Twitter but follow and even flirt with me on Instagram. One guy said, 'I also follow Modi. I want to fit into that Football Twitter group, which is why I did not show it in front of them, but I would vote for Modi in any case.'

She is also ridiculed because Disha's father has a gaushala in Thane's Yeoor Hills.

> We have rescued a lot of cows and even a few buffaloes. We have a caretaker, but my father pays for everything. So, we would go there. My friends think, 'Gaushala!' They joke about gaumutra or cow piss, but I don't mind. I am totally okay with that.

Disha's display photo, petting a cow, secured labels like 'Sanghan', 'Right-winger', 'bhaktan' more tightly around her neck. But she does not care. 'Liberals are one of the reasons I am becoming more Right-Wing. I always thought I was a liberal. For me, the nation is more important than the BJP or the Congress,' she asserts.

She says she has been able to change the views of some of her friends. She talks about a girl named Keki, who used to be 'a hardcore liberal'. But after she witnessed the minority appeasement and violence in Bengal, she started questioning why liberals were blind to that issue. Disha then made her watch Vivek Agnihotri's movie, *The Tashkent Files*. 'The conversion was complete,' she says.

Disha's rants on social media echo some of the issues that people across age, geography, and gender have been raising:

- What kind of mindset prompts politicians and celebrities to question and insult the defence forces after the Uri surgical strikes or the Balakot airstrike?
- Why can't those who call themselves secular fiercely condemn Muslims who, after the Pulwama terror attack killed more than forty troops, mocked the forces saying, 'How's the Jaish?'

- How can one call oneself a feminist and yet support burkha in 45-degree heat or instant triple talaq or nikah halala?
- Liberal actors like Swara Bhaskar talk about Hindutva politician Sadhvi Pragya being a terror-accused. Then why does she work with murder accused Salman Khan? What about murder suspect Tharoor? Or terror convict Sanjay Dutt? Or out-on-bail Rahul Gandhi?
- Why pick on the Railways for the new-age Vande Bharat train or the Indian Space Research Organisation (ISRO) for some launch over minor technical snags? Why deliberately miss the big picture of development? The BJP doesn't make the trains or space shuttles, talented Indians do.
- Why a Gurmehar Kaur, daughter of an army officer killed in battle, achieves instant celebrity status among so-called 'liberals' by holding up a placard: 'Pakistan did not kill my father. War did.' Why are you demeaning your father's sacrifice and thousands of others killed by Pakistan?

She proudly proclaims that her most treasured possession is a T-shirt with a straight, simple message: 'Indian Army: Saving our ass since 1947, whether you like it or not.'

However, her cultivated air of girliness disappears when she starts knowledgeably speaking on digitisation, tech shifts, infrastructure-building, healthcare schemes, and ease of doing business happening in the last few years. She wears her love for the nation on her sleeves, even if it means having to detach herself from the 'cool', urban milieu she could have comfortably slipped into.

CHAPTER 2

Making Constitution Meet Civilisation

Colonialists rise and fall, but long after they are gone, they often leave behind vestiges of their domination and tyranny. These contaminate our language, our clothes, our books, and crucially, the laws that regulate our lives.

These remnants of colonialism have penetrated the Indian Constitution. Prominent legal minds of the Indic wing believe that these cripple the great civilisation and hinder its progress. Wheels are in motion at the individual, ideological, and government levels to rid India of these vestiges of slavery.

In December 2017, the Lok Sabha passed the Repealing and Amending Bill and the Repealing and Amending (Second) Bill, eliminating 245 antiquated and unnecessary pieces of legislation. It has identified over 1,800 more.

Some of the legal baggage invokes embarrassing irony. The Salt Satyagraha, immortalised by Mahatma Gandhi's Dandi March, was a significant turning point in India's freedom struggle. The protest aimed to end British colonial taxation on salt, which Indian farmers produced. Despite that, a salt tax exists in most Indian states even today. When Jawaharlal Nehru became the head of the interim government in 1946, he repealed the tax. But his own government brought in the Salt

Cess Tax Act in 1953, which is still in force. This tax is imposed as a sub-tax to pay for a specific administrative cost, costing 14 paise per kg of the body weight of salt. Salt manufacturing facilities, whether privately or publicly owned, are subject to this levy. A little more than 1.4 lakh people are employed in India's salt industry, and 92 per cent of the salt is produced by private companies.

Take, for example, another notorious symbol of British repression of Indian resistance—the Dramatic Performances Act of 1876. It came into effect to stop public performances of nationalistic plays. The colonial government was rattled by Dinabandhu Mitra's 1860 play *Nil Darpan*, which depicted how the British mercilessly tortured and pushed Indians into the doom of unrepayable loans and slavery.

After a couple of performances of the play staged by the National Theatre, which paved the way for more such plays critical of the British Raj, the rulers feared that this would incite audiences to oppose the government. The British government passed the Dramatic Performances Act in 1876, citing the threat of social unrest. It outlawed 'scandalous' and 'defamatory' theatrical performances. After Independence, amended and updated versions of this same law were introduced and implemented in several states, with the exception of Delhi and West Bengal.

Another archaic and problematic piece of legislation, akin to blasphemy laws of Abrahamic religions, is Section 295A of the Indian Penal Code. In 1927, publisher Mahashay Rajpal wrote a book named *Rangila Rasul*, which was a satirical take on Prophet Mohammed's personal life. It was published in Lahore, already on the communal boil because of the rise of Muhammad Ali Jinnah's Muslim League, which was demanding the creation of Islamic Pakistan to be carved out of India. The book also delved into the radical aspects of the Hadiths. It was first written in Urdu and challenged certain dogmatic beliefs and the pitiable condition of women in the Islamic world, discussing Mohammed and his wives.

Rangila Rasul was believed to be a retaliation to a nude painting of Sita, which a Muslim group in Lahore had published and referred to as a prostitute. When the *Rangila Rasul* matter went to the Lahore High Court, Justice Dilip Singh found Rajpal not guilty. However, succumbing to the wanton Islamist violence that erupted around the book, the British amended Section 295 and introduced Section 295A, a softened version of blasphemy laws:

> Whoever, with the deliberate and malicious intention of outraging the religious feelings of any class of citizens of India, by words, either spoken or written, or by signs or by visible representations or otherwise, insults or attempts to insult the religion or the religious beliefs of that class, shall be punished with imprisonment of either description for a term which may extend to three years, or with fine, or with both.

After a stormy trial, Mahashey Rajpal was acquitted in 1929. However, Islamic mobs openly lusted for his Sharia-style beheading. After many failed attempts, they finally got him on 6 April 1929. Ilm-ud-din, a fanatical carpenter, stabbed Rajpal to death.

A haunting replay of that barbaric episode seems to be unfolding nearly a hundred years later in the Nupur Sharma case. As a BJP spokesperson, Sharma engaged in a heated, on-air debate with her co-panellist, Social Democratic Party of India (SDPI) leader Tasleem Rahmani, who made uncharitable remarks about the Shivling found in the Gyanvapi mosque. Sharma then referenced Mohammed's child marriage, as mentioned in the Hadiths. In the tornado of Islamist violence that this has triggered, more than half a dozen Hindus have been killed—most of them beheaded—simply for supporting Sharma.

In the UK, the country of the colonisers who created the legislation, any writing that insulted the Bible or Christianity and disrupted public order was potentially criminal until 2008. The demand by UK Muslims to use blasphemy laws against Salman Rushdie's *The Satanic Verses* ultimately sparked a drive to repeal the statute.

In 1985, the UK Statute Commission recommended that the law be abolished, citing both the right to free speech and the law's irrelevance in today's society. The UK government stated that rarely used laws like blasphemy served no purpose and instead encouraged religious organisations to attempt to limit artists. The law was abolished in the UK in 2008.

In India, however, hundreds of lives have been lost over accusations of blasphemy since Rajpal's murder, yet the colonial relic Section 295A has persisted.

In the new Indic upsurge, however, a growing number of lawyers and legal activists have started challenging laws and parts of the Constitution that are steeped in colonialism and a history of bloodshed. The Modi government's strong and steady weeding out of colonial and oppressive laws has energised these individuals and groups to reform India's legal framework in ways not witnessed for many generations.

J. Sai Deepak

One of the foremost names in this battle to reform the Constitution and save civilisation is J. Sai Deepak. Originally an aerospace engineering aspirant, the thirty-eight-year-old is now one of the country's most talked-about Supreme Court advocates. He is a rousing orator with formidable argumentative skills.

Sitting in a grey tracksuit at his Noida residence-cum-office, Sai adjusts his tall frame and thickset glasses as he begins his story.

> We are basically Iyers. Our ancestry is from the Kaveri Delta, specifically Thanjavur. That's where both sides of the family trace their origins. I was born in Chennai but was brought up entirely in Hyderabad in undivided Andhra Pradesh. It was a joint family setup that was still climbing its way up the social ladder. It straddled the red line between the lower middle class and the middle class. So, there was this typical Tam-Bram obsession with education, education, and education. Because you don't have any land or property. Nothing else. I'm a product of the convent education system. It's a Christian school from Hyderabad, St Anthony's High School.

One of the earliest influences in Sai's life was Atal Bihari Vajpayee's historic 1996 speech on secularism during the No-Confidence Motion that felled his government. He also carries vivid memories of the 1993 riots in Hyderabad after the Babri Masjid demolition.

> I've lived in Muslim-dominated localities too. I've seen the attitudes of young children around that particular period, how they would make a mock gun with their fingers and target the tricolour. This was Hyderabad, not Kashmir. If you grow up in that kind of place, there is a gradual, unspoken, subconscious awareness that not everybody is necessarily pro-Bharat. The ability to articulate comes much, much later. I think as time

goes by, our experience only informs our instinct with little logical reasons, but the seed has already been sown. Kargil was also a major trigger. In several parts of Hyderabad, they celebrated the mutilation of our soldiers. Even after 9/11, the gloating and the concept of a global Umma were very visible in Hyderabad, which has more than 40 per cent Muslims. Then there is the legacy of the Nizam. Many see themselves as descendants of Nizam.

In 2002, at the age of sixteen, he left Hyderabad to study engineering in Coimbatore, Tamil Nadu. His major influence during that period, when India was churning out missiles, was Dr A.P.J. Abdul Kalam.

On Tamil Nadu campuses, both Dravidianism and its direct descendant, anti-Brahmanism, were in full force. Absolutely full force. And if you're a Tam Bram coming from outside, your language is relatively uncorrupted by the changes it has undergone in Tamil Nadu. So, the fact that you're a Brahmin is immediately reflected in your language. They'll immediately know. They'll say, 'Iyer'. The other word that they use is 'thayir cātam' or 'curd rice' because curd rice is something that Brahmins eat. Another stereotype is that if you are a Brahmin, you are expected to be fair. Since I'm not, they called me 'Black Brahmin'. Imagine, this is how race politics is in Tamil Nadu. We are not talking about America. For a state that is heavily invested in Dravidianism and would call themselves blackshirts, with black being the colour of Dravidian ideology, many would vote for MGR because he was fair. They had such an inferiority complex. And what is the stereotype in Tamil movies? A dark hero and a fair heroine. Typically, get a north Indian heroine and *dono ko mila do* [part them together].'

He says that ever since the Dravidian movement, activists have been known to remove vibhuti from others' foreheads and cut the tuft of hair of a shikhadhaari Brahmin.

> They would actively incite their youth wings to go and hug Brahmin women in public and molest them. So Gopalpuram, where Karunanidhi ultimately passed away, was largely populated by Brahmins. DMK cadre would go house to house and rape people. This is a known fact. It never came out. The current chief minister has a lot to answer for on these subjects. Kashmiri Pandits suffered at the hands of Muslims. Tam Brams suffered at the hands of so-called Hindus. Unfortunately, we have not even showcased the story properly.

It was at this point that Sai Deepak began to ask himself how one could address the situation dispassionately, setting emotions aside. As an engineer with a background in mathematics, physics, and chemistry, he had no training to counter the narrative and no exposure to history, humanities, or economics.

> The only thing I had was a decent command of the language. The standard practice in the south is to be told, 'Read the *Hindu*. Do not forget to read the editorial brilliant opinions.' What brilliant opinions? Lousy opinions. Now you look back and wonder, our parents did not know that they had been pushed, and then they were pushing us into brainwashing.

But he found journalist and writer Cho Ramaswamy to be outstanding.

> Ah, fantastic. Fantastic. My initiation to the man came about after 2004. He realised that things were going from bad to

worse. One thing he was clear about was how Jayalalitha's reputation and work changed post-1996, how she had surrounded herself with a pack of wolves.

The year 2004 was also the year when Sai started asking himself questions.

> *Kya ho jayega* engineer *bann ke? Lakhon to hain already* [What will change if I become an engineer? There are lakhs of engineers already]. I never quit engineering because I was not interested or because I was suffocating. I had gone into engineering with a lot of interest. I realised that if you want to speak on a subject, do not do so just on the basis of being an autodidact. It is important to have a qualification. Otherwise, why do you need someone who's a qualified lawyer to speak on the law? I was absolutely clear that I would never be content leading the life of a self-sufficient engineer. Maximum, what would I do? Sit in California and start writing about Bharat.

Sai's father is a retired State Bank of India employee, and his mother still teaches children out of passion. Sai says he has always had the reputation of being 'uddand' (stubborn or defiant) of the first order.

> Unless I'm convinced, nobody can change me. Even my parents have not been able to change me, *tum kya hi change kar loge mujhe* [how will you change me]. I thought that I was decent with articulation, and I was surrounded by friends and people who would not just encourage my reading, they would flood me with books. My initiation to Arun Shourie was by my Malayali friend's uncle. He gave me two seminal books: *The World of Fatwas* and *Missionaries in India*. Whatever may have happened with Dr Shourie subsequently, according to

me, is irrelevant. These people did this in a generation in which people's careers were being destroyed left, right, and centre for even speaking on those lines.

Sai's next choice was between civil services and law. He was still unsure, aware of the nepotism in the legal ecosystem, and the existence of 'blue-blooded' families that control the profession.

> I think the Constitution tells you about the mentality of the system, about its neural network. But if you happen to choose law in my generation, the stereotype was that you would be found on this very popular bridge in Hyderabad called Chikkadpally Bridge, wearing mismatched Hawaii chappals, riding a Hercules cycle, and looking for clients.

He completed his BE in mechanical engineering in 2006. During his fifth semester, he went to IIT Kharagpur for a paper presentation. The then-director mentioned that they were about to start a new specialisation in Law and Intellectual Property Rights, exclusively for engineers, doctors, and MBAs with a science background.

> The best part is that you could sell it to your parents because it is LLB from IIT. Had it been from anywhere else, parents would have said, '*Bhaag jaao, koi shaadi nahi karegi* [Run away, no one will marry you].' Once I entered law school, it was like this out-of-body experience when the atma enters the soul again, where you realise, 'I've come to my place.' Suppose I had collected a rupee from everyone who has asked me this question, 'Why Law after Engineering?', I would have been a billionaire by now. It so happens that the legal profession had gone through a slump in the seventies and

eighties. And the erosion of public confidence in the entire establishment was massive. In every other movie, black coats [lawyers] or khaki [cops] were the villains.

Sai Deepak says he was fortunate to have taken to the profession, and the profession also took to him. Among the brilliant minds he was surrounded with in law school was visiting faculty Professor N.L. Mitra, who served as the second vice-chancellor of the National Law School of India University (NLSIU), Bengaluru, and the founding vice-chancellor of the National Law University Jodhpur (NLUJ).

Mitra recommended Sai Deepak to Gopal Subramanium, who had then become the solicitor general of the country. Subramanium was impressed by his CV but could not meet his financial expectations. So, he advised him to join a law firm. Sai started with intellectual property law. By the sixth year, he had become an associate partner. In the seventh year, he transitioned to working as an independent practitioner focusing exclusively on serving as arguing counsel.

> I realised that when competence meets opinions, it is a deadly combination. I was perhaps the first law student in Indian judicial history whose blog post was cited by the division bench of the Madras High Court in the Bajaj vs TVS patent dispute on 18 May 2009. But once I came out into the profession, I realised that doing well in law school is one thing. But it is a massive fraternity out there, with lakhs of people from across the country, including those from established national law schools. So, for the first seven years, I kept my head down and focused on delivering results in court. Like any other lawyer, I made myself useful to the team, the seniors, and the clients I worked for. Then gradually, I started voicing my opinions.

One of the major milestones came in his second year in the profession when the Ram Janmabhoomi judgement was delivered by the Allahabad High Court. Current MP Bhupinder Yadav was one of the members of the legal team, along with Vikramjit Banerjee (whom he called Vikramda). They were assisting Ravi Shankar Prasad, who was one of the counsels for the matter before the court.

This was in 2011. Sai conducted a fair amount of research around that time on the concept of deity and their rights under the Constitution, including privacy and other matters; little did he know that it would come in handy in the Sabarimala case in 2018. Ram Lalla was to take the Sabarimala argument forward.

An anonymous Twitter handle recommended Sai Deepak to contact the individual managing the @People4Dharma handle and take up the legal challenge on behalf of the movement to uphold the Sabarimala temple's tradition. In 2015, C.S. Vaidyanathan, who represented Ram Lalla in the Ayodhya case, invited him to join the 'Temple Freedom' petitions filed by Swami Dayanand Saraswati.

He adds, 'You can say that my involvement in civilisational causes began tangibly with my association with the Free Temple petitions from 2015. It was further solidified once I became part of the Sabarimala team.'

But the Sabarimala case did not proceed as favourably as the Ayodhya matter.

Perhaps there was a saviour complex influencing the judiciary at that point, leading them to believe that they had to somehow liberate women who were under Brahmanical patriarchy. Interestingly, the sole female member of the bench felt otherwise. The dissenting opinion came from

Justice Indu Malhotra, essentially stating that women know how to protect themselves, echoing the sentiments of Swami Vivekananda.

On 28 September 2018, the four-to-one decision came out in favour of allowing the entry of women. Subsequently, a massive number of review petitions were filed. Before retiring on 14 November 2019, Chief Justice of India Ranjan Gogoi delivered the judgement that there was a case for a review. He identified seven questions for consideration by a bench of nine judges.

When Sharad Arvind Bobde became the chief justice, Advocate Indira Jaising, who appeared for the petitions, went to court seeking security and protection for the entry of women under the age of fifty.

> Justice Bobde took the position that seven questions had already been identified for the review, and compared to the new 2018 judgement, the practice had been around for at least 300 years. So, the balance tilts in favour of the practice. Therefore, we cannot provide any security at this stage. You will be allowed entry if the temple believes that your entry is consistent with its own traditions and practices. So, effectively, that was the status quo. Hence, there is no question of women under the particular age group going. The Kerala government backed out badly. It realised there was not just revolt from people but also from the CPM cadre. They said, 'All these years we have been bleeding for the red flag, now we will bleed for the Aiyappa.' Second, a lot of those who stood by me were Malayali Christians. Many of these Christian families had rented their homes to people who were observing that vrata away from their families. The BJP initially sided with the petitioners but quickly changed its

stand. In all this, the Left did not see an incentive to keep pursuing it.

The nine-judge bench began hearing the review in February 2020, but the proceedings were interrupted by the onset of COVID-19. Additionally, one of the judges, Justice R. Bhanumathi, retired during this period. Consequently, a new bench will now have to be constituted to continue the proceedings.

The struggle for Ram Lalla or Aiyappa is a component of Sai Deepak's broader endeavour to align the Constitution more closely with Indian civilisation. As he eloquently articulates in his book, *India That Is Bharat*:

> While the adoption of national constitutions facilitated the creation of political entities which could now be called nation-states, this was largely a product of colonial imposition through 'international law', as discussed earlier, and not necessarily reflective of the irrelevance of other forms of political organisation. The irony of the situation was that on the one hand, former colonies had to rely on their past to stake a claim for their nation-statehood, and on the other hand, to be accepted into the 'commonwealth of civilised State', they had to embrace modernity and sever ties with their past. Naturally, those tensions affected the making of their constitutions, with coloniality more often than not having the upper hand. Consequently, under constitutions imbued with coloniality and a strained relationship with the past, the colonialised nation-states donned the robes of a contemporary Martin Luther, holding forth from the bully pulpit and calling for the reform of the native under the authority of the new Bible, namely the constitution.

He further explains:

> I hold great respect for the Constitution. However, it is imperative to question whether this Constitution has facilitated civilisational awareness and empowerment or has it come in the way? Alternatively, is it the judiciary's interpretation of the Constitution that has led to a clash between civilisation and the Constitution? This is the fundamental question I'm trying to ask. Whether the mindset has to be changed or the document, I have yet to arrive at a conclusion. Nonetheless, one thing I firmly believe is that the alterations made to the Preamble in 1976 and 1977, adding the words 'secular' and 'socialist' during the Emergency without parliamentary approval, need to be corrected. A couple of petitions have been filed, but it is incumbent upon the legislature and the current government to take the lead. It is time for a reset.

The second crucial change that Sai envisions pertains specifically to Article 25 through Article 30, which address religious rights. He believes that within these articles, the concept of dharma should be firmly entrenched. 'For a country that swears by dharma—the Supreme Court's motto is "*Yato dharma sthato jaya*", which means where there is dharma, there is victory—dharma does not feature in the Constitution anywhere. Religion is not dharma,' he says.

Sai Deepak passionately advocates for change in another area—education. He firmly believes it must be approached holistically.

> It is astounding that there are gurukuls outside this country. We see videos of gurukuls in the UK where children are openly chanting Sanskrit, and they are not necessarily children of Indian origin. And what is happening in Bharat?

It is relegated only to Veda pathshalas. Mainstreaming has to happen, which was the position until 1835 [when Thomas Babington Macaulay introduced the English Education Act]. We have to invest there.

The conversation shifts to one of the most contentious issues in Hindu activism—State control of temple funds. Hindu temple trusts are subject to State control and taxation, while minority religious trusts enjoy exemptions.

Why does the [Indian] State believe that corruption is exclusively Hindu and limited to Hindu institutions? Second, is it the position of the State that corruption can only be addressed if the State takes over the institutions for eternity? Let me give you a simple example. The government intervened after the Satyam scam, took over the company, reconstituted the board, and moved on. If it can do so in the case of private companies, why can't the same be done with religious institutions? These are community institutions. This is community money. When the State wants to exercise its right to march in, it must show that there was no other option and this was the last resort. But now it is the first resort. Which means Hindu institutions are up for grabs.

He argues that temples, like every charitable institution, should be exempt from tax under Indian laws. 'But the problem lies elsewhere,' he says. The State extracts wealth from temples not as tax but as service fees. There is a growing backlash because the State exerts control over temples, imposes high service fees, fosters casteism by establishing electorally favourable caste equations on the temple board, and does so selectively, targeting only Hindu institutions.

He also discusses government regulations that incentivise conversion to Islam and Christianity.

> There is a state corporation for SC and ST Christians in Kerala, with a very clear scheme and allocation of budgets. I don't understand how this is even constitutional. In the name of social empowerment, you are facilitating conversion. Is it your position that you want to break jatiwaad or casteism? To achieve that, are you encouraging people to simply switch from one religion to another? Which means, your grievance is not with casteism. You want to dismantle Hindutva. How is that different from Dr Ambedkar's original position that the only way to destroy caste is by eliminating Hindus? He had mellowed down subsequently because Gandhi forced him to. So, when a structure is put in place to facilitate conversions from the Hindu fold—whether direct, indirect, intended, or unintended … it does not matter—you have effectively walked into the largest organised religion in the world, Christianity. Therefore, the sole surviving indigenous civilisation, which has put up such stiff resistance against colonisers and invaders, is being forced to open its doors for the exodus of its people to another religion under independent, secular Bharat.

He mentions that in Andhra Pradesh, funds from the Tirupati trust are being allocated for the construction of flyovers, a move that CM Jagan Reddy has acknowledged. He also raises concerns about the state's subsidy for the Holy Land Pilgrimage for Haj. Where does the money come from?

> The state can instead provide excellent facilities at the airport or guest houses for crowd management or law and order purposes. But why provide a Haj subsidy when there is

no subsidy for the Amarnath, Kedarnath, or Kanwar Yatra pilgrimages? The police force recruits Muslims under the OBC category. How is that allowed? The next argument presented is that we should recognise the concept of a Dalit Christian. No. The premise of Christianity and Islam is that they are casteless. The day you choose to leave Hinduism, you have chosen to sever all ties with your previous caste. We have the right to protect our demographics and identity as much as anyone else, if not more. For two reasons: one, we have suffered at your hands, and two, our faith system is native to this land. Malini Parthasarathy claims that Christianity is one of India's oldest religions. What utter nonsense! Why were these apostles murdered? Because they were going around converting people and calling their religion the faith of Satan. And then they were made martyrs.

He cites the case of the Kapaleeswarar Temple in Mylapore, Tamil Nadu. It is not in its original location. The board states that the Portuguese destroyed it. Originally, it was situated at Saint Thomas Mount, where the Basilica now stands. The murti were transported and re-established at its current site, which used to be a beachside temple.

'With all this going on, I don't see how even equality is not available to us. There should be greater affirmative action in favour of Hindus as a consequence of what they have suffered,' he says.

When asked in what ways are Hindus considered less equal in the eyes of the law, he answered:

> Let's consider the control over our institutions. The interpretation of Article 29 and Article 30 with respect to our autonomy over traditional educational institutions, and the Right to Education (RTE) Act, for example. Minority

groups have argued that including their institutions in the RTE Act would violate their right to conserve their language and culture, as defined in Article 29, and their right to establish and administer educational institutions, as defined in Article 30. The Supreme Court has upheld this view. Why is an exception carved out? If you believe that they're equal citizens, then social responsibility must be equally borne by them. Then, who is creating the concepts of secession and separatism? It's the State doing this. What is the basis for saying that Christian and Muslim institutions shall not bear the duty of educating underprivileged children as much as Hindu institutions? If you have accepted them as different, why do you call us 'fascist' when we say they are different? Minoritism is another name for a state within a state. Perhaps that is the intention ... to shield this particular group entirely from the State's interference. When it comes to personal law, you can't touch them. When it comes to conversions, you can't touch them. Their religious institutions, educational institutions, and central aspects of their life are completely untouched by the State. What remains of their ability to become part of the mainstream? How do you then hope that they will become part of the mainstream? How does integration even play out after that? It's a mirage. It's a pipe dream. And the Constitution is facilitating it at this point. Since this has been the norm for seventy-five years, it is no longer seen as an opportunity but as a right. It has become an entitlement. Anything less is viewed as an infringement and an attack on minority freedoms.

You'll have reports written by the United States or Amnesty International, and India will certainly defend itself. One mention in the *New York Times*, and we become defensive about it. Clearly, there is a lack of civilisational confidence. China says, 'Go do your worst. This is my State. I do what I want.' Instead, they will come up with their own report on the United States, authored by a Chinese academician. No wonder Trump was going after institutions with a lot of Chinese presence. That is why I keep saying that Bharat obviously has to protect its interests from China. But we have to learn from the way China deals with the West. This is the language that the West understands. The world's biggest intellectual property thief is the West.

China tells the West that when it was developing, it stole everything. Now, when the West is at the top, it tries to change the rules of the game for others, whether it is climate change or World Trade Organisation negotiations.

The young lawyer, with profound clarity on India's civilisational place in the world, believes that the nation has reached a critical inflection point in history. He cites the Bhagavad Gita, stating that everything has both a worldly and a metaphysical aspect.

The worldly response is that there has been a certain degree of pent-up frustration at being treated as human doormats. That frustration sought an outlet in the age of print media by sending letters to the editor, which the editors would not publish. The letters went to the trash. The internet has opened the doors to the democratisation of opinion, allowing the common people to shout and say, 'Enough is enough!' Of course, it has its downsides. But the essential question is, is it doing what it was meant to? Yes, it is. The monopoly over opinions and facts held by the mainstream media has been completely undermined. That citadel has been broken, and there is no going back.

Sai says that often the responses to posts by celebrity journalists are more educated and informed. This phenomenon has also exposed the abysmal understanding and fieldwork in journalism. He cites the scene in the United States, where specialist blogs on economics, climate change, and other subjects have taken over from mainstream newspapers. He notes that a similar trend is also occurring in India.

As for his metaphysical response, he explains:

> People believe that Narendra Modi is the harbinger of this change. I believe he represents the change and the churn that was already present. It is time and situation that always throws up the individual, not the other way around. Then it is up to the individual to realise his or her civilisational responsibilities. Look at the number of options across streams today. Whether it is history, science, journalism, academics, law, or climate change, we are offering some fantastic options. And the bluff of the Left that the non-Left is bereft of talent and intellectual heft has been blown to smithereens. The arrogance of the Nehruvian establishment has been smashed.

He further notes that the Left ecosystem's advantage has always been the existence of a well-oiled machinery, which continues to be its strength. It will take time to dismantle it. But we are seeing a response word for word, woman for woman, man for man, child for child.

> Youngsters in schools, fourteen- and fifteen-year-olds, have started taking this particular position ... There is a beautiful thinker from Odisha, just about eighteen years old. His name is Anvesh Satpathy. He wanted to interview me on his podcast after reading my book. For some reason, it didn't work out because I was busy. But these kids have already read content that I started reading only in my early thirties. These people have understood the message to play to your

strengths, whether it is law or science or anything else, and contribute to the cause. Computer science grads are telling me we will create alternatives to Twitter or Facebook. That is so fantastic to hear. You're creating a society where people are realising why we can't create better? That questioning has begun. They will take this forward, come what may.

When he went to Coimbatore for a book talk as part of the book tour, Union Public Service Commission (UPSC) aspirants from Bengaluru travelled to listen to him.

> They cried. Their first reaction was that more people need to speak for us, for our people. These are kids in their teens. They are saying you are not alone. We are joining this. One boy had taken sanyas … proper sanyas. He came back and joined the UPSC to serve the nation. He said his generation has to fight in this world. The other world can wait. They took Vivekananda's message to heart. When you see this, how can you feel hopeless? I don't think we should estimate our sense of hope based on what happens at national-level politics. The ground is changing, and it will change a lot more. And therefore, this is going to be one of the most troublesome periods for Bharat. Hindus will ask all the uncomfortable questions which will have to be answered.

His books, *India That Is Bharat* and *India, Bharat and Pakistan*, have received bestseller reception. There was an eager audience waiting to consume them.

> I just happened to be giving shape to those thoughts and pushing them in the right direction. They lapped it up. They have taken ownership of the message. They have gone to a different level altogether. And some of these people are so

vastly read, I realised that I could have said a few things better and differently. As someone who believes in the Vedic approach to life and its approach to cosmological balance, I would seriously believe that dharma rests on rita. Rita is the natural state as things are meant to be. And therefore, the movement towards rita and dharma has begun.

What tipped the balance, he states, are events like the 26/11 Mumbai attacks and rampant corruption under the Congress. People felt that the country was up for sale. A movement like India Against Corruption showed that Indians did not want to put up their country for plunder and sale again. It started from a secular issue of corruption and has now taken on a civilisational dimension.

> When you realise that your civilisation and culture are at stake, it is the deepest realisation. And that is what has happened now. No single individual can take credit. It is a movement. As a Hindu, I can say that there are prayers of several seers across the place for this lady, Bharat Mata, saying 'Protect us, this lady needs to rise again.' I don't think Swami Vivekananda was ever operating from a 'vyavaharic' or worldly perspective. He goes there, sits on the rock, and says, 'This lady will wake up again.'

At this point, J. Sai Deepak's voice becomes coarse and his eyes well up. There is a long pause before he continues.

> When he [Vivekananda] says that you have to ask yourself, which generation will finally grasp that? It can't be an endless adjournment like you get in court. Some generation has to wake up and say, 'In our lifetime, not any further.' The transformation may not always be beautiful. It could be

all sorts ... beautiful, ugly ... everything. But one thing is certain ... it is going to be 100 per cent exciting. If there was ever a time to commit, this is that time.

Vinay Joshi

Calls for justice often fail to make their way to the courts from across the 3.287 million square kilometres of this nation. Thousands of small and big tyrannies eat away at the very foundations of India. Many of these are not merely personal in nature; they have a profound civilisational effect.

An imam delivering an inflammatory speech in Maharashtra's Beed, the Church taking over tribal land in Jharkhand, lynching of a Hindu boy for marrying a Christian girl in Assam's Lakhimpur, defacing of the national flag at a Muharram procession in Kanpur ... every day, in parts of India either not accessed or deliberately ignored by the media and our legal system, events unfold that slowly alter the spirit and composition of this nation.

It is these events that the Legal Rights Observatory (LRO), an organisation ideologically aligned with the RSS, monitors. Vinay Joshi, forty-four years old, a former RSS pracharak, heads an important chapter of it. Fluent in Marathi, Hindi, English, Garo, Koch, Hajong, Assamese, Bengali, Urdu, Konkani, and currently learning Pashto, Joshi is married with two children—an eleven-year-old girl and a six-year-old boy.

His introduction to RSS started with his father, an RSS pracharak, who first took him to a shakha in Dapoli, a coastal hill station in Maharashtra's Ratnagiri district, when he was just three years old. After completing his BSc in horticulture from the Konkan Kushi Vidyapeeth, he joined the Sangh as a pracharak at the age of twenty-two. He was then sent to work in the missionary-dominated Garo Hills of Meghalaya. Garos are the second-largest converted tribe after the Mizos, with almost 90 per cent having converted to Baptist Christianity. Joshi worked with the Songsarek Garo community, who have not converted.

Talking about his challenges as a pracharak in the Garo Hills, Joshi states:

> There were no-go zones for me. I faced life threats from radical Christian groups and armed militant outfits. Still, I managed to penetrate 100 villages in the west, east, and parts of south Garo Hills. Mass reconversion may not be possible at this juncture, but many converted Christians repent of losing their ancestral faith. About twenty-five powerful Garo Christian citizens are working with us.

Joshi traces the earliest year of the Hindu resurgence movement to 1925, with the birth of the RSS. Following that, there was tremendous persecution of Hindus after M.K. Gandhi's assassination in 1948 and during the Emergency in 1975, he notes.

> After both occasions, the RSS continued to grow, albeit slowly and steadily. The watershed moment was the Ayodhya agitation. However, for any ideology to be sustained, it must have social and political power simultaneously. At the peak of the Ram Janmabhoomi movement, there was enough social momentum for Hindutva organisations like the RSS, VHP, and Bajrang Dal. But there was no formidable political power. The next watershed was in 2002. It was the Godhra train burning incident. There was a concerted attempt to capture and incriminate Modi and Amit Shah. But they

kept growing, and their political persecution led Hindus to recognise them as their representative.

That feeling of persecution was exacerbated after the Malegaon blast when Sadhvi Pragya, Swami Aseemanand, and Colonel Purohit were falsely implicated and hounded, he adds. He cites the Communal Violence Bill of 2011 as another example of the deep anti-Hindu bias of the Sonia Gandhi–Manmohan Singh-led UPA government.

Then came 26/11. The Mumbai attacks left another deep mark on the Hindu psyche, says Joshi. 'It again reminded us that although we are the majority in India, we are bound to face persecution for years to come,' Joshi adds.

He further claims that even though at the organisational level, LRO has no formal relationship with the RSS, 'there are ideological synergies.' The LRO has emerged as a mass movement, now comprising more than 5,000 highly motivated lawyers and writers who work pro bono. Joshi says that the LRO operates on donations, funding from patron trusts, and sometimes money from one's own pocket. There are only about a hundred paid workers. 'It has a loose structure. Different professionals volunteer for different issues,' says Joshi. 'Our focus is the persecution of Hindus by the Church, especially of the indigenous people in the Northeast and tribals all over India.'

It also addresses jihadi violence and investigates shadowy foreign funding of NGOs. The organisation has offices in Mumbai, Guwahati, Ratnagiri, and an NGO monitoring unit in Bengaluru, which handles the Foreign Contribution Regulation Act (FCRA) or foreign funding-related issues.

The LRO has made about 250 interventions in different courts so far. However, it has also written thousands of letters and notices to gram, taluka, state, and central governments, filed complaints, made repeated follow-ups, and issued intimations of legal actions. In most cases, the issues are resolved outside the court simply because somebody is pursuing them instead of giving up.

Among LRO's recent successes, Joshi counts a case from Arunachal Pradesh. In 2021, an additional district collector handed over a government quarter to a church organisation in Arunachal Pradesh. Joshi explains:

> They started building a church on government land without any documents. We issued an intimation of legal action. The militant group National Socialist Council of Nagaland (NSCN) was slowly getting involved. Whistleblowers were being threatened. After around twelve legal notices and exchanges, the government land was cleared, and the additional deputy commissioner (ADC) was demoted and transferred.

But one of LRO's ongoing and most crucial interventions has been against the shadowy funding of NGOs. From October 2020 to February 2022, the organisation took action against about 550 NGOs with the home ministry's FCRA department. It submitted nearly 8,500 pages of complaints. Joshi adds:

> Following this, a massive cleanup has started. In May 2022, the CBI raided forty-two locations across India and arrested more than fifty people, including seven home ministry officials. These officials were sharing IB reports with NGOs, facilitating illegal clearances. The bureau has charged all of them.

One of LRO's major breakthroughs was the case in which, for the first time in India, the Church faced action for grabbing tribal land. In 2017, it took action against the Simdega diocese in Jharkhand for the unauthorised purchase of land in violation of the Chhotanagpur Tenancy Act and the Santhal Parganas Tenancy Act. The state reclaimed the land. However, since the BJP government fell and the JMM-Congress Hemant Soren government came to power, it has not taken physical control of the disputed land.

LRO's legal activism has reached even the hallowed benches of the Bombay High Court. In July 2021, sitting judge S.S. Shinde heaped praise on Stan Swamy after the death of the Naxal activist and terror accused in the Bhima-Koregaon violence of 2017–18. LRO lodged a complaint with the chief justice of India and the registrar of the Supreme Court regarding the behaviour of the judge. The LRO's letter to the CJI said:

> In our considered view, Hon'ble Mr Justice Shinde, in making this comment, has crossed the line of judicial propriety, since he was the judge hearing the bail applications of Stan Swamy and he has also been hearing other matters involving the Bhima-Koregaon incident. A judge who has to adjudicate on the merits of extremely serious criminal charges, commenting openly about being appreciative of the work of one of the accused, casts a shadow on his impartiality and fairness.

After its relentless campaign, which involved collecting 850 signatures from anguished citizens, Justice Shinde recused from the Bhima-Koregaon case. Although later he was promoted as the chief justice of the Rajasthan High Court, LRO kept up the pressure on the Union law minister to not accept the recommendation of the collegium.

Joshi outlines a stunningly intricate and ambitious roadmap for LRO.

> For 1.35 billion Indians, we need two to five legal activism forums for every walk of life: omen, health, civic issues, education, politics, environment, senior citizens, children, video game addiction ... in such a huge country, raising such issues and for the government to rectify these is part and parcel of a healthy ecosystem. LRO has identified at least 5,000 such verticals related to ordinary citizens for which there should be at least one active forum for each. A likeminded government can't solve all the issues of citizens by itself. In many cases, it cannot take up issues on a suo motu basis. One needs legal activists to identify and raise the issues.

He also underlines how social media has rendered mainstream media irrelevant, 'It has reduced many so-called star journalists to mere YouTubers.' He quotes from Sanjaya Baru's book, *India's Power Elite*, on how individuals from small towns are now shaping policy and government. In the new India, there's little regard for the elitist and once-influential St Stephen's alumni. He further says the RSS has left no social vertical untouched, ensuring it has at least ten serious representatives in each

Towards the end, he casually makes a vital revelation—he will be handing over the responsibilities of LRO to a capable successor within a year. While he claims not to have a new assignment, RSS seniors privately smile and deny it. Joshi is among the finest in the ranks, and his next assignment has long been decided. It will be revealed when the time comes. And then, he makes a prophecy—by 2034, India will have just two Hindutva factions fighting it out at the top.

The decline of the Congress has been more rapid than any thinker, intellectual, journalist, or politician could have predicted. At some point, a party will rise to fill that vacuum. Gradually, there will be only two parties with a common agenda of national security, religious demographics, Hindu cultural values, and indigenisation of political culture. This is bound to happen in the next ten to twenty years.

Ashwini Kumar Upadhyay

One of the most combative legal warriors of the Indic wing has been Ashwini Kumar Upadhyay. He has taken a slew of legal challenges to India's highest courts, addressing issues ranging from reclaiming temples destroyed in invasions to fighting for a Uniform Civil Code. Upadhyay has also tackled the culture of garnering votes by promising freebies, advocated for broader laws against forceful or fraudulent conversions, and worked to ban instant triple talaq. Additionally, he has questioned statewide minority status, challenged the Wakf Act, the Police Act, and the Evidence Act, and appealed for drugs and human trafficking to be brought under the National Security Act for harsher action.

The forty-seven-year-old Supreme Court advocate has filed over fifty public interest litigations (PILs) in just five years. He hails from a middle-class family in Prayagraj, Uttar Pradesh.

The father of two sons started off as an engineer, quit his job at Maruti-Suzuki, joined Anna Hazare's IAC movement, and was expelled after he started questioning Aam Aadmi Party chief Arvind Kejriwal over overseas funding, ticket distribution, and an alleged secret alliance with the Congress. He then joined the BJP.

When Islamist violence raged on Indian streets after Nupur Sharma's remarks about Prophet Mohammed, Udaipur tailor Kanhaiya Lal was beheaded on video for supporting her on social media, followed by more than half a dozen others. During this time, Upadhyay was advocating for a longer-term legal solution to the problem.

> The main issue is Kanhaiya's death, which was trending on Twitter and led to several national protests and riots. This also happened during the brutal killings of Rinku Sharma and Dr Narang. There is a fixed pattern: protesting in the streets, collecting donations, and providing financial help. The public is doing all it can. However, the government has a role. In France, when a man was beheaded, five laws were changed. Since Kamlesh Tiwari's murder, we have had 400 to 500 similar cases, especially if you include Kerala and Bengal. However, in India, not one law has been changed. Behaviour depends on the laws. For example, because the law is strict, no one litters in the airport or the metro. But since there are no such laws or CCTVs in railways, they remain dirty.

Upadhyay's main battle has been against colonial laws. He argues that the subjugation of India's judicial system to colonial masters begins with the dress—the attire of lawyers, judges, and court officials. Why would one sweat in black coats, ties, and wigs during a sweltering Indian summer? Additionally, proceedings and orders are in English, a language many ordinary Indians do not understand.

> The judicial proceedings are all colonial, even the holidays. When the British came, they introduced summer holidays, which still continue today. The laws the British made were not designed to deliver justice but to punish the people here.

The 1860 Indian Penal Code, the 1861 Police Act, and the 1872 Evidence Act give the judiciary unbridled power. For the same section and under the same conditions, one judge can grant bail while another can deny it and jail the person. There are so many loopholes that a district court can sentence someone to hanging, but a high court can reverse it.

He cited the case of former cricketer and now Congress leader Navjot Singh Siddhu. The Supreme Court initially pardoned him for allegedly beating a cabbie to death, but after a review petition, he was sentenced to two years in jail. Upadhyay says these loopholes must be corrected as they waste hundreds of man-hours.

The Indian Evidence Act of 1872, enacted by the British government, currently governs all court processes, including court marshal. However, arbitration proceedings are not subject to the provisions of this act. It specifies which items can be used as evidence and which ones must be reported in advance to the court of law.

In cases such as a child born out of wedlock, for instance, it relies on the judge's moral judgement rather than DNA tests, as DNA testing was not available in 1872.

Moreover, there is no mechanism to ensure the unbiased nature of an expert whose opinion the court seeks. Contradicting an expert's opinion is left to the discretion of the judge, and experts often receive little protection for providing their opinions in sensitive cases.

Upadhyay's legal activism is aimed at a comprehensive overhaul of many core laws. He believes these legislations were not crafted to address the nation's current or future challenges. He argues that a series of Islamist violence incidents—the killings in Bengal or Kerala, the case of Kamlesh Tiwari and

Dilbar Negi in the Delhi riots, the stabbing of Rinku Sharma, as well as the spate of *'sar tan se juda'* killings in Udaipur, Ballabgarh, Palwal, and Maharashtra—highlight India's inadequacy in dealing with the issue.

> Why does this problem exist only in India? Why not in China, America, or Singapore? Muslims live there too. Why are Muslims there law-abiding, why not in India? Are their leaders more capable or patriotic than our prime minister? Chanakya had said 'Iron cuts iron'. If we know this, why aren't we changing our system accordingly? If we had executed Kamlesh Tiwari's murderer within six months or a year, it might have prevented more murders. There were hundreds of murders after this. We have Section 302 of the IPC against murder. When is this applicable? If you're on the road and there is road rage between two people, then Section 302 is applicable. In Kanhaiya's case, Section 302 was applicable too. We don't have any separate laws to deal with jihad. We have not defined hate speech in the Indian Penal Code until now. This has resulted in Wasim Rizvi [who had called for the expunging of violent verses from the Quran, getting death threats and becoming a Hindu named Jitendra Tyagi] spending three months in jail for hate speech. However, many others don't even get charged with an FIR for hate speech. In Rajasthan, there have been numerous cases of hate speech, yet no charges have been filed. Why? Because the 1861 Police Act was designed by the British for their benefit so they could book whoever they wanted for any offence. Similarly, the 1860 Indian Penal Code. If these were good, then some Britishers would also have been arrested. Those who attacked Tilak, Savarkar, or were involved in Jallianwala Bagh. Not one Britisher got arrested.

He pointed out that the legal system was designed for the British, not Indians. These laws were not intended to provide justice or resolve crimes, jihad, or religious conflict. Yet, India continues to utilise the same laws to address these issues.

> You need to understand that no matter how skilled the driver is, if the car is faulty, the journey will not be safe. Similarly, no matter how proficient the doctor is, if the medicine is ineffective, you will not be cured. The crux lies in the law. With the escalating religious tensions, addressing each issue individually is not feasible. I have delved into history extensively. Initially, I pursued engineering, and my journey into law was accidental. Before that, my passion lay in history. It took just a hundred years for Purusapura to transform into Peshawar, for Persia to become Iran, for Takshashila to evolve into Rawalpindi. The history and culture of these places swiftly changed. If we fail to amend colonial laws, the identity of our ministers will become inconsequential.

Upadhyay points out that the Judicial Accountability Bill was introduced by the Congress, but unfortunately, it lapsed in 2014. Since then, the Lok Sabha has not made any attempt to revive it, not even through a private member bill. He maintains that until the judicial system undergoes reform, the underlying mindset will remain unchanged.

> The Nupur Sharma matter is not for the Supreme Court to decide. What will be uncovered in the investigation, no one knows. There has been no chargesheet for this case so far. Commenting despite this is unwarranted. 'She faces threats or she has become a security threat? This lady is single-handedly responsible for what is happening in the country,' said Justice Surya Kant. I don't believe the comments that have been

made are by the Supreme Court. I believe they are the judge's personal comments. And those comments have only been made because we have given the judiciary unbridled power with no accountability. Until now, in the district courts, there have been so many wrong decisions taken; why have there been no hearings against those judges? There have been so many cases of judges being bribed in district courts with Rs 10–20 lakh so that they issue a favourable judgement. The high courts understand that these judgements are wrong, they reverse the charges but don't hold the district judges accountable. Because there is no judicial charter or judicial accountability bill. There are so many countries with a judicial charter and a judicial accountability bill. If we simply use those same laws, other countries will not ask us for royalties. Until now, we have raised more than fifty private member bills in the Lok Sabha. We can very easily change these laws.

The only solution to ending the murders of individuals or the demise of this civilisation, according to Upadhyay, lies in prioritising judicial and police reforms. For him, this stands as the only lasting solution.

Indianising Colonial Laws

One of the foremost legal reforms currently under consideration for the nation is the establishment of a Uniform Civil Code (UCC). Article 44 (Part IV) of the Constitution, forming a part of the Directive Principles of State Policy, says, 'The State shall endeavour to secure for the citizens a Uniform Civil Code throughout the territory of India.'

The argument originated with the October 1840 Lex Loci Report, which emphasised the need for uniformity in criminal legislation. But it also proposed that the personal laws of Hindus and Muslims regarding marriage, inheritance, and maintenance remain exempt from such codification. This distinction was further reinforced by Queen Victoria's Proclamation in 1858, affirming 'non-interference in religious issues'.

When crafting the Constitution, B.R. Ambedkar harboured doubts about the distinction maintained by personal laws, especially its impact on women and religious minorities. He claimed that while the UCC was recommended as one of the Directive Principles, it was incorporated into the Constitution with the intention that it would be implemented whenever the country was prepared to adopt it.

With ostensible good intentions, Nehru introduced the Hindu Code Bills in the 1950s, leading to the abolition of numerous Hindu traditional personal laws and practices. True to form, Nehru left the Muslim personal laws untouched, including the most regressive practices such as polygamy, nikah halala (which involves a woman marrying and sleeping with another man to remarry her former husband), instant triple talaq, and inadequate alimony protection. Syama Prasad Mookerjee cautioned against the risks of this action in 1951, arguing that codifying the personal laws of only one religion would be unfair and pose long-term challenges.

The initial move towards rectifying this injustice was made by the Narendra Modi government through the passage of the Triple Talaq Bill, which became the Muslim Women (Protection of Rights on Marriage) Act of 2019. This legislation liberated Muslim women, such as Shayara Bano, from enduring longstanding religious norms that rendered them invisible and powerless in the face of their husbands' unilateral authority to divorce them by uttering the word 'talaq' three times, at times even through a WhatsApp message. It was also the first and decisive step towards a UCC. A UCC may bring about the most radical and overdue changes in Muslim personal law, but even Hindu laws may need further reform. For instance, the Hindu Succession Act was amended in 2005, yet it still considers married women as members of their husbands' families. If a Hindu widow passes away without leaving a will or any heir, her assets automatically pass on to her husband's family. Similarly, under the Hindu Minority and Guardianship Act, men (fathers) are deemed 'natural guardians' and are given preference. A UCC could rectify these gender inequalities.

Apart from the UCC, Indianising colonial laws and aligning the Constitution more closely with our civilisation will be the major legal frontiers in the coming years.

Little quirks, such as the police's khaki uniform—approved by Officer Sir Harry Burnett Lumsden in 1847 for its colour resembling 'khaak' or dust—and the continued use of left-hand drive, a British legacy, while most of the world employs right-side driving, still persist. But the focus will primarily be on addressing larger issues, such as freeing temples from government control, rationalising caste reservations, combating terrorism and incursions, implementing population and demographic control measures, establishing criteria for citizenship, and initiating the process of establishing a Hindu Rashtra—making India the natural homeland for Indic faiths.

The next twenty-five years could witness a transformation of the Constitution that the nation could not have imagined in the last seventy-five years.

CHAPTER 3

History: The New Kurukshetra

In the multi-theatre ideological war being fought in today's India, the central battlefield is history. The new nationalists believe that reclaiming this ground is crucial. They argue that this civilisation could have been kept in slavery for approximately a thousand years mainly by distorting and obliterating its past, thereby breaking its confidence and self-esteem.

The British, for instance, enlisted well-known Indologists like Max Muller to manipulate India's history. Muller was appointed as an examiner for the Indian Civil Services examinations. In 1868, he wrote to the Duke of Argyll, George Campbell, who was then the secretary of state for India, 'India has been conquered once, but India must be conquered again, and that second conquest should be a conquest by education.' Thus, the colonial factory of recasting the past sprang to life. Army officers and administrators of the East India Company took charge of mass-producing half-truths and lies about India's past.

The word 'Dravidian', for instance, was first used by Robert A. Caldwell as late as 1856 in his book, *A Comparative Grammar of the Dravidian or South Indian Family of Languages*. Over a century and a half, Dravidian politics has portrayed itself as torchbearers of an identity exclusive of larger Indianness and not just distinct from but inimical to the north's 'Aryan' influence. This is despite early texts showing fluid cultural exchanges, spiritual unity, and genetic studies indicating there was no Aryan invasion as claimed by colonial 'manufacturers of history' and their Leftist successors in independent India.

Historians like Michael Danino and David Frawley argue that the British concocted the thoroughly discredited Aryan Invasion Theory solely to denigrate Indians and propagate the notion that fair-skinned men from Europe, mounted on horses, invaded India and intellectually fertilised the land. Studies on genetic migration, as well as recent excavations, have conclusively debunked the Aryan Invasion Theory.

The Indic wing accuses India's first prime minister, Jawaharlal Nehru, of outsourcing history and education to the Leftists, who created a brutal ideological hegemony on campuses. For about seven decades, Indian universities, and particularly history classrooms, were prototypes of vicious 'cancel culture' and victimisation of ideological opponents, akin to what the West has been experiencing now.

But luminaries like Chakravarti Rajagopalachari, Minoo Masani, R.N. Majumdar, Jadunath Sarkar, Sita Ram Goel, Arun Shourie, and more recently Meenakshi Jain continued to counter the narrative, despite facing discrimination and bullying.

The foundation of distorted history lies in deracinated education. The English Education Act of 1835, a masterpiece by Thomas Babington Macaulay, eradicated Sanskrit and Persian, replacing them with English, with the stated motive of producing brown coolies of colonialism. Jawaharlal Nehru opted for colonial continuity in education.

Nationalists like Rajnarayan Basu, Nabagopal Mitra, and Rabindranath Tagore's father and elder brother, Debendranath and Satyendranath, along with Bal Gangadhar Tilak a little later, attempted to establish a bulwark against colonial education through initiatives such as the Hindu melas. But swa-shiksha remained a bruised, unfinished project.

Under Narendra Modi, the National Education Policy of 2020 (NEP) and the National Curriculum Framework of 2023 (NCF) bring hope that the river that once devastated the age-old knowledge landscape of Bharat may finally reverse its course and begin to fertilise its banks.

According to the Ministry of Education:

> [The NEP] envisions a massive transformation in education through – 'an education system rooted in Indian ethos that contributes directly to transforming India, that is Bharat, sustainably into an equitable and vibrant knowledge society, by providing high quality education to all, thereby making India a global knowledge superpower.' ... It also proposes the revision and revamping of all aspects of the education structure, including the school regulation and governance, to create a new system which is aligned with the aspirational goals of 21st century education along with India's tradition, culture and value system.

Traditions and roots are repeatedly underlined in the policy:

> The vision of the policy is to instil among the learners a deep-rooted pride in being Indian, not only in thought, but also in spirit, intellect, and deeds, as well as to develop knowledge, skills, values, and dispositions that support responsible commitment to human rights, sustainable development and living, and global well-being, thereby reflecting a truly global citizen.

The educational policy acknowledges the need for value-based education, as emphasised by the Radhakrishnan Commission of 1948–49, the Mudaliar Commission of 1952–53, and the Kothari Commission of 1964–66. It aligns with the perspective of eminent educationists like Atul Kothari, who advocated for the incorporation of moral values and spirituality to give education a soul, as well as for courses to be taught in one's mother tongue.

Without much fanfare, the government rolled out the National Curriculum Framework in 2023. It aligns both in letter and spirit with the National Educational Policy, consistently emphasising the importance of Indianness.

Take this guideline, for instance, which seeks to ensure that the student not only recognises the evolution of numeration throughout human history but also values the significant contributions made by India:

> [The student] understands the development of the representation of numbers through human history, from tallying (e.g., on the Lebombo bones), to Roman numerals, to the Mayan and Babylonian systems, leading up to the development of zero in India and the modern Indian system of writing numerals (from the Yajurveda, the story of Buddha, the Bakshali Manuscript, Vasavadatta, Aryabhatiya, Brahmasphutasiddanta, the Gwalior inscription, etc.) and its transmission to the world (due to Al-Kharizmi, Al-Kindi, Fibonacci, etc.) … [Also, the student] recognises important mathematical contributions of India (e.g., zero, Indian numerals, ideas around infinity, concepts of algebra, etc.) as well as the contributions of specific Indian mathematicians (such as Baudhayana, Panini, Pingala, Aryabhata, Brahmagupta, Virahanka, Bhaskara, Madhava, and Ramanujana).

Some of the curricular goals of NCF include appreciating the importance of being an Indian by understanding India's glorious past: its cultural diversity, heritage, traditions, literature, art, philosophy, medicine, and geographical diversity. The student must also understand the idea of a nation and the emergence of the modern Indian State.

Interestingly, starting in Class VI, students are required to research their own family history and the history of their neighbourhood. History textbooks for Class XI and XII have subtly shifted focus from the Mughals to Bharat between 900 CE to 1200 CE, highlighting the Cholas, Palas, Pratihars, and Chalukyas.

A twelve-member committee, headed by space scientist K. Kasturirangan and including members such as American mathematician Manjul Bhargava, French Indic historian Michael Danino, National Book Trust chairman Govind Prasad Sharma, and trainer and social activist M.K. Sridhar, was formed to create the new NCF.

This process bears the Modi stamp of a grassroots-up consultative approach. Inputs were gathered from over 13 lakh interested citizens, including students, parents, and 1.5 lakh teachers and educationists from across the country. Additionally, over 1,550 district-level consultations were conducted in thirty-two states and union territories, along with thirty-five groups of institutions. These efforts were supplemented by over 600 papers on twenty-five specifically relevant themes, authored by groups comprising over 4,000 experts. All this input was distilled by twenty-five focus groups, each consisting of about six experts.

The new textbooks are set to roll out in phases in 2024, potentially marking a historic shift in how Bharat tells its own story and history.

Meenakshi Jain

Her slender frame and gentle smile belie the fierce, almost unassailable intellectual warrior within. Even the most outspoken Leftist historians typically avoid crossing paths with Meenakshi Jain. Against her, the best weapons in their arsenal—ideological narrative, selectivity, whitewashing, distortion—fall silent. The publicity-shy daughter of the legendary editor–intellectual Girilal Jain stands as one of the most diligent and well-trained custodians of history.

With the efficiency of a seasoned librarian, she deftly opens the correct drawers and dusts off from the appropriate shelves the most authentic and indisputable accounts of the past.

And she does not mince words. In her book *Rama and Ayodhya*, she writes:

> In an astonishing act of daring, a handful of Leftist historians attempted to counter a centuries-old belief and vociferously assert that the Babri Masjid was built on vacant land. They remain undeterred despite mounting evidence stacked against them. Some of these historians even appeared as experts for the Babri Masjid Action Committee (BMAC) [during negotiations] between the Vishwa Hindu Parishad, BMAC and the government in 1990–91. Yet, throughout they have maintained the charade of being 'independent historians'.
>
> In his recently published autobiography, Njan Anna Bharatiyan [I Am Indian], Dr K.K. Muhammad, former regional director (north) of the Archaeological Survey of India [ASI], has stated that a set of Leftist historians systematically derailed attempts at a peaceful resolution of the issue.

Meenakshi Jain sees herself as a textbook example of a colonised mind attaining freedom. Her family was deeply entrenched in the ethos of this land. Her father, Girilal, studied in a village school near Sonipat before moving to Delhi when he gained admission to Hindu College. There, he forged lifelong friendships with prominent Indic thinkers such as Kapila Vatsyayan, Ram Swarup, and Sita Ram Goel. Meenakshi received an English education in a convent school before pursuing higher studies. Her teachers were leading Marxist historians of their time. She says:

> My father was careful not to try to influence me. He was confident I would find my path, just as he did. In a fundamental sense, my journey reached its fruition with the Ayodhya movement. The surge of nationalism has been long in the making but was stifled by certain forces for various reasons. As a student of Indian history, I was struck by the continuous vigilance our leaders demonstrated in guarding against potential denationalisation.

Nationalism animated much of the debate in 19th-century Bengal, adds Jain. Rajnarayan Basu (1826–99), hailed as the first prophet of Indian nationalism, had declared, 'No reform is accepted by a nation unless it takes on a national form.' In 1861, he prepared a *Prospectus for a Society for the Promotion of National Feeling among the Educated Natives of Bengal*. She explains:

> It was arguably the most radical proposal by an Indian nationalist at that time. A blueprint for the regeneration of the youth, it included physical training aimed to 'restore the manliness of Bengali youth and their long-lost military prowess'; the establishment of a school of Hindu music for the 'composition of songs for moral, patriotic and martial enthusiasm'; the founding of a school of medicine to revive

'our own medical sciences'; and the promotion of 'Indian antiquities' to illuminate the 'glory of ancient India'.

In 1872, Rajnarayan Basu delivered his famous lecture on the grandeur of the classical Hindu tradition. A journalist attending the lecture wrote, 'Hinduism was dying but Rajnarayan saved it.'

In his final testament, *The Hopes of an Old Hindu,* Rajnarayan Basu expressed the wish that Hindus and Muslims, under the aegis of the Indian National Congress, would together 'help build a glorious future for their common motherland'. Despite lingering memories of Muslim rule, leaders of the era endeavoured for Muslim participation in the creation of a new India.

Jain states:

> The stream of leaders thereafter, who emerged from all corners of India, strongly articulated the nationalist sentiment. I believe the movement was derailed when the Indian National Congress aligned itself with the Khilafat cause. India rallied behind a cause that had nothing to do with its own interests. Furthermore, Turkey abolished the institution of Khilafat soon after. But it inflicted tremendous damage in India.

Jain has dedicated years to exposing distortions in Indian history. Her first serious attempt to rectify deliberately introduced misrepresentations in Bharat's history was with the Medieval India textbook for Class XI, which she authored for the National Council of Educational Research and Training (NCERT). She states:

> I had to write within the framework of the syllabus provided. I tried to provide a comprehensive overview of the period,

focusing on the unifying forces at work in the realms of culture and religion. This was a departure from the previous emphasis on frictions and divisions. I provided brief summaries of various dynasties and their tremendous contributions, such as the Chandellas, who built the Khajuraho temples, the Paramara king Bhoja, who authored over two dozen books on subjects ranging from medicine to religion, the Chauhans, who fought Mohammad Ghori, King Lalitaditya of Kashmir, and many others.

Jain demonstrated that, by and large, Indian rulers were talented and enlightened. In that textbook, she also shed light on the exploitative nature of the Muslim ruling class, which appropriated almost the entire agricultural produce, leaving peasants on the verge of starvation. She exposed the restrictive nature of the ruling elite, noting that almost all ministers were from outside the subcontinent, and highlighted the extremely limited participation of groups like the Rajputs.

She explains:

> My book survived only for one year. When the UPA government returned to power, it removed the book, even though there was no replacement ready. As a stopgap arrangement, the old textbooks written by leading Marxist historians were reinstated!

Meenakshi wrote two books on the Ayodhya movement, which remain the standard references. She was relentless in exposing the duplicity of Left historians and archaeologists based on their articles and depositions in the Allahabad High Court. 'It is important to note that there was no rejoinder or rebuttal from their side,' she quips.

Her book on Sati exposed the role of British Baptist missionaries in falsifying data to present it as a common custom. 'Many senior officials of the East India Company themselves admitted it was a slander campaign; the missionaries sought permission from the British Parliament to proselytise in India. Thus, they fabricated the debate on Sati,' she says.

In her book *Flight of Deities and Rebirth of Temples*, Jain wrote about the efforts of ordinary people to protect their sacred heritage during the attacks on temples in the medieval period. 'In my book, *Vasudeva Krishna and Mathura*, I provide literary, epigraphic, and sculptural evidence of the antiquity of Krishna worship and his age-old links with Mathura,' she says.

Jain is currently researching the state of indigenous judicial and educational institutions in Bharat as they existed when encountered by the British in the 18th–19th century. She questions why their early admiration for these institutions eventually changed.

In the next twenty years, she hopes to see an India that has overcome the memories of its contentious past and has grown into a nation confident and proud of its civilisational heritage. 'For that, a strong reconnection with our spiritual heritage is most important. Due to shortcomings in our educational system and failings in the family system, there has been a disconnection from our cultural and spiritual heritage. Reestablishing that connection is crucial,' she says.

Sanjeev Sanyal

One of the most influential younger authors who has shaken India's Leftist bastion of historians, Sanjeev Sanyal, offers a fresh perspective on the post-independence battle for the past. While Sanyal's books on Indian history enjoy immense popularity, he also serves as a member of the Economic Advisory Council to the prime minister of India and is the former principal economic advisor in the Ministry of Finance. Sanyal says:

> There is now a clear and discernible intellectual challenge after more than half a century. If you go back to the 1950s and 1960s, there was an intellectual challenge to the colonial approach. There were individuals like Rajaji, Minoo Masani, and others associated with the *Swarajya* magazine of that time, as well as B.R. Shenoy and R.C. Majumdar. Savarkar was still alive. Interestingly, the early years of independence saw the continuation of non-Leftist thinking from the colonial period into the 1950s. However, it gradually disappeared in the 1960s, became a memory in the 1970s, and was almost erased in the 1980s and 1990s. But over the past decade, it has resurrected itself. There were people who, even during the dark ages, so to speak, raised opposing views, such as Arun Shourie. But the current lot is different. Shourie, or even Sita Ram Goel, limited themselves to being critics of existing thinking. They did not present alternative worldviews. What sets apart the work now is that these are not critiques; these are alternative worldviews. My history books offer alternative worldviews. You may agree or disagree, but it is an alternative worldview. I am not spending a significant amount of energy critiquing the other side. I am simply pointing out that there is another way of thinking about this.

At fifty-four, Sanyal looks younger with his lean frame and sharp features, with a hint of dark circles under his eyes. He was born in Kolkata. Delving into the family history reveals the revolutionary foundation upon which it stands. On his mother's side, they are refugees from Kushtia in East Bengal. Originally, large mill owners, the family continued to live there for a while after the Partition. They migrated in the 1950s, with some members staying on until the 1960s and fleeing just before the 1971 genocide.

His father's family are Bengalis from UP who settled in Varanasi in the late 18th century. From the 19th century until around 1927, they resided in Kashi. During his grandfather's generation, many family members were involved in the revolutionary movement.

Sanjeev is the grand-nephew of freedom fighter, Sachindranath Sanyal, the author of *Bandi Jiban*. Sachindranath was involved in the Anushilan Samiti and later in the Ghadar Movement alongside Rashbehari Bose. Lahiri Mahashay, the man who initiated modern Kriya Yoga, also hails from the same family.

> It is basically a Varanasi-based family. Many of my father's brothers, cousins, and others were involved in the revolutionary movement in the early 20th century. When Rashbehari was leading the Ghadar Movement, he was living in our extended family home in an area called Bengali Tola, located in the Madanpura area of Varanasi. There is still a school there, established by my family in the 19th century, called Bengali Tola Intercollege.

After returning from Kala Pani or the Andaman jail, Sachindranath co-founded the Hindustan Socialist Republican Association in the 1920s. This initiative led to the recruitment of the iconic revolutionary Ram Prasad Bismil. Sachindranath was sent to Andamans again in connection with the Kakori case.

Sanyal further states:

> My mother's family was also involved in the revolutionary movement. Nalinakshya Sanyal, my great-grandfather, participated in Bagha Jatin's Yugantar group. So, one major influence on my thinking comes from this concept of resistance, particularly armed resistance. Another aspect that is not appreciated entirely is that much of this drew heavily upon Shakta Hinduism—an ideology centred around worshipping Adi Shakti, especially in her militant forms like Durga, Bhavani, Kali, and others. This has had a very big influence on my thinking. If you examine Bankim Chandra's 'Vande Mataram', the first two or three stanzas may appear somewhat secularist, but the latter half is clearly imbued with Shakta imagery of Durga. Similar ideas can be found in the works of Vivekananda, which are also clearly influenced by Shakta traditions. The notion of Bhavani is strongly present in Bal Gangadhar Tilak's imagery, and the idea of Chandi is prominent in Punjab, for example. This ideological anchor of Shakta Hinduism has greatly influenced my thought process, derived from centuries of resistance.

Sanjeev Sanyal's father was born in Allahabad. He joined the Indian Administrative Service (IAS) and was assigned to the West Bengal cadre. Sanjeev was born in Kolkata in August 1970, amid two major crises. One was a huge flood at that time, while the other was the influx of millions of refugees from Bangladesh.

> When I was born, amidst all this chaos, my mother had no idea of my father's whereabouts because he was serving as the sub-divisional magistrate or something similar in one of the border districts. He was actively involved in flood relief

and refugee assistance. Three days after my birth, my mother opened the newspaper and found on the front page of *Anandabazar* a photograph of my dad accompanying Indira Gandhi on a tour of some refugee or relief camp. That's how she found out where my dad was.

He spent his early years in Kolkata, then moved to Sikkim, followed by a relocation to Delhi, and eventually returned to Kolkata for his formative years from the age of eight to eighteen. This explains why he speaks Bengali with a Kolkata accent. He attended St Xavier's school and later enrolled at St James.

> I was one of those fellows who didn't take very well to education, in the sense that I mostly ignored my teachers and did my own thing. I was heavily involved in everything else in school, so my teachers left me alone. And I was good at taking exams. I was much into debating, drama, and choreography. Break dancing was a cool thing in the 1980s. I was Kolkata's break-dancing champion for a while, of all things. And then I trained for state-level swimming, but I didn't pursue it, so I switched to athletics. I was a middle-distance runner for a while in school. Then I moved to Delhi, where I attended Shriram College of Commerce. There I participated in athletics, but I eventually switched to adventure sports, which I took pretty seriously. I am from the first batch of Indians to get a paragliding licence in 1990 or 1991. I also have an instructor-grade licence for kayaking and canoeing.

Sanyal insists that one cannot take a fifty- or hundred-year view of India. Instead, one must take a thousand- or a million-year view.

India is a long-lived civilisational nation. The modern Indian republic is the latest manifestation of this ancient civilisation. Even though its borders and rules may be modern, it is a manifestation of the ancient civilisation that has existed from the beginning of time.

Sanyal says that as Indians, we have always had a conception of ourselves as one people. The way we think about the world is very ancient and has a civilisational anchor.

For example, Shankaracharya built the matths. He erected them in four corners of a certain landscape. The Shakti peeths are scattered across a certain landscape. The northernmost is Sharda Peeth in Pakistan-occupied Jammu and Kashmir. The southernmost is in Kanyakumari, or northern Jaffna, depending on how you look at it. The westernmost is in Hinglaj Mata in Balochistan, and the easternmost is in Tripura—Tripurasundari. Scattered in between are fifty-two peeths. Is that a random distribution?

You can clearly see how the idea of Jambudvipa or Sapta Sindhavah evolved from the Rig Veda to Puranic times, where it became Sapta Sindhu or seven great rivers scattered all over India. You can clearly see a conception of India that is civilisational. Not only do we recognise it, but the rest of the world also recognises it in the words they use to describe India. After all, we don't have anything called the South Asian Ocean. There is something called the Indian Ocean. And the term used for the people over here, whether it is Hindu or Al-Hind.

When the Constitution was drafted, it began by saying 'India that is Bharat'. It is not the case that it just means that Bharat is its Hindi translation. That is not. Those who wrote the Constitution deliberately used both versions in both languages, suggesting 'India that is Bharat', that today's

India, the republic, is part of the civilisational idea of Bharat. It is just the modern manifestation of it. This obviously is a very different view of the world than the Nehruvian view of the world. In the Nehruvian world, you have the 'Discovery of India'. Now, we cannot discover India. We live here. Similarly, you have the idea of 'Father of the Nation'. How can you have a 'Father of the Nation'? If there is a 'Father of the Nation' at all, it would be the Rig Vedic chieftain of the Bharatas, Sudas, and his guru Vasistha, or Shivaji with his conception of Hind Swaraj. But how can you have somebody who is a 20th-century character as the Father of the Nation? Were the freedom fighters pre-dating Gandhi such as Tilak or Rashbehari not fighting for anything? It is ironic because in his own independence speech, Nehru wrote, 'A nation so long suppressed.' How is it long-suppressed if it didn't exist?

Sanyal says that this conception of India was clearly aimed at constructing the narrative that India is some sort of a modern construct. Everywhere colonialists went, they wanted to claim that the place was terra nullius, or territory without a master until they arrived and 'civilised' them. For instance, they went to Australia, displaced the locals, and declared that the land was empty and available for colonisation.

But when they came to India, there was a problem. It was evident that there were people already living here.

> If you read 18th- and 19th-century colonial writers, they clearly see Indians—Hindus in particular, but Indians in general—as having a national identity of some sort, even if they are politically divided. Later on, through the 19th century, they propagated the idea that Indians were regressive and needed to be civilised. They did this everywhere in the world. When they discovered ancient ruins in Zimbabwe,

they claimed that Africans could not have built this ancient city. Instead, they proposed that it must have been built by Caucasian migrants called the Hamites. So, just as we have the Aryan Invasion Theory in India, you have the Hamitic Invasion Theory there.

The conception of a white ruling race that brings civilisation to the rest of the world, Sanyal says, is very much a 19th-century construct, emerging after Europeans became the dominant force. There was this idea of the superior race which the British and Germans held, and it manifested itself in Nazi mythology. It was prevalent in 19th-century British thinking. The term 'white man's burden' was coined by Rudyard Kipling.

> If you read the nationalist histories, they were contesting this. Whether it is Tilak or Sri Aurobindo, who, by the way, was one of the fathers of the freedom movement, now remembered as a spiritual guru. Or Savarkar or Vivekananda. All of them are clearly guided by a certain conception of nationhood with which they are contesting the colonial story. After Independence, more than Nehru himself, the ecosystem of Nehruvians and the Marxists then built on the colonial idea for their own political gain. Because after all, unless you have the 'Father of the Nation', how do you have the 'Chacha of the Nation'? Or the 'Damad of the Nation' and so on? So, India is the family of the Family's India.

By doing this, he says, the Congress–Left ecosystem tried to achieve two things—to break down the existing idea of nationhood and to tie it to a certain dynasty or ideology.

Many of the Leftist historians had collaborated with the British. It was in their interest as well to create this historiography because you can't be a traitor to the nation if there was no nation. The Left was very happy with this historiography, and it suited the Congress ruling dynasty's cause by undermining the idea of an Indic nation.

The author of *The Ocean of Churn*, a book that tells the story of Bharat's influence in the Indian Ocean, says he began to write it 'to simply write our history from our perspective'.

> In our history books, we often say Fa-Hien came, Hiuen Tsang came, or somebody else came and told us about ourselves, and that must be the truth. But what about our own views of ourselves? There are lots and lots of inscriptions. How often do you hear about the Gurjara–Pratihara inscriptions? You don't. You will hear much more about what Hiuen Tsang said about India, but you won't hear what we said about ourselves. For example, the *Kamasutra* may have a lot of sexual positions, but it also has brilliant descriptions of city life in the Gupta period. But you don't actually learn very much about it. I write about it in one of my books. An Indian is much more likely to read Shakespeare but not learn much about Kalidas, even in translation. It is possible to grow up in India and never have read the *Arthashastra*, but you probably have read Plato in various courses. And we are taught that the author of *Arthashastra*, Kautilya, was the Machiavelli of India. Or Samudragupta, one of the greatest generals of human history, as the Napoleon of India. The reference point is somebody else's. One of the things I am trying to do, whether I am succeeding or not, I will let you judge, is to simply reference it from our perspective. Tell our own story.

Sanyal insists that new writers must not replace the colonial or Marxist–Nehruvian lies with random jingoistic speculations. The alternative story must be properly referenced.

We all have the right to our opinions, but we don't have the right to our own facts. The Nehruvian, colonial, Marxist milieu began overdoing some of their storytelling and simply denying that Aurangzeb was a bigot, despite plain evidence all around us. In an earlier time, the response would have been much more muted. However, because we now have the confidence, resources, and information, we can counter it. Much of this is coming from people not so cultured in the history departments. I am often criticised because I am not trained as a historian. You will notice that whether it is the *Caravan* magazine or *The Wire*, they never contest any of my facts or arguments. What they are effectively saying is that I have not been cultured by their system.

On the accusation that Sanyal does not use primary sources to write history, he says, ironically, he very often uses their primary sources.

In many cases, I deliberately go out of my way to quote sources that they reference. Very often, even when I am quoting a primary source, I use the version found in their books. For example, I have somewhat heretical views on Ashoka the Great, who I believe was not so great. It is well documented in their own texts that he became a Buddhist before he invaded Kalinga. They quote *Ashokavadana*, or they will quote edicts. I quote the same edicts; I just quote some different lines from them. So why are they objecting to my point? I have no problem with different people having different stories. After all, why should people object to historians having different views of what happened 2,000 years ago? Put on any television channel, you can see that we have varying views of what happened yesterday. Historians should have different views. Just that they do not have a right to their own facts.

Sanyal mentions a crop of non-Left thinkers emerging in different spheres.

> Vikram Sampath is an interesting character. Those, like him, who do incredible work don't always emerge from a formal system. Take someone like Amish Tripathi as part of this phenomenon. He brings out the Indian essence in a field where, at one time, it was simply not permissible to do so. He struggled to publish his book because writing mythological fiction in his style was not considered acceptable. Yet, it turned out to be a massive bestseller. You can observe this trend in Bollywood as well. In the films of the 1950s and 1960s, there was a lot of nationalist sentiment. But by the 1970s, they shifted towards themes of angry men raging against the mill owner, symbolising oppression. Recently, there has been a revival of interest in our history.

He says that in movies like *Baahubali*, Hindu imagery is no longer apologetic. In popular culture, it is now considered 'cool' to embrace things that are Indian, specifically Hindu. Hence, the resistance against banning Jallikattu or against secularising many Indic rituals as seen in the Sabarimala issue. This does not mean that the Indic wing simply wants to continue the outdated tradition for the sake of it.

> If you trace it back to its origins in the 19th century, this is a thoroughly modernist phenomenon. Ishwar Chandra Vidyasagar, for instance, was very much a modernist. On one level, he was a Sanskrit scholar, and on another, extremely modernist. He advocated for widow remarriage and spent the second half of his life—often overlooked—among the tribals in Burdwan or Purulia. Look at Sri Aurobindo; he, too, was a modernist. Savarkar is famously a modernist.

Rammohun Roy could be seen as both a modernist and a Westerniser, but many others were modernists despite their suspicion of Westernisation. Even Savarkar, though strongly nationalistic, wore Western clothes. I would even include someone like Ambedkar in the non-Left category. Ambedkar is now claimed by the Left, but highlighting some of his writings would greatly embarrass them. He was clearly against State control, and his writings on Islam are quite brutal.

He says the Indian non-Left—'one can call it the Right, but I think it's more non-Left'—is not a monolith. Sanyal refers to himself as a complexity theorist or 'Kautilyan'.

It is as if time has come full circle. One of Bharat's sharpest minds continues to inspire and spawn change agents 2,400 years later.

Vikram Sampath

One of the writers of history most acutely targeted by the Left cabal's criticism is Vikram Sampath. Sampath was born in Bengaluru, which has remained his hometown. Vikram's parents were private sector bankers. He studied at Aurobindo Memorial School and then at Bishop Cottons for high school. His interest in history was ignited at a very early when he was in Class VI.

> That was when Sanjay Khan used to produce the TV serial, *The Sword of Tipu Sultan*. It aimed to highlight the greatness of Tipu and Haider. However, the maharaja of Mysore was depicted in a poor light, portrayed as an obese retard preoccupied with dancing with a court dancer. Similarly, the

maharani was shown as a scheming woman. The idea was just to make them appear like buffoons. This portrayal sparked numerous protests in different parts of Karnataka. The Mysore royal family, which ruled for 600 years, continues to enjoy a lot of regard and reverence from the people of Karnataka even today.

As a young boy who was not particularly interested in the way history was taught in school, Sampath was captivated by these protests and stories. There was also a studio that caught fire, and people were saying that this was the curse of the Wodeyars, the Mysore royals. 'My curiosity was ignited at that age. Every vacation meant travelling to Mysore from Bangalore with my parents and maternal grandmother. It became a family project—a self-motivated journey without any agenda,' he says.

Sampath met with the royal family, historians, and went through the archives. Starting from the king-and-queen stories, his interest slowly progressed to encompass the entire dynasty spanning 600 years. 'One of the most modern and enlightened dynasties of India, and much of what Karnataka is today, the foundation was laid by the Wodeyars,' he states.

Even while he was engaged in other pursuits, his fascination with Mysore persisted. He gathered copious material over ten years. At this point, his well-wishers and family suggested that he publish it as a book. In 2008, he released his first book, *Splendours of Royal Mysore: The Untold Story of the Wodeyars*, while working in the corporate sector.

Despite coming from a family of non-historians, his parents keenly supported his project. He later pursued his PhD in history from Queensland. His academic journey included a degree in engineering in electronics from BITS-Pilani, an MSc in Maths, an MBA in finance from SP Jain, and he worked at Citibank and Hewlett Packard in risk management.

Sampath's weekends were dedicated to travelling for research. While he was employed in the corporate sector, he was also working on his first three books. *My Name Is Gauhar Jaan: The Life and Times of a Musician* won the Sahitya Academy award and gained recognition abroad as well.

The story of Gauhar Jaan was close to Sampath's heart. Born Eileen Angelina Yeoward in 1873, an Armenian Christian who later converted to Islam, in 1902, Gauhar Jaan became the first Indian voice to be recorded. She recorded nearly 600 records, was the most famous female musician of her time, and led a life destined to be depicted in books and movies.

This book finally gave Vikram Sampath the courage to become a full-time historian. As a result, the University of Queensland offered him the opportunity to pursue a PhD on the topic, 'Advent of the gramophone and its impact on India'. It is ironic that an Australian university, rather than an Indian one, awarded him a scholarship for this. Sampath, incidentally, is also trained as a musician in Carnatic classical music.

In 2011, with the help of entrepreneur and business leader Mohandas Pai and others, he established India's digital sound archives for vintage recordings. It is the first online archive for gramophone recordings and has so far collected 15,000 records.

> The first books I read were those of Arun Shourie. Through him, I was introduced to Jadunath Sarkar, R.C. Majumdar, Radha Kumud Mukherjee, Dharam Pal, and Sita Ram Goel, who were part of the non-Left. These individuals, at

that point, did not receive much support because the state was backing Marxist historians. There has to be an honest and nationalistic viewpoint to Indian histography. These historians were called nationalistic even during the British era, as they held a nationalistic perspective. With the National School of Historiography promoting a colonial viewpoint, Vishwanath Kashinath Rajwade, Ramakrishna Gopal Bhandarkar, and other historians from Maharashtra wrote rebuttals under pseudonyms like 1st Hindu, 2nd Hindu, 3rd Hindu, Parsi Boy.

Sampath remarks that the irony is that even at the peak of the British colonial era, there were historians who wrote with a nationalistic viewpoint. However, post-Independence, people who write with a nationalistic viewpoint are called 'Sanghis'.

His two-book series on Vinayak Damodar Savarkar, a revolutionary freedom fighter and radical Hindutva ideologue, has exhumed the ghost that the cabal had worked tirelessly to bury. Both books, *Savarkar: Echoes from a Forgotten Past* and *Savarkar: A Contested Legacy*, stand out as particularly celebrated at a time when there has been a sudden surge of literary interest in the man. Whether it is Vaibhav Purandare's *True Story of the Father of Hindutva* or Uday Mahurkar's *Veer Savarkar: The Man Who Could Have Prevented Partition*, it seems as though a pharaoh's tomb packed with buried secrets has been opened about the revolutionary.

Here is an excerpt from Sampath's second book, *Savarkar: A Contested Legacy*:

> Savarkar asked India to emulate the example of Israel which came into existence in May 1948 after almost a 2,000-year struggle by the Jews for a homeland of their own. Israel, he said, 'is besieged by its staunch enemies, the Arab nations.

But this tiny nation has given military education to its men and women, procured weapons from Britain and the U.S.A., established arm [sic] factories in its own nation, intelligently signed treaties with foreign nations and raised its own strategic power to the extent that its enemy Arab nations would never dare to invade them'.

He claimed that it was still not too late for India to wake up from its slumber and similarly increase her military and strategic strength as the world recognizes only that. The Chinese prime minister Zhou Enlai was accorded a warm welcome in New Delhi on 26 June 1954 and Nehru coined his favourite phrase '*Hindi Chini Bhai Bhai*'. In an interview on India–China diplomacy in the *Kesari* on 4 July 1954, Savarkar welcomed this bonhomie with a sense of cautious optimism.

He said: 'In politics, the enemy of our enemy is our best friend. Enlightened self-interest is the only touchstone on which friendship in political dealings could be tested since there is no such thing as real and selfless friendship in the political arena. If the meeting between Chou En-Lai and Nehru angered the U.S.A., Indians should not pay attention to it because the U.S.A. too did not care to pause and think about India's sensitivities if America entered into a military pact with Pakistan. All the policies of India must be dependent on what was good or bad for India herself. If it was advantageous to India she should not in the least worry or care whether anyone felt enraged, insulted or irritated.... The general principles that are being propagated as fundamental in this visit are very good and sound, so far as their language is concerned. Nothing is lost in proclaiming wishes for world peace, prosperity and brotherhood. But so long as India does not have any effective practical remedy or measures to check the transgressions, such visits have no more than a formal status. While crying from the rooftops about these principles it was worth noting that China, by swallowing Tibet, had ruthlessly trampled those very principles of world peace, brotherhood and peaceful co-existence. That was the funniest part of the whole deal, and it at once raised doubts in Indian minds about the bona fides of China and Chou En-Lai. There was at that time a political party in Tibet aiming at independence.'

'My foray into Savarkar began at my mother's house, where he was spoken of in hushed tones. That family was a victim of the 1948 Brahmin massacre following Gandhi's death,' he says.

After half a century of hiatus, during Vajpayee's time, Savarkar's bust was erected in Parliament. There was very little written about him, at least in English. The last comprehensive history of Savarkar in English was a 1960 biography by Dhananjay Keer.

Sampath started researching on Savarkar in 2015. It took him five years of intense research, alongside pursuing his PhD, to retrieve documents on the legend and the revolutionary movement that had been subdued and suppressed. He spent a lot of time at the archives and libraries in London. For him, one visit would mean sifting through 20,000–30,000 pages of material on the Indian freedom movement.

For the Savarkar book in India, he obtained a senior research fellowship at the Nehru Memorial Museum and Library. A lot of the material was in Marathi for primary sources and secondary sources. The research involved meeting his family and also visiting places associated with his life such as Nashik, the Cellular Jail in the Andamans, and Ratnagiri.

> In my book, I have not tried to sweep Savarkar's faults under the carpet or whitewash him. It is not hagiographical. I have

also mentioned where Savarkar erred so that everything is laid out in front of the media for them to make up their minds about Savarkar and his ideas. I had an idea that there would be backlash but didn't imagine it to be this massive. One of the major reasons for the hate is because Savarkar propounded Hindutva. Whereas all he did in those troubled days during Partition was to give Hindus of this country a political voice in the face of extreme Muslim separatism and violence.

The scenario changed from pre- to post-1857 with the Aligarh Muslim Movement, Sampath believes. That is where the seeds of the two-nation theory were sown by the Muslim elite. They felt that they were wrong in siding with the Hindus in the 1857 revolt.

'It was about how close you could become to the British, encouraging English education so that Muslims could enter the civil services,' he says. 'The two-nation theory emerged when Savarkar was just three years old.'

Savarkar gave Hindutva a more practical and logical sense. While the first seeds of Hindu nationalism were sown in Bengal, Shivaji Maharaj's Hind Swarajya inspired every Maharashtrian revolutionary, including Bal Gangadhar Tilak.

Flowing as thick and fast alongside the attacks, the sales of Sampath's Savarkar books have been robust. The books became national bestsellers, with eight editions translated into Marathi, Hindi, and other languages.

What was disappointing was that the print media, in particular, ignored the book. Some bookstores even refused to stock it, with some owners saying, 'We don't want to pollute the store with a book on Savarkar.' However, through social media and word of mouth, the books did very well.

The second volume delved into very controversial areas such as partition and Gandhi's assassination, in which Savarkar was implicated. Sampath knew that the second volume would receive more backlash than the first.

He recalls:

> Hitjobs by Left-leaning websites began. They launched personal attacks such as 'he is not a technical historian, has no peer reviews'. There is a war going on on my Wikipedia page. A TV anchor introduced me as a 'historian' while introducing another panellist as a 'professional historian'.

What lies behind the resurgence of nationalism and Indic consciousness?

> Post-2014, Modi has been a catalyst. It has overtaken both a person and the party. In every field, alternative and strong nationalistic voices are emerging. Nationalism and Hindu awareness have outgrown even the Sangh or Modi. Over the years, the community has been pushed so much to the wall that there is a resurgence happening from all sides. If things had not been made so intense, Hindus as a community would not be so aggressive. With certain instances like the 'Dismantling Global Hindutva' conference in the US, the patience of ordinary people has run out. There is no going back, even if the regime changes. It is competitive Hindutva now. All the potent symbols important for national pride, like the Ram Mandir, are out there in the open.

Sampath's next book is titled *Bravehearts of Bharat*. It will feature unsung heroes from different times and geographies. 'The narrative is that we lost many battles. But we won quite a few,' he says.

Sampath is spearheading an initiative by the Motwani Jadeja Foundation and Indic Academy for history fellowships. Every year, around ten scholars will receive support for historical research and writing. They must produce a manuscript by the end of the fellowship period. Historians and those with a strong historical inclination are eligible. Scholars can include professors as well as rookie historians. The target is to have 100 such history scholars within ten years. They will receive a substantial stipend and have their book published.

He also felt the need to create cultural spaces. Backed by the Zee group, he started a multiregional cultural event called Arth, which is now in its fourth year.

> History is the biggest contestation today. Everything hinges on the legacy wars. It came to the fore with the Ayodhya movement and judgement. This is why books like Meenakshi Jain's *Rama and Ayodhya* are so important. It is crucial that things don't go uncontested. He or she who controls the past and the future controls the present.

True Indology

One of the most influential and enigmatic entities that ripped through the Left-liberal fabric of history is True Indology. Over the last six years, this anonymous handle has become iconic and immensely popular, especially among young nationalists.

As it became the online history fact-checker, debunking lies that glorified genocidal Islamist rulers like Babur, Aurangzeb, or Tipu Sultan, the account was repeatedly suspended, especially on Twitter. Recently, it posted on

Twitter from @BharadwajSpeaks and publicly declared that he was a young man named Bharadwaj. He also added a profile photo.

But even that account was suspended, and the suspension has been contested in court. True Indology, or Bharadwaj, now has active accounts on Facebook and Instagram.

Although the person has chosen not to fully disclose his identity, citing safety concerns, we shall take him at face value for what he has put out in public and confirmed for his book.

True Indology became an instant hit as his Twitter threads started debunking claims of history writers like Audrey Truschke, Rana Safvi, and S. Irfan Habib, often leaving them without a retort. He contested, for instance, a widely circulated photo during Eid by the likes of politicians Shashi and Yogendra Yadav, writer William Dalrymple, actor Shabana Azmi, and others like Safvi. Purportedly, it showed an 18th-century (some said 17th-century) Rajasthani painting in which Lord Krishna is pointing at the moon along with Eid devotees.[1]

True Indology challenged it with a thread from his now-suspended account. Prominent Indian art critic and historian B.N. Goswami later rubbished the fake and forced effort to secularise Eid by citing the painting. He wrote:

> I must confess that I had not seen this image before, despite being quite familiar with the Bhagavata Purana and this series of paintings from the Tehri-Garhwal collection (painted by one of the members of the first generation after Manaku and Nainsukh). However, the present 'reading' of it is completely meaningless based as it is, chiefly I think, on the appearance of Nanda who is dressed like a Mughal courtier: with that kind of beard, and wearing a long jama and a sloping turban. The anachronic impossibility of a Muslim figure to be seen

in the Bhagavata Purana or this series apart, this is the way Nanda appears in every single folio of this series whenever we see him! Even in this regard, if one notices from close, the jama Nanda wears is clearly a Hindu style jama, tied as it is, in Hindu fashion, under the left armpit. There is not the slightest doubt about this. Topped by that is the silly statement that it is a Rajasthani painting! Of course, it is not. It is a Pahari painting from the series to which I have referred above.

On another occasion, Truschke had tried to whitewash Mughal Emperor Aurangzeb's repression of Diwali celebrations, saying he even clamped down on Eid and Muharram. True Indology challenged her again. He argued that since Aurangzeb was a Sunni fundamentalist, he naturally banned the Shia from grieving during Muharram, degraded the rank of any mansabdar found participating in Muharram, and beheaded anybody abusing the Prophet's companions (whom Shias see as usurpers).

True Indology challenged Audrey to cite texts that showed that the Mughals restricted Eid. He posted the testimony of Italian traveller, Niccolo Manucci, who recorded the grand celebration of Eid held during Aurangzeb's regime.[2]

Such exposés became so frequent and savage that his ideological opponents started hounding him. Unable to beat him with facts, they began mass-reporting him. His account was a direct target, and Twitter seemed to oblige time and again. There was, however, no concrete occasion of True Indology being abusive or calling for violence, which should be the grounds for suspension, if any.

True Indology responded to a mailed questionnaire for this book in September 2019. The responses are being reproduced in the original question-and-answer format:

Q: Are you a professional historian or a keen student of history? If it is the latter, please give me some idea about your profession.
A: I have always referred to myself as a student of history. 'Professional historian' means different things to different people. That is a label I wouldn't use to describe myself. However, I am familiar with professional historical methods, and I have a background in publishing papers.

Q: Are you male or female, based in India or abroad (which city), one person or a group of individuals (like a sort of think tank)?
A: I am male. I am a single person. I am NOT a 'group of individuals' or a think tank. 'True Indology' is a name I have chosen for my online work because it is my intention to ensure that history isn't manipulated to serve political and ideological ends. I have chosen not to make it a 'think tank' or involve anyone else precisely because I wanted 'True Indology' to exclusively represent my thoughts and perspectives on everything under the sun. While I would always welcome coordinated efforts from a 'think tank', that would not represent 'True Indology'.

Q: A bit about you. Age, growing up, family, schooling, college and university, strong intellectual influences, etc. What shaped your ideology? Which personal and political events/tipping points made you lean Right/Indic, honed your nationalism? Please be as detailed as possible.
A: I was born into a traditional Hindu family. As is common in such backgrounds, an innate protestant spirit dominated my early teens. But traditional Hindu families place significant importance on education. I developed an interest in geography at a very young age, followed by a subsequent fascination with

history. During my early teens, I was a sceptic and questioned everything, yet I maintained a constant and avid reading habit.

My parents imparted the Akhyanas from the Ramayana and Mahabharata, which left a tremendous influence on me. Later on, I read the works of Sita Ram Goel and Ram Swarup. Their writings made me realise the extent of the blatant distortion of Indian history by Leftists. But the tipping point was the Leftist noise surrounding Ayodhya. The irrational arguments they made and the disingenuity they exhibited convinced me that their stance had to be opposed tooth and nail.

Q: When and why did you feel compelled to challenge the Leftist–colonial version of history on social media? How did you go about it? Is there somebody who helps you with the research?

A: I was a subscriber to *The Hindu* news magazine. It frequently published articles by eminent historians like Romila Thapar and Irfan Habib. Their pieces convinced me that there was a blatant distortion of history that needed to be challenged. I began by reading as many books as I could. When it comes to examining primary resources, nobody can 'help' others with research. One has to learn the source language and examine the sources available in online or offline libraries. Yet, many expert researchers and 'Indologists' in this field are quite helpful. If one needs any clarification, one simply has to drop an email, and they would be kind enough to respond. I have personally experienced it.

Q: Which three or five episodes do you consider to be your best busting of lies on social media?

A: That is not how I see it. My intention is to objectively dig out and present history as close as possible to the discernible facts. As such, I value every single tweet and post of mine.

Q: Would you be as optimistic about the ideology, or done your work as True Indology, if it were not for Modi emerging on the scene?
A: Even before the emergence of Modi, I had been on another platform, writing many posts on ancient Indian history. My ideology and work have nothing to do with politics and the ascent or descent of any political party.

Q: Have you gotten into serious trouble for running True Indology?
A: Apart from stray threats I have received from many powerful politicians and civil servants, I have never encountered any serious trouble.

Q: What are the positives and negatives you see in the Modi government?
A: Positives: The government is bold enough to take tough and positive decisions that could attract a lot of outrage and criticism. A case in point is the revocation of Article 370 and the implementation of CAA. In the long term, these steps will ensure national integration. The government has also made significant progress in opening bank accounts and constructing toilets in rural India. The Swachh Bharat campaigns have been effective in making the environment cleaner.

Negatives: I particularly did not approve of the Modi government's erstwhile alliance with separatist elements like the People's Democratic Party (PDP) in Jammu and Kashmir. Additionally, some politicians with serious cases/accusations of corruption and crime from other parties have found entry into the BJP.

Q: Which parts of Indian history have been distorted the most and why?

A: Without any question, pre-Buddhist Ancient India has been the most distorted section of Indian history. Apart from religious texts, which hardly elaborate on social, political, and economic conditions, there are hardly any sources available. This period is less understood, and even the most objective historian's account is marred with startling bias when it comes to evaluating this period.

Q: What specific steps are needed to correct our view of history and culture?

A: Every single line written hitherto has to be examined, and if found to be false, discarded. Historical opinions passed off as history have to be discarded. Anything that does not have a backing of primary sources needs to be questioned, and every single line rewritten has to be backed by proof. There should be no 'appeal to authority'. There are no two ways about it.

Q: Why haven't you written a book yet? What are your plans to build on your work as True Indology?

A: I am currently working on a very comprehensive book that involves a lot of research on a wide range of historical topics. My professional life and job also keep me busy. Writing such a book is a significant undertaking that could consume years of work and research, but I have always been prepared for it. My immediate plan as of now is to finish my book.

Q: Why have you stayed anonymous? Will you ever reveal your identity?

A: I have chosen to remain anonymous because I prefer to keep my personal life separate from my work on social media.

This is particularly important because I engage in discussions about history, which can be contentious and controversial. However, I plan to go public with my identity upon the release of my forthcoming book. That is when I will reveal my identity.

Q: What kind of India would you like to see in twenty years?
A: In twenty years, I would like to see an India where farmers never have to commit suicide, where India becomes the world's biggest agricultural country (overtaking China by gross value of agricultural production), and where healthcare facilities are available in every nook and corner of rural India.

David Frawley

One of the foreign Indic scholars who has been at the forefront of breaking the Leftist–colonial–Islamist narrative—along with the likes of Michel Danino, Koenraad Elst, and Francois Gautier—has been US-born David Frawley. Born in La Crosse, Wisconsin, into a Catholic family of ten siblings, he later embraced Sanatan Dharma. Frawley was given the name Vamadeva Shastri in 1991 by his teacher, Dr B.L. Vashta, and an Arya Samaj group in Maharashtra.

Frawley has been married to Yogini Shambhavi for fifteen years. She was born into a Sikh family and was given a Christian name, Lorraine Gill, which she no longer uses. She is also involved in yoga, Ayurveda, and astrology. She is a strong speaker and vocal advocate on women's issues, championing the traditional idea of Shakti against the modern concept of feminism. The two met in Delhi through work and a mutual friend, Lokesh Chandra.

Frawley's son from a previous marriage is a prominent naturopathic doctor in the US. He is also interested in yoga and Buddhism. 'He didn't grasp the Indian side the way I have. He is more focused on the healing aspects,' he says.

Frawley, sitting on the lawns of Delhi's India International Centre with the winter sun shining on his flowing white beard and thin, tall frame, says that he lives close to the earth and does not lead an urban life. He owns two acres of land in a semi-forested area near the national forest in New Mexico, in the southern Rocky Mountains. He adds:

> My grandparents grew up on farms. They had a very large farm, not just a small one. But that was the generation that moved away from the farm and into the city. We moved to Denver, Colorado, which was a bigger city where we were able to grow up, see more things, and enter college. That was in the late 1960s. I was involved socially and politically in the anti-war movement and all those things, but also in the counter-cultural movement.

He was part of the Students for a Democratic Society, a prominent New Left organisation, during his early years.

> But I was always a bit more of a pacifist or anarchist. Besides that, I mainly stayed with the spiritual side … yoga and Vedanta. It was through the study of the gurus of that era … Aurobindo's teachings, Vivekananda's, Ramana's, and Yogananda's … that I was introduced to India, particularly through Aurobindo's work.

Frawley was also involved with the Hippie Movement and helped with some college anti-war demonstrations, but he quickly became disillusioned. It is hard to believe that a scholar like Frawley did not finish college.

> I started off initially and left with the anti-war movement. I went to the University of Southern California and found out that my library of Indic–Yogic–Vedic things was better than theirs. I went to Colorado University and took cosmology and metaphysics and found out it was neither cosmology nor metaphysics nor psychology. I felt they were not studying the subjects, and the way they teach them is wrong. So, I studied with people in India, people from ashrams, people in my fields. We started the first Ayurvedic schools; there weren't any in the West. Even in Vedanta, there was hardly anything, but then we eventually found people like Swami Dayananda, Ramana Ashram, Aurobindo Ashram, and so on. That's why I have always been outside academia. I don't trust academicians because they are brainwashed, they have peer pressure, and they have no sadhana. Mostly they don't know Sanskrit, and they are coming at these things with the Western mindset. I wasn't resonating with the Left or Right in America. I wasn't resonating with American intellectuals and artists. I found them very shallow. I understand Western civilisation and its limitations. I wouldn't say I am part of it because I don't have their mindset. I spent a lot of time studying the mind, brain, consciousness, intellect, and I tell people that the Western mind has never gotten beyond the rajasik buddhi. They were unaware of the idea of atma, sattvik buddhi.

Interestingly, he was born on 21 September 1950, just four days after Narendra Modi and ten days after RSS chief Mohan Bhagwat.

> There is also astronomy there. All of us were born between two total eclipses. It only happens ten or eleven times in a

century that you have one total eclipse followed by another. It is said to be a kind of doorway in time to the timeless. I always had an interest in history. But what drew me to India was Aurobindo's work and my study of the Vedas. Along with the Vedas, I was also very active in the field of Ayurveda. I was studying all this personally. I was more connected to Indian gurus. I didn't like the local people so much. I was connected to Anandamayi Ma in my twenties. For example, the main influence I had with my writing was on M.P. Pandit of the Aurobindo Ashram. He was the secretary of the ashram, and I had done a series of books on Vedic research: the Upanishads, Rig Veda. When I met him, it must have been 1978 or 1979, I showed him my work, and he said, 'This is very good. I will publish this for you in India', which he did.

Pandit began publishing Frawley's work through all the Aurobindo Ashram publications and books. While studying the Vedas, Frawley says he discovered that the historical model was completely wrong. 'That was one of the first things I wrote about. The spiritual and religious interpretation of the Vedas by the West was blatantly wrong, and their historical interpretation was also incorrect,' he states.

When he came to India in the 1980s to study Ayurveda, his teacher was Dr B.L. Vashta from Pune, who was a major leader in the RSS. He had been an editor of *Kesari* in Pune and had also authored books on Savarkar, Guru Gobind Singh, and RSS ideologue M.S. Golwalkar.

> I got to meet the RSS before I knew about the propaganda against them. I also noticed that the Left in India was much more communist and Leftist fundamentalist than even the Left in America. Gradually, in the 1980s, I became a spokesperson, bridging the gap between the East and the West

in various ways based on Yoga–Ayurveda–Vedanta, and also encouraging people in India to uphold their own traditions. I was able to meet a lot of groups—teachers, writers, and publications. I was part of that discussion in India for more than thirty years and I have a sense of what it is, where it came from, where it is going, and I was even able to meet Sadashiv Dange of the communist era. I met RSS and VHP leaders like Ashok Singhal.

Frawley's scholarship has stemmed from personal studies with individuals such as M.P. Pandit, K. Nitesh of the Ramana Ashram, Sivananda Murthy, Swami Dayananda.

Some of the main books one studies on Ayurvedic medicine have been written by Frawley, along with contemporaries like Dr Vasant Lad. They set up schools. He took Hindu thoughts from the Vedas, Ayurveda, and Vedanta into yoga groups, yoga ashrams, and yoga movements. He also experimented with Vedic astrology.

His *Ayurvedic Healing* was the first book in English to be published in India, promoting Ayurveda in a new way. Then he wrote books on ancient India like *Gods, Sages and Kings*. What made him more well-known in the long run was his work with the Delhi-based nationalistic publishing house, Voice of India, which began in the early 1990s. His books like *Myth of the Aryan Invasion*, *Arise Arjuna*, and *Awaken Bharata* kept shattering long-held Leftist narratives on history.

> I also write on the misinterpretation and distortions of history, theology, and politics. I came out thirty years ago against this idea that all religions were the same or some of these platitudes. In the Vajpayee era, I did a whole series of talks in Delhi. I remember doing some programmes and talks in which I was there with Swami Dayananda, Murli Manohar

Joshi, and other speakers. We did a big programme in JNU in 1999 on ancient India. We did programmes in the Northeast as well.

Recently, Frawley has finished a book on Upanishadic thought, particularly focusing on the four states—waking, dream, deep sleep, and the fourth dimension of being, turiya. He believes that the West has yet to fully encounter India.

The West has its own civilisational narrative, and India and China would be footnotes, perhaps growing footnotes. Maybe Native Americans would be a footnote as well. There has been no real direct examination of India as a civilisation, or India's civilisational terminology, or even the fact that India has its history. India's view of history is ignored, and India's theology is reduced to Western theology. India's view of the State is ignored. The British and Westerners took the Vedas outside of India and rewrote them according to the rules of Western thought. They created things like mythology, anthropology, comparative religion, and terms like polytheism and animism. They established a line of interpretation that negated the Indian tradition. They would not study the Indian teachers and totally ignored the Indian living gurus. They would never mention Aurobindo or Vivekananda. They would pick up some obscure verse from the *Manusmriti*, and that would be their understanding of India.

Frawley argues that during the colonial era, instead of looking at India or China as great civilisations, the West tried to portray them as regressive—primitive, filled with superstition, widow-burning, caste, and idol worship. That narrative was intentionally changed. The British also destroyed the educational system in India, and then they claimed the Indians were illiterate. They shut down the Ayurvedic schools and claimed Indians didn't have medicine. 'Ironically, they borrowed a lot from Ayurveda. The West borrowed linguistics, mathematics, and many other things without crediting India properly. The United States followed the British narrative,' he says.

Frawley adds:

> So far, India is the only country today that has not rewritten its history in the post-colonial era. Its colonial views are still there, and they have been reinforced with a Marxist tinge. The narrative about Native Americans has changed in America, as has the narrative about native Africans. However, in India, the narrative hasn't changed; it worsened since Independence. In the pre-Independence era, you had a strong revivalist tradition with Gandhi, Aurobindo, Tagore, Vivekananda. They were seeing a civilisational awakening. After Independence, the communist–Marxist–Fabian–socialist Left took over. They tried to pretend there was no India before 1947. They negated all these teachers, removed their works, and put up people like Romila Thapar and Irfan Habib who did a lot of tactical groundwork on local customs but they had no sense of India as a country, a culture. They had a political bias to negate it because they did not want the Hindus to come out.

He then narrates a short story. There was a huge conference on ancient India at JNU in 1999. About 500 students attended. Besides Frawley, archaeologist S.P. Gupta, poet Bhagwant Singh were among the speakers.

> We were wondering what kind of questions we would get. There were only two, and one I remember specifically. A student

said, 'Look, you have shown us clearly from data that there was no Aryan invasion of India, that the Indian civilisation has this great continuity. But because this information is politically advantageous to the Hindu fundamentalists or the Hindu Right Wing, it should be suppressed even if it is true.' And that is how I learnt about their mindset. It is not about the truth. The Marxist view of history, whether it is in China, the Soviet Union or India, is propaganda. Even in America, there are more Marxist professors in humanities than there are Republicans. Now we have this hijacking of the narrative of India. Anti-Indians, Marxists, communists, or even just Christians, Muslims, or Fabian socialists have created the views you find in Indian textbooks. They try to whitewash Aurangzeb, but Shivaji is hardly mentioned. Great Hindu and Buddhist kings receive little mention.

Frawley argues that there is no sense of civilisational continuity. Leftists have distorted history to imply that people arrived from outside and that there was no indigenous culture, despite India maintaining the same customs from Kanyakumari to Kedarnath for thousands of years, preserving epics like the Mahabharata, and boasting the world's richest literary traditions.

It is essential that the narrative is changed because it poisons the minds of children and youth, alienating them from their own culture. They are often taught a negative view of the dharmic tradition—that their caste is sexist, intolerant, violent. The history of oppression from Muslims to the British is carefully covered up. There needs to be an honest historical model and a reclamation of the civilisational model through science, economy, literature, art, music, dance, a new syllabus, new teachings, new textbooks, new experiences. They say,

'Oh, the Puranas have idol worship and metaphysics, so you shouldn't use them as historical works.' The Bible has that, the Quran has all this religious stuff. The ancient works of the Greeks and the Romans have gods and goddesses. You have to bring back that literature too, not just as history but as culture.

Frawley says Modi is honouring India's civilisational past by rebuilding Kedarnath, Kashi Vishwanath, and other places of deep cultural significance.

It is something that Vajpayee could not do. He was a poet. He had to be a kind of harmonising figure. But Modi is in a much stronger position in government. 'In foreign policy, Modi has put India on the world stage. India is no longer apologetic. It is no longer in the shadow of the Soviet Union or kowtows to China or the Islamic world. It has an identity. He has awakened it economically,' he adds.

Frawley says it was difficult to believe during the Ram Janmabhoomi movement or Kashmiri Pandit exodus of the 1990s that a grand Ram temple would come up after a unanimous order of the Supreme Court, or that Kashmir would suddenly be reintegrated with India. Or that India would bomb Balakot in Pakistan in response to the 2019 Pulwama attack when it did not militarily retaliate even after the 2008 Mumbai attacks.

He states:

> Modi prioritised infrastructure improvements, such as electricity, toilets, running water, over other reforms. Politicians don't really take the time to address these critical issues of the people, focusing simply on civilisational and cultural matters. He is going after black money. So many

changes are there, despite tremendous resistance from bureaucracy, media, foreign groups like NGOs.

Ordinary Indians are connected with this movement, the changes in attitude, and on the ground, he says. He recalls an episode when he was writing *Myth of the Aryan Invasion*:

> A lady named Meera Nanda from *The Week* called me 'the well-known fascist William Frawley'. She didn't even get my name right. There is an actor in America named William Frawley. But in any case, I became 'a well-known fascist' simply for criticising the Aryan Invasion Theory and promoting Ayurveda, yoga, and non-violence. Now, we have a very excellent group of young writers like Sanjeev Sanyal. We have them in positions of power in the government; we have an intellectual awakening. Hindu is no longer a bad term. Earlier, one said, 'Oh, I am a Hindu, but I accept the Quran, the Bible as well.' The apologetic approach is no longer there, and the Left has been deflated. It is still in power in certain areas of the media, but it has lost control of the narrative. Now, you see politicians of all parties running to Hindu temples, trying to play soft Hindutva, however insincere. They at least know they cannot get elected by just catering to their minority vote banks. Earlier, they would get elected just by one Hindu segment like Yadavs, Reddys, or whatever, allying with the Muslims. Now, even with AAP's Arvind Kejriwal, you could see suddenly Hanuman is there this time. Some of these changes are going on. But it is still in the initial phase. There is much more to come.

One of the biggest challenges India faces in the next ten, twenty, thirty years is demographics, according to him.

> The CAA is under attack because it represents the first attempt to reverse demographics or address demographic issues. Muslims have long believed that demographics would enable them to gain power. If demographics no longer favour them, it will cause panic. Even Yasser Arafat once said to the Israelis that whatever happens, 'the womb of the Arab woman is my strongest weapon'[3]. Also, India's development and Pakistan's decline are causing a lot of resentment. The positive aspect is that Modi knows how to address Islamic countries diplomatically.

He says English-speaking, upper-/middle-class urban Indians are also returning to their roots, 'like Hindu yatras to go to the Himalayas'.

> That's why you have contemporary gurus like Sri Sri Ravishankar or Sadhguru Jaggi Vasudev, who can address in a language and idiom that is urban. They can also incorporate other aspects like ecology, global issues, and psychology, which are more relatable to them. In America too, Hindus from science and business backgrounds remain respectful of their traditions. It is the people from the humanities who are being influenced by Marxist education. The wild card is the youngest generation, which is emerging with heavy technology, infotech, smartphones, media, and Bollywood. We don't know what's going to happen to them as they get older and develop their political leanings. In America, for instance, the Left was defeated in terms of the economy in the 1970s, 1980s, and 1990s. But now they are making inroads through education, and a lot of gender issues. How this next generation handles technology and what that technology teaches them is very important. That is why we need to change education. We need to bring culture and tradition in a positive and futuristic way.

The new wave of nationalism makes Frawley optimistic. He says that Indians now take pride in their culture and civilisation. It is not just 'British created us' or 'Mughals created us'.

> I don't want to be critical of Gandhi, but Gandhi is not the best image for a country. Why? One, as a man in a loincloth, he doesn't represent economic development. You should have Goddess Laxmi or Ganesha on your money. And then Gandhi is a secular figure. But no secular figure wears a loincloth. That's a religious figure. His many good teachings are there, but that's not a model the youth can follow. They are not going to be wearing a loincloth, they are not going to be spinning wheels. I think Aurobindo had a better model. You need a model here that can be spiritual, hip, educated, scientific, and technological, and able to deal with the whole world today.

CHAPTER 4

Whoosh of an Economic Tide

Rahul Gupta's roadside pani puri stand at Noida's Sector 93 market is a microcosm of India's new economy. Customers savouring the crisply fried hollow wheat balls filled with mashed potato and dunked in tamarind water no longer need petty change to pay the twenty-year-old. Money flows from customers' phones via the barcode at his stall to an e-wallet, which is ultimately linked to his bank account. He had opened the account along with 47.8 crore (478 million) mostly low-income Indians under Prime Minister Narendra Modi's Jan Dhan scheme.

Changes in Rahul's life and business embody the shift in governance that the Indian economy has experienced under the prime ministership of Narendra Modi. Today, nearly 50 crore, or 500 million, Indians have accounts under the Jan Dhan financial inclusion scheme. Almost 55 per cent of Jan Dhan account holders are women, and 67 per cent are in rural and semi-urban areas. Around 86 per cent of accounts are operational.

Such is the transformative power of the scheme that during the COVID-19 lockdown, Rs 30,945 crore (nearly $3.73 billion) was credited to the accounts of women Jan Dhan account holders. Approximately 5.1 crore or 50 million

Indians mostly receive direct benefit transfer (DBT) from the government under various schemes in these accounts.

The economic approach under the new administration has shifted from ideology to pragmatism. It has been building a transparent social welfare network alongside capitalism, minimising leakage and ensuring that benefits are directly transferred.

From the Nehruvian era to the time of Indira Gandhi and through the coalition era, India has heavily relied on Fabian socialism, with the nationalisation of key industries and the State acting as the arbiter of all disputes. Then in 1991, the Narasimha Rao government led India into its path-altering economic liberalisation. It freed the nation from its socialist shackles, but the Bretton Woods system or the World Bank–International Monetary Fund school of thought presumed that India had missed the manufacturing bus. It predicted that India's growth would be chiefly services-led.

But the new India has turned that hypothesis on its head. From being the biggest importer of arms from 2017–21 and for decades relying solely on defence imports, India today is among the top twenty exporters of weapons and defence products, much of it being manufactured by private companies under the Indian government's Make in India initiative. With defence, electronics, and semiconductors, India has leaped into the league of the most sophisticated manufacturing.

The COVID-19 pandemic, which exposed the 'brittle bones' of India's healthcare system, triggered a resurgent India's resolve to overhaul the health system, build capacity, invest in quick-turnaround research, and develop vaccines for itself and the world. India sent its Covaxin to nearly seventy-five countries. From Rs 34,985 ($35 billion) in 2019–20,

India's pharmaceutical industry is predicted to nearly double to $65 billion in 2024.

In the automobile sector, for instance, Hyundai, which refrained from bringing its gearbox technology to India for many years, has now introduced it under the Make in India initiative. So, from being a manufacturing sector laggard, India is advancing to the middle rung of manufacturing. A manufacturing export-led economy is widely considered robust.

Three factors that have powered India's economic engine and attracted investment under Modi have been policy consistency (except on land reforms and farm laws, which the government withdrew due to chaotic protests), political stability, and law and order.

A large number of states ruled by the BJP, which also governs at the Centre, has been helpful. The government has not been distracted by the pressures of a coalition.

Sanjeev Sanyal

One of the most notable changes in the economic approach of the new Right under Modi has been the shift from Keynesian and Ashokan approaches to the Kautilyan approach.

Kautilya, also known as Chanakya, was a Hindu statesman, philosopher, and chief counsel to Emperor Chandragupta Maurya around 300 BCE. His seminal treatise on polity and economy, the *Arthashastra*, still forms the bedrock of understanding material wealth and success, as well as the nuances of governance and statecraft. His work has inspired numerous modern interpretations, and his relevance has endured the passage of time.

Sanjeev Sanyal, formerly the principal economic advisor of the Department of Economic Affairs, Ministry of Finance, and now a member of the Economic Advisory Council to the prime minister, explains India's departure from the Keynesian approach and adoption of the Kautilyan path. He says the Keynesian approach is purely demand-driven, with the supply side seen as given.

> We are supply-siders. So, we clearly see the world as driven by the supply side as an important part. Yes, demand is important but only meaningful in the context of supply. You can see what's happening in the world ... all the inflation. The chip shortage, or the container shortage ... all these are supply-side issues that have suddenly popped up because the rest of the world was pumping up demand without paying attention to the supply.

On one side is the socialist-leaning view, with strong parallels to Emperor Ashoka's model, which used to be the cornerstone of Nehruvian economics. Sanyal adds:

> The socialists believe that a group of government bureaucrats, individuals in the Planning Commission, or wise men will know the direction in which the economy should go and guide it accordingly. It is an interventionist approach, which is also reflected in the Ashokan idea. If you read Ashoka's edicts, he always states, 'I have entrusted my people to the dhamma mahamatras...'. Officials would distribute benefits to citizens, akin to a parent giving something to a child. It was a very 'mai baap' or paternalistic approach. But the alternative to the socialist view is the market or neo-classical perspective, which suggests that this equilibrium can be achieved by mostly allowing markets to operate freely, leading to a laissez-faire system.

Sanyal argues that these two worldviews are actually close cousins because they are both based on the idea that there is a 'known or knowable or fixed optimal equilibrium'. The dispute between the marketwallas and the neo-classicalwallas is that their methods of reaching this equilibrium differ.

Those who rely on Complexity Theory are making the case that there is no such equilibrium. The world is completely uncertain, and even if such an equilibrium exists, it is fleeting. By the time you formulate your policies, it has already shifted elsewhere, argues Sanyal.

> It's a waste of time thinking about this equilibrium. You basically need to create State institutions that provide for things that the market is unable to do. There is a very important role for the State in the Complexity universe, which is not so laissez-faire because there is a need for coordination and navigating in this rather foggy world.

Sanyal argues that anchors need to be created, whether it's regulation or enforcement of contracts, among other things, to prevent this system from drifting off. There is a role for leadership and vision, which is absent in laissez-faire. So, there is a certain role for the State. He says there is a case for a strong but limited State.

> Now, if you trace our intellectual lineage, who is the person who made this case? Well, it turns out that the Indian intellectual tradition has made such a case, and it is by Kautilya. The two views—Kautilya's and Complexity—are not separate. The idea is that there is a role for the State. The role is not minimalistic, serving merely as a referee. Rather, it is to provide leadership, vision, and coordination. But it is a limited role. You don't want the State to engage in excessive regulation, akin to the

licence/permit raj. Therefore, this is the third view. It does not align with the traditional socialist vs neo-classical linear trade-off. In this view, the State intervenes where necessary with a serious demeanour. That's the Kautilyan perspective. In areas like internal and external security or currency issuance, the State exercises complete control. The State also has a significant role in municipal governance and in regulating, though not banning undesirable practices.

He cites the case of prostitution in the Kautilyan State. The polymath was very clear. He did not favour prohibition, but he clearly stated, 'I prefer regulation.' He regulated it quite severely. Where the State holds supremacy, he has no sense of humour.

But Chanakya was suspicious of the State and its officials. He had a reputation for employing a wide network of spies. However, the espionage was not directed at the average citizen but at officialdom, nobility, and external enemies.

Kautilya granted the State significant power in certain areas but was extremely suspicious of the officials who enforced these laws. He also imposed limitations on the State. It was not meant to interfere with your life, even in matters like alcohol. The State-regulated drinking places. 'This is exactly in line with the views of Complexity Theory. Complex systems have a role for the State, but it is a limited role. The Chanakyan State is strong but limited. Not weak and limited like a Libertarian State,' Sanyal adds.

He says the State has no business interfering in a large part of the economy. He prefers fluid evolution over grand plans.

Even in town planning, I am against rigid master plans, for example. That's why I much prefer Gurgaon over Chandigarh,

> despite all its flaws. And of course, Singapore, which I often use as an example. Singapore is a well-managed Gurgaon. It is not an evolved Chandigarh. No matter how Chandigarh develops, it will never become a Singapore. If you manage Gurgaon better, it could, in theory at least, become a better Singapore.

Sanyal refutes the criticism that the Modi government has failed to deliver on its promise of 'minimum government, maximum governance'.

> People hear what they want to. Some hear only 'minimum government', while others hear only 'maximum governance'. But in some ways, 'minimum government, maximum governance' is a restatement of a strong but limited State. Again, I will let you judge whether we are doing a good job of it, but this is consistent with the fact that you have a government that is interventionist in various ways, yet at the same time, is deregulating and privatising. Some people feel there is a contradiction. There is not. If you adhere purely to a neo-classical view, then you can't do both, which is privatise on one side and implement a PLI [Performance Linked Incentive] scheme on the other, which involves intervention. Or provide a huge incentive for FAB [semiconductor fabrication] plants because the neo-classical perspective would question why you are interfering? PLIs, FAB plants, or providing special incentives are also forms of intervention because they focus on a particular thing.

The Modi government, he says, is in a different place. It is willing to intervene where necessary; however, it does not encourage a licence/permit system. So, one may be against rigidly master-planned cities but fine with occasional, limited interventions like the Kashi–Vishwanath corridor or building the Central Vista.

As mentioned in earlier chapters, Sanyal comes from a family deeply involved in the Indian freedom movement. His father's side of the family follows the Shakta worldview, which sees the world as an unstable, uncertain place. He says his approach to economics, derived from Complexity Theory, is closely aligned with the intellectual heritage of Shakta Hinduism. The other factor that influenced his economic thought was growing up in Jyoti Basu's Bengal.

The sheer absurdity of the economic policies carried out in the late 1970s and 1980s, the destruction not just of Kolkata but of Bengali culture, entrepreneurship, everything, has had a deep impact on me. Today, people don't realise that Bengal was famous throughout history for entrepreneurship. If you read Bengali folklore, it is full of merchants who would travel to other countries. Bengal, like Gujarat, is a coastal state. So, Bengalis were travelling all over the world trading. The Sinhalese, after all, derived their lineage from King Vijaya from Bengal, who migrated there. So, there was always this idea that Bengal did not have a trading culture. It did, and it was very strong. That is why all the Europeans went and set up shop in Bengal along the Hooghly because there was such a strong business culture there. There is a long history of this. And of course, as I told you, my mother's father's family were businessmen who had set up at that time one of the largest cotton mills in India—certainly the largest in Bengal—called Mohini Mills in Kushtia, Bangladesh. They were entrepreneurs, and they set it up following the 1905 division of Bengal and the Swadeshi movement the same year.

The 1905 Swadeshi movement was one of the reasons his mother's father's family got into business.

> If you search from that time, Bengalis were known for their highly competitive businesses, challenging the likes of British entrepreneurs. So, I come from that background on one side, and then I see what Jyoti Basu did to Bengal and how the mindset destroyed the work ethic and artistic culture. I am a first-hand witness to the amount of violence that accompanied it, which is often forgotten. When the Marichjhapi massacre happened, I was nine years old. I didn't quite understand the massacre until I was much older, but the whispers of this violence were always there. It was quite common for random violence to occur, like the burning of Ananda Margis. This is a very important influence on my thinking.

The third major influence on Sanyal's thinking was the 1991 economic reform. He was at Shriram College in Delhi at that time. It coincided with the collapse of the Soviet Union and the fall of the Berlin Wall. 'I was overjoyed when this happened, coming from Kolkata and having witnessed this. It was almost like I was from the Soviet bloc, and what was going on in Poland was happening in my head as well,' he states.

So, Sanyal, one of the leading intellectual figures of the new nationalism, is a product of these three influences: a family experience of resistance against the British rule derived from the Shakta religious tradition; witnessing the destruction of Bengal and Bengali entrepreneurship and culture under Jyoti Basu; and the collapse of the Berlin Wall, the Soviet Union, India's own economy, and the redemption with the reforms of 1991. The last one, particularly, had a significant effect on his thinking and his consequent suspicion of excessive State control, licences, and permits.

He then went on a Rhodes scholarship to Oxford for three years, joined the financial markets, spent years in Mumbai, and then went to Singapore. He also had stints in Hong Kong and London. He witnessed the Asian crisis firsthand. He was the chief economist for South Asia and Southeast Asia for Deutsche Bank.

Professionally, he witnessed the transformation in East Asia and how these countries rebuilt themselves. Many of them were as poor as India in the 1990s, but within one generation, they shifted from the Third World to the First World.

Even while working abroad, Sanyal was quite vocal about what India needed to do. In 2009–10, he took a two-year sabbatical to drive across India with his wife and their two boys, then nine and six. The research resulted in *Land of the Seven Rivers*, a book on how India's history was shaped by its rivers, mountains, and cities. At some point in 2015–16, he says he was 'sounded out by the government' about whether he wanted to move back to India. He said yes.

Sanjeev says that, in many ways, this point in time is extremely important in the life of the nation.

> One is, you have a government with a clear mandate, clear vision, and a very unapologetic approach to various issues. Whether it is economics, privatisation, civilisational, or geo-strategic issues, this is not an apologetic approach of '*Hindi Chini Bhai Bhai*', 'we will fidget along the way by doing non-alignment', or 'we will try to protect ourselves'. Atmanirbhar Bharat is not about protectionism. We want to compete with the rest of the world. We will occasionally provide support to companies and/or sectors that we think are globally

competitive, and we are not apologetic about it because East Asia built its capacities by providing those kinds of protection to industries.

Sanyal insists that currently there is a market orientation, but not the classical or neo-classical view of economics. Much of this is influenced by a philosophical framework called the Complexity Theory.

Some of its insights seem obvious and not entirely new. Early economists like Friedrich Hayek thought about the world in the same way, but Complexity Theory was formalised not too long ago. In 1972, Edward Lorenz, a North American theoretical meteorologist studying weather systems, famously said, 'A butterfly flapping its wings in Brazil can produce a tornado in Texas.' He set the scientific world aflutter, implying that small differences in a single variable can affect a system's evolution in significant ways and set the stage for Chaos or Complexity Theory.

It has now pervaded other fields of knowledge, including economics. Figures like the Lebanese–American statistician, option trader, and risk analyst Nassim Nicholas Taleb, for instance, have taken these ideas and developed them.

> I arrived at this line of thinking from a slightly different angle because of Shakta Hindu philosophy. When I formalised my thinking around this from the 1990s onwards, reading up on Complexity Theory gave me a much more rigorous, formal framework on many issues. So much of my economics—not just macroeconomics but also my ideas on how cities should evolve, or even history-writing—is heavily influenced by it. It is becoming more mainstream. Although most college courses still do not really teach Complexity Theory, institutions like

the Santa Fe Institute in the US are at least discussing it in a more systematic way.

Sanyal says the Modi government has applied many of these ideas to deal with COVID-19. India's economic surveys have over time incorporated a lot of Complexity Theory principles. 'So, I can at least claim to have mainstreamed Complexity Theory in policymaking for the first time anywhere in the world,' he says.

A critique of the Modi government has been that some of its policies seem random, knee-jerk, and not well-thought-out. But Sanyal says that there are meticulously studied methods in motion: creative destruction, Black Swan Theory, Complexity Theory, etc.

> If seen from the perspective of traditional economics—whether neo-classical or socialist—many of our responses may not make sense. But once we explain them, they seem like common sense. See, Complexity Theory posits that the world is composed of a vast number of agents: companies, governments, random shocks, technologies, politicians, nature. All these entities are continuously interacting in various ways, interconnected through diverse networks that transmit these shocks. Many of these events are unpredictable, such as COVID-19, but this applies to geopolitical shifts, technological shocks, and more. So, the starting point of Complexity Theory is that the world is inherently unstable and unpredictable. It is not a deterministic world. This is not about constructing a more brilliant model of the world; it won't improve. Even with all the information in the world, you would still be caught off guard. So, this is not about grand five-year plans, because the world is too complicated to predict.

How do you navigate in a non-deterministic, complex world? 'First, invest in a good, real-time understanding of where you are,' says Sanyal. It is not about your ability to forecast, but rather your current situation awareness and analysis. He prescribes a Bayesian approach, updating the probability of a hypothesis as more evidence and information emerge, while simultaneously hedging for the worst-case scenario.

> If you look at our COVID-19 response, we did not come up with these grand trillion-dollar packages in the beginning and were criticised for it. But what did those trillion-dollar packages achieve for other countries that implemented them? Not much. We, on the other hand, took the view that this is a marathon through unknown territory, not a sprint. So how do you navigate a marathon through unknown territory? Well, first of all, you continuously update your position, responding to the challenges of the moment. As you may have observed, the finance minister implemented a series of medium-sized packages.

He further states that the government viewed this crisis as both a demand- and supply-side shock. The Narendra Modi government announced a special economic and comprehensive package under Atmanirbhar Bharat amounting to Rs 27.1 lakh crore—more than 13 per cent of India's GDP—to combat the impact of the COVID-19 pandemic and revive economic growth. The package included in-kind and cash transfers for households, jobs under Pradhan Mantri Garib Kalyan Rojgar Abhiyaan, increased allocation under MGNREGS, credit guarantee and equity infusion-based relief measures for micro, small and medium industries and non-bank financial companies.

Under the Rs 2.76 lakh crore Pradhan Mantri Garib Kalyan package, it released free food grain for eighty crore people, free cooking gas for eight crore families and direct cash transfers to more than forty crore farmers, women, elderly and the poor.

Also, if one does not know much about the future, how does one deal with it? Particularly when the post-COVID-19 world is fundamentally different from the pre-COVID-19 world.

He explains:

> Thus, you invest in two things—flexibility and resilience. Look at all the reforms we have undertaken; they are all aimed at one or the other. Flexibility entails a significant amount of deregulation. We deregulated drones, geospatial data, trade finance, and telecom regulations in the BPO sector. We are investing in startups and risk-taking. We also invested in how to shut down companies effectively, in churning, in creative destruction. We focused on the Insolvency and Bankruptcy Code (IBC). We don't become overly sentimental about the closure of large companies like Jet Airways. As long as new companies can emerge, we don't worry about the closure of old ones. The idea is to have a system that facilitates this process in an orderly manner. Therefore, the IBC is a crucial part of this thought process. Framework reforms like GST are aimed at creating a level playing field.

The economic thinking in the Indian 'Right' is far from homogenous, unlike among Western conservatives. There is the RSS-backed Swadeshi Jagran Manch, led by S. Gurumurthy, who insists on protecting Indian traders and integrating the staggering unorganised sector into the formal economy.

Sanyal says:

> Then there are the traditionalists, the Savarkarites, the Ambedkarite constitutionalists, the Kautilyans, and Complexity Theory proponents like myself. Additionally, there are individuals derived from the first principles of individual rights like Harsh [Gupta Madhusudan] and Rajeev [Mantri], who are aligned with my line of thinking but also have some differences.

Sanyal says the process of making the rupee a reserve currency has begun, but it is a long-term, step-by-step endeavour.

> You suddenly cannot wake up one morning and make the rupee a reserve currency. It requires a certain degree of confidence in ourselves, in terms of the kind of capital controls and international clearance capabilities we have. It is not impossible. After all, the Chinese have effectively transformed their currency into a hard currency over twenty years. We need to take the first steps. We are beginning to think along those lines.

S. Gurumurthy

At the other end of the spectrum of Indian economic thought is RSS ideologue S. Gurumurthy. His emphasis on small businesses finds an echo in Prime Minister Narendra Modi's approach and actions.

In his 2016 essay 'Indian Economy for Dummies' for the Vivekananda International Foundation, he addresses head-on the perception that multinationals and big companies run the Indian economy. Citing a July 2013 study by Credit Suisse

Asia Pacific India Equity Research Investment Strategy, he argues that the share of the corporate sector in the national GDP is just about 15 per cent, despite drawing a whopping Rs 18 lakh crore credit. Furthermore, the corporate sector created only 2.8 million jobs. In contrast, the 'informal sector' generates 90 per cent of jobs in India.

> Indian public and private—domestic and foreign, listed and unlisted—corporates together improved their share of the national GDP from a mere 12 per cent in 1991 to just 15 per cent—by a mere 3 per cent over two decades of a policy regime that rolled out the red carpet for corporates, particularly foreign ones. The share of listed corporates in the national GDP is still only about 5 per cent. Moreover, the share of companies listed in the Sensex is minuscule. These obvious facts conceal some fundamental truths about the Indian economy. But economists often fail to see the hidden truth behind the obvious facts. They even blame the obvious facts for the economic ills of India. They fault Indians for not investing in stocks and for not producing risk capital. Indians invest in gold, thus rendering their savings unproductive, they argue. Yet, they overlook the underperformance of corporates altogether.... The elitist nature of the guild of economists in India, who seek solutions from the West to address India's problems, is the reason for their ignorance about the hidden truth behind obvious facts.

PM Modi echoed Gurumurthy's thoughts when unveiling the Mudra finance scheme for the non-corporate sector on 9 April 2015. He said, 'People think it's big industries and corporate houses that provide higher employment. The truth is, only 12.5 million people are employed by big corporations, compared to 120 million by the MSME sector.'

The Credit Suisse study mentioned that unlike in the West, where the informal sector is largely illegal, in India, legal businesses remain informal only because the government has failed to reach them.

In his essay, Gurumurthy lashes out at both the bureaucracy and economists:

> Their objection is that if informal financing is formalised, that would add to systemic risk. Is allowing close to Rs 12 lakh crore sub-monetary cash economy sourced in black and illegal monies to operate and gain interest rates ranging from 24 per cent to 360 per cent, distorting formal savings, investment, and interest rates, not systemic risk? Will Raghuram Rajan and the Department of Financial Services answer?

Gurumurthy is one of the leading ideologues of the Swadeshi Jagran Manch (SJM), an organisation that promotes the RSS's economic views of self-reliance. Formed in 1991, the year India liberalised its economy, SJM has consistently cautioned governments, including Atal Bihari Vajpayee's administration, against reckless liberalisation and sacrificing the self-interest of Indian trade and industry.

Lately, SJM has had the ear of the Modi government and has wielded influence in significant policy decisions. It was one of the organisations whose objections and concerns led the Centre to shelve the Land Acquisition Bill. SJM also opposed the Regional Comprehensive Economic Partnership (RCEP)—possibly the world's largest free trade agreement among fifteen countries including China, Japan, Australia, and Korea. The government carefully weighed the argument that it would hinder India's manufacturing sector and decided to stay out.

SJM then took on the bill and Melinda Gates Foundation (BMGF), accusing it of ties with Big Pharma, and successfully had a foundation member removed from the RBI board for conflict of interest. BMGF receives foreign funds, which are cleared by the RBI board. SJM maintains that the Gates Foundation engages in shadowy activities under the guise of philanthropy. Eventually, the Modi government excluded the Gates Foundation from the country's immunisation programme due to the alleged ties between BMGF and pharmaceutical companies.

Over the years, the SJM has become an extremely vocal and vigilant watchdog that is not averse to liberalisation and globalisation but swiftly reacts to any hint of threat to local trade and industry. While many of its critics label it as 'protectionist', others believe that Prime Minister Narendra Modi's strong push for Atmanirbhar Bharat or self-sufficient India is influenced by the approach of the Manch and Gurumurthy.

Harsh Gupta Madhusudan

One of the youngest evangelists of the new, economically strong, and assertive India is Harsh Gupta Madhusudan. The thirty-six-year-old economist, investor, and author has become an articulate voice of Bharat's economic resurgence and self-reliance on social media, at events, and on television. His columns and books, like *Derivatives* and *A New Idea of India*, capture the optimism of a generation. Harsh says he adopted the pen name Madhusudan because it is anti-caste. It is also one of the many names of Lord Krishna, whom his grandfather was a devotee of.

The Kolkata native from New Alipore did his schooling at Birla High. He attended IIT Delhi for BTech but dropped out to study economics at Dartmouth University. He then joined the team of Abhijit Banerjee and Esther Duflo at MIT Poverty Action Labs. He currently serves on the board of directors of the National Stock Exchange and the International Financial Services Centre (International Exchange, GIFT City). Additionally, he is a visiting lecturer at the Indian School of Business. He is involved in public marketing investments and invests in the stock markets.

From academia, Harsh shifted to the private sector. He started his own financial consulting firm in Singapore and India. Then he pursued his MBA at INSEAD in Fontainebleau, France, and worked for Bain & Company, a global strategic consulting firm in London and Houston.

He then moved to Mumbai, got married in 2017, and joined a fund as a fund manager. Around that time, he co-authored a book called *Derivatives* with Anantha Nageswaran and T.V. Somanathan. He was also writing columns with Rajiv Mantri.

> [Rajiv and I] settled down, and we wanted to release the set of columns as an anthology. But then we realised that we were not really famous, and nobody really cared about our seven-year-old columns. So, the process of updating them eventually made it into an entirely new book, *A New Idea of India*. At least half of the content was kind of new. The book did decently well. The prime minister endorsed it, and a lot of people read it. We got good reviews, and it was published by Amazon Westland.

He is working on his third book, *Long India*, on why to be bullish on the Indian economy. Harsh says one cannot be a public intellectual and a party member at the same time, at least in India. That is one reason he attributes to Shashi Tharoor losing debates with J. Sai Deepak, Vikram Sampath, or him.

> I actually messaged him [Tharoor] and meant it seriously. I told Shashi that if you didn't have this albatross around your neck, you'd probably have a much better chance. You have to defend the indefensible. It was really not fair to him. In many ways, he shows his graciousness by agreeing to these debates.

Gupta, like Sanyal, says that growing up in communist West Bengal shaped his political and economic views.

> If you're born into a business family in a communist state, your economic instincts are not aligned with communist philosophy anyway. That, I think, was subconsciously the initial seed. My family, before moving to Kolkata, had been in Delhi. They were old Jan Sanghis. In Kolkata, we have Bada Bazar. In Delhi, we have Chawri Bazar ... central areas where small traders are. I already had an anti-Left vaccine growing up in Calcutta.

Gupta narrates an incident upon landing in the US for college. He studied in a state called New Hampshire, whose motto is 'live free or die'. It is a libertarian state and also one of the richest states in the US in terms of per capita income.

> My very first memory of the place is very strong. What we call a 'jamadar' in India, they call a janitor. The janitor at our student housing had a massive SUV pickup truck. Once he got his job done, he'd take the gloves off and wash his hands. If you talked to him, he'd shake your hand just like

any other person. A lot of my ideas on economics, class, caste … it's not like I anticipated it, but actually saw it. It was a bit of a culture shock. It was so impressive. Human beings are human beings; they're always complaining. Americans complain about tough times and this and that, but as a new outsider, I could see how wealthy this place was and how, in a certain sense, socially egalitarian. I remember that when the janitor retired, he gifted a grandfather clock to the reading room at our dorm.

The other stark difference that he found in the US compared to India was the teachers' approach to students asking questions.

I remember when I was at IIT Delhi for around four months, there was one professor who told me, 'If you ask one more question in class, I'll fail you.' Whereas at Dartmouth, I only received praise and citations for asking questions. So, that was the difference in style, pedagogy, and the encouragement of curiosity. I must say, US academia has worsened in the last ten to fifteen years. It has become very woke. When I was there from 2006 to 2009, there were early signs of that, but you could push back. Anyway, it's difficult to call a brown guy from India a racist, right?

He recalls that in 2011, there was a very famous article in *Newsweek* titled 'We Are All Hindus Now' by Lisa Miller. She wrote that Americans are becoming less Christian, and even those who are Christian are open to multiple paths to salvation.

As we become more powerful and influential as a country, you won't find that article being written today. Shashi Shekhar, who was in Prasar Bharti, wrote a column on the anti-India Left-liberal propaganda in America, funded indirectly by the Chinese Communist Party. Also, a convenient global alliance between the Left and Islam has occurred in the last forty years. The Frankfurt school pushed liberalism to Left-liberalism. I've realised that if you use the word 'liberal' as one of the defining attributes, the genealogy ultimately gets deciphered by people in the UK and the US. They'll say, 'Wait a second. John Stuart Mill and this and that.' I don't want to play that game. I don't want to be adjudicated based on their premises and semantics.

Harsh says even the word liberalism is relatively new. The French Revolution was about liberty, equality, and fraternity. 'Liberalism' came later, just like the word 'Hinduism', which appeared just 200 years ago. 'Raja Ram Mohan Roy was one of the first people to use it, and I feel he has been unfairly attacked by some people,' he says.

Till his early twenties, Harsh would call himself an atheist.

I think religion should not be worn with what Milind Kundera called 'kitsch' in his *The Unbearable Lightness of Being*. He defines kitsch as the 'absolute denial of shit'. He says that we tend to have these idealised images which were not true at all or very selectively true at most. Somebody will be like, 'Oh my god, you were an atheist at some point, how can you talk about Hinduism?' That makes it better because there's no faith without doubt. I'd question someone's sanity if they have never doubted at all. I came to religion in a very roundabout manner: economics to politics to philosophy to civilisation to religion. There are many things on which you can disagree with Ambedkar, but there's one thing he said famously, 'Religion is for man.

Man is not for religion.' The more I read about RSS and their idea of Hindu sanghatan and dharma sanghatan, the idea of creating a third pole because there are two very well-organised poles in the world, it all kind of converged.

Harsh admits some of his views may change in the next ten years, but he is very excited to be alive, to be Indian, and to be Hindu at this point. He explains:

> I am privileged to be able to write, talk, or do something about it. Because after a thousand years, we are rising. We now have a civilisational state. We have nuclear power. We started from a low financial base but are growing fast. And while retaining the diversity, Hindus seem to be intermingling better. It's easier to settle across cities, make friends, and marry across caste or linguistic communities. Without losing diversity, centrifugal forces are reducing. In the discussion with Shashi and Rajdeep [Sardesai], Rajdeep asked me a question, 'Don't you think divides are increasing? Even among Hindus, north and south?' I said, 'Look how popular South Indian movies are becoming in the rest of India.'

Gupta debunks the artificial north-south divide. He cites Brahmins going from south to north and from east to west, and vice versa.

> I met this very eccentric and brilliant billionaire, Sridhar Vembu, in his village called Tenkasi in Tamil Nadu. Tenkasi literally means 'southern Kashi'. And then there's Uttar Kashi. So, there's this civilisational geography, and we're bringing it back. Naipaul wrote about it beautifully in the aftermath of the Babri demolition. He said something very constructive is happening in India.

He draws a parallel with Hagia Sophia in Istanbul, which used to be an orthodox church before the Ottoman Turks conquered it and turned it into a mosque. Kemal Ataturk then made it a museum. But under Islamist Recep Tayyip Erdogan, it has been reconverted into a mosque.

> There have been debates over what it should have been made into. I would gently raise my hand and say that before it was a church, it was a pagan temple. There's a broader history. Right after Independence, the Somnath Temple was reclaimed, and Ayodhya is being reclaimed now. It is not necessarily about the number. Even RSS chief Mohan Bhagwatji said we are not trying to find a Shivling under every mosque. But if you're going to call people bigots for trying to get their mandirs back, then you can't even have a conversation. A maximalist position gets a maximalist response. Shashi Tharoor also said that the past is never past. We are getting '*sar tann se juda*' crowds on the streets even today.

Gupta's paternal grandmother was born in Lahore. Within her lifetime, the Indian geography shrunk. He says that if the violent Punjab partition was 'jhatka', in Bengal it was 'halal'—slow and dreadful.

He also points to geo-religious shifts, stating Christianity is declining in its core areas like Europe and North America, but not so much in Africa, where money goes a long way in converting people.

Pointing to large-scale reconversions in Iran to atheism and Zoroastrianism, he says:

> In 1979, after the Iranian revolution, one of the earliest prime ministers of the Islamic Republic of Iran said, 'We wanted rain, we got floods.' Now, the youth in Iran seem to despise

the regime. One thing which even the Islamic Republic of Iran could not fully take away was the celebration of Navroz. Even in the Gulf countries like Saudi—maybe Qatar is an exception—what MBS and MBZ (crown princes of Saudi and UAE, Mohammed bin Salman and Mohammed bin Zayed, respectively) are fast liberalising.

Harsh says that while their opening up is driven by the waning oil economy, there is a broader recognition that the region and religion have run out of ideas, and they have to accept modernity. He also believes that many in India dislike Hindutva, not understanding that it is fundamentally a modernisation movement.

> It is modernisation but not Westernisation. Pakistan is clearly in a cul-de-sac. It can't move forward with its current policies. The way Narendra Modi gave them a blow on 5 August 2019 [abrogation of Article 370 in Kashmir], they are probably never going to recover from that. It's an interesting time to be alive. These things happen over long periods of time. Things may keep happening even after our lifetime. In India, economics drives culture and vice versa. As India becomes richer, women become more educated and financially independent. People move around different cities. They mix and match. This [bigotry] automatically becomes less important.

Civilisation is all about larger and larger entities, he says. We start with the tribe, then an agricultural community, then a small village. Somebody builds a larger village, a city, a state, and so on. 'What Abrahamism brought to the world was not equality as some people say. It was organisation. It was the sense of the other,' he explains.

On the inception and evolution of the modern nation-state, Gupta says the Protestant-Catholic wars led to it. He disagrees that the modern nation-state is inherently Christian in nature.

> It's like comparing the vaccine to the virus. The vaccine contains elements of the virus, but it's meant to kill the virus. France serves as a good example of a modern nation-state. Remember, at one point, 30 to 40 per cent of Germans killed themselves in the name of Christianity. It sounds silly today. They were as bloodthirsty as ISIS is today.

Modern nation-states, for the first time, allowed for the establishment of larger, more structured empires with defined boundaries. They were not always defined by religion. Similarly, your schools and health services could be provided in the name of national service, rather than relying solely on religious charity.

> Some hundreds or thousands of people could have just come from Afghanistan and captured India because we didn't have a nation-state. The Rajputs and the Marathas could not unite. The only person who had this vision [of a nation-state] was Shivaji Maharaj. But the modern Indian State allows for unity. Therefore, while 1947 was a pivotal year, the second key year was 1977 when the Emergency was revoked. Because 1977 ensured that the democracy of this country would endure. People like Narendra Modi were young during the Emergency. Indira Gandhi came back in 1980, but the point was made that India would remain democratic. China, unlike India, has been an incipient proto-modern state for 2,000 years. So, they had more time to mix and match. They are at a level of homogeneity where a dictator can rule them.

Harsh says India is a State that allows us to build the economy to scale, with massive factories and infrastructure, while also enabling people from different backgrounds to unite. 'That is something very new. Dharmic forces prosper in this modern state context, while Abrahamic forces weaken,' he states.

Gupta goes on to explain why Pakistan is a failed State. It thought Afghanistan would be its strategic depth, which is why it created the Taliban. Now, it realises that with the Taliban in power, they will not recognise the Durand Line or Pakistani dictators. He says even an iconic Urdu poet and another founding citizen of Pakistan, Iqbal, realised that Pakistan would be a makeshift movement at best.

In contrast, while Hindu communities may identify as Agarwal, Brahmin, Mahar, Kshatriya, or Yadav, there is an overarching Hindu identity. The kind of Hindu consolidation in the voting for Yogi Adityanath in Uttar Pradesh could not have happened if people were solely divided by caste, he says. And that identity spreads and strengthens with urbanisation.

> The Hindu identity becomes more pronounced when you travel and meet other Hindus instead of being restricted to your Agarwal community. In Kolkata, for instance, Ganesh Chaturthi is celebrated almost like in Mumbai, just as one now finds thousands of Durga Puja pandals in Delhi, Bengaluru, and Mumbai. Even Ganesh Chaturthi was revived by Lokmanya Bal Gangadhar Tilak just 120 years ago. Today's reform becomes tomorrow's tradition, and then that further extends nationally and globally.
>
> So, this idea of the Opposition saying 'Bengal *mein* Ram *nahi chalta*, *vo* Vaishnav *hai*, *vo* Shaivaite *hai*, *vo* Shakti worship *karta hai*' is all nonsense. In spite of these beautiful contradictions, India has always been one integrated cultural landscape.

He says a modern economy and resulting intermixing are prominent factors that have made Hindus more cohesive. The other factor is Islamic radicalisation since the late 1970s and the Muslim population growing from under 10 per cent to around 15 per cent after Partition. The threat of real and perceived radicalisation has encouraged Hindus to mingle more internally. Polytheism has never been a stumbling block to mingling.

> From a child's point of view, what is the Marvel franchise of movies? It's a child's version of a polytheistic universe. They literally have the Scandinavian God Thor in it. When Hindus were poorer and more divided, they were afraid to openly show their identity. The sangathan [power to organise] was missing. As they become richer and more cohesive, it becomes more acceptable to openly flaunt your spirituality, religiosity, and the symbols thereof. As India becomes richer, you will see more questioning, more intermixing, but also more pride. Imagine a billion-plus cohesive Hindus, prosperous and proud of their traditions.

He further asserts that times have produced leaders in India, emphasising that these leaders were shaped by their environment.

> Even about Ram Mohan Roy, people now say he was speaking against idolatry. But they forget that he was the biggest roadblock for the Anglican missionaries in Bengal. To label him Christian simply because you don't understand his beliefs is very unfortunate. Similarly, Nehru was a product of his time. Perhaps fifty years from now, people will consider Modi a moderate. They may even argue that Yogi had compromised. It's very easy to sit in the present and judge the past.

In 2018, Harsh gave a lecture on 'Modinomics'. He spoke about Atmanirbhar Bharat and the Production-Linked Incentive Scheme for large-scale manufacturing, for instance. Early on, Narendra Modi attempted to implement the classic Washington Consensus of market principles—the term coined in 1989 for ten free-market economic policies supported by prominent financial institutions such as the International Monetary Fund, the World Bank, and the US Treasury. It involved 'minimum government, maximum governance' and 'government has no business being in business'.

> But around 2017, maybe, he realised that manufacturing was not catching up. We had to think a bit outside the box. And that's the beauty of the man in terms of how practical he is and ready to adjust his mindset. He does not have a formal affiliation with this or that school. He has a very Gujarati pragmatism. So, he goes on and says, 'Okay, let's put some mild tariffs.' Now, mild tariffs go against twenty-five years of a unidirectional trend. It's not so much that the tariff going from 5 to 7 per cent makes a difference; it's the symbolism of it. And the message it sends to everybody—to economists, to analysts abroad who suddenly said, 'Oh, *yeh toh* Licence Raj wapas *aa gaya hai* [Licence Raj has come back].' Classic over-the-top reactions from Raghuram Rajan, Arvind Subramaniam, and others. Or more importantly, domestic industry. The small businessman thought, 'Let me go to China, import from there, and sell it here because the government doesn't want to manufacture. Because manufacturing needs a minimum ten-year gestation period.'

But at the same time, Modi decided to invest in infrastructure, which entails short-term pain and long-term gain. While the roads in south Mumbai are congested due to the Metro, the Delhi Metro is in a much better state than it was ten or twenty years ago. That, Gupta says, is limited intervention in industrial and trade policy, going against free-market orthodoxy.

Third, Modi triggered ground-up demand. While India has the demographic dividend of a 1.4 billion population, many people do not have bank accounts, proper roads, sanitation, or drinking water. They could not take part in the formal global economy. Then the private sector came to help; Jio was a great leveller in lowering data costs.

> Suddenly, in the last ten, fifteen, twenty years, India has gone from being a set of autonomous villages in the default economy with few clusters of technology in urban areas to potentially this whole mass being globally connected in another 5 years. There are issues, but at least you are connected now. If you have some elementary education, you can do a basic KPO job working from home. There is running water; you don't have to be unsafe going out to the toilets, especially as a woman. You don't have to go out to get water, and you're getting clean cooking gas. Just imagine the difference in the quality of life. That makes a huge productivity difference.

Modi, he says, realised there is a small window before China becomes too dominant, during which the West is displeased with China for its increasing aggressiveness. He cut corporate tax, which is never easy for a politician to do.

He also started negotiating treaty agreements—not with China though; we turned down RCEP—with the UK, Australia, UAE, and Saudi Arabia. So, India is not against trade and globalisation. But there is a particular issue with China, which has a highly government-distorted system of its own. They provide substantial industrial subsidies, which forces India to respond in kind.

What economic decisions by the Modi government set India on a very different path?

> GST is number one. There will be some issues with GST in terms of federal policy, but broadly, it's a big positive. It has allowed us to leverage the scale of one market, with godowns in every state. People talk about bringing petrol, diesel, and alcohol under GST, but then for the states, the entire revenue autonomy goes away. Number two is the IBC, which declogged the financial system. It was painful, but now it's done. Number three, I would still say, was demonetisation. They did not follow that up with personal direct tax reforms, but they did implement corporate direct tax reforms. If they had followed it up by lowering the top tax rates, they would have had more tax revenue. You used a heavy stick but forgot the carrot. So, I would call it a half-reform.

Gupta says that while developing infrastructure is not a reform per se, it is of utmost importance. The bulk of India's population lives away from the seas and oceans. The nation's rivers—Modi has started working on it now—had until recently stopped being navigable. While southern and western states had sea access, UP, Bihar, the northeastern states, and many others suffered because of poor infrastructure and connectivity.

He states that a decrease in high-level corruption, increased state capacity and infrastructure, a smarter industrial trade policy, respect for free markets (such as privatising Air India), and disinvesting from a few PSUs are among the significant achievements. Also, managing geopolitics without losing the US camp, such as obtaining cheap crude from Russia in the middle of the Ukraine war, has given India a moment of advantage.

'It is analogous to what China experienced when the US was using it against the Soviet Union,' he says. 'Throughout the 1980s and up to 2001, the US was helping China.'

Harsh adds that certain factors, such as the COVID-19 pandemic coinciding with exogenous technology changes, have also helped India.

"It made this Zoom conversation normalised. Earlier, the technology was there, but we used it only for personal reasons. Now, if this can happen, imagine the productivity increase. I didn't have to fly down to meet you. If somebody is transferring a job from New York to Austin, Texas, because it is cheaper, they can send it to Bengaluru or Hyderabad as well.

While some factors were external, Harsh believes Modi's encouragement of the startup ecosystem has yielded results. Despite India's low per capita income and other layers of complexity, it now has the world's third-largest startup ecosystem after the US and China.

But broadly speaking, we have reached a position, because of our scale, where a very smart young Indian need not leave India. That tipping point is very important. Unlike many other emerging markets—including parts of China, even though it's richer—because of its political authoritarian system, many people don't want to live there. In India, because of UPI, for example, you can onboard to a Mumbai brokerage firm in five minutes while sitting in Delhi. In a deglobalising world—on goods, not necessarily on services yet—your scale matters. In a totally America-dominant globalised world, you could be a Singapore and do very well. But for real economic growth, now you need your own hinterland, your own domestic base. Because if Bangladesh or Nepal today turns around and says, 'We have some tariffs and PLI, take it or leave it,' some people will say, 'Fine, we'll leave it.' But nobody can say that to India because of the sheer scale. Which is why Samsung is here, which is why Apple is here through Foxconn, etc. They are saying one out of four iPhones will be assembled in India by 2025.

Gupta says that access to the Indian market has been made easier, with PM Modi acting as the chief salesperson. While economic policy has been a continuum from Narasimha Rao to Atal Bihari Vajpayee to P. Chidambaram to Manmohan Singh, Modi is massively scaling it up, especially with schemes like Jan Dhan. Millions of bank accounts have been added, benefits are directly flowing into them, and financial inclusion has been kickstarted.

> I have worked in the villages as part of my MIT research. I remember when people were receiving National Rural Employment Generation Scheme (NREGS) money for real or perceived work, they had to go to the local post office, and to get Rs 5,000, they had to pay Rs 2,000 as a bribe. Now, money from schemes goes directly into their bank accounts. Our digital goods infrastructure (we could say no to crypto last year because we have our own payment systems, own digital system, own breaker system), extending healthcare with universal health IDs, and our evolving e-commerce have changed things. Mastercard and Visa are very unhappy with the Indian UPI infrastructure because they got sidelined. One doesn't need a card anymore.

India has just launched a Central Bank Digital Currency (CBDC). It functions like an RBI app where one keeps their money, nullifying the role of banks as intermediaries. He says it will roll out slowly because banks rely heavily on current account savings account (CASA) money. If people start putting money directly into the RBI, banks will have no role. This is why, he says, nobody is talking about it loudly. India implemented it because China did, and to keep the technology infrastructure ready. India has also started using blockchain technology for land records. There is an IIT Kanpur project for Andhra, for instance.

India decided that crypto as a private currency was not required. No modern state would allow any competing currency as a means of exchange, says Gupta. So, instead of banning it, they just taxed it, and it died. 'Regarding economics, the PM has consistently made sensible decisions, one after the other,' he says.

Gupta, however, criticises the Modi government for not opening up as much as it could have on the inclusion of Indian rupee bonds in global indices.

> That is something they have discussed for almost three years now, but they have not yet acted upon it. Ultimately, India's future lies in the rupee becoming a global reserve hard currency. The European Union has its own issues; it's not yet a unified nation. China is not geopolitically aligned with the broader West or Japan. India is relatively small now, accounting for 3–3.5 per cent of global GDP at market exchange rates, but it will soon be much larger. That is one missed opportunity where they have been too conservative. Second, they didn't follow up demonetisation with direct personal tax reform. The top tax rate, including surcharges,

in India is 42.7 per cent. Instead of paying 43 per cent, many people will take the risk and keep their money in the black market. I think the government got caught up in politics because reducing personal tax rates can always be perceived as pro-rich. They had already slashed corporate tax rates.

The third thing the government did not do, he says, is incentivise urban infrastructure or urban government reforms. His fourth and final concern is that while the government performed admirably in public health, it failed to significantly improve teaching quality and teacher attendance in education. However, he finds the National Education Policy very encouraging.

He says the government may face some blowback on federalism because the initial five-year guaranteed remuneration to the states for GST at a compounded annual growth rate has been rescinded. The states may feel the need for more control over taxes.

By 2047, he predicts India will be the world's largest economy. However, he says that even if the Indian economy overtakes the US in the 2040s, in terms of per capita income, America will still be four times richer.

> Amrit Kaal would be a good way to formalise it. We have always been diffident about our ambitions. I remember after the nuclear tests, and during the India Shining campaign, Sonia Gandhi referred to an 8 per cent growth rate as *'Mungeri Laal ke haseen sapne'*. The funny thing is that under her government, 8 per cent growth was delivered, but that was due to Vajpayee's reforms and global liquidity. My point is, any Indian is as good, as bad, as ugly, or as interesting as any average human being in the world. So, if we are going to have the world's largest population, we should have the

world's largest economy, provided we get the basic social and physical infrastructure, human and financial capital. There's nothing jingoistic about it. To actually not agree with this proposition is to assume that the average Indian is somehow less human than the average non-Indian.

A hundred years ago, the Japanese were famously called lazy, he says. Made in Japan goods were mocked even sixty to seventy years ago. Now, they are considered the pinnacle of quality.

> Perceptions change. But per capita income should be our aim. The average Indian should be as rich or as poor as the average American or Chinese. That will happen a bit later than 2047. But, if by 2047 we are the world's largest economy, we will be ahead of most current projections. Most people in business, finance, academia, and government are underestimating how fast India will grow because we have never seen this kind of growth in a democracy on this scale. It happened in China, but within a very State-dominated model in terms of finance, external policy, etc.

The attacks on India, calling it a fake democracy and quasi-dictatorship, are because the rest of the world is unable to digest it, avers Gupta. India will also bring its understanding of dharma.

Harsh says, unreservedly optimistic about India's future:

> Whenever we have seen economic inflorescence, there is also cultural inflorescence. There might be a lag, but they have never happened separately. I was talking to Sanjeev [Sanyal], and he mentioned the same happened in Venice and during the European Renaissance. The same happened in Bengal.

> Enterprise flourished with people like Ram Mohan Roy, Dwarkanath Tagore, and Ram Dulal Sarkar. Why did Kashi become the spiritual capital of India? Because it was also a very strong riverport. It was the commercial capital of north-central India. The rich kings and saints would endow big temples and mutts. When I talk to these young people, I am super impressed. I feel like an idiot talking to some of them.

Besides number-crunching to support his positive bias, he reads a lot of history. He is convinced that this is a unique moment in the nation's history and that many things will go right.

> What fascinates me about human nature is that the default reaction is pessimism or cynicism: '*Kaise hoga, sab bekar hai*'. But there is a small but growing young section who are genuinely very optimistic about the economy. In politics, people used to talk about the Modiji succession crisis. A. He looks quite fit. B. He has Amit Shah, Yogi Adityanath, and others to succeed him. C. Even if the BJP doesn't win in 2029, the polity would be irreversibly Hinduised, despite real demographic challenges. There are broader global changes where it's no longer possible to have a modern economy without having women liberated. Very orthodox forms of religion will just wither away. The transition period might be long.

He quotes a V.S. Naipaul speech at the Manhattan Institute titled 'Our Universal Civilisation':

> This idea of the pursuit of happiness is at the heart of the attractiveness of civilisation to so many outside it or on its periphery. I find it marvellous to contemplate to what extent, after two centuries, and after the terrible history of the earlier

part of this century, the idea has come to a kind of fruition. It is an elastic idea; it fits all men. It implies a certain kind of society, a certain kind of awakened spirit. I don't imagine my father's parents would have been able to understand the idea. So much is contained in it: the idea of the individual, responsibility, choice, the life of the intellect, the idea of vocation, perfectibility, and achievement. It is an immense human idea. It cannot be reduced to a fixed system. It cannot generate fanaticism. But it is known to exist; and because of that, other more rigid systems, in the end, blow away.

Harsh Gupta Madhusudhan concludes the conversation much like former Indian cricket captain M.S. Dhoni would seal a victory with his helicopter shot—unorthodox optimism rising from a sea of doubt and pessimism.

> I'm very bullish on India and its economy. I returned to my country and am happy to invest in India in whatever small ways. I have skin in the game, both family-wise, finance-wise, and philosophy-wise.

CHAPTER 5

Narrative War: Mainstream Media vs Social Media

Once upon a time, India only had one TV channel—the public broadcaster Doordarshan. Today, India boasts about 900 private satellite TV channels, with more than 400 focusing on news and current affairs. The Ministry of Information and Broadcasting has granted permission for 237 new TV channels in the last six years and for five TV channels in 2023–24.

According to Forbes, as of June 2023, India has over 5.7 million websites. It has over 1.1 billion cell phone connections, which accounts for 77 per cent of the total population. Nearly half its population—692 million or 48.7 per cent—was connected to the internet at the beginning of 2023. In 2023, there were 20,821 newspapers and 1,25,767 periodicals.

This vast, turbulent ocean is the battleground of a fiercely fought information war. In its waters roam only sharks, piranhas, and poisonous jellyfish, not friendly dolphins. Whoever rules this ocean controls the political landscape of India.

While the Congress and the Left have traditionally dominated these waters, their century-long establishment has deep anchors of loyalty here. However, the BJP and those ideologically aligned with it have grown in influence phenomenally, challenging and upstaging the liberal–secular legacy media and intelligentsia. They outsmart them with a well-planned, robust, and innovative approach, overwhelming them with numbers, especially on social media.

While Indian and foreign media kept crediting the gargantuan social media might to the BJP's undoubtedly formidable IT cell, they remained in denial, to their peril, that a spontaneous, generational wave of hitherto unknown men and women has been the real driving force behind the counter-narrative coup.

Shefali Vaidya, Nupur Sharma or @Unsubtledesi, Priti Gandhi or Mrs Gandhi, @Coolfunnyshirt, @TheSkinDoctor, @BefittingFacts, Muglikar, @SquintNeon, Aabhas Maldahiyar, Akhilesh Mishra, Abhijit Chavda, @TrueIndology, Smita Barooah, @OpinionBakery, Sanjay Dixit, Ramesh Solanki, @DesiMojito, Pratyasha Rath, Nandini, Vikas Pandey, Raghav Awasthi, Amit Paranjpe, Ankur Singh, Abhinav Prakash, Abhinav Agarwal, Sankrant Sanu, @TheLyingLama, Sushant Sareen, Minhaz Merchant, Sandeep Ghose, Ankit Jain, Mr Sinha, @Jogakhichudi, Seemantini Bose…. There are so many more names from various walks of life—economists to lawyers, marketing experts to businessmen, academicians to entrepreneurs, doctors to bankers, and some still in the mist of anonymity—that a whole book could be filled with just their names.

They emerged from the faceless masses that legacy media and its minions would earlier simply speak to, not bothering to listen. Then mobile phones and social media arrived. The unseen, unheard but brilliantly argumentative Bharat started speaking back. Aghast at losing arguments, mocked, and being challenged on facts, the ones who enjoyed a monopoly over opinion for decades labelled them all as 'trolls'.

When that did not work, Congress minister Kapil Sibal amended the IT Act to add Section 66A, which gave the State and police sweeping powers to arrest and jail 'trolls' or those who disagreed.

But even that did not kill the mockingbird. In fact, the fiery surge of nationalistic opinion on social media became one of the chief reasons for the crumbling of the old establishment and paved the way for Narendra Modi's ascent to power. The wave of 'untameables' placed Narendra Modi at its crest and carried him to the shores of power.

In this section, we speak to a few of them—extraordinary personalities spearheading the social media war against the old establishment.

Swati Goel Sharma

It is challenging to find someone in today's Indian journalism who conducts ground reporting as distinctively as Swati Goel Sharma. She ventures into spaces that even the boldest reporters have carefully sidestepped. She delves into subjects previously considered untouchable, meticulously documenting hate crimes that have been largely overlooked until now. In short, Swati is the stormtrooper in the netherworld of politically incorrect truth.

Her work on real-life instances of love jihad, cow smuggling, and Islamist radicalism has earned her several prizes, including the Sanskritik Yoddha Award, which she received from UP CM Yogi Adityanath.

She has been exposing everything that the so-called liberal establishment wants to be whitewashed. However, her journalistic journey began in a hyper-conservative, urban cocoon in UP's Ghaziabad, where she aspired to break free and explore an open, liberal world.

> I come from a lower middle-class family, although we belong to the Agarwal business community. I attended the Catholic Sister's Holy Child School for my education. Later, I pursued a BSc in physics from Miranda House because of my academic proficiency. Despite my papa being in service, everybody around us was involved in business ... tailors, shopkeepers, etc. My sole ambition was to escape Ghaziabad and its trading culture, which I found too conservative. Our movements were restricted. Nearby was a cinema hall, Manohar Talkies, which screened B-grade Bollywood films. Whether it was noon, 3 p.m., or 9 p.m., we couldn't leave the house during showtimes due to the type of people who frequented the area.

It was perhaps the beginning of Swati's contentious relationship with Bollywood and its content. Later, she teamed up with Sanjeev Newar of Agniveer to start Gems of Bollywood, a handle that relentlessly exposed brazenly anti-Hindu, misogynistic, and pro-violence and pro-rape tropes from commercial Hindi movies.

While growing up, she looked up to the *Times of India* as her window to the 'liberal' and 'progressive' world. She read the newspaper from end to end. So, when she saw a job advertisement in the paper, she applied and got the job. 'But after working there for a year, I started thinking, "This is not what I had signed up for." *TOI* looked big from the outside, but from the inside, it was not,' says the thirty-five-year-old.

After quitting *TOI* in Hyderabad and a stint with a market research company, Swati got married. Then she joined the *Hindustan Times* and shifted to Mumbai. Even there, she felt stagnant. Online media was gradually rising, and she started questioning whether her mainstream reporting experience was teaching her any worthwhile new skills. Swati stepped out of print journalism and joined ScoopWhoop.

She says:

> I joined because they knew how to make content go viral. Soon, I realised that they were not interested in news; they were only interested in viral content. It was very enriching in terms of experience because you get instant gratification and immediate response online. In a newspaper, you end up writing for your own circle, but online, you write for a real audience. That was my biggest learning from ScoopWhoop.

When Swati entered the media industry, she was fascinated by liberal ideas such as late marriage, opting not to have children, and being career-ambitious.

> *TOI* used to write amusing pieces about the so-called nosy 'aunty culture'. But the problem with the liberal ideas of the media is that they steer clear of criticising Muslims. I grew up with Muslims but came to know about 'nikah halala' just two or three years ago. The media doesn't talk about it, although it is quite common in the community.

It troubled her that while the media told you how M.F. Hussain was hounded (for painting Devi Saraswati in the nude), it did not mention that Swami Shraddhanand was killed in 1926 for doing ghar wapsi. Or that *Rangila Rasul*, a satirical book on the marital life of Prophet Mohammed, ushered in the draconian Section 295A of the Indian Penal Code, which states: 'Deliberate and malicious acts, intended to outrage religious feelings of any class by insulting its religion or religious beliefs.' The publisher, Mahashay Rajpal, was stabbed to death by a twenty-year-old carpenter named Ilm-ud-din in Lahore. Or that the media whitewashed the Kashmir exodus. Or that Muslim politicians and goons caused a Hindu exodus from UP's Kairana.

> My turning point was 2014. The Modi government had just come to power. I started sensing how much had been hidden from us. I decided not to work for this pseudo-liberal media. Mainstream media creates a narrative with stories like Muslims not getting houses on rent or Akhlaq being lynched over beef. But I have seen from childhood how cow smuggling gangs would come, shoot farmers, and take away their cattle. If cows are not the source of livelihood, then why is Chhattisgarh, which does not have a BJP government, working on the cattle economy?

The Chhattisgarh government, in which the Congress is a coalition partner, procured cow dung worth Rs 247 crore from cattle herders since the launch of the scheme in July 2020.

She highlights the media bias against the BJP. Since the Congress came to power in Rajasthan in 2018, newspapers stopped carrying reports of mob lynching of cow smugglers in the state.

> I have done ground reports on four or five such lynchings after talking to farmers. More than twenty farmers have been killed by cattle smugglers. But this data doesn't reflect reality at all; it is based solely on Hindi reports. If you read the

court orders on cow slaughter cases, the community has been mentioned for years. All of them are locked up under the Arms Act. It is a deadly mafia. I began to see that liberalism is good, but some people are using its principles and pushing us towards Sharia rule. They call Hindu dharma regressive. Then I started ground reporting. I have been very rigorous, unlike these people who just make sweeping statements about the so-called rising crime against minorities without any data.

Swati says one of the biggest problems with Indian newsrooms is their colonised, 'liberal' humanities education and lack of scientific temperament. But, when she joined *Swarajya*, she found that, except for the editor R. Jagannathan and herself, all the staff members were BTech graduates. Journalism not backed by facts disturbed them, she says.

In science, you observe broad patterns and treat exceptions as exceptions. In the Asifa case in Kerala, they set the narrative that Hindus are creating the bogey of love jihad. Only very dishonest and low-IQ people do this. I have covered many cases of Hindu women being tricked, cheated, and killed. If I can find so many cases, imagine how many such incidents exist. Even Ambedkar wrote that Hindu women were disproportionately targeted by the Muslim community in riots. *Swarajya* markets itself as a media house, but it should brand itself as a group of science graduates trying to break the hegemony of arts-dominated journalism. No offence to art students; this is not an art vs science debate. Most people join the media without understanding these issues.

Swati also points out that a number of staff members at the nationalistic news and opinion platform OpIndia come from science backgrounds. She takes pride in her reporting on the killings of cow rearers and the smugglers who rob their cattle in the dead of night, slaughtering them and leaving no proof. She also cites her work on love jihad, although accusations of a religious angle in such incidents have been stubbornly brushed aside by liberals, who describe them as simple gender-based crimes.

> My counter question is, if there are so many cases of Hindu women accusing Muslim men of trapping them with false names and cheating them, and so many cases of them being murdered by Muslim men for not agreeing to their nikah proposals, shouldn't one see a pattern? Also, there are examples of Hindu men getting murdered for daring to fall in love with Muslim women. Give me five cases where Muslim women have accused Hindu men of cheating and converting them. In fact, Christians in Kerala were the first to accuse Muslims of love jihad. One has to see the pattern. In Pakistan, Hindu women face this far more acutely. There, you won't even find a single case of a Hindu man who has married a Muslim woman. Films also perpetuate the same stereotype.

She cited the grooming gangs in Egypt, the US, the UK, and Pakistan. She says most of these are part of the Tablighi Jamaat conversion mission. However, to date, no Hindu outfit has opposed the marriage of Hindu women to Christians, Jews, Sikhs, Zoroastrians, or Buddhists.

> Under the Dawa mission of the Tablighis, if you convert someone, you get jannat. Muslims have found a very easy way to carry out this mission through women. Christians don't target women to increase their numbers. The UP ATS exposed a conversion mafia in Jamia. An overwhelming

majority of the women were converted to Islam through marriage.

Swati finds a pattern in the course of her reporting on cases like those of Nikita Tomar and Neetu Yadav. For instance, Neetu met a man named Aksh after getting divorced. When she became pregnant, Aksh turned out to be Akram Qureshi. He then began pressuring her to be his second wife and convert to Islam. Akram was arrested on charges of rape and cheating and is now in jail, while Neetu struggles alone to raise the baby.

> Although people often blame the woman for not inquiring enough or staying in such relationships, there is an emotional angle as well, and I recognise that. Nobody easily wants to break off a relationship. Even a person who wants to go to jannat or heaven could be a regular man. Sometimes he too feels he is doing something wrong. I don't see people as villains; they have many shades. That is why my reports run more than 3,000 words. In love jihad cases, I include the minutest details. For example, if a woman is lying at any point, I grill her. I have not been insensitive. How can they claim victimhood when they gave consent all along? Neetu Yadav's interview is one-and-a-half hours long. I keep the raw recording as a document, without any cuts.

As mentioned earlier, her disgust for the sexism and communal overtones of Hindi commercial cinema led her to team up with Sanjeev Newar to create a Twitter handle called Gems of Bollywood, which became virally popular. In Bollywood movies, she found the same patterns she had started spotting while reporting on cases of love jihad, cow smuggling, and Hindu exodus.

In 2019, Sanjeev and I were sitting in a café in central Delhi. We shared the same disgust for Bollywood. The industry is a master at showing exceptions as the rule. For example, in the 1973 film *Zanjeer*, Sher Khan, the Pathan played by Pran, is shown as a wonderful person. Why show a good Pathan as an exception when, in the 1971 war, Pakistani Pathans unleashed the worst atrocities against Hindus? Why do they claim to break stereotypes only in such instances, while in every other movie, they reinforce stereotypes like women who step out at night getting raped? They are fine showing gender threat perceptions but want to mitigate religious threat perceptions of a certain kind. This is why the 2002 Delhi riots caught so many off guard, despite the looming threat. Our media and movies played a significant role in ensuring that many people did not even perceive the danger. If I am scared of a drunk man at night on a street, am I a bigot? No, I am only being alert and conscious of a looming threat because I know the pattern. But if I get scared of communal violence or religious persecution—even after a brutal partition or riots—I am called a bigot.

Swati travels across India for reporting with her notebook and smartphone, which she sometimes uses as a camera. Recently, she has also purchased a digital recording gadget. She explains that over the last three or four years, she has come to understand the events unfolding around her, but she feels disheartened by the fact that very little has changed in the last hundred years.

When I pick up Ambedkar's 1945 book *Pakistan or the Partition of India*, I find that what happened then is happening again today; the way we tried to defend then, we are trying to defend the same way now ... except that there was no video then, but there is video now.

However, Swati remains skeptical about the much-touted civilisational revival.

> I don't feel there is a Hindu revival. If there was one, then Hindu texts and symbols would have been revived, people would read the Vedas and Upanishads in every home. When Islamic society gets more Islamised, we see a sea of skullcaps and namazis. What seems to have happened is a gradual push toward Sharia rule, and that may have slowed because of growing awareness about the past (like the 1971 Bangladesh genocide) and threat perception. One sees some protests during the love jihad hearing, which was unheard of earlier. Or how Gurugram residents got together to stop the takeover of a public park for namaz. Or that people are vocal about the whitewashing of the genocide and ethnic cleansing in Kashmir. These were not taught in schools nor talked about in families. That has changed. But we are still not acting on the threat perception.

Swati aims to go beyond ideological lines and inform people about the looming threats. She explains:

> For instance, the liberal media has deceived Muslim women by subverting truths. Pakistan, for instance, is a nation designed for men. Women are told that on the one hand, there is dignity, and on the other there is jannat. I have heard Muslim women in villages talk about jannat.

She cites the example of the honour killing of twenty-three-year-old photographer Ankit Saxena reportedly plotted by his girlfriend Shehzadi's mother. This woman was said to be obsessed with the idea of attaining jannat or paradise, as neighbours had told Swati during her reporting assignment.

Swati wants to take a break from reporting and write a few 'quick books' from the material she has gathered from her journalism and experiences.

Amit Malviya

His opponents call him 'He-Who-Must-Not-Be-Named'. They both loathe and fear him. They have speculated about his so-called 'evil powers' so much that they have both elevated his political status and embarrassed themselves with messy, botched-up hit jobs. Amit Malviya privately chuckles about it. His haters making him seem like the dark lord of the BJP IT cell seems to only advance his and his party's scheme of things.

For instance, the ideologically adversarial platform *The Wire* did an 'investigative piece' on how Malviya influences Facebook to remove posts. The report later turned out to be based on fake documents. A slew of red-faced retractions and deletions followed.

Under the forty-four-year-old former banker, the BJP's IT cell has taken its core messaging strengths—short videos and memes—to the next level. These videos and memes then race through the fibre-optic lines and wi-fi to millions of mobile phones, delivering the message with the precision of a heat-seeking missile.

In the 2022 Uttar Pradesh elections, for instance, the BJP utilised more than 90,000 WhatsApp groups. For the 2023 Gujarat elections, another 50,000. The party has at its disposal over a million WhatsApp groups across India and tens of thousands abroad. Hundreds of pro-BJP pages spend over Rs 2 crore per month on Facebook ads, according to some estimates. Malviya oversees this entire operation.

Amit was born in a military hospital in Prayagraj. Three generations of his family had served in the forces. He says three things shaped his political views. First, his father, who was in the army, was transferred to Srinagar. This was in the 1990s when Pakistan-backed separatism and terror were at their peak in the Valley.

> I saw the rise of militancy in front of me. I witnessed Kashmir becoming a fortress by 1992. Islamist jihad was rapidly taking over the Valley. Every day, I didn't know if my father would come back from work. But when I came out of Kashmir, I saw the narrative was completely different from what was happening in the Valley.

While the Left, 'liberal' and Islamist elements in the national and local media kept hiding or whitewashing the ethnic cleansing of Kashmiri Pandits and other non-Muslims in the Valley and portrayed Pakistan-backed terrorists like Yasin Malik as freedom fighters, Indian soldiers were shown as occupational forces.

Malviya's second profound influence was the Ram Janmabhoomi movement. Along with a whole new generation awakening to the long-buried tyrannies of history, he witnessed the political chicanery that had denied Hindus peacefully demanding their destroyed heart of spirituality back for more than 450 years. He read reports of the UP police killing dozens of kar sevaks in Ayodhya for peacefully marching towards Ram Janmabhoomi. Official estimates put the number of deaths at seventeen, while many reports suggest the actual toll was approximately forty to forty-five.

It conveyed to millions of Hindus that they had no right to reclaim the 40,000-odd temples that invaders had destroyed and that the governments and media were against them.

And the third factor that shaped his views very early on was the Mandal agitation, which started in 1990.

> The Mandal Commission report was taken up when I was in Class XII. In the middle of fierce protests, a string of self-immolations, and reignited caste fury, one question was topmost in my mind—was affirmative action actually helping them?

Amit Malviya went on to complete his BBA and MBA. He lived most of his life in south India and travelled widely. Eventually, he ended up as a banker in Mumbai. He joined ICICI and worked there for some time before shifting to the French bank, Crédit Lyonnais, then to HSBC. Finally, he joined the Bank of America, heading business for the South.

> At twenty-nine, I was the regional head of HSBC. I got bored. Destiny had other plans. We wore black suits, met clients in the plushest of suites. My life was not real. My father studied in a village school till Class VIII. His parents lived in a house with a thatched roof.

In the course of his banking career, Malviya visited Japan, Greece, the US, Hong Kong, and China. Travel gave him a global perspective.

> Back home, most of my peers lived in a Railway Colony or studied at NIIT. One day, I visited my village and saw squalid poverty. When I returned to Mumbai, I had no connection with politics. Never thought I would enter it one day. But destiny had other plans. There was this one occasion when BJP stalwart Murli Manohar Joshi was in Prayagraj. He was my father's physics teacher. The BJP had just lost

the election in 2004. The party was having its 'Chintan Baithak' [collective introspection] at the Renaissance Hotel in Mumbai. I called Joshiji. We could not meet on that trip. I finally met him in Delhi. He gave me a unique perspective. 'India's poorest district is Kalahandi in Odisha. But why is there no terrorism there and only in Kashmir?' he asked me. That set me thinking.

Joshi asked Malviya to meet lawyer, politician, and BJP MP Bal Apte. The meeting took place at his home in Mahim. 'It was a dilapidated building. I met a simple man in a frugal house. The sofas had thin foam on them. Apte put me in touch with BJP leaders Piyush Goyal and Vinay Sahasrabuddhe,' he says.

In 2009, Goyal called up Malviya and asked him to set up Friends of BJP for the urban middle class. It was meant to enrol through a simple process and galvanise large and productive sections of society comprising doctors, lawyers, bankers, writers, and other professionals who have an affinity towards the BJP but cannot participate in its daily activities. 'In 2010, I had the option to go to Hong Kong. I didn't. Nitin Gadkari made Friends of BJP a cell within the party. I was the co-convener,' he says.

Malviya then moved to Bengaluru and met P.V. Krishna Bhat, who was the ABVP national president. They set up a team of around twelve people, known as Friends of BJP, with no money, spending Rs 2,000–4,000 from their own pockets. Bengaluru was then the epicentre of the Right-Wing movement.

We organised a programme on Hindu temples. Swami Dayanand Saraswati, Subramanian Swamy, and heads of all the matths in the city attended. Malviya's team collected a princely Rs 35,000 from the event. One of the people involved was T.R. Ramesh, a prominent activist in the movement advocating to free temples from state control.

Malviya says the Sangh nurtured him. Senior RSS functionaries like Dattatreya Hosabale, B.L. Santhosh, and Ram Madhav mentored him. Amit first met Narendra Modi, who was then the chief minister of Gujarat, in 2010 in Indore. 'I told him that he should be PM. He was poker-faced. No reaction. None.' He then met Modi in May 2013. He did a presentation on communication for forty minutes. 'He hardly said anything. Occasionally, he scribbled something. I said repeat communication was important. He said, "I have a different view." He asked me to crowdsource ideas. He is a very powerful listener,' says Malviya.

Amit was appointed as the convener of the BJP's IT and social media cell in 2015. It was then that he met Amit Shah.

> We decided to focus on content, aiming to reach out to a large mass of people, including social media users aligned with us. I was on the other side of the table, creating and working through volunteer groups. To Amit Shah's credit, he took up what I suggested and executed it across the country. Social media played a vital road. He provided budgetary support and infrastructure, establishing social media as an institution within the party from 2015 onwards.

As the author of this book, here is a personal anecdote which puts Amit Malviya's work as head of the IT cell in context. When I was the resident editor of *Hindustan Times*, I met Amit Shah at Delhi's Gujarat Bhavan in late 2013 when he was actively overseeing UP as the state's election in-charge. Even at that time, when social media had not yet become a prominent feature in the electoral campaign plans of other parties, Shah told me that he was establishing war rooms of 200–300 young men and women to counter the narrative of the Congress and self-proclaimed secular parties. 'Wait a couple of weeks. We will hit them out of the park,' Shah had smilingly told me back then.

Amit Shah was the chief architect of the BJP's dreaded IT cell. Modi and he foresaw something that would later become the primary weapon in the electoral warfare of the future.

Malviya further recalls how he organised large-format meetings to mobilise social media volunteers in auditoriums with a capacity of 5,000 people.

> It was an atmosphere akin to a rock concert. Attendees filled out forms, and all our platforms are standardised. We utilise handles like BJP4India, BJP4Gujarat, BJP4Bengal across Facebook, Twitter, Instagram, YouTube, and other platforms. Lakhs of volunteers flocked to these enrolment events. There were 14 lakh registrations across all Indian languages. A volunteer would disseminate the message—there weren't briefings, but they were provided with a wealth of resources and skilled handles to follow and amplify the message.

Malviya highlights the grassroots nature of the BJP's social media cell, as demonstrated by its volunteers from Trichy to Sambalpur and Kishanganj to Rajkot. 'The focus is not just on Delhi,' he says. The party has institutionalised social media and technology like no other, long before its opponents recognised its power. The BJP advises its local mandal presidents to examine PM Modi's website and create their own pages.

Amit says those who cannot defend their views are labelled as pro-BJP handles, which are then dismissed as 'trolls'.

He acknowledges that the use of derogatory language is indefensible and makes it easy to discredit the content of what is being said.

'Why should any party be controlling what they write? They have their own experiences. How can a volunteer, who doesn't have any affiliation with the party, be managed? Does the Congress regulate what its leaders are saying? They are not school students,' he says.

Malviya mentions that thousands of pro-BJP handles have supported so-called progressive issues like decriminalisation of Section 377, while in reality, the Congress opposed it. He accuses the Left and Congress student unions like the SFI and NSUI of historically mistreating women, leading some of them to mental and physical collapse.

He states that the objectionable content occasionally posted by pro-BJP handles should be attributed to the views of that individual and not to that of the party. But there is another sinister aspect to social media activity, which Malviya points out. It is akin to false flag operations. 'Some handles post with Hindu names about Hindu gods, and then we find out it is a fake handle. That is why we encourage our volunteers to meet, so they can get to know one another and easily spot an imposter,' he says.

Initially, despite its considerable dominance on other social media platforms, the BJP was weak on Instagram. It used to be the playground of urban, English-speaking youngsters from affluent backgrounds with 'liberal' or Left-leaning views.

> They were using children on Instagram for anti-CAA protests. Now, interesting Right-Wing handles have emerged on Instagram. We make considerable efforts to ensure that individuals with a nationalistic ideological leaning are

connected to one another. Why do the faithful go to church on Sunday or mosque on Friday? It sends a message to others that they are not alone. It was the same with social networks. If the internet was disruptive, social media is disruptive to the power of ten. It has given people a chance to come together. In such a scenario, leadership matters.

Malviya attributes this rallying together of like minds for the well-being of the nation to the emergence of a nascent Right-Wing ecosystem. For over seventy years, the Left enjoyed a near-monopoly of thought and influence in academics and media. Challenging the Left ecosystem seemed almost unimaginable. It faced suppression at the admission, classroom, or peer review levels. Even capitalists helped bolster that ecosystem. 'Ashoka University is a classic example of capitalists investing money to establish a communist-dominated institute,' he says.

But things are changing rapidly. Asserting that market forces are responding to social change, Malviya cites a plethora of Right-leaning annual literary festivals that have emerged from Bhubaneswar to Gorakhpur, Indore to Puducherry, Mangalore to Delhi.

Publishers like BluOne Ink and Garuda Prakashan are releasing books that other legacy publishing houses have thus far declined to publish.

Seats of learning like Rashtram School of Public Leadership at Rishihood University in Haryana, Chinmaya Vishwa Vidyapeeth in Ernakulam, MIT School of Vedic Sciences in Pune, Hindu University of America in Florida, and Vivekananda Yoga University (VaYu) in California, among many others, are emerging with a strong foundation in Bharat's civilisational values.

Leading TV channels have been compelled to adopt a nationalistic line, while portals like Swarajya, OpIndia, and PGurus have garnered wide audiences. Additionally, dozens of influential Right-Wing YouTubers have emerged in the last decade, asserts Malviya, pointing to patterns of enduring change.

Anand Ranganathan

Here is a tantalising irony—some of the fiercest attacks against the Left-liberal ecosystem in the war of narratives come not from a journalist or a historian, but from a scientist.

A biochemistry professor and researcher at JNU, Anand Ranganathan is widely popular today for using an invisible dissecting knife to tear apart opponents' arguments. He approaches subjects with the sharp edge of logic, not with melting dollops of emotion. The common ingredients of his laboratory are not optics, perception, and innuendo but data, facts, and instances. He spares no one, not even those who have embraced him as their ideological—albeit loosely—compatriot. His list of accusations against the BJP and the Right is long as well. He recently won a case after refusing to apologise to the Supreme Court in a contempt case.

How does Anand Ranganathan manage his work, life, and everything else?

> I live a split life. From 9 to 5, it is science. And when the sun goes down, I do other stuff. As far as science is concerned, our laboratory is now delving more and more into finding a cure for malaria, tuberculosis, and many other pathogenic diseases. We are using techniques developed in our laboratory

in collaboration with Professor Shailja Singh, Professor Goverdhan Das, and others.

Instead of targeting the proteins of pathogens, which tend to develop drug resistance through millions of years of evolution, the team is working on attacking the human host proteins that are hijacked by these pathogens.

Parallel to his scientific pursuit, Anand, now fifty-one years old, started writing twelve years ago.

> Maybe I was bored with science. There's a lot of drudgery involved in it. So, I just wrote a page, and I liked it. But I didn't know how to judge it, and I was too embarrassed to share it with others. So, I decided to read because, by virtue of being in the STEM field, I hadn't read much literature. I read great books by great authors.

Ranganathan then put his writing into the public domain. His first book was *The Land of the Wilted Rose*. Around that time, Madhu Trehan started Newslaundry, and Anand was invited to write for it. He also began writing for Swarajya and Firstpost.

After publishing four fiction books, he wrote his first nonfiction, *Hindus in Hindu Rashtra* in 2023. In the first two weeks, it sold around 30,000 copies and had a rerun of another 30,000. Week after week, it stayed on the bestseller list.

But before that, TV happened to Anand in 2018. Republic owner and editor Arnab Goswami invited him to participate in his Sunday debates. By then, public consumption of ideas was shifting from reading to watching videos.

Ranganathan, now famous for his punchline 'give me thirty seconds' before he demolishes an argument, explains:

The readers were transitioning into viewers. I think I arrived at just the right time. I realised that in an hour-long show, I would only have a few minutes to speak. So, I made sure to prepare thoroughly. People appreciate that I get straight to the point. You can waste time speaking slowly, insulting someone, or getting off-topic. Before you know it, your two minutes are over. Or you can efficiently fill it with 500 or 600 words, three or four facts, a bit of humour, a punchline, and more. I prepare for these debates meticulously. I insist on knowing the topic three or four hours in advance.

Till he was ten, Ranganathan grew up in Delhi. One of the stories from outside the world of science that Anand cherishes to this day is how his parents met and fell in love. Some would say that is the most magical chemistry of the universe.

Both of my parents were chemistry professors at IIT Kanpur. It's a beautiful story about how they met. There was a chemistry symposium. My father was a speaker, and my mother asked a question he could not answer. He later wrote her a letter explaining the answer. In the postscript, he added, 'I'm an eligible bachelor. If you deem me desirable, perhaps we could get married.' I still have that letter. My mother said yes, and my father brought along a baraat of fellow scientists, and the marriage took place in my mother's house. She then moved to IIT Kanpur with my father and stayed there for thirty-five years.

His late father was a Tamilian, an Iyer from the Palghar region. His late mother was Punjabi.

I had a lovely childhood. My parents were absolutely obsessed with science and chemistry. Instead of coming home from school to our house, I would head straight to the lab, where I'd spend all my time. There was a small cubicle built for me where I would study and dump my school bag. Our dinners would take place in the lab, and my father would often make pizza in the oven where the TLC [thin layer chromatography] plates used to dry. God knows how much silica I have consumed as a pizza topping! We used to experience very frequent power cuts, but luckily, we had the NMR instrument, and there was an uninterrupted power supply to that NMR room. Many times, we slept in the NMR room at night. It was an absolutely magical childhood. I knew I was very, very lucky. From the fifth or sixth class, I wanted to become a scientist … specifically, a chemist.

Anand, like his father, went on to marry a Punjabi woman. 'I'm in this very enviable position to pick and choose between two beautiful cultures, Punjabi and South Indian. Between chhole bhature and filter coffee and Mysore pak … the best of both worlds,' he says.

Growing up in IIT Kanpur, Ranganathan went to the Kendriya Vidyalaya on campus. He pursued his chemistry honours from St Stephen's College and went to Cambridge for his BA, MA, and PhD post-doc before returning to India in 1999. He set up a lab in India and has been based in Delhi since then.

So, what shaped his ideology and convictions? His parents weren't very religious, but they were culturally Hindu. They followed all the practices. His maternal grandmother, with whom he spent the first ten years of his childhood, was very religious. Like any other Indian child from that era, he grew up watching *Ramayana*, *Mahabharata*, *Hum Log*, and *Chitrahaar* on TV.

> I used to adore Vinod Dua back then. It wasn't until much later, when I saw his work with The Wire, that I thought, 'Oh my gosh, many of our heroes revealed their true selves after 2014.' I grew up without any ideology, and I still don't have one. *Main* science *ke taraf se hoon* [I lean towards science]. Whenever one is confused and doesn't know what to follow or where to go, the simplest thing to fall back on is science.

Ranganathan says the closest he has come to defining himself is as 'non-Left'. He finds the Left's stance comical and criticises its hypocrisy—rejecting the concept of nationhood in the context of India while displaying staunch nationalism in support of communist countries like China, the former USSR, and North Korea, or when allying with Islamic nations.

He believes Hindu dharma transcends nationalism and exists in the realm of universalism.

> It is all about questioning. The religion itself encourages atheism. Can you imagine? I don't even consider Hinduism a religion. Hinduism is able to change because the very ways of life evolve, but religion doesn't. In Islam, the way of life is an offshoot of religion. In Hinduism, it is the other way around. I am a product of Hindu civilisation; it has nothing to do with religion.

He continues, acknowledging that a party like the BJP cannot have ambiguity when communicating with the electorate, 'I suppose if you have to win elections, you have to be absolutely concrete about the ideology. And that is Modi's masterstroke.'

Anand further states that his father taught him never to worship anyone, but he counts B.R. Ambedkar as one of his biggest influences.

> While I have disagreed with him, [Ambedkar] was absolutely fearless. The tragedy is that a lot of Hindus have misunderstood him. He was not against the Vedic school of thought in Hinduism; he was against something that poisoned Hinduism. The clarity and fearlessness with which he criticised people ... in today's age, he would likely have been beheaded by the very people who worship him.

Other than Ambedkar, I wouldn't say politicians have inspired me, but there have been policies of politicians I admire. I'm a fan of a lot of what Rajagopal Rajaji did. I'm an absolute fan of Kamraj's mid-day meal scheme. I thought it was one of the greatest, if not the greatest, policies by any politician, living or dead. And Sardar Patel, of course, although I don't quite like that he worshipped Gandhi. He had many differences with Jawaharlal Nehru. I don't like Nehru as a political figure at all. I think he is the quintessential communist—a person who creates a liberal image for himself but is the most illiberal person you can find. Arresting and jailing people, amending the Constitution, banning films, and so many other things.

Ranganathan laments the turn that India took in siding with the Soviet Union instead of America, even though Kennedy and many other American presidents were very friendly with Nehru and India. The US even offered India a UN Security Council seat, but Nehru declined it, saying China should get it first.

Ranganathan then turns his attention to Mohandas Karamchand Gandhi.

> I don't blame Warren Anderson of Union Carbide for escaping after the 1984 Bhopal gas tragedy. He was a criminal. It was his job to escape. But people let him escape. Similarly, I don't

blame Gandhi. It was his job to be like that. I blame people like Sardar Patel and other powerful figures who did not stand up to Gandhi. Just imagine, we are having a war with Pakistan and Mahatma Gandhi says, 'Please give Rs 55 crore that we owe them.' And Patel said, 'What are you talking about? God, Gandhiji, they are going to use this money to procure weapons and attack us.' And Gandhi went on a fast until death, and Patel had to succumb.

To what does Ranganathan attribute this new surge of nationalism, this revival of Indic consciousness?

> I think the nation is tired. I believe the internet age has revealed a lot of things that were deliberately hidden from us. This includes even the present government, whose minister said he was proud to not even change one comma in the school textbooks. Let's be very honest about it. People are choosing between the lesser of two evils. Also, the BJP is not as disastrous as the Congress towards Hinduism. Although, as my new book gives you eight reasons why Hindus continue to be treated as second-class citizens and the BJP has also done precious little to remove the stigma that afflicts Hindus. But the BJP would not go down the route that Congress did. The Congress almost brought the Communal Violence Bill, 2011. In the aftermath of a riot, no matter who perpetrated it, no matter who was responsible, the majority would have been held responsible. Even in Kashmir, where Hindus are a minority, if there was a riot, Hindus would have been held responsible. The person who wrote it, Harsh Mander, said Muslims, being minorities, are oppressed.

Anand criticises the BJP for being cowardly and hesitant to amend the Places of Worship Act, Waqf Act, and numerous provisions of the RTE.

Anand says technology has ensured that people are no longer fooled, and facts can be easily accessed and tabulated. Seven years ago, he started compiling, in two separate Twitter threads with authentic citations and references, the number of times the Congress and the BJP breached freedom of speech.

He documented 275 instances and 50 books, plays, and films that Nehru alone banned, despite being hailed as a 'liberal' by historians like Ramchandra Guha. The first amendment to Article 19, which is supposed to safeguard freedom of expression, was made by Nehru. Tripurdaman Singh captures it in his book, *Sixteen Stormy Days*.

Ranganathan believes that the current period we are living in, this moment in the nation's life, is absolutely critical.

> It is because of the openness with which views that one might disagree are being accepted and are reaching people. Someone like me, for example … I'm not affiliated with any political party, nor am I from the humanities. I am a guy who was dabbling in science and decided to pursue something other than science. Ten years later, people are listening to me, agreeing with me, disagreeing with me. You may hate me or love me, but I'm here. There are many like me. We are getting a lot of coverage. That is not to say that people like us did not exist. People like us existed before the internet age. The most prominent one who comes to mind is [historian] Sitaram Goel. We must never forget their contributions. They are the ones who built the foundation, and we read them, imbibed their values, saw how fearless they were, and how shamelessly they were rejected by their own. Sitaram Goel was arrested, and nobody came to help, and he died almost a pauper. R.C. Majumder and so many others died like that.

Ranganathan says that the ramifications of this moment will be profoundly felt in the future. He believes that after the BJP's electoral defeat in 2004, Narendra Modi went into isolation and planned India's future for the next twenty or thirty years.

In 2008 or 2009, he said he was going to create a nano class and soon 120–130 million people will be in that nano class. He first gave them bank accounts, then toilets, Ayushmann Bharat and other schemes, tap water ... he is first satisfying the basic needs of subsistence. The real revolution is going to come in ten years' time when most Indians will have a toilet, tap water connection, house, health insurance. When they will be relatively more prosperous. About 431 million people have come out of abject poverty, which is remarkable. People aren't talking about it.

Anand says that once the basic needs of every Indian are fulfilled, they will begin to prioritise cultural aspects—the core of the Indic civilisation. He predicts that the results of the inflection point are ten years away.

While he overwhelmingly credits Modi for it, he acknowledges that the seeds were sown by P.V. Narasimha Rao and Manmohan Singh, goaded by the World Bank, who brought about India's economic liberalisation. In the nine years of Modi's administration, Anand lists nine of his most spectacular achievements:
- Vaccinating a billion Indians twice.
- Providing 170 million new LPG connections under the Ujjwala scheme.
- Withdrawing Article 370 from Jammu and Kashmir.
- Conducting the Balakot airstrike against Pakistan, which exposed Pakistan's nuclear bluff.

- Constructing 112 million Swachh Bharat toilets.
- Implementing the Ayushman Bharat health insurance scheme.
- Building 50,000 km of highways.
- Privatising Air India.
- Implementing the CAA.

And here is Anand's list of nine of the Modi government's failures:
- Repealing the farm laws.
- Still maintaining government control over temples.
- Implementing demonetisation.
- Allowing the Shaheen Bagh agitation to persist.
- Failing to scrap the Places of Worship Act.
- Not establishing a public sector unit bank for privatisation.
- Taking no action regarding the post-poll violence in Bengal.
- Abandoning the Land Acquisition Bill.
- Yielding to international pressure in the case of Nupur Sharma.

Ranganathan has consistently held up a mirror to Islam. However, he takes a non-traditional approach to criticism by simply quoting from Islamic scriptures. He explains, noting that he has received death threats via email:

> Every Muslim, by definition, must believe in every word of the Quran. So, I always turn to the Quran overwhelmingly. And I always quote, never criticise ... never, ever. I get trolled and abused on Twitter. But I take it in stride because I am certain that I will never criticise the Quran, because the day I do, that will be the end of me. People are just waiting. Some

individuals have created a kill list. You are on it. I'm on it. J. Sai Deepak is on it, Vikram Sampath is on it ... many people are on it. They handle it very subtly. They don't call it a kill list. They call it the Hindutva Watch. They're just waiting. It's a battle of attrition.

Here is an example of Ranganathan's signature style of attack. He hypothetically asks his audience, what if he calls Muslims the worst of creatures? Would it be considered hate speech? Promptly, the response comes, 'Of course, you communal bigot!' He then quietly states, what about verse 98:6 from the Quran? Suddenly, silence descends.

Verse 98:6 says: 'Those who disbelieve—be they from among the People of the Book or among those who associate others with Allah in His Divinity—shall be in the Fire and will abide in it. They are the worst of creatures.' Ranganathan did this with a communist leader from Kerala and received the exact response.

Does he believe that Islam can reform from within?

It's impossible. You see, it's one of those things—a Newtonian Three-Body Problem. It's intractable, forbidden. So, you can leave Islam, but apostasy carries the punishment of death. So, forget about redaction. Waseem Rizvi had to convert and become Jitendra Narayan Singh Tyagi. And now he's a marked man. Each one of those ex-Muslims is a marked man because even people from different sects of Islam are marked. Ahmadiyyas, for instance, carry a death sentence on their heads, although Jinnah himself was Ahmadiyya. When he was buried, his plaque said: 'The First Muslim Nobel Laureate'. So, a gang of Muslims went there to protest, to rip out the grave and the plaque. They were prevented at the last moment. However, they were allowed to remove the word 'Muslim'. So now, Jinnah's plaque says: 'The First Nobel Laureate'. Can you imagine? If you read J. Sai Deepak's authoritative book, *India, Bharat and Pakistan*, you will know Ahamdiyyas were at the forefront of Partition.

He mentions the irony that before the current Taliban regime, there was a Pew survey in Afghanistan wherein more than 90 per cent of Afghans voted in favour of Sharia law. And they got it.

Anand says he has tremendous hope for India's new generation.

> We were nothing when we were young compared to how intelligent they are. We were laughable. I'm so embarrassed. But while I have great hope in the new generation, there are so many opportunities available to them that if the State fails them, they will simply say, 'I don't give a ****, and leave'. And that worries me. The State is so overpowering, meddling in everything. We don't even need 60 per cent of the ministries. We have around eighty-odd ministries [there are fifty-eight ministries and ninety-three departments of the Union government]. We should have no more than fifteen, for heaven's sake. Look at the Bharatiya Nyaya Sanhita. The language is more complicated than even Macaulay could have envisaged.

Anand says he supports logical regulation, rather than a nanny state or State control over everything. He debunks socialism and praises PM Modi for the phrase 'the government has no business to be in business'. However, he criticises Modi for not making much progress in that direction over the past nine years.

- What kind of Bharat does Anand want to see in twenty years? Ranganathan presents a four-point agenda:

- First, minimal government control, particularly over business. He suggests having very few regulations, but ensuring they are effective.
- Second, he hopes for a future where people don't have to worry about feeding themselves. For that, he says, one has to rely on science. But he warns against another Green Revolution and the 'poison' it has brought. He advocates for genetically modified food.
- Third, he asserts that the nation needs large-scale projects like river linking, as Bharat cannot afford to have large areas of land suffering from drought while other areas are flooded.
- Fourth, he highlights that almost 45 per cent of India's active labour force of 550 million people is involved in agriculture. In the West, only 2–3 per cent are involved in agriculture. He cites a recent survey that indicates 58 per cent of these farmers don't want the next generation to continue farming. He argues that if India does not reintroduce the farm laws that the Modi government rolled back under pressure, the country will face significant challenges.

Rahul Roushan

The story of resurgent nationalism and Hindutva, in the fiercely fought war of narratives, cannot be told without mentioning Faking News or OpIndia. Faking News, the Indian version of the *Onion* with a twist, managed to infiltrate the Left-liberal ecosystem undetected. And before they could decide whether to laugh or grimace, it surprised them with its wit and satire. OpIndia, on the other hand, had a different mission. It aimed to deliver a powerful blow to the anti-Hindutva, anti-nationalist propaganda. It fact-checked, broke stories, investigated important documents, and relentlessly exposed the lies and hypocrisy of 'the other side'.

Both digital platforms have something in common—the same founder, Rahul Roushan, an MBA from IIM by training. Born in 1980 and raised in Patna in a Brahmin-Bhumihar family, his earliest political memories are of the two defining movements of the 1990s: Mandal and mandir. And the advent of economic liberalisation, which had a profound impact on the nation.

> Growing up in that decade obviously had its challenges. So, just like any other Bihari growing up in that era, I had only two options: either become a doctor or an engineer. If you didn't choose one of these, you would certainly aspire to become an IAS officer later. So, I skipped all three. To be honest, I did try to become an engineer. I was good at maths. But my chemistry was pretty poor, so I couldn't qualify for IIT.

Rahul graduated in mathematics. While studying for his degree, he became attracted to arts, literature, and music (specifically ghazal). His father was a professor of literature, so he was introduced to the novels of Mark Twain, Charles Dickens, and D.H. Lawrence. Then came his crush on journalism. 'That's how I got into journalism. The late 1990s saw the rise of television journalism. So, even though my initial love for journalism was because of writing, I ended up studying broadcast journalism because of the glamour around it,' he says.

Rahul got admission to IIMC, New Delhi. In his book, *Sanghi Who Never Went to a Shakha*, he writes that he was not a very political person and definitely not an ideological one. He joined Sahara TV and worked there for two-and-a-half years. He became a news anchor in a short time and also started producing bulletins. But disillusionment began to set in.

> It was a pretty good experience. But I got to understand the world of journalism, including the dark and ugly part of it. Sahara Shri Subrata Roy is now no more. He was very close to the Samajwadi Party, and there was an unwritten rule that we wouldn't cover anything negative about the state government. Mulayam Singh Yadav was the chief minister. He once humiliated a Sahara reporter so badly that if there had been social media then, the clip would have leaked and gone viral. I don't exactly remember the context, but Mulayam was so upset. How can a reporter of Sahara, who is like his own employee, ask him a question? *'Meri billi mujhe hi meow'* type. I felt that if this is just another job that I have to do, then why not get one that at least pays handsomely?

He has an interesting take on science and journalism:

> In science, you gather data, analyse it, and come up with a theory. In journalism, you have a theory, and then you cherry-pick the data to fit it. In fact, it is not just journalism versus science but liberal arts versus STEM. People would scoff at this comparison, but that's how it is.

Rahul then took the CAT to get into the Mudra Institute of Communications, Ahmedabad (MICA), to study advertising and communication. He found the CAT aptitude test pretty easy and cracked it. The road altered its course, and he was shortlisted by three IIMs: Ahmedabad, Kolkata, and Kozhikode.

'Ahmedabad was a big name. I completely forgot about my love for media. I landed there, and life took a very different turn. I vicariously lived the life of an IITian there because the culture of IIMs is a derivative of the IIT culture,' he says.

At IIM Ahmedabad, Rahul started leaning towards the libertarian ideology. He began reading Richard Dawkins' book, *The God Delusion*. 'After two years at IIM Ahmedabad, I emerged as a classical liberal or libertarian. I was definitely not a Sanghi. That happened a little later,' he says.

While at IIM, Professor Sunil Handa inspired him to become an entrepreneur.

> He has that capacity to influence, to brainwash you. There were at least a dozen guys in the second year who decided not to take part in campus placements and instead tried to do something on their own. I happened to be one of them. That story is pretty funny. We won a business plan competition about setting up an ethanol factory in Bihar. We were two guys, me and Kartik Laxman from BITS Pilani. We didn't have any understanding of business. We came from typical middle-class families, and we were thinking of putting up an ethanol factory when we had absolutely no idea how big businesses work. But Professor Handa was so supportive that he gave us a car and driver to go to Bardoli in Gujarat to learn how sugar is extracted from sugarcane because ethanol extraction is just two steps ahead of extracting sugar. I'm sure Professor Handa knew there was no way we could do it, but he just wanted to encourage us.

After meeting with a minister from the Nitish Kumar-led Bihar government in 2007, they also spoke to one of the biggest sugar barons. He asked them about the capital needed to set it up, which they did not have. But more importantly, he warned them that there were so many criminals in Bihar that they would have to run the very next day after setting up their business. The ethanol dream ended there.

Rahul and Karthik then set up a cricket stock exchange, Crick Stock. It got a phenomenal response. NDTV and Star News (now ABP) offered to use their data and create shows out of it.

> For a startup, that obviously was a very good thing. On national television, you were getting half an hour weekly or maybe even a daily show of 5 minutes of the stock exchange. That's crores of marketing coming free to you. Obviously, we were pretty interested. Star News offered a licensing fee because it was using our data. That was our first earnings. Unfortunately, the 2007 World Cup was the worst in many ways. India and Pakistan both were kicked out in the first round. You know, Bob Woolmer died suddenly. We didn't know how to run the business when the chips were down. Coming from middle-class families, we wanted to pay off our loan. So, whatever money Star News had given, we paid off our educational loans with it. This is one mistake we made by not listening to Professor Handa. He said that if you are going to become an entrepreneur, debt is going to be a friend for your lifetime. Don't run away from debt.

It was curtains for Crick Stock. But in late 2008, Faking News happened. That was Rahul's comeback to the world of politics and journalism. Some of Faking News's spoofs and satires were so convincing that *India Today* did a story based on one of its stories, claiming that IRCTC servers were running slow because of fog! Things started going viral. Faking News became a hit venture. After a successful run, Network 18 bought it out.

Then came 2014. Roushan could not believe the scale of Narendra Modi's victory, one of the reasons being that he still considered himself in the classical liberal bucket. He, however, had started warming up to Modi and wanted him to win. Coincidentally, Faking News had become extremely popular.

> Normally, humour and satire are supposed to be Left-Wing domains. And here, it was being done by the Right-Wing. It's like the universe was conspiring to make the right guys win. Modi was, and he remains, an enigma. Everyone could see a little bit of Modi in themselves. I, as a libertarian, could understand that many of the things he says match with that classical liberal position. But people who were completely about Hindutva, religion, and all that could also associate with Modi. Many of them have fallen out, but many continue to be with him. And now, it's no longer about destiny. Now, he is the guy driving it. Whatever is happening, it's because of Modi.

Along came OpIndia. Launched in 2014 and immediately in the Left-liberal ecosystem's crosshairs for unrelenting fact-checks, it faced multi-pronged and concerted attacks over supposed 'trolling', 'Islamophobia', 'partisan', and 'Right-wing propaganda platform'. It has survived that daily slander and grown.

The founding team comprised Kunal Kamal, an academician, Gaurav, whose popular Twitter handle @bwoyblunder is no longer active, and Rahul Raj, who runs the Facebook page Bhak Sala. After initial disagreements, the core team moved on. OpIndia passed into the hands of Rahul Roushan as CEO and Nupur Sharma (@Unsubtledesi) as editor.

'With OpIndia, we decided, why not take a side like Fox and Breitbart, or CNN and The Guardian. Swarajya gave us shares. In early 2018, we received some seed money from a couple of guys,' says Rahul. 'That is when I asked Nupur Sharma to come and lead the editorial. We became a lot more vocal.'

Nupur, extremely outspoken on social media, had to leave her home and business in Kolkata after being hounded by the Mamata Banerjee regime. She faced at least three or four legal cases.

Nupur wrote in a note posted on Twitter (now X):

After enduring unrelenting persecution by the Mamata Banerjee government and facing threats over the past few years, I have decided to move to Delhi. Staying in West Bengal under the current regime, it is next to impossible to report the truth. For the safety of my family and to contribute to upholding Dharma, as OpIndia has been doing since its inception, leaving my home of decades has become a necessity.

Besides being under open attack from its ideological opponents, Rahul says OpIndia has been on the receiving end of Big Tech manipulation.

The machine learning systems themselves are biased. Then there is manual intervention. But now OpIndia links come up. They may not be on the first page itself, but certainly on the second or the third. We are three times bigger than The Wire in traffic.

We are ahead of Scroll as well, but not The Print. We operate through crowdfunding. We were surprised that people started paying voluntarily. We book it as revenue and pay GST on it.

Roushan predicts more political churn and increased polarisation in the coming years. He says the Overton window has shifted on both sides. 'After farm laws, I have personally been threatened by Khalistanis and Islamists. I would not say it does not matter. It does worry you sometimes,' he says.

Does Rahul feel that this surge of Hindutva or nationalism is just momentary? Or are there very strong elements in this movement that are irreversible or very difficult to reverse?

> Hindutva politics has always been reactive. The other side has entered a zone where Hindutva politics will always remain relevant. The Left has now completely delved into identity politics. So, even at a surface level, I would say Hindutva/nationalistic politics is not going away. This is not just a blip. People thought the Vajpayee era was a one-off thing. The more the Left becomes fixated on identity, the more relevant Hindutva politics becomes. When you are fixated on identity politics, you don't see people as individuals. Everyone is either a woman or a Dalit or a Brahmin. There is no individuality left. How do you react to that? Either you become a mirror image and reply with identity politics, which is also in Hindutva, or you go the individualist way, which is also covered by Hindutva. There are too many shades of Hindutva.

What has been OpIndia's most impactful work?

> The most impactful thing is that we have shifted the Overton window in the journalistic space. We realised that many of the

stories that only we would cover are now coveted by others as well. I will very immodestly claim that we have changed the grammar. Previously, when certain things occurred—like a Hindu being persecuted for his identity—we could cover the story after a cup of tea. Who else would cover such a story other than us? But now, mainstream channels like *India Today* cover such stories. We have compelled many media houses to correct their stories. We have done to the mainstream media what MSM does to others.

Shefali Vaidya

Very few women receive the kind of hate, abuse, and trolling from their ideological adversaries as Shefali Vaidya. Even fewer achieve the impact that her posts do. From getting PETA on the back foot over its activism against Hindu festivals while sparing other religions to forcing Indian companies to not discard Hindu symbols through her 'No Bindi No Business' campaign, Shefali can deliver blunt force trauma by hammering in her point with relentless facts.

Vaidya was born in Goa into a cultured, nationalist Saraswat Brahmin family. She grew up in a small village called Cuncolim in south Goa, with a joint family.

> Our family was different from other families in the neighbourhood in the sense that my grandfather and his brothers believed in modern education for boys as well as girls, supported widow remarriage, and encouraged the habit of reading in everyone, including women. My grandmother learned to read after she came to the Vaidya household after marriage. My aunts could swim, cycle, and climb trees at a time when girls used to be married at a very young age. Both

my mother and my uncle's wife worked after marriage, which was again a departure from the norm.

The Vaidya family held strong opinions and were not afraid to express them. Shefali reminisced:

> Dinner time at home was always full of arguments, but no one was censured for that. There was space for opinions across political ideologies. The packed bookshelves of the household captured a vibrant diversity. My grandfather was a Savarkarite. His brother turned Gandhian in his later years, while my father was a rebel who actively participated in the Goa liberation movement as an armed revolutionary. When I was growing up, you could choose which political party to support, but patriotism was non-negotiable. My father could have chosen to get into electoral politics after Goa liberation. He was a hero who was immensely popular, but he chose to focus on education. He started an educational institution to provide quality education with a nationalist flavour in our village, which now runs a full-fledged degree college. My brothers and I are products of the same institution.

Growing up in Cuncolim in the 1970s was far from drab. Everyone knew everyone else, so there was no concept of 'safe neighbourhoods'; every neighbourhood was safe. People had a strong sense of community and looked out for each other.

'I spent a lot of time exploring my village after school. Cuncolim was the first village to offer armed resistance against the Portuguese missionaries in 1583. I grew up listening to those stories of valour. I think I inherited my fighting spirit from there,' she says.

After graduating in Goa, Shefali pursued her master's in mass communication from Pune University. A promising orator and quizzer during college, she represented both Goa University and Pune University in numerous intercollegiate events. Her time at Pune University instilled in her a sense of independence and the courage to uphold her values amidst peer pressure.

Following her master's degree, Shefali embarked on a career in various media-related fields, including entertainment television, news television, e-learning, and print journalism.

She now resides in Pune with her husband and their triplets. She deliberately chose her life partner from outside her birth community. Reflecting on her personal journey, she remarks, 'It has been an intriguing and fulfilling adventure, spanning three continents, four countries, and approximately ten cities.'

Vaidya holds a keen interest in Hindu temple architecture, Indian textiles, arts and crafts, and the history of her home state, Goa. This interest evolved into a passion and ultimately became her area of in-depth study.

She began discussing the forgotten history of religious persecution in Goa when it had faded from public memory. She has authored five books in Marathi covering various subjects, including one dedicated to temple architecture. She has also contributed research papers on textiles, temples, art history, and civilisational issues.

Talking about the impact of social media, she states:

> I discovered social media way back in 2013. It was liberating to find a platform free from moral policing or editorial gatekeeping. I had always spoken my mind, but now I had a means to reach readers directly. I soon realised that my words held the power to shape people's actions. Through

persistence on various issues, I gained enough credibility with my audience for them to stand behind me.

Her hashtag #NoBindiNoBusiness sparked a mass movement, resonating with the sentiments of tens of thousands of Indians. She articulated the frustrations of many who may have struggled to express themselves similarly. The 'No Bindi No Business' campaign instigated tangible changes in advertising campaigns for Hindu festivals. 'Many major brands such as Tanishq, PNG, and FabIndia were compelled to alter their advertisements due to this campaign. It has even become a case study in some business schools,' she says.

Vaidya also raised funds for weavers in Bihar, Odisha, Tamil Nadu, Assam, and Karnataka through her online campaign #HelpTheWeaver during COVID-19. The campaign connected weavers directly with customers and assisted them in selling unsold stock.

> Every weaver I recommended sold products worth at least a couple of lakh rupees within two or three days of my posting about them. I have also raised funds for causes that I personally support, such as Vedic education, gauraksha [cow protection], and women's welfare. I am a brand ambassador for at least three different NGOs that work in these fields. I also helped raise Rs 30 lakh in two days for the family of the driver who was the victim of the Palghar mob lynching along with the sadhus.

Another of Shefali's successful campaigns was against the multinational animal rights NGO PETA. 'Senior PETA officials attacked me personally on social media because I questioned their anti-Hindu campaigns,' she says. 'I have always been opinionated and felt I had the intelligence and logic to defend my opinions.'

What made Shefali so vocal and combative? To what extent do trolls affect her life?

> The haters are toxic. I've been trolled, abused, and threatened in the most abominable way. I have had to lodge police complaints twice and got two people arrested for giving me rape and murder threats. The abuses still continue, but I am a strong woman, and it is nothing I can't handle. Outspokenness has always been a strong personality trait, but social media opened the floodgates to both adoration and abuse. Suddenly, I found people who appreciated me for the values I espoused, as well as detractors who hated me for the very same thing.

Similar to Roushan, she shares the belief that the Overton window has shifted gradually but dramatically, and the journey was far more difficult for women who started speaking out for Hindutva and nationalism a decade or so ago.

> Today, there are millions of women on the internet who think like me, but when I started talking about civilisational issues, it was a very lonely journey, particularly as a woman. Now, Hindus are becoming more assertive in every field, and I think a large part of that is because Modi is at the helm of affairs. By 2047, I see good things coming Bharat's way. We are a young, aspirational country that has just woken up from a deep slumber. This is our moment in the sun, and we are doing it our way—development with civilisational ethos.

However, what worries Shefali is the impending demographic change. Already, many districts in Bharat are experiencing a drastic demography shift, she says. 'Hindus are vacating their ancestral lands and moving to cities as they are edged out by minorities with aggressive birth rates. I really want this issue to be addressed at the policy level somehow,' says Shefali.

India's majority religious population has reduced by 7.81 per cent from 1950 to 2015, while the share of the Muslim population has risen by 43.15 per cent during the same period, according to a working paper published by the Economic Advisory Council to the PM (EAC-PM) in May this year. Among the 167 countries analysed in the paper, the decline in the majority population is second only to Myanmar, which witnessed a 10 per cent decline.[1]

Her latest initiative is the Akshayya Hindu Puraskar, which rewards work done for the Hindu cause. Since 2023, these awards have been given in five different categories to grassroots activists who are doing stellar work in gauraksha, social assimilation, art, culture, literature and media, welfare activities in tribal regions, and protection of dharma.

'We talk a lot about how there is no Hindu ecosystem that institutes awards or fellowships for people who work on the ground. But all talk and no action never helped anyone,' Shefali posted on X.

The award includes a cash prize of Rs 10,000 each, a murti or statue of Kodanda Dhari Shriram, and a set of books by various authors that promote cultural nationalism.

Shefali and her friends are in the process of forming a trust under the aegis of the Humanist Indian National Democratic Union, HINDU for short. As with Shefali, there is hardly any ambiguity in that name.

Kushal Mehra

Of the various shades of the new nationalism, a particularly interesting voice is that of the atheist or non-theist Hindu. The forty-three-year-old who has captured this 'nirīśvaravād' and sparked renewed interest in the Cārvāka (pronounced Charvaka) philosophy is Kushal Mehra, who runs *The Cārvāka Podcast*. It has over 1,00,000 subscribers on YouTube.

The fourth-generation textile entrepreneur is a Mumbaikar whose lineage goes back to Amritsar, a city known for the silk trade.

> I belong to the Khatri caste. The Hindu Khatris were removed from the forces, I think both during the Mughal period and the British period. As a result, a large group of Khatris and Mehras went into business, particularly silk, and migrated to Bombay. The Orkay-wale (entrepreneurs who set up Orkay Silk Mills Ltd) were also part of that group. From there, it has been my great-grandfather, grandfather, and father who have taken this business forward. I am actually the last one. Among my cousins, I am the only one still in textiles; all the others have exited.

Mehra maintains that the entire Indian political landscape is Left of Centre, including the BJP in terms of policy. He laments that no political party in India supports free speech.

'The BJP today resembles what the Congress was years ago. The Congress has shifted towards the hard Left. Even yesterday, when I saw the Congress video on Twitter, it was evident that they have become a hard-Left political outfit now,' he says.

He describes himself as 'non-Left'. Does he hold a purely free-market economic view?

A pure free market would be a libertarian utopia. I am not against some form of redistributionism. In a country like India, where there are so many poor people, to advocate for pure laissez-faire economics would be self-deception. We should approach issues on a case-by-case basis. The BJP is far more state-driven than I would prefer. But, I didn't believe India is ready for laissez-faire, and I say this not as someone who supports socialism, but based on my personal experiences working in rural India and Mumbai slums. Russell Peters once joked that India is the only country where he could find someone poorer than himself. That's how impoverished we are. When people lack access to basic amenities like toilets, discussing laissez-faire is impractical.

Mehra says his primary reason for liking Modi was that he was the first leader in seventy years to acknowledge and address India's peculiar problem—half of the country was defecating in the open. Now, as even UN reports acknowledge, this is no longer the case.

Anybody who says 'I vote for the BJP because of economics' is actually lying. The only reason that the BJP and the Congress can be differentiated is purely socio-cultural. When a prime minister comes to the Red Fort and tells people to stop defecating on the road, I thought, 'I want to follow this man.' He is raising the Indian standard. The first time a prime minister comes to the Red Fort and we start telling our son, 'Better watch yourself', not the daughter what she is supposed to wear. These are small messaging. Things like giving women gas stoves, which is such a basic thing. I remember in a speech, he had said, '*Sab log badi badi baatein karte hain, main chhoti baatein karoonga* [Everybody talks

about macro issues, but I will focus on the more basic ones].'
I can relate to that because I actually work in villages.

Kushal says that as an avid reader of philosophy, he could not relate to Veer Savarkar's perspective on Hindutva, which he perceives as primarily ethnic in nature. 'Will Julia Roberts fit into Hindutva?' he wonders. Roberts is not ethnically Indian, but she has embraced Hinduism.

And on the other side, he calls out the deep bias of Leftist historians like Romila Thapar. For them, he says, India was a garbage dump, and all the good things that happened were done by Buddhists, Muslims, Jains, or the British.

I remember when I was seventeen or eighteen, I told my mom that I don't believe in God. I run a podcast and I talk to so many ex-Muslims, and they have such horror stories! With every Muslim and Christian, I have seen this childhood trauma of 'hell'. They go through this. We [Hinduism] don't have that concept of hell. The concept of 'narak' in Hinduism is like a pit stop, where your car is there for a while and then according to your karmic cycle, you go wherever you are going, into the next life. So, I never had this issue. I don't have specific problems with Hinduism, I have multiple problems with it. I belong to the nastik darshan, which is Cārvāka. I don't think Hinduism can be classified as theistic and atheistic. It can be classified in terms of people who say Vedas are the authority and those who say Vedas are not the authority. I fall in the latter category. Having said that, I could take something genuinely nice in the Vedas. I like the concept of nishkaam karma at a practical level from the Bhagavad Gita. So, for me 'Hindu' has always been a civilisational, geographical identity, and it is multi-layered. It is a cultural identity. So, I am a Hindu culturally, and I believe

> Julia Roberts is also culturally a Hindu. A lot of people might find my statement uncomfortable, but I think even Richard Dawkins is a Hindu. Because he is compassionate and believes in mutual respect and non-violence. Anybody who believes in these principles may not take the label 'Hindu' for himself. That's why I don't say I am a nationalist or a patriot; I am a civilisationalist.

Mehra's Muslim or Christian friends sometimes ask him why he calls himself a Hindu if he is an atheist.

> I start talking to them about why I believe in this. Then I ask them certain classic questions about their core religion, and then they just lose it. If they are open-minded, you just have to see the window. Are they open-minded? Are they willing to consume other views about their religions? I never force it upon them. I have a rule. If you start a conversation, I will end it, but I will not start a conversation about your religion. I am not an anti-theistic atheist in the Western parlance. I always call myself a 'nir-ishwar-vadi'. But we live in the 21st century, and unfortunately, if I describe myself as a nastik nirishwarvadi, everybody will think I am mad. So, I used the word 'atheist' out of no option. I don't hate religion. I think it has problems, but it is the most powerful mythopoeic. So, we need to work with it. There are a lot of people who say that Islam talks only about peace. I say, yes, it talks about peace in two verses, but it talks about violence in 150 verses, and I share those verses. I tell them, 'You seem to be a nice guy, but how do you reconcile Surah an-Nisa where God tells you can beat your wife up? How do you reconcile with that?' I am talking about reasonable, educated Muslims. And they confess that they can't. when I am sitting with a Christian, I say, 'You are pro-gay rights, right?' They say, 'Yes.' I ask, 'How can you be Christian,

man?' There are clear-cut verses that say you should be stoned. There is no way out. No matter how much mental gymnastics you do, you have to reject the verse, and that is where their problem comes. In Hinduism, if somebody says *Manusmriti* has a verse that says for the same crime a man should be punished less than a woman, a Hindu will say, 'I will dump it.' Hindus can reject verses. They can't.

Kushal says he does not hang out with most of his upper-class friends these days because they are deracinated. He is not a socialiser. He has four or five very close friends who are 'grounded'. He says he does not spend a lot of time on Twitter and believes that the best way to communicate is to sit across the table with someone.

> Even if you say something atrocious, I will not think that you are saying it out of evil. I use Hanlon's razor—never attribute to malice that which is adequately explained by ignorance [stupidity]. And when you do that to the other person, I have seen it break all barriers. They open up to you. I will share the story of a Bengali communist girl. I have been chatting with her for a long time now. She followed my podcast and felt this BJP supporter was interesting. One day, she said, 'How can you be an atheist and not support the women in Sabarimala?' We had a conversation, and I asked her only one question—can you name one scripture of that temple that says women are impure and that's why they can't be allowed inside? She googled, did everything, but could not produce one primary source. Then she said, 'Oh, I was sold a lie that the scriptures say they are impure.' I said, 'I will never go to Sabarimala. I find that whole practice stupid.' That's what I said. It is a pointless belief, but there is the Kamakhya Devi case also where men are not allowed. I find both of them

stupid. Believe me, in that one hour, that girl had almost abandoned communism.

Mehra has worked with his friend and BJP MP, Poonam Mahajan, on the Sansad Adarsh Gram Yojana, which he thinks is PM Modi's best scheme.

> I remember it was Jai Prakash Narain's birthday or something when the scheme was launched. I was on my sofa watching TV, and I saw it. Immediately, I messaged Poonam [Mahajan] saying, 'You are not giving this scheme work to anyone else other than me. Otherwise, I will troll you for the rest of your life.' And she replied, '*Haan mere baap, tereko hi doongi* [Yes, my father, I will give it to you only].' I seized that opportunity. I had the chance to literally work in two villages as a full-time job. One was Charoti, the other was Vaghadi. They were adopted by Poonam Mahajan under the Sansad Adarsh Gram Yojana. I learned so much. I am a changed person after that. We went there, surveyed the village, went door-to-door, formed teams, identified who needed bathrooms, solar bulbs, pump sets, and so on. Now, every single house has a washroom. Today, Anita Dongre has a garment manufacturing unit there. Around 100 women are working in that village. Their lives have changed. Imagine Global Desi dresses being made in a village. We built roads. I could not sleep for three nights after my first visit there. I used to get nightmares thinking about the luxury we live in. Children had to walk 4 km to go to school, leading to dropouts. Then we built a simple bridge and distributed cycles to the children under a government scheme.

Mehra says that to change India, one does not necessarily need to join an NGO but leverage politics instead. With India having 6,64,369 villages, he believes that if even that many Indians get involved, they can make a massive difference. What distinguishes the Indian Right-Wing of yesteryear from this new wave?

> There is a good side and a bad side. The good side is, I think they are not shy now to speak their minds. The bad side is, they are not nuanced. I think Narendra Modi has given them the confidence but not the intellectual tools. I will give you an example. Go to the office of the BJP MPs. Count how many BJP speechwriters and question writers are ideologically aligned with the BJP. You will be shocked. Many of those who write questions for the BJP to be raised during the question hour are communists and Leftists. I am not making this up. I was an Advani guy. I remember when the Babri Masjid happened, and how it changed me at a personal level. I was around twelve at that time. I didn't understand what was happening. Not in a bigoted way, where I was saying, 'Wow, *tod diya*.' I didn't like the breaking part of the Babri Masjid, but I did understand the part about asserting themselves because I grew up in an India where Hindus were scared of Muslims. Literally scared. If we were travelling on a bus and happened to get into an argument with a Muslim, my parents would immediately ask me to be quiet.

An M.K. Gandhi fan himself, Kushal values Modi's admiration for him. He says the RSS does not support Gandhi's assassin, Nathuram Godse, but rather the much less influential Hindu Mahasabha does.

> And then, to see a prime minister openly invoking Gandhi in every fifth speech … that resonates with me. If you admire Gandhi, you are automatically denouncing Godse.

The man killed Gandhi. He is the murderer. The way he [Modi] appropriates Sardar Patel's legacy, I absolutely love that. Look at the reduction in the number of riots in India. All the lynching thing is nonsense. Let's not even get into that. India does not have a cow lynching problem. India has a law and order problem. People get lynched for stealing chappals.

Mehra says even his wife, who was born and raised in Canada and has no in-depth knowledge of Indian politics, carries the image that the Congress is too anti-Hindu. She is a typical liberal, Western girl who supports gay and transgender rights.

His mother, a staunch Arya Samaji, was a Congress voter until Indira Gandhi's era. After that, she shifted to the BJP. His father has been a BJP voter all his life. Even when the BJP's predecessor Jan Sangh had minimal electoral success, he would still vote for it.

Kushal's biggest grievance against Indian politics is that priorities are messed up. He feels that the law and order is pathetic, and there is too much identity politics, and somewhere down the line, the individual is lost.

'I don't want people to be killed for eating a cow, or anything for that matter. My biggest criticism of Narendra Modi is that he has done no police reforms. Look at the cop-to-citizen ratio in India. For a democracy, we have one of the most pathetic citizen-to-cop ratios in the world,' he says.

Once the government fixes law and order, it will be much harder for the mainstream media to casually hang tags like 'fascist', 'bigot', and 'authoritarian', concludes Mehra.

CHAPTER 6

Reviving Hinduness in Popular Culture

The blue-painted face of Pushkar Nath Pandit woke India from its slumber to a nightmare it wanted to forget. The story of the elderly Kashmiri Pandit man, living in exile in a small, dingy Delhi house after the 1990 genocide and exodus tore him away from the snow and warmth of his home in Srinagar, stopped the nation's blood in its veins in thousands of multiplex theatres. The unspeakable brutality of Pakistan-sponsored separatism and terror, the Islamic holy war that took away lives and homes of minority Hindus, Sikhs, and defiant, nationalistic Muslims, was depicted vividly, graphically, and truthfully for the first time on screen in Vivek Agnihotri's *The Kashmir Files*.

The Kashmir Files marks the latest crescendo in the steadily rising note of the new nationalism in Indian commercial cinema. Since the turn of the century, a new strain of patriotic movies has been emerging. Until then, films like *Border* were woven around the bravery and sacrifice of the armed forces. *Lagaan* captured the fervour of an India buoyed by the second wave of strong reforms, global assertion, nuclear tests, and the Kargil War victory against Pakistan during the Vajpayee era.

But it was *Swades* (2004) and *Rang De Basanti* (2006) that introduced the ordinary Indian as the protagonist, restless to contribute to the nation and change a corrupt, uncaring system. If Shah Rukh Khan's *Swades* inspired a generation of Indians in the diaspora to want to return and give back to the motherland, Aamir Khan's *Rand De Basanti* provided India with a template of revolutionary protest. This was utilised by millions of young Indians to challenge the Jessica Lal murder verdict, exert pressure on an apathetic government after the 26/11 attacks, and demand accountability from politicians and the police following the Nirbhaya gangrape and murder.

Soon, India's sports glory started being celebrated in movies like *Bhaag Milkha Bhaag, Chak De! India,* and *Dangal*. Bollywood began to recreate the stories of revolutionary freedom fighters such as Mangal Pandey, Bhagat Singh, and Surya Sen.

Indian forces and intelligence operatives were being celebrated in films like *Uri: The Surgical Strike, Baby, Raazi, Shershaah, Aiyaary,* and *Airlift*. OTT series such as *Family Man* and *Special Ops* became huge hits.

The stunning successes of India's space scientists were captured in *Mission Mangal*, while *Parmanu* told the story of the Pokhran nuclear tests. Hinduness went overt and muscular with *Baahubali, Padmavaat, Kesari,* and *Manikarnika*.

South Indian movies have more than kept pace with Bollywood on patriotism. In Telugu, *Sye Sa Narasimha Reddy* told the story of a freedom fighter, while *Ghazi* was a war film. In Tamil, A.R. Murugadoss's blockbuster *Thuppakki* featured an Indian intelligence officer busting an Islamist terror cell. In Malayalam, Mohanlal starred as an army major in *Keerthi Chakra*. In Kannada, *Sarvabhouma* depicted a war prisoner escaping from prison to return to his homeland.

Other recent high-profile nationalistic films from the South include Mohanlal's *Marakkar: The Lion of Arabian Sea* in Malayalam and Rana Daggubati's Telugu flick *1945*. The Telugu film *Major* portrays the life of NSG commando Sandeep Unnikrishnan, who was killed while rescuing hostages during the 2008 Mumbai terror attack.

But the fire of reel patriotism would have been extinguished quickly without the fuel of box-office collections. S.S. Rajamouli's *Baahubali* earned well above Rs 1,000 crore, while *Uri* and *The Kashmir Files* have crossed Rs 350 crore despite being made with modest budgets. Rajamouli's *RRR*, featuring superstars from both south and north, has also crossed Rs 1,000 crore.

Rajamouli's lush, muscular, and unapologetic Hindu symbolism almost immediately alarmed Leftists. Many critics called *Baahubali* casteist, supremacist, and a celebration of Kshatriya pride. However, such predictable attacks could not stop the movie and its sequel from becoming runaway hits.

There is no sign of the trend ebbing. India's revivalism has influenced cinema, with a range of movies from Nitish Tiwari's *Ramayana* to Rajamouli's *Mahabharata* in the queue.

Anupam Kher

The protagonist of *The Kashmir Files*, Pushkar Nath, is portrayed by one of India's finest living actors, Anupam Kher. Kher's defining performance draws from his own personal loss and memories as a Kashmiri Pandit whose family left the state early but witnessed the unfolding tragedy with every visit home and through the accounts of tormented relatives. He has emerged as an outspoken voice of nationalism amidst the prevailing anti-Hindutva currents in Bollywood.

If Anupam Kher was the face of a common man's anger against a corrupt and slothful system in the award-winning *Saraansh* in the 1980s, his portrayal embodies the essence of a whitewashed genocide in *The Kashmir Files*.

> It is the truth about the exodus of Kashmiri Pandits that people had somehow hidden away. The judiciary, media, politicians, intelligentsia, writers … everybody just tried to sweep it under the carpet. It was not a simple matter. It was not just ten to twelve people who were killed. Countless people were killed, women were raped, houses were burnt. And then came 19 January 1990. More than 4 lakh people were thrown out of their houses that particular night. My mother's younger brother was also there. It is the biggest exodus and genocide in independent India.

Kher, much like his character Pushkar Nath, has been the voice of a wounded civilisation. Six years ago, he made a video titled *Haan Main Kashmiri Pandit Hoon*, which went viral.

> When Vivek approached me about this film and offered me the role after I heard the script, I knew I had to be a part of this story being told to the world. In a movie, you cannot depict 4 lakh people running away. You cannot show all that actually happened. So, I had to channel my soul to portray that. In *Saraansh*, I had to rely on craft. I was preparing to portray an old man. But *The Kashmir Files* required both the actor and the person to be on the same page.

And this is where Anupam Kher becomes one with Pushkar Nath Pandit. The actor and the character are both in exile from their beloved Valley.

In his Delhi home, Pushkar often drifts into reveries of his Kashmiri home. Like a mother comforting her child, Pushkar wraps his arms around himself when he feels the chills from the snowy winds of his imagination and sings to himself in Kashmiri.

> There is a silent scene in the refugee camp where he eats a biscuit, cries, and slaps himself. Or the scene where he feels cold and starts singing that Kashmiri song. Even the death scene ... when we were filming the truck scene, there were actual Kashmiri Pandits in the truck. In the movie, when they were told that two people are hanging, the lady next to me started howling. I asked what happened. She said that her cousin brother had also been hanged.

The Kashmir Files was released on 11 March 2022. Made with a budget of Rs 15 crore, the movie amassed Rs 350 crore within two months. Filmmaker Vivek Agnihotri, known for films like *Hate Story* and *Dhan Dhana Dhan Goal*, found his calling with *Buddha in a Traffic Jam* and *The Tashkent Files*. India's popular imagination had begun to be coloured by the new nationalism and a wave of vocal anger against the Nehruvian system. Agnihotri delivered a blockbuster simply through solid research on Kashmir and powerful storytelling.

> Vivek used to make a different kind of cinema. I'm glad he found this calling from *Buddha in a Traffic Jam*, which I was part of. He'll be remembered for the kind of cinema he is making, but look at the opposition he is facing from all quarters ... the threats he is receiving. They are obsessed that the film will expose what happened thirty years ago. We have seen characters like Radhika Menon [a far-Left character in the movie believed to be loosely based on JNU professor

Nivedita Menon and her worldview]. We know journalists in real life who said the same things as that journalist in the film, claiming that Kashmiri Pandits were affluent, which is why the Muslims were upset.

That dialogue mirrored the narrative that journalists like Barkha Dutt promoted while covering the bloodbath in Kashmir at that time.

He also mentions his own experiences as a Kashmiri Pandit. Even in the 1970s and 1980s, whenever Kher went home to Kashmir, people would say, '*Aap India se aaye ho* (You've come from India)?' The address he quotes in the film—84, Karan Nagar, Srinagar—was his own maternal house. He states that by the mid-1980s, sporadic killings had started.

> Otherwise, I have beautiful memories of Kashmir. I have memories of Handwara and Sopore. My uncles were professors in a medical college and a girls' college. In Baramulla, cherries would come into my house through the window. I remember Kheer Bhawani, Nishad Garden, Dal Lake. It is the most beautiful place in the world, and I have travelled the whole world.

Kher says the public interest litigations, smear campaigns against the movie, negative reviews (sometimes without even watching it), and attempts to cancel it are all designed to make Kashmiri Pandits relive the pain and experience the trauma again.

> It is not that the terrorists have only killed Pandits. They killed young Muslim officers and Sardars as well. And why should good infrastructure, hospitals, and education not reach Kashmiris? Jews have kept the memory of the

Holocaust alive. Films like *Schindler's List* were made. Why not films on Kashmiri Pandits or anti-genocide museums?

The film has reignited the demand for the Supreme Court of India to reconsider the cases related to the Kashmir genocide, which it had twice dismissed appeals to reinvestigate. The court had previously cited the lapse of time as a reason not to reopen the cases.

So, why didn't Bollywood make movies like *The Kashmir Files* earlier?

> Because everybody wants to be liked. The problem begins when you want to be liked by everybody. But I will tell you why I am the way I am. I'm eight years younger than my country's independence. We grew up with those feelings. The 1962 war, the 1971 war. We were still talking about how we got independence. We were still talking about Bhagat Singh, Gandhi, Nehru, Lala Lajpat Rai. It's in my bones, my blood. I can't change that. I need to respect myself. That can only happen if you stick to your convictions. Who can stop me? I have come from the gutter. I came to Mumbai with just Rs 37 on 3 June 1981. Today, I am a crorepati and doing so well. I have been trending for the last six hours on Twitter because of my birthday. I have 522 films in my kitty. Who can threaten me now?

Kher lives in a rented apartment, which is unheard of for a multi-millionaire Bollywood star. But such decisions set him apart from the rest of the industry, giving us a glimpse into his mind. 'The day I decided I would not buy a house and stay on rent, I became the richest man on earth. I have a car. I have an AC in my room. What else do you need? Our needs make us feel small,' he says.

For Kashmiri Pandits, 'home' is a very layered word. One movie cannot erase the jihadi slogan from mosque speakers or neighbourhood walls: 'Raleev (convert), galeev (be killed), ya chaleev (or flee).' But it did bring some catharsis.

> When you leave home, you don't leave concrete. You leave behind memories of corners, of smells, of aab-o-hawa. The film is not going to change that. But sometimes, catharsis happens when people cry—in Jammu, in Delhi, in Mumbai, all over America—because they did not even have the chance to experience catharsis about it.

Kher says India is changing and has a great future,

> [Because] we are comfortable being who we are. We endured a thousand years of slavery, and emerging from it in just seventy years is an extraordinary achievement. We feel the power of that awakening when some British journalist says something ignorant on social media about India and 50,000 Indians demand they first return $45 trillion in reparations for looting our country and give us back the Kohinoor. As written in the Mahabharata, truth prevails in the end.

His vociferous nationalism has not made his journey in Bollywood easy.

> I was the darling of everybody. I was the darling of the media. I was the darling of the film industry. But I am not anymore, which is fine. I need to be popular with myself and then with the world. And that can only happen when I stick to my convictions. If somebody tells me a soldier of this nation has been killed, how will it not affect me? If somebody says good things about my country, how will it not make me feel

great about that person? If somebody targets my country for their own agenda, how will it not upset me? Our government has done the most remarkable job of rescuing Indians stuck in Ukraine, and then some people say it hasn't done this, it hasn't done that. Will it not upset me? There are two kinds of people in the world: doers and critics. I am the former.

For Kher, this moment in our nation's life may dazzle those looking back fifty years later.

You or I may not be alive then, but our coming generations will marvel at how Jammu and Kashmir's special status under Article 370 was scrapped, putting the state on the path of integration and development. Change happens silently. You can't see it overnight. As the Mohammed Rafi song goes: *Gam ki andheri raat mein/dil ko na bekaraar kar/subha zaroor aayegi/subha ka intezaar kar* [In this dark night of grief/do not get restless/the dawn will surely arrive/wait for the light to break).

Amish Tripathi

A common Leftist taunt in India used to be about the Right Wing not having enough books to fill up the glove compartment of a car. Today, much of the airport bookshop shelf space has been usurped by books from the new nationalists. One of the first bestselling Indian novelists in English from outside the Leftist ecosystem has been Amish Tripathi.

Even after achieving the kind of commercial success most Indian writers can hardly dream of, forty-seven-year-old Amish remains grounded, earthy, and unapologetically

Indian and Hindu. Born in Mumbai to a deeply religious family, Amish says, 'My parents, who had studied in Hindi medium schools, sent us four siblings to schools beyond their social status.' Amish attended Cathedral and John Convent for schooling, went to St Xavier's College for graduation, and then got into IIM Calcutta.

> The shoes my friends wore cost more than my father's salary. While the atmosphere at school was very Westernised, our home was totally Indian. We learned our scriptures and culture at home. My family was not intimidated by the English-speaking elite as many from our social status usually are.

Amish then entered the corporate world, little knowing that destiny had a very different plan for him. He worked at Standard Chartered, DBS Bank, and the Industrial Development Bank of India.

In 2004, at the age of thirty, Amish started writing alongside his finance career. He was with DBS Bank at the time. The first book in the Shiva trilogy, *The Immortals of Meluha*, began with a philosophical idea before Amish transformed it into an adventure.

> I was rejected by every publisher. Most did not even respond. Some said, 'Look, it is a religious book. Our target audience is the youth, who are not interested in religion or spirituality. They want campus romance novels or office scandals. They are also not into long books. Also, there are "gyaan sessions" every four or five pages. Why don't you dumb it down?'

The publishers were going by anecdotes, assumptions, and marketing presentations. They could not have been more wrong about Indian youth not being interested in culture. The nation was already riding a new wave.

Undeterred by rejections, Amish decided to self-publish the book in 2010. It took off in the first week itself. Trained in the world of business, he employed some innovative marketing techniques, including a trailer video and distributing free booklets containing the first chapter for potential readers to sample. The book sold 40,000 copies in the first three months. Then, the same publishers who had turned him down started coming back to bid for a book deal.

> The demand for content on Indian culture and spirituality has always been there. The anglicised elite in this country is just 20–30 million. The real India, which exists beyond that demographic, was not part of the conversation; it was struggling to survive. The real change began in 1991 with economic liberalisation. We started seeing the impact in one sector after another. The corporate sector used to be dominated by the boxwallahs, the anglicised elite. That began to change with the revolutionary reforms.

In the financial sector, Grindlays, Standard Chartered, HSBC, Citibank, and other multinational banks, which exuded a certain culture foreign to India, were being replaced by HDFC and ICICI.

> Slowly, elbowing out crisp English, Hindi chatter crept into the workplace. The advertising world started flaunting desi wit with figures like Piyush Pandey and others. The real India was emerging. The last bastions of colonialism are the English media and the legal world. But with more money in the hands of Indians from the hinterland, small towns, and villages came more confidence. I just happened to be there at

the right time, right place. Forty years ago, my book would have been a flop.

As success visited Amish counterintuitively, entirely against the templates of that time, his engagement with the nation's past grew deeper. In *The Legend of Suheldev: The King Who Saved India*, he tells the story of the king who defeated and killed Ghazi Miyan, a Ghaznavid general, in UP's Bahraich in 1034 CE. Suheldev was from the backward Rajbhar caste, and his life shatters the narrative that in ancient or medieval India, kings and great warriors came only from the upper castes. But his story also gave Amish an occasion to speak directly and politically about India, its past, and present in the introduction of his book:

> A giant tide of history in the last 2,000 years was defined by horrific violence. It wiped out the ancient cultures of the world: Pagan Rome, mystical Egypt and mythical Greece; Zoroastrian Persia, idol worshipping Central America, and even martial Norse… and too many others. Some might say some still exist; heartbreakingly though, in wilted forms that fuel, at best, the tourist industry and some museums. No, they no longer are living, breathing [entities]. But one ancient civilisation stubbornly refused to die. One proud culture refused to be overwritten. It retreated at times, even withdrew permanently from some lands, became silent, but is one of the rare few still left standing. And breathing. It is India.
>
> Heroes and heroines arose, magnificently, whenever invaders came to our land. They led us. Defended us. There were many—Harihara and Bukka Raya, Maharana Pratap, Lachit Borphukan, Rani Abbakka, Raja Marthanda Varma, Maharaja Ranjit Singh, Chhatrapati Shivaji,

Mahatma Gandhi, Netaji Subhash Chandra Bose—and countless other courageous men and women with a steely determination to fight. But, a careful reading of our history tells us that the biggest challenge for these heroes and heroines was to somehow unite our fissiparous society, to fight those foreigners. We had a national consciousness, as the millennia-old Vishnu Purana evidences, but the default tendency in us Indians is to fight each other; tragically, to this day. Infighting is our favourite pastime, which ceases only briefly when the enemy is at our doorstep. The challenge, always, was how to stop our constant infighting.

These leaders succeeded where others failed. They united us, albeit briefly. And, we prevailed.

Sadly, many of these heroes and heroines have been airbrushed out of our history books. I believe these great men and women demand from us, their descendants, that we remember their tales. That we share their stories. That we celebrate them. And learn from them.

Today, more than ever, we need to hear the chronicles of these great people who united us and saved our land by making us confront brutal foreign invaders, beat many of them back, and most importantly, survive.

This book is of one such hero, a fictional story inspired by real events. It is the story of the magnificent King Suheldev of the 11th century.

Being an Indian writer in English, Amish detects colonialism in the language and grammar. 'Most Indian media outlets and publishers follow the English grammar rule of capitalising the male God but not the female goddess. I insist that Goddess should also be capitalised,' he says. After *Sita: Warrior of Mithila* was released, a website published its excerpts after editing Goddess into lowercase. Amish put his foot down.

'They accommodate woke pronouns like "they/their", but are reluctant to readjust grammar according to the Indian cultural ethos.'

How does the Left-liberal literary ecosystem treat him? 'To be fair, they always invited me to the Jaipur Literature Festival. I have openly declared at the Jaipur LitFest that I am a proud Hindu. The public responded with a roar of applause,' he says.

The problem often lies with nationalists and those aligned with Hindutva, whom he refers to as 'Dhartiputra' or children of the soil, in contrast to 'Macaulayputra', the ideological offspring of Thomas Babington Macaulay, the British historian who influenced education in India.

> A conversation is needed among Dhartiputras to determine whether we want to embrace open-mindedness, confidence, and knowledge-driven approaches, or adhere to close-mindedness and mirror those who we oppose. Dhartiputras still seek validation from the West and the Left. We should not waste time with Macaulayputras. Creators don't need to disparage others, engage in arguments, or seek approval from others.

He says the West and the Left have created a smokescreen of myths about Indian culture. Caste is portrayed as something that was always birthbound, rigid, and inherently evil in Indian culture. However, our texts are littered with examples that demonstrate the flexibility of the Varna system.

Lord Ram's chief priest, Satyakam Jabaali, was born to a Shudra or low-caste single mother, Amish states. By virtue of his knowledge and wisdom, little Satyakam grew up to be Jabaali Maharishi or a sage.

Also, many Leftist and Western scholars propagate the lie that our ancestors did not write anything down and we are an oral culture. Well, according to the National Mission for Manuscripts, an autonomous organisation under the Union Ministry of Tourism and Culture, about 3 million manuscripts in Sanskrit and other Indian languages still survive [which is more than the rest of the civilised world combined]. This is despite millions being destroyed during the invasions and plunder of Taxashila and Nalanda universities. Only about 20,000–30,000 Greek manuscripts exist today.

Those manuscripts are not just religious texts or philosophical treatises. They are a tightly shut treasure trove of mathematics, chemistry, biology, physics, astronomy, economics, and other subjects.

At this moment, a revival is palpable, he says. Films like *Baahubali* and *Uri* and web series like *The Family Man* are evidence of that. In March 2022, Shekhar Kapur announced that Roy Price, CEO of International Art Machine, would adapt Amish's book *The Immortals of Meluha* into a web series, with Suparn Verma as the director.

Amish predicts that the new wave of rooted Indian writing, cinema, and art is going to become more and more powerful. It is inexorably linked to the nation's economic might. 'When our economy is $10 trillion, they will respect us. We should simply focus on our work and achievement. Write books, make movies,' he says. 'And market them well.'

Ayurveda and Yoga

The surge in nationalism has yielded rich returns on ancient health systems and homegrown textiles. The export of the soft power of yoga and Ayurveda has never been so visible and extensive in modern times.

Narendra Modi succeeded in persuading the United Nations to unanimously designate 21 June as International Yoga Day. From the West to Africa, the Middle East, Central Asia, and Russia to South Asia and the Pacific, more than 190 Indian embassies around the world have been actively promoting yoga and Ayurveda with remarkable energy.

The prime minister established a new ministry called AYUSH (Ayurveda, Yoga and Naturopathy, Unani, Siddha, and Homoeopathy) right after coming to power in 2014. From about $244 million in 2012, India's export of ayurvedic and herbal products more than doubled to $540 million in the financial year 2021. After India officially adopted the AYUSH systems to fight COVID-19 in 2020, exports of Ayurvedic products increased by about 45 per cent compared to 2019. 'In many countries, turmeric-based drinks are becoming more popular. Prestigious medical journals are also expressing new hope in Ayurveda,' the PM said.

At the Fourth Global Ayurveda Festival in 2021, Modi said:

> In June 2020, I came across an article in the *Financial Times*. The headline was: 'Coronavirus gives health halo products a boost.' The piece referred to turmeric, ginger, and other such spices whose demand is steadily rising in the context of the COVID-19 global pandemic. The current situation presents the right time for Ayurveda and traditional medicines to become even more popular globally. There is growing interest in them. The world is recognising the importance of both modern and traditional medicines in promoting wellness. People are realising the benefits of Ayurveda and its role in

boosting immunity. They are making kaadha, basil, black pepper integral parts of their lives.

The market has exploded with herbal and traditional products. Starting from a small pharmacy in 1997, Yogi Baba Ramdev has built an empire with his Patanjali enterprise, whose annual revenue in 2021 was nearly $1.3 billion.

While India's herbal giants like Dabur, Nuralz, Hamdard, Zandu, Himalaya, Vicco, Baidyanath, Navayur, Vopec, Charak, and Sandu have grown, a swarm of startups like Kama Ayurveda, Kivashots, Aadar, Oziva, andMe, and Akiva are carving out their space.

The path that Mohandas Karamchand Gandhi paved with homespun Khadi products has widened into an expressway. The Khadi and Village Industries Commission (KVIC) in 2021–22 posted a turnover of Rs 1.15 lakh crore ($14.8 billion), setting a record for an FMCG company in the country. That represents a growth of 20.54 per cent from the previous year. From 2014–15, production in Khadi and village industry sectors in 2021–22 registered a 172 per cent growth, while gross sales during this period increased by more than 248 per cent. This was achieved despite a partial lockdown in the first three months of the 2021–22 financial year due to the second COVID-19 wave. Khadi's single-day sales at its flagship Connaught Place store in New Delhi hit a record of Rs 1.29 crore ($170,000) on 30 October 2021.

Hari Kiran Vadlamani

Hari Kiran Vadlamani, aged fifty-nine, is one of the foremost drivers of India's new cultural awakening. Quietly, almost self-evasively, and with money and resources, the serial entrepreneur powers some of the most impactful and sophisticated media and cultural ventures today.

Born in Hyderabad, Hari Kiran grew up in Guntur. His father was a chartered accountant. He became a CA too, specialising in taxation and investment banking. In 1996, he entered the power sector. His work transitioned into wind energy. He moved to Singapore in 2008 and eventually ventured into the coal sector. From traditional industries, he gradually moved to the virtual realm, investing in a dotcom venture.

Internally, a more profound change was afoot. While Vadlamani remained focused on balance sheets, he was also gravitating towards a new equilibrium—spirituality. He became a student of Vedanta in 2000 and established the Advaita Academy in 2010. His passion for art became entwined with his spiritual quest and flourished. In 2015, he initiated the Indic Academy.

> There are three kinds of civilisational action: protection, preservation, and promotion. These are distinct capabilities. Many individuals in the media and on social media are dedicated to protecting our history and culture from Leftists. Personally, I am more into promotion. I started the Indic Academy because of the need to promote and protect.

He says there were immediate challenges. Protection and promotion of Indic culture were uncharted territory. 'There was initial backlash from friends. I deleted my Facebook account in 2014 and my Twitter account in 2018. There were too many value judgements I could do without.'

Vadlamani makes two kinds of investments. One category is profit ventures, while the other focuses on people. He has been a major shareholder in Swarajya Media since 2014. 'It was a passion investment,' he explains.

Another organisation he founded was NICE.org, which expands to the Network of Indian Cultural Enterprises. NICE serves as the Nasscom or TIE for cultural enterprises, lobbying, promoting, and bringing together investors. It operates similarly to an angel network.

His other flourishing venture is Indica, a platform for Indic education. 'When you think of me, think of two buckets: entrepreneurship and education,' says Vadlamani.

He makes a sharp distinction between narrow race-bound or language-based Western nationalism and Indian civilisationalism. He is much more comfortable being called a 'civilisationalist' than a 'nationalist'.

He expounds on 'dharmic liberalism'. In his essay 'Dharmic Liberalism Is Classical Liberalism + Social Liberalism +', he writes:

> Liberalism has acquired different connotations across different countries and within a country across different time periods. Over the years, it has changed several shades as people try to define themselves better as to what they stand for. So you have various adjectives defining liberalism: economic liberalism, social liberalism, conservative liberalism, etc. So when I use dharmic as an adjective to define a liberal, it is defining the liberal further wherein dharma plays a defining role in my being a liberal.
>
> From a guna point of view, dharma is sattvaguna and liberalism is rajas. When you do your duty with a sense of service, with an attitude of seva to your nation, or the world, then you are predominantly sattvic in your disposition. Likewise, when you pursue your right to liberty and material happiness, the predominant guna in play

is rajas. So a dharmic liberal is equally endowed with both the gunas. Such a person is simultaneously a universalist and an individualist.

Similarly, being liberal is about your ego; being dharmic is about humility. So you can say it is a combination of being humble and being confident of your abilities at the same time. Strains of this thought can be found in the concepts of 'servant leadership' and 'level 5 leadership'.

He believes that a dharmic or Indic liberal is not conservative, nor does he or she possess an unwillingness to change. He refers to himself as a 'NOTA person' (none-of-the-above person). According to him, here are some of the cornerstones of an Indic liberal's belief system:

- India is part of a 5,000-year-old unbroken civilisation.
- The timeless profundity of the scientific and philosophical insights of our ancestors is acknowledged without making any grandiose claims.
- India is intrinsically pluralistic socially, culturally, and economically.
- A liberal is willing to accept diverse views and is open to new ideas.
- Advocates for limited government.
- Promotes free markets.
- Upholds individual liberty.
- Ensures equality of opportunity.
- Advocates for an assertive defence policy, socially non-dogmatic, evolving, and self-reforming.
- Does not encourage superstitious practices.
- Does not claim exclusivity.
- Is not predatory.
- Respects non-believers.

- Is not discriminatory based on gender or class.
- Encourages spiritual inquiry and reasoning.

Vadlamani says the new nationalism was accelerated by the excesses of the Congress.

> It is a pan-India movement, encompassing Bengaluru, Pune, Mumbai, NCR, Coimbatore, Chennai, and Hyderabad. Events between 2004 and 2014, such as the 2008 Mumbai attack, contributed to this momentum. A lot of people who became engineers in the 1990s or 2000s began contemplating the meaning of life. In the last twenty years, the frequency of attacks against us has increased. The hope is that millions of people have awakened. They are searching for meaning. Many Hindus still believe it is acceptable to be denigrated or to belittle our own culture. But the tide is turning in our favour.

He says the Indian Left gains momentum from the global Left, Islamists, Khalistanis, and similar forces. Today, India's battle is against the global Left.

'The issue here is cultural revival, not roads or buildings. The problem is that the day a politician gets elected, he or she thinks of getting re-elected. Cultural revival is seldom at the top of his or her mind,' he says. He criticises the Right Wing for wasting a substantial amount of time 'building castles in the air' and fighting the wrong battles. He feels that while an inordinate amount of time and attention goes into dispelling the Leftist narrative or sometimes trolling people, not much is done to further the cultural agenda and promote minds that can enrich the civilisational discourse.

'I'm seeking to change the narrator and not the narrative. I believe we can transform the world. We have to think of our culture as a natural resource with which we have been blessed. We will become a "viswaguru". The solution to the world's problems lies with us. We have yoga, ayurveda, cuisine, crafts,' says Vadlamani. This is why, he says, it is so important to invest in Indian culture.

Advaita Kala

From living under the threat of being kidnapped by the Dawood Ibrahim gang as a child to writing the story of the hit Bollywood movie *Kahaani*, to tireless writing and exposing the political murders of Hindutva activists carried out by the Left in Kerala, her life has always had a crime thriller element to it. Today, author and scriptwriter Advaita Kala is also one of the most prominent voices of the resurgent Indian nationalism.

Long associations with the film and hospitality industries gave her exposure to glamorous India. It also enables her to understand the creativity and visibility, hubris, and hypocrisies of that world. Her experience and articulation sometimes make leading politicians consult her. She is also a familiar face on television and social media.

Advaita's journey in the outside world started very early. She went to boarding school—Welham Girls, Dehradun—when she was just eight.

> I left home at a very young age and was thrust into an environment where parents aren't there, and you have to fend for yourself. There were kidnap threats. The Dawood gang was threatening my father because he was in customs and then the Directorate of Revenue Intelligence, and was

> targeting gold smuggling in Mumbai. So, there were a lot of threats on us as a family, and there were attempts to kidnap me. As a result, I had to be pulled out of school. I had 24/7 security. It was bad. My sister was a baby. It was 1982–83. She was safe because she was obviously with my mother all the time, being nursed. I dropped out of school at seven. Imagine. And then they [parents] told everybody that I was going to Panchgani, but I was sent to Dehradun because my mother is from Welham as well. So, she felt like, 'This is my alma mater'. She went to the principal in tears and said, 'Look I don't have a mother, I can't send her somewhere. This is the only home I know.' They were very kind. It is a very snooty school, but they were very sweet. They took me in mid-term.

Thus, for Advaita Kala, real-life drama began quite early.

> It was quite dramatic. I think it has kind of made me a thriller writer because I was surrounded by it—being seven or eight years old and seeing a gun in the house, living in that environment. In fact, in *Kahaani*, one of the characters was very clearly based on an uncle of mine. Nawazuddin's. That kind of frenetic energy. My uncle's name is Dayashankar. He was very well-known in customs ... anti-smuggling units. He used to come home a lot because he was my dad's junior and used to work very closely with him.

Advaita went to the US for four years and returned to complete her college education in Meerut, where she studied political science. After that, she pursued hospitality at the Oberoi Centre of Learning and Development (OCLD). She underwent two years of training with the Oberoi in Jaipur, Shimla, Kolkata, and Bengaluru. Later, she accepted a position at Madinat Jumeirah's Dar Al Masiyaf spring-side villas in Dubai. She describes the experience as less than satisfactory and resigned after just eight months, returning to India.

It was then that her mother suggested that she start writing because she was good at it. At twenty-eight, she wrote her first book, *Almost Single*. HarperCollins published it, and it went on to become a bestseller.

'It's about being single and a woman, dating, love, and such stuff. It is a fun book. I was crowned the queen of "chick lit" for a while. And it was published in the US. The American publisher Bantam House picked it up for its Bantam Dell New Voices,' she says. After that, she moved to Bollywood scripts with *Anjana Anjani*. Then came the award-winning *Kahaani*.

> *Kahaani* was great because I took on the very 'masculine' genre of thrillers and made the protagonist a female. She is pregnant on top of that. I was sure that we were not going to use sexuality, make her a honey trap, or some such trope, but give her an actual role and a character with layers. For me, it was very challenging … gratifying. It also gave me a break from chick lit and not being taken seriously. Suddenly, people were saying, 'Oh, this is art', and I felt it was the same writer who wrote something fun and light and frivolous because that was the subject. She can also write something intense with feminist undertones.

After writing *Almost Single* and the script of *Kahaani*, Advaita moved to Yangon in Myanmar to work at the Shangri-La in 2012. It was a time when the country was transitioning from a military junta to a democracy.

> I went to a press conference in the hotel with Burmese journalists. After the talk, they asked, 'Any questions?'

And nobody raised their hands. I said, 'What kind of press conference is this? No journalist is asking a question.' A Burmese friend said, 'Don't laugh. You don't know right now.'

After a few months, she came back to India and started writing again. It was around the time 26/11 happened. From that day, Advaita's political shift began.

> I had just quit working for the Taj. The Mumbai attacks shook me up. One of my closest friends was the assistant front office manager, Abhimanyu. The first shots were fired in the Oberoi lobby, not the Taj. And he used to work in the Oberoi. Abhimanyu was a bachelor, and I know that he used to work until really late. Ironically, there was a HarperCollins party at the Taj Palace, Delhi, that night. We had just come down and we were hanging around outside when the news started coming in. I had a work phone and a private phone, and I realised that I did not have his number on the phone I had with me. So, I completely freaked out. I drove home and called him. His number was busy. So, I thought that's sort of a good sign. And then I got through to him, and he told me that he had gone to Udaipur that morning for his brother's wedding. He said that something bad was happening, something really bad was going to happen. So, that was the beginning for me. Then I was just glued to the TV. My student trainees, one of them was killed, another was shot, some were trapped overnight in the chambers. And that kind of made me start looking at politics, looking at issues of security and terror in a way that I had never done before.

Advaita, like millions of Indians, felt deep rage during 26/11. She felt the nation was not able to protect itself the way it should have.

A space that I love is hotels. That has transformed irreversibly. Now you walk into a hotel and you have to go through all kinds of security checks and frisking. I felt a big shift post-26/11, and that's why I wrote *Kahaani*. I don't think I would have written a *Kahaani* had I not felt the anger and a sense of vigilantism.

Why did she choose Kolkata as the backdrop for *Kahaani*?

I had worked in Kolkata, and filmmaker Sujoy Ghosh is Bengali, so he was keen on doing something in Kolkata. The protagonist played by Vidya Balan had to be an outsider who experiences the city as I experienced it, which is its multiple realities. It could be beautiful and polite and cultured on one hand and also unionised to such an extent that I have seen the two unions—Left and TMC—fight viciously at the Oberoi Grand. I have seen them surround the skinny HR manager, shake his table, and keep a goat's head on it. *Kahaani* was really about exploring that underbelly. There is a streak of violence because any place that has enough Left politics will have that underlying violence there. I would not necessarily say Delhi has that underlying violence, although it has overt aggression.

She then started writing a column for *Mail Today* and delved into politics. TV appearances followed suit.

She says, adding that Modi made her more and more interested in Indian politics:

I saw Narendra Modi, the prime ministerial candidate at that time, and I found him to be very compelling in terms of narrative, in terms of his persona, where he came from, and where he was headed. Then Twitter happened.

Everything came together at the same time. It was sort of a political awakening. I think he is a very charismatic politician. And here he was saying something that was very different because we had ten years of a prime minister who was really not saying anything. So suddenly you have somebody articulate, passionate, who has something to say, who has a vision, and a great personal story. Going from abject poverty to aspiring for the highest office in the land was a very compelling reason for me to get involved.

Advaita reiterates that the Right and the Western sense don't exist in India.

I am a Hindu, and I think Hindus are generally liberal, so I consider myself a liberal. I don't associate with any Right or Left. Some people may find security in that kind of association, but I don't believe in that kind of tribalism. I feel that there are issues and there are responses to those issues, and they don't necessarily have to be consistent, but they have to be consistent with a view of the world, which in my case is decidedly a Hindu view. It is not necessarily Hindu in a religious sense but cultural. Nationalism was always there. This surge is new because there is somebody like Modi who is really talking about India and making it the centrepiece of discourse. Bal Gangadhar Tilak and all of these people were great nationalists. It was believed that after Independence, the goal of nationalism had been achieved, and it was time to abandon it and be part of a larger world community. So, for the last seventy years, we had this rush to catch up with the rest of the world while ignoring and setting aside our own truths, wisdom, and realities.

She calls out the West for grappling with the breakdown of society and social structures because of certain aspects of so-called liberalism. That brand of liberalism is failing, and the whole world is taking this so-called Right turn or this new nationalistic approach. and the Left has overused and misused identity to the point of being tyrannical to the majority, she asserts.

> My best friend, for example, is a white American man. Very often he tells me about how he feels targeted. He says, 'You know, I have never in my life indulged in a lot of the things that they say about the white man—white privilege. The white man is typified as a colonialist, imperialist, slave-owner. It is a kind of reverse racism of sorts, and the Left kind of wraps it up in righteousness.

From English-medium boarding schools to the hospitality industry to Bollywood, Advaita Kala never exactly inhabited the RSS's core sphere of work. But as she started becoming more politically aware and involved, she slowly and organically started gravitating towards the Sangh's universe.

> On Twitter, I met a few friends. One of them happened to be a swayamsevak. And he said, 'You know Dinanath Batra? Would you like to meet him?' I said, 'Not really because I don't agree with anyone who wants to ban books [Wendy Doniger's] and all of that.' He said, 'No, that's not what he is about. That's how he has been projected, and it would be very nice if you could meet him.' I met him, and I didn't entirely agree with him, but I saw commitment. He is a ninety-year-old man. He goes to court for every hearing and stands up for what he believes in. He is not using violence. He is using the civil means available to every citizen of this country. And the publisher won't even go to court. Here is someone who is standing up to his beliefs, and on the other hand, you have

a publisher who is not standing up for their author. As a writer, I found that pretty offensive because I would want my publisher to stand up for me.

Slowly, she started interacting more with the RSS. She found the interactions 'open-minded'. She thought that if this organisation is growing at the rate that it is, if it is finding more and more people to support it, then one has to figure out what it is about. Her writer's instinct came alive.

> I had heard a lot about their anti-woman reputation. So, I wondered how they would react to someone like me—female, outspoken, and English-speaking. But I found them surprisingly open, willing to share and engage ... very egalitarian. Not once have I felt the need to hold back from expressing myself or voicing an opinion. I found this particularly revealing, given the propaganda that the RSS doesn't favour women. I didn't anticipate such receptiveness and decency.

Advaita ventured into Kannur, Kerala, where the Left cadre reportedly engaged in frequent attacks on Hindutva activists, making it one of the most politically violent places in India. She delved into the ground reality ahead of the Assembly elections in 2016. As a woman, she found herself amidst hundreds of men in this mini-conflict zone.

'The narrative depicted the RSS as fascist and spreading hate. But here I saw them being killed despite having no access to [local] political power. They were literally sequestered, rounded up, hunted, and killed. The police, under the control of the state government, failed to protect them,' she says. Moreover, the media remained silent on these incidents, which emboldened politicians to let the culprit go unpunished. During his visit to Kerala, Prime Minister Narendra Modi had to ask why the Delhi media was not speaking about the violence.

> The Kerala experience—travelling there, interacting with the locals, providing laptops for kids, rallying people to contribute for some of the slain individuals, extensively writing about it, making TV appearances—took two years of my life. But I actually feel very happy that for many years now, there have hardly been any killings. It was crucial for me to mainstream that discourse, to be partisan, to take a side and then advocate for it. I believe that the criticism I faced really helped put an end to the killings. The last recorded killing was in August 2017. That's a positive development because when the communists are in power, they can be very brutal.

In Kannur, she met pracharaks and swayamsevaks whose commitment to their cause is remarkably unwavering. They don't know if there is political power at the end of the dark, arduous tunnel. They don't know how their lives will end. Most of them are very poor, and there is no tangible payoff for risking life and limb. Yet, they are committed to the ideology, the nation, and Bharat Mata, or Mother India.

> And the strength ... you hear about Dr Keshav Hedgewar and how he initiated this mission of vyakti nirman [building an individual], especially because this is a country that has been enslaved for generations and centuries. They were resilient people; they knew no fear. They were unafraid of expressing their opinions, risking their lives; fear simply did not exist for them. I believe that more than I helped them, I learned

a lot. I grew stronger, bolder in expressing my opinions. When I went there, I was scared. As I mentioned, I am not a journalist, I have not engaged in conflict reporting or any of those things. I pretty much just hopped on a train and went. Ignorance has often aided me in my life.

Advaita was very young when the Babri Masjid dhancha (structure) was brought down because it was built on the site of the destroyed Ram temple. She says that event set the ball rolling for Hindu nationalism, which has now taken on a bigger and more concrete form.

She also states that although her political awakening led her directly to Hindu nationalism and aligned her closely with the views held by the BJP or the RSS, she would readily acknowledge if AAP or the Congress did something good.

When asked how diverse is the new Right, she says:

Much more than the Left. It is hugely diverse. And that's what is lovely. It is like Shivji's baarat. You have the gays, you have the trans. You have moderates like me or liberals. Someone in the media was telling me I am defined as a Right-Wing liberal. People just make up their definitions so that they can label people. The so-called Left-liberal ecosystem expects conformity. I remember once mentioning something to a doyen of the Left-liberal ecosystem at a party and he shouted me down. This is a very aggressive idea of liberalism. I can't go with that. I went to a liberal arts school where people have different views. You could agree with them on six or eight out of ten points. It is rare that you will agree on all ten. How can you not accept people for their views? I found that a lot more in the Sangh than I found among Left-liberals. Because of my success in the writing world, I had access to the people at the forefront of that kind of thought, and I found that they were far more rigid in their views. And the Sangh, which is considered rigid, is far more flexible and open because they were essentially Hindu in the cultural sense.

Advaita believes there has been a fundamental and decisive shift in the way Indians think, but one has to be careful that it does not become codified.

> That's my generation's work. The challenge will be to ensure that this pride remains, that it nurtures and nourishes, but it does not start crowding out people's personal experiences and choices. This awakening was definitely needed. Anyone who has studied in an English-medium school knows that if you spoke in Hindi, you were punished or looked down upon. It was just not acceptable. Our generation's task will be to ensure that we maintain the liberal equality that is part of Hindu culture and civilisation, while still moving forward with pride. That's a challenge. The world is becoming a much more violent place. We have a role to play—a spiritual role, not a reactive one.

CHAPTER 7

Nationalism and Mission Northeast

Very few life forms smell sublime while being skinned, but cinnamon trees do. In Manipur's tiny Bungte Chiru village, they are everywhere. You can casually peel off a few inches of bark, baring the tree's pink-brown flesh, and a riot of sweet, woodsy fragrance erupts.

Bungte Chiru and the many villages dotting the lush green hills surrounding Imphal comprise Leishi Kabui's karmabhoomi.

Less than a hundred kilometres from Imphal, in the surrounding hills, twenty-six-year-old Leishi from the Rongmei tribe is helping to undo profound demographic and cultural changes that this part of Northeast India has witnessed for over a century. Her real name cannot be revealed because of the risk associated with her work.

She teaches eight children in the village and also goes door to door, networking and collecting information. She is comfortable in English. Additionally, she babysits her little sister, one of her four very young siblings.

She is a purna-kalik, or full-timer, with Vanvasi Kalyan Ashram (VKA), the wing of the RSS that works in tribal areas. VKA runs about 18,000 projects and claims a presence in well over 50,000 tribal villages across the country. A purnakalik in these parts receives a stipend of Rs 5,000–10,000 ($65–$130) per month. Her job begins at the foothills on the edge of Manipur's picturesque capital, Imphal, winding through predominantly Christian villages on foot or by bike. She goes from door to door, village to village, chatting with families about everyday matters like a daughter's studies or a grandma's illness.

Most days, she comes here alone. On some days, an elder mentor from VKA accompanies her. The mentor is equally familiar with the hilly roads, barebones houses, and the simple people who live here.

Today, Leishi is visiting the home of a younger purnakalik. Large jackfruits hang from a tree next to the scrawny bamboo gate. Cinnamon trees and bay leaves grow in the unkempt front garden. Like Leishi, the young woman also teaches children in the village.

In almost every village, there are young persons like her, many of them Christians, who are part of the Sangh Parivar's massive and silent community outreach. They run schools and clinics, work to revive indigenous culture and traditions, and help people with their day-to-day problems. Leishi connects with her part of this vast and growing network every day. In hundreds of households, they are a family outside the family.

Northeast India is one of the fastest-growing catchment areas for Hindu nationalism. This development is a response to extensive and organised missionary activity, mass conversions of tribals, and the rapid spread of Christianity that began during British rule. Much of the Christian expansion in the Northeast occurred between 1931 and 1951, especially from 1941 to 1951, and continued unabated even after Independence.

In the last count, Nagaland stands at 87.9 per cent, Mizoram at 87.2 per cent, Meghalaya at 74.6 per cent, Manipur at 41.3 per cent, and Arunachal Pradesh at 31 per cent Christian. Of India's 2.78 crore Christians counted in 2011, 78 lakh are in the Northeast. The region is home to India's largest concentration of Christians after the coastal stretch from southern Tamil Nadu and Kerala to coastal Karnataka, Goa, and Maharashtra. The 2011 Census showed Assam had 34 per cent Muslims. Today, the real number is believed to be around 40 per cent, mainly due to illegal immigration from Bangladesh and Myanmar, tribal land takeover, and widespread conversion efforts.

Leishi explains:

> Sometimes, in these Christian villages, people have approached me and said, 'You have come to convert us to Hinduism.' They usually say these things when they are drunk. Then I explain to them that I do not represent a religion; my work is cultural. Other villagers have also come to my rescue and reasoned with those who got aggressive.

Being a nationalist in the Northeast can entail untold perils. One of the most high-profile cases of abduction and murder occurred in the then Communist Party of India (Marxist)-ruled Tripura in 1999. Very senior RSS leaders—Shyamal Kanti Sengupta, zonal general secretary of West Bengal, Assam, and the Northeast; Dinendranath Dey, a pracharak working in southern Assam; Sudhamay Dutta, Agartala area-in-charge; and Subhankar Chakravarty, district pracharak—were kidnapped on 6 August 1999, from a VKA-run students' hostel in Tripura's Kanchanchhada area. The National Liberation Front of Tripura (NLFT) held them captive for months, tortured them, and finally executed all four in February the following year. Two decades later, Tripura has a BJP government.

While a BJP-backed government also rules Manipur today, the groundwork in the state was also laid with much blood and sacrifice. Madhumangal Sharma is a striking example. Born to Samurailatpam Ibohal Sharma and Uttarani Devi in 1938 at Khurai Chingangbam Leikai, Imphal, he was the first mining engineering graduate from Manipur. He retired as the additional director of the state industry department and joined the BJP. He served as the BJP president of Manipur from 1985 to 1990. His grassroots work for the RSS, VHP, and other organisations began far earlier, dating back to 1950. He would sometimes travel 75 km on his bicycle to the remote areas of his state, combating drug addiction and extremism. He was well-versed in the Bhagavad Gita and wrote patriotic songs.

On 11 February 1995, Madhumangal Sharma was shot by unidentified gunmen belonging to one of Northeast's many militant groups. He had a copy of Deendayal Upadhyaya's *Integral Humanism* with him that day.

Sharma's murder was not an isolated incident. According to a local leader of the Sangh, who wishes to remain anonymous, militants also killed another prant karyakarta or zonal office-bearer of the RSS. Imphal's autowallahs, for instance, formed a strong information network for insurgents, he says. 'Before the BJP-led government came to power, there would be a strike or violence almost every day. That has lessened drastically now,' he adds.

Undeterred by the dangers, grassroots workers of the RSS bodies continued their focused, quiet work, even when the BJP was not in power. And gradually, things started to change.

In 2017, Manipur elected twenty-one BJP leaders to the assembly, and the party now leads the state's ruling coalition. Since 2014, there has been a significant increase in the number of RSS shakhas in Manipur, with more than 120 shakhas and mandalas now active. Across the Northeast, the RSS and its affiliated organisations ran about 650 educational units in 1995. This number has grown to more than 6,000 today. Additionally, there are more than 3,000 ekal vidyalayas or single-teacher schools in the region.

Education has been one of the focus areas of the Sangh Parivar in the Northeast. Its many organisations, such as Sewashram, ekal vidyalayas, VKA, Sewa Bharati, Kisan Sangha, ABVP, Vidya Bharati, Friends of Tribal Society or Van Bandhu Parishad, Vishwa Hindu Parishad, Bharatiya Jan Seva Sansthan, Bharat Kalyan Pratishthan, Bal Sanskar Kendra, and the Akhil Bharatiya Rashtriya Shaikshik Mahasangh, run educational institutions across Manipur and most other northeastern states.

These centres are not only cultivating a new generation of nationalist students but also exerting significant influence on parents. Local RSS leaders proudly mention that even children of some extremist and separatist leaders of Nagaland attend English-medium schools operated by a Sangh wing.

In addition to education, Sangh organisations operate in the most remote, Christian-dominated areas to re-establish connections between converted tribes and their indigenous cultures. The underlying belief is that the arrival and rapid spread of Christianity have disconnected local populations from their traditional roots, uprooted them, and incited revolts against their own motherland.

Reviving Indigenous Traditions

Meanwhile, in Sadu-Chiru village, Leishi arrives at the home of a Baptist family and is warmly greeted. The matriarch is seated outside in the sun on an old, rickety wooden chair. She beckons Leishi towards her with a hand gesture, her face lighting up with a smile.

The Manipur Kalyan Ashram had assisted the family in accessing benefit funds under PM Modi's Ayushman Bharat, which claims to be the world's largest health assurance scheme. The assistance covered the elderly woman's angioplasty operation, which cost Rs 1.7 lakh (about $2,300). With a monthly income of about Rs 15,000 ($200), the family would not have been able to afford the medical expenses. Representatives from the Kalyan Ashram spoke to the private hospital to negotiate a reduction in the matriarch's fees. Now, they are trying to secure a follow-up surgery at a discounted rate.

To them, Leishi has become like family. They express concerns that the biggest government hospital in Imphal is not empanelled under the scheme, while a large private hospital has been included. So, the scheme isn't providing significant financial assistance to the local community. Leishi listens attentively. Providing such feedback is part of her role, which she reports back to her seniors in the RSS. They, in turn, periodically present it to the government to refine its schemes and address gaps in policymaking and implementation.

The other central scheme that has impacted the villages of the Chiru tribe is the Pradhan Mantri Gram Sadak Yojna, aimed at building rural roads. Along the roads, local boys and girls sell homemade juice made from pineapple and other fruits that grow in the area. Picnickers driving to a nearby waterfall often stop to buy the juices. Women apply turmeric paste to their faces before heading to the rice fields to protect themselves from sunburn caused by the reflection of the sun on the water in the croplands. Pomelo and pomegranates hang from the trees by the road, while women sell spring onions freshly picked from the fields, with mud still clinging to the bulbs.

In these parts, underground militant organisations had banned the hoisting of the tricolour and displaying other national symbols since the late 1990s. However, with the extensive groundwork of the RSS, the national flag and anthem have made a comeback.

A more significant success for the Sangh has been what it terms 'sanskriti jagaran' or cultural awakening.

The VKA has revived over 300 long-lost or dying tribal folk songs. According to a local RSS senior, Christian missionaries had dismissed this aspect of indigenous culture as evil. The Kalyan Ashram is forming core teams that work with specific tribes such as Kom, Moyon, Maring, and Tangkhul. The revival required meticulous and exhausting work. Ground workers like Leishi convinced community leaders and identified elderly individuals, some nearly seventy years old, who still remembered the songs. They painstakingly recorded the words and tunes from oral traditions onto paper. These songs had ceased to be passed down due to the demonisation of the indigenous way of life by missionaries, he explains. The collection of over 300 songs has been released on DVD and distributed for free in the villages.

The revival work did not stop there. More than fifteen traditional village games from nine tribes have been resurrected. These local games are not only fascinating but also serve as strong societal bonds. For example, Osu Kaka, a game of the Mao tribe, is played during the Chiithuni harvest festival. During breaks from work in the crop fields, unmarried villagers challenge the married ones. Another beloved game of the Mao tribe is Lerii Kaphi Cho, a spear sport held during the Saleni festival, reminiscent of past wars. Nakinje–Nakinje, a game of the Mon tribe involving singing, has been revived after mining the memories of elders from Khoirentak Kom village. Manipur also revived its own version of polo called Sagol Kangjei. According to ancient texts, around 33 CE, Manipur's iconic king, Nongta Lailen Pakhangba, introduced his companion Laisana to his friends and other chieftains through a game of Sagol Kangjei.

Even three forgotten folk instruments—dang dung, roshem, and sarangdar—have been revived. Roshem is a local bagpipe made of bamboo, while Sarangdar requires horsetail hair. Dozens of idioms and local expressions that had disappeared have also been rediscovered. Sangh organisations in the Northeast are also actively involved in the People's Biodiversity Register, documenting local tribes' knowledge of their environment. This initiative serves as a defence against environmental destruction and the erosion of traditional ways of life, including agriculture, wetlands, forests, local fish, and wildlife habitats.

At the forefront of the RSS agenda is the preservation of traditional seeds. Native or heirloom seeds have evolved organically over generations and are well-adapted to local soil and climate conditions. The excessive use of chemicals in commercial farming often results in depleted nutrients in food, malnutrition, reduced yields, and even farmer suicides. There is a global movement—from the highlands of Guatemala to Oklahoma in the US and the valleys of

Manipur—to conserve seeds of traditional cereals, vegetables, and fruits.

While revitalising indigenous traditions, the RSS closely monitors infiltration and demographic changes. The BJP government has reintroduced the Inner Line Permit, an official document issued to allow Indian citizens to enter a protected area for a limited period. This permit serves as a shield against illegal immigrants. For similar reasons, local RSS leaders support the demand for scheduled tribe status by the Meiteis, the largest community in Manipur.

There is already concern about Rohingya Muslims from Myanmar illegally entering and settling down in towns like Jiribam and Lilong. It is a battle that cultural nationalists are determined to fight and win, rallying local populations to their cause.

Reconnecting People with Their Roots

India's cultural nationalists argue that reclaiming each inch in the Northeast metaphorically requires the effort of building many miles of roads. Large portions of the region's geography and mindset have been stripped of indigenous local traditions, leading to skewed demographics and the usurpation of jobs and livelihoods.

This is why the RSS dispatches activists from its core areas of influence to work in regions where sensibility to national interest has waned and its organisation is still developing. Though not always strictly adhered to, the Sangh tends to assign individuals from specific strongholds to particular areas in the Northeast. For instance, pracharaks or purnakaliks from the Pune region of west Maharashtra are often sent to Meghalaya's Khasi and Jaintia Hills. Those from Devgiri in Maharashtra typically find themselves in the Garo Hills. Swayamsevaks from Konkan and Mumbai are directed to Nagaland, while those from Karnataka are deployed to Manipur. Many from Vidarbha are assigned to Arunachal Pradesh. In Assam, the largest northeastern state, RSS workers from several states converge. Barak Valley (including Silchar and Karimganj) and Tripura see a significant number of volunteers from Bengal, mainly because Bengali is widely spoken by both locals and illegal immigrants in these areas.

Thirty-five-year-old Pratham Sambre, whose name has been changed upon request, came to work in the Khasi and Jaintia Hills of Meghalaya. He reminisces about his initial days in the region seven years ago:

> I was travelling on a bus, and an elderly woman was sitting next to me. I struck up a conversation with her, and she invited me to visit her home. I took her mobile number and eventually visited her family. That marked my first entry into a house in Meghalaya as a pracharak. Teachers, doctors, lawyers, and people from various professions here hold us in high regard. All pracharaks are addressed as babus.

The RSS commenced its operations in Meghalaya in 1946, with the establishment of the first shakha by Vasantrao Oak in Shillong. At that time, the state was a part of Assam, achieving full statehood on 21 January 1972. Oak, one of the Sangh's earliest pracharaks, had previously played a pivotal role in establishing the organisation in Delhi. His organisational skills were so remarkable that his colleagues began referring to him as 'Dillishwar' or the king of Delhi. Recognising the importance of extending the Hindutva movement to the hills, he, along with Dadarao Paramarth and Krishna Paranjpe, set up the first Northeast shakhas in Guwahati, Dibrugarh, and Shillong.

An incredibly challenging and uphill journey commenced. Thousands of volunteers sacrificed the prime years of their lives to work silently in the Northeast, resisting the demographic and cultural takeovers, and reconnecting people with their roots.

RSS leaders state that the aim of the Sangh in Christian-majority states like Meghalaya and Nagaland is to create nationalistic leadership with strong ideological moorings at the local level. The emphasis is on inculcating the right cultural values rather than engaging in religious conflicts.

In Manipur, for instance, even church schools have gradually been persuaded to incorporate nationalistic content, activities, and songs into their syllabus.

Shankar Dinkar Kane, fondly called Bhaiyyaji, established the Purva Seema Vikas Pratisthan to connect communities with the mainland and mainstream. Hailing from Chinchani Tarapur in Maharashtra, this mathematics and science teacher left his home in 1971 to pursue his dream in Manipur. He started his work in Imphal, later moving to Ukhrul and eventually settling in Tusom. Over the next fifteen years, he facilitated the relocation of more than 500 children to stay with families supportive of his cause in Maharashtra. They pursued their studies there before returning to Manipur to further their mission. After Kane's death, his pupils built a school in Kharason, about 15 km from the Myanmar border, and named it Oja Shankar Vidyalaya.

Integrating the Northeast with mainstream India can be as challenging as drying clothes in the open at the world's rainiest place, Mawsynram, located in Meghalaya. The Mongoloid features of Indians here, coupled with limited population exchanges due to decades of neglect and poor infrastructure, tend to alienate northeasterners from those in the heartland and southern India. Moreover, the seven states of the Northeast comprise over 200 tribes, speaking more than 200 languages according to the 2011 Census, with over a thousand dialects in existence.

Pratham says:

> Ekta Kapoor's serials often accomplish what we cannot. There are women living just 100 km away from Shillong who don't even know the city exists. Yet, even in these villages, women request the red mark ([tilak or bindi] for their foreheads because they have seen it in TV dramas. Young boys imitate characters like Chhota Bheem. In villages where Hindi isn't spoken by anyone else, only the children speak it, influenced by television, the internet, and now mobile phones.

The pracharaks endeavour to bridge the gap between the present and the past. Nagaland's capital Dimapur, for instance, was formerly known as Hidimbapur. According to legend, Pandava Bheem from the Mahabharata was married to the rakshasha princess Hidimba. In Dimapur, there is an overgrown park where one can find large, mostly broken chess pieces strewn around. Legend holds that Bheem used to play chess there with his and Hidimba's son, Ghatotkach.

The Idu Mishmi tribe of Arunachal Pradesh considers themselves descendants of Rukmini, the wife of Lord Krishna. When she fell in love with Krishna, her brother Rukmi vehemently opposed their marriage and attempted to compel her to marry Shishupal instead. Rukmini then secretly sent Lord Krishna a message. But Rukmi caught wind of the couple eloping and confronted them. In the ensuing duel, Krishna defeated him. however, at Rukmini's plea, instead of beheading him, Krishna shaved his head using his Sudarshan Chakra, the spinning disc. Thus, the Idu Mishmi tribesmen still cut their hair in a manner resembling a disc-shaped chop. They are referred to as Chulikatas. It is believed that they wear Lord Krishna's punishment as a badge of honour. Rukmini is revered and worshipped by them as Inyi Maselo, the Great Mother.

The Khasis of Meghalaya, renowned for their skill in archery, trace their lineage to Ekalavya, the tribal boy-warrior who famously sacrificed his thumb for Guru Dronacharya. Similarly, many Bodos of Assam believe themselves to be descendants of Brahma, while the Karbis of Assam claim ancestry from King Sugriva of the Ramayana. Throughout the Northeast, the tales of the Ramayana and Mahabharata intertwine intricately with life and tradition. Following these delicate threads, swayamsevaks painstakingly endeavour to sew the region's psyche into the broader tapestry of the nation.

A more challenging aspect for the Sangh in the Northeast is the consumption of beef. While staunchly opposed to cow slaughter in most other regions, the RSS demonstrates remarkable flexibility in the Northeast by accommodating the dietary preferences of the local populace.

Thousands of shakha-goers consume beef here. Pracharaks readily accept beef and liquor when offered, recognising it as local hospitality and a means to establish lasting bonds.

'In the Northeast, the RSS works like a river, navigating around large rocks. There is no fixed method; one has to be flexible. But one must know what one needs to achieve,' says Pratham. He cites the practicality of the RSS's second sarsangchalak or chief, Madhav Sadashiv Golwalkar, also known as 'Guruji', in uniting Hindus despite their remarkable diversity. Swayamsevaks say it is not uncommon to see a cow carcass hanging on the porch of a house, while photos of RSS pioneers Hedgewar and Golwalkar adorn the drawing room walls.

Golwalkar himself preferred the tree metaphor to explain the Northeast's relationship with the rest of India. In his book, *The Greater India Experiment: Hindutva and the Northeast*, scholar Arkotong Longkumer from the University of Edinburgh delves into Golwalkar's vision.

Longkumer writes:

> Golwalkar too uses arborescent imagery to explain national identity in his *Bunch of Thoughts*, ideas that are recycled in images and words in the Northeast. He uses the tree as a spatial metaphor to argue for a single way of life [Hindu] despite India's evident heterogeneity [language, customs, habits, etc.]. These variations, he says, are of the same tree, the 'same sap running through and nourishing all those parts. They are no more a source of dissension and disruption than a leaf or a flower is in the case of a tree. This kind of natural evolution has been a unique feature of our social life'. He calls on the national workers to nourish and strengthen the roots, without which the fruit will be sour and dry, so that 'we can stand free and erect amidst all tempests in the world'. Question those 'separatists' [in the Northeast], he says, who argue that tribals are animists and not Hindus. Isn't worshipping trees, stones, and snakes the common principle that links both the tribal and the Hindu? In fact, anima, or animus, is the principle of all life that is immanent in creation. 'Do not the Hindus all over the country worship the tree? Tulasi, Bilva, Ashwattha are all sacred to the Hindus.' This arboreal metaphor of the tree is an apt blueprint for the nation. Take away the place

names, the artificial state boundaries, the towns and cities, and all you have is a nation of trees and roots: it plots a certain order, fixes a point—one nation, one people, and one culture.

For Pratham, it is a constant process of learning, adjusting, assimilating, and thereafter, taking action. First, most local societies are matrilineal. Almost 80 per cent of the property is in women's names. Traditionally, the youngest daughter inherits the mother's land because she is left to take care of the parents while other siblings marry before her. Mama, or the maternal uncle, is the most revered relative in the family.

The elderly are always cared for within the family. It's rare to find old-age homes in the area. Also, strong family values ensure there are very few thefts. But men still find their way. 'People often have ten or eleven wives, with eight to ten children. They believe it is wrong to reject God's gifts,' says Pratham.

Nationalistic Identity and Pride

The march of Hindu nationalists in Meghalaya picked up pace after 1985. The RSS began working with the Garos, Jaintias, and Khasis, as well as the Hajong and Koch communities, which are tribes from the plains. Seva Bharati organises medical camps and provides educational aid. Today, Sangh outfits run medical camps in more than a thousand villages in Meghalaya. They also operate more than fifty schools in each of the eleven districts in the state.

Just in Shillong, there are fourteen RSS organisations operating, including Seva Bharati, Rashtriya Swayamsevak Samiti, ABVP, Sanskar Bharati, Seemanta Chetna Manch,

VHP, and Purva Sainik Parishad. The RSS has its own activities and runs community programmes in the Jaintia, Khasi, and Garo Hills.

In Shillong's Laitumkhrah, the local church head recently hoisted the saffron flag at an RSS function. Local swayamsevaks say that while the church leaders may not agree with the Sangh's ideology, they have a healthy respect for its social work. Additionally, they appreciate the importance the RSS gives them. 'Every local Christian leader loves being the chief guest. That is how we get them to our functions and open lines of communication,' says Pratham.

One of the Sangh's biggest challenges in Meghalaya is that the indigenous people lack many nationalistic icons to celebrate. This may be due to their reliance on oral traditions to pass down stories of valour and patriotism. The absence of literature and documentation makes it easier for imperialists and evangelists to erase stories of indigenous pride and identity. However, three individuals stand out.

The first is U. Kiang Nangbah, a Khasi freedom fighter who waged a guerrilla war against the British and led an uprising. He spearheaded the local resistance in the Jaintia Hills against the imposition of British taxes and the establishment of a police station in the area. The tipping point came in Yalong when the British police confiscated weapons intended for a traditional dance called Pastieh Kaiksoo and burned them in a bonfire as the locals watched helplessly.

Nangbah and his people retaliated by building barricades, stocking grains, and launching an armed attack that destroyed the police station, burned down Christian settlements, and seized a military post. He was arrested after one of his men betrayed him. The British publicly hanged him in Jowai town of West Jaintia Hills on 30 December 1862. A government college in Jowai was named after him in 1967. A postage stamp was issued in his memory in 2001 during the Vajpayee years. But, to this day, Nangbah has yet to receive a prominent mention in any of the nation's textbooks.

Then there was U. Tirot Sing Syiem, a Khasi chief who declared war against the British as they attempted to take over the Khasi Hills. He fought with traditional weapons like swords, shields, bows, and arrows, which were no match for the modern British weaponry and firepower. Despite his disadvantage, Tirot's men held out for four long years, engaging in guerrilla warfare, ambushing, and frustrating the imperial forces. He was shot and captured after one of his generals betrayed his location in exchange for gold. Tirot died in Dhaka on 17 July 1835 at the age of thirty-three.

Another local tale of daring is that of Pa Togan Sangma, the first Garo freedom fighter and a daredevil 'a-chik mande' (hill people) warrior. In 1872, he led a nighttime attack on a British contingent that had come to conquer the East Garo Hills while the British troops were sleeping. After the initial shock, the troops retaliated with modern firepower, completely overwhelming the tribe's traditional weapons. Sangma's innovation of using large shields made of plantain stems proved ineffective against bullets, and he was killed on the spot.

The Sangh has its own pantheon of martyrs in Meghalaya. One of them is the iconic local leader, Rijoy Sing Khongshah, hailing from Umniuh Tmar village in the picturesque Pynursla area of Meghalaya's East Khasi Hills. Rijoy was an RSS member and president of the local Seng Khasi Ri-War Mihngi unit. Seng Khasi is a cultural organisation dedicated to preserving and reviving the religion and traditions of the Niam Tre. It originated as a resistance movement against

British colonial rule in the Khasi and Jaintia hills and the widespread religious conversions carried out by Christian missionaries among the Khasi-Pnars.

Rijoy soon became a local hero. As his popularity continued to rise, he began receiving death threats from local militant organisations. However, he paid no heed to them. On 1 March 2001, while on his way to a meeting, he was kidnapped and never returned. Despite extensive protest rallies and a CBI inquiry, his body was never found.

Rijoy Sing Khongshah is the inspiration behind Pawnamshisha Khongsai's turn to nationalism and the initiation of social work. The wiry twenty-nine-year-old serves as the RSS secretary of Khasi Hill in the Ri-Bhoi district.

Khongsai joined the movement following Rijoy Sing's kidnapping and, in all likelihood, murder. 'Thanks to Rijoy, nearly every village in the Khasi Hills now has an RSS activist,' says Pawnam, whose father was closely associated with the locally renowned activist. 'I first met him when I was in Class III. I witnessed his tireless efforts, travelling from village to village, working for the indigenous people.'

He criticises the 'heavily pro-Christian media' in the state, alleging that it conceals regular atrocities committed by Christians against the indigenous people while sensationalising isolated incidents where Christians are the victims.

Pawnam resides in his wife's home, which is 20 km from Pynursla. He mentions that it was only after Narendra Modi became the prime minister that his village received infrastructure such as roads, electricity, toilets, and cooking gas cylinders.

'People never imagined they would have all these amenities in just five years. My village, Tynriang, is just one kilometre from the Bangladesh border, yet we now have access to all these facilities. Even the border fencing began after Modi took office,' he explains. He adds that indigenous youths admire Modi. Even many Christian youngsters began praising the prime minister after the Balakot air raids in response to the Pulwama terror attack. Interestingly, the local BJP block secretary is a young Christian man.

Pawnam, an MSc in physics, teaches in Pynursla. With the help of the RSS and the Seng Khasi, he has established a local higher secondary school. He is also associated with the Ramakrishna Mission, which works extensively in the interiors of Meghalaya and Arunachal Pradesh.

Sitting outside his modest, rustic house, one can observe hill dogs with furry tails basking in the sun amidst intermittent rain showers, a brood of hens pecking around, and goats bleating. The formality around the conversation slowly peels off, and a larger picture begins to emerge.

He mentions that about sixty families used to revert from Christianity to indigenous Hindu faiths every year in the Khasi Hills. But that number has significantly increased. He estimates that over 500 families have undergone ghar wapsi in the last five years.

If a young Khasi woman is affluent and educated and marries a Christian man, he sometimes undergoes reconversion on his own after marriage. Pawnam says in Pynter village, ten families were reconverted through his and RSS's efforts.

'We do not force anyone into reconverting or deceive them into returning to their original religion. We observe, maintain contact, and closely monitor their daily lives. When they face difficulties and the Church is unable to assist, they reach out to the "nong knia" or the Indigenous priest-doctor,' says Pawnam's fellow activist, Ba Engestar. 'From there, their journey back to their roots, their 1,000-years-old faith, begins.'

A Seng Khasi school supported by RSS was established in the area a few years ago. Several students were sent to Maharashtra, Delhi, or Assam for their education. They returned as doctors and lawyers, forming strong connections with the mainland.

The movement frequently encounters intense hostility. Outsiders are referred to as 'dakhar'. Pracharaks trying to enter a village or establish connections with residents have sometimes faced attacks and even fatalities. 'Last year, members of a church-backed NGO threatened me, asking, "Why are you bringing those dakhars?"' says Pawnam.

But Rijoy Sing Khongshah's spirit seems to have instilled a gentle yet steadfast determination among his followers in these areas. They do not back off easily; instead, they persistently chip away at everything that stands between them and their goal.

Reconversion from Christianity

On the way to Pynter village, nestled deep within the heart of the East Khasi Hills, the weather serves as a reminder that you are merely two hours away from two of the wettest places on Earth—Mawsynram and Cherrapunji. The car winds through narrow, rain-lashed roads flanked by pine, betel nut trees, broomgrass, and bay leaf plants. Beneath the sodden soil lie the niap seeds, harvested from a wild creeper and used as soap to cleanse the bodies of the deceased before cremation.

The annual rainfall in these parts, exceeding 10,000 mm, surpasses London's by more than fifteen times, painting the world outside the car window with the graceful blur reminiscent of a Turner painting.

In Pynter village, a group of five or six men sit in a dimly lit room, savouring the local rice beer, kyat, their voices barely audible over the constant patter of rain. Thirty-one-year-old Nikelson Khongmawloh serves as the Seng Khasi village prabhari or chief. He introduces Eliphiles Nongrum, who was formerly a Christian. In Nongrum's family, only his mother remains a practising Catholic; all others have undergone reconversion.

Then there is Jovenstone Nongkrot, sixty-two years old, with a white, unkempt shadow on his tanned and wrinkled face. He also underwent reconversion from Christianity.

Nikelson says:

> When Christians encounter troubles, they seek puja and indigenous rituals performed by a Seng Khasi priest. In their darkest hour, they revert to their roots. We simply aid them in reconnecting with their ancestral ties. Earlier, it was dangerous to do so. Since Modi came to power, we have shed our fear.

The men recount that three months ago, forty Christian families underwent reconversion in Mawngap in the East Khasi Hills. This occurred during a programme organised by the Lympung Sengkhihlang, which merges the Seng Khasi and Seinraij organisations.

Meghalaya

While Hindu nationalists strive to restore the demographic balance, in the same geographical area, almost as if in a parallel universe, Christians serve as foot soldiers of India's new nationalism.

Take Plielad Khongtiang, for instance. The thirty-five-year-old BJP worker is currently spearheading enrolment efforts for the party's local unit. Employed in the insurance sector of an Indian financial giant, he is a father to a three-year-old daughter. Khongtiang became a member of the BJP in 2013.

'Unlike many Christians, I hold a different perspective on the BJP. It is a corruption-free party, and that value aligns well with the teachings of Christianity,' says Plielad. 'When implementing schemes, the BJP does not consider caste or religion.'

He has the air of a man constantly on the move. He speaks while holding his black helmet, his mud-caked bike parked a few metres away. 'I oversee the village durbar, akin to a panchayat. Additionally, I lead the Catholic church in Pynursla. My role involves presenting facts to my community. The problem in Meghalaya is that people like to get things for free.'

He mentions that the local BJP leadership is weak. According to him, the local honcho is a good man but not a very effective leader. Additionally, there is something else that bothers Plielad a bit—he often doesn't get reimbursed for the fuel he uses for the extensive local travel demanded by his party work. Did he join the BJP for money? 'No,' he chuckles. 'I actually paid five rupees to join the party.'

He mentions one of the concerns shared by Hindus and Christians alike in Meghalaya—the increasing number of illegal Muslim settlers from neighbouring Bangladesh. 'Right now, the main issue in Meghalaya are the illegal Muslim immigrants. Many arrive from Bangladesh and reside here without proper documentation. In the church, they have started openly discussing the Muslim problem.'

Plielad believes that the people of his state and his community lack exposure to the world. He observes that they neither recognise real problems nor appreciate true progress. 'People here need to experience the world outside and learn more about our vast nation. I pursued an MBA in Bengaluru, so I have firsthand exposure.'

Nagaland

Even Nagaland, a state that has experienced almost uninterrupted insurgency and separatism since 1947, has witnessed the emergence of the BJP. The BJP currently holds power in Nagaland in alliance with the Nationalist Democratic Progressive Party (NDPP).

The tumultuous political history of modern Nagaland traces back to the arrival of British imperialists in the Naga Hills in 1832. The expedition was led by Captain Francis Jenkins and Lieutenant Robert Boileau Pemberton.

During World War I, the British government dispatched nearly 3,000 Nagas as part of the Naga Labour Corps to serve in the trenches as labourers and porters. Upon their return, they fostered a sense of shared Naga identity. In 1918, some of these individuals established the Naga Club in Kohima, which advocated for the British departure from their ancestral land.

Seventeen Naga tribes and twenty more sub-tribes united under the Naga National Council (NNC) in 1947, demanding an independent Nagaland. On 14 August 1947, the Nagas declared their independence. By 1954, the Indian Army moved into the Naga Hills to safeguard sovereign territory. Nagaland, initially a district in larger Assam, attained statehood as the sixteenth Indian state in 1963.

The Nagaland conflict is a complex blend of ethnic identity, foreign powers fuelling secessionist movements, and decades of governmental neglect of the region. Militant groups advocate for a distinct Constitution and flag.

In the report on the militant National Socialist Council of Nagaland (Issac-Muivah) [NSCN-IM], the South Asia Terrorism Portal of the Institute of Conflict Management writes:

> Over the years, the NSCN-IM has developed extensive linkages both within India and outside, and has also been receiving substantial assistance from neighbouring countries. The form of this assistance ranges from the supply of arms and ammunition and other logistical support to the provision of safe havens, camping and training facilities. Till 1971, the US was a major provider of arms, finance and intelligence. The erstwhile East Pakistan had also provided assured supplies of money and arms. Till the late 1980s, China also provided support to the organisation. Pakistan's Inter-Services Intelligence now provides a large component of finance, arms and logistic support to the NSCN-IM. The outfit has linkages with the Naga groups operating in Myanmar, and drug trafficking from Myanmar is a major source of income.

But even amidst this swirling current, the BJP's election symbol, the lotus, managed to find a way to bloom. 'The party's initial presence began to emerge in Nagaland in the early 1980s. I joined only because of Vajpayeeji,' says James Vizo, an executive member of the BJP. Vizo became a BJP karyakarta, or worker, in 2000, inspired by Atal Bihari Vajpayee's personal outreach in the region. He initially joined as district youth president, then ascended to district president, followed by becoming the Nagaland president of the Bharatiya Janata Yuva Morcha. Subsequently, he served as a spokesperson and became the first general secretary of the party from the state.

Vizo's rise in the BJP paralleled the party's staggering growth in Nagaland. Starting with just twenty to thirty members in the 1980s, it now boasts approximately 300 full-time karyakartas. However, the journey was far from easy for individuals like Vizo.

Vizo explains:

> They have falsely created an anti-minority image of the BJP and used it as a weapon. We, the karyakartas, know the truth. I have faced disdain in the past. Some believed we compromised our religion, Christianity, to work for the BJP. Churches discouraged us, and there was a lot of hardship. In 2018, my friend ran for office on a BJP ticket from Chizami. Opponents started pasting photos of Hindu deities on the church compound, implying the BJP's involvement.

He says Manmohan Singh never visited Nagaland during his ten years as the prime minister. But Vajpayee did. He even travelled on the state's narrow and dilapidated roads and constructed a four-lane highway from Kohima to Dimapur. A journey that previously took over three hours now takes one-and-a-half hours.

And then, in 2014, six months after being sworn in as the prime minister, Modi attended and inaugurated the internationally renowned Hornbill Festival in Nagaland.

'He has ushered in drastic changes. People have started receiving benefits such as rice, LPG, and medical insurance under central programmes. There is significant emphasis on highway construction,' says Vizo.

But insurgency persists in otherwise captivating Nagaland, like thorns to a local bijou flower. Vizo adds:

> It is not a straightforward matter. In the past, almost everyone was involved, but attitudes are changing. Today, insurgency still persists due to the involvement of various vested interests. Funding comes from external sources, serving as an alternative income for many. But people are becoming increasingly disillusioned. They remain silent because they are afraid of bullets. I won't use a strong term like nationalism, but the desire for a separate country is diminishing. Nobody wants to be part of China or Bangladesh.

But the ground of peace in these parts is riddled with unforeseen setbacks. On the early evening of 11 December 2021, a special unit of the Indian Army mistakenly opened fire on a pick-up van transporting coal miners from Tiru to their village of Oting, approximately 15 km away. Six individuals were killed on the spot. An hour later, seven more civilians and a soldier died when villagers retaliated. As a special investigation team delves into the facts, what appears to be an intelligence mishap sends years of hard work and trust-building spiralling backwards.

Despite such setbacks, the RSS quietly persists in carving out its presence in the state, much like the local alder trees. One of its most successful campaigns has been to delve into the story of the legendary Rani Gaidinliu. She revitalised the indigenous Heraka religion and spent her life fighting against first the British and then the missionaries who sought to convert local tribes to Christianity.

She was born in 1915 in Tamenglong district of present-day Manipur and passed away in 1993. As a Naga spiritual and political leader from the Rongmei tribe, she led an armed uprising against the British in Manipur, Nagaland, and Assam. Gaidinliu joined her cousin and guru, Haipou Jadonang, in the Heraka movement when she was just thirteen. Arrested by the British in 1932 at the age of sixteen, she was sentenced to life imprisonment. Following her release in 1947, she resumed her activism. Nehru referred to her as the 'daughter of the hills' and bestowed upon her the title 'Rani'. She was awarded a Padma Bhushan. A statue was erected in Silchar in her honour, and a postal stamp, a film, and a coin have been issued in her memory.

The Sangh began to incorporate her legend into their work in the 1970s, aligning with her Heraka religious movement. The church became alarmed, but Gaidinliu's story began to take root in the Naga psyche.

Portraits of Gaidinliu adorn every Kelumki or Heraka temple. The Zeliangrong Heraka Association (ZHA) maintains a close alignment with the RSS. Zeliangrong individuals who had converted to Christianity are now returning to the Heraka fold. A team of hingdepaupeus or preachers actively encourages people to reconnect with their roots. Operating in villages across the Zeliangrong region, which spans parts of Assam, Manipur, and Nagaland, the ZHA assigns preachers to each circle. RSS-backed institutions and schools like the Saraswati Vidya Mandirs collaborate in these efforts.

In her paper titled 'Rani Gaidinliu, the Iconic Woman of Northeast India', Ajailiu Niumai of Hyderabad University wrote:

> She strategically combined the Heraka religion with politics to fulfil her goals in fighting against the British rulers. Her story illustrates a rationality that would encourage marginalised

and invisible women to become leaders in both socio-political and spiritual spheres. Such empowerment would bring about social inclusion and supersede patriarchal structures at home as well as in the public space. She showed how her community, in particular, and the Nagas could integrate with mainland India. Rani Gaidinliu managed to encourage her people to preserve their traditional and cultural heritage as she stood at the intersection of many important events such as religious currents, the Naga movement, and the freedom struggle.

Assam

One of the most intense frontlines in India's battle against illegal immigration and demographic change is Assam, the largest state in the Northeast. At the turn of the last century, Assam's Muslim population stood at 12.4 per cent. By the time of the first census conducted after Independence in 1951, it had doubled to 24.7 per cent. In 2011, the Muslim population had further increased to 34.2 per cent, and it is now believed to have reached 40 per cent. Districts such as Barpeta, Bongaigaon, Darrang, Dhubri, Goalpara, Hailakandi, Karimganj, Morigaon, Nagaon, Hojai, and South Salmara already have more than 50 per cent Muslim population.

The profound demographic shift has not happened organically or indigenously. It has been driven by rampant illegal migration, mainly from Bangladesh. It started along the riverine islands in the Brahmaputra, starting from the bordering Dhubri to Darrang and beyond, with thousands of boats surreptitiously entering Indian waters over the years. The immigrants subsequently spread to the state's cities, towns, and villages, encroaching even upon parts of tribal belts such as Bodoland, Tiwa and Mising autonomous councils, Karbi-Anglong, and north Kachar Hills. Political interests aiming to secure a loyal vote bank from thin air, unchecked corruption within civic and police administrations, and public complacency have created fertile ground for this systematic cultural, geographic, and economic takeover.

The last National Register of Citizens (NRC) exercise in Assam led to a significant number of genuine citizens being excluded from the list, while millions with questionable claims to citizenship managed to make their way onto it for similar reasons. Assam has long been known as a hub for the production of fake documents and manipulation of legacy data. Activists assert that the police are heavily influenced by those who facilitate the settlement of illegal immigrants in the state, resulting in complaints of encroachment being seldom addressed and sometimes met with silence or even violence.

Demographic change lies at the core of Assam's political landscape like an ischemic heart. The Assam agitation of the 1970s and 1980s centred around the 3 Ds: detection, detention, and deportation of illegal aliens. The backlash against immigration was so intense that after six years of turbulent movement, the Assam Accord was signed in 1985 to protect the cultural, economic, and political rights of the ethnic Assamese.

But the Illegal Migrants Determination by Tribunal (IMDT) Act, introduced by the then prime minister Rajiv Gandhi of the Congress, proved disastrous as it made the first step—detection—nearly impossible. The complainant had to prove that a person immigrated illegally. On 5 December 2006, Supreme Court Justice S.B. Sinha and Justice P.K. Balasubramanyan struck down the IMDT Act. Justice Sinha observed that the Rajiv Gandhi regime had enacted 'an act which had no teeth and which, instead of aiding identification, was intended to obstruct it'.

The repeal of the IMDT Act coincided with the arrival of Badruddin Ajmal on Assam's political horizon. He epitomised everything that both Assamese Hindus and Muslims dreaded—a wealthy perfume merchant who became the bellicose voice of the immigrant Muslim Bengali population.

A staunch, homebred nationalism began to rise, akin to the spirit of the great Ahom Lachit Borphukan, the king and naval master strategist who famously defeated the Mughals on the Brahmaputra in the Battle of Saraighat.

Politicians like Tarun Gogoi began embracing soft Hindutva, often participating in overt pujas for the cameras. Young leaders such as Sarbananda Sonowal and Himanta Biswa Sarma—both of whom would later become chief ministers in Assam's recent and current BJP governments—adopted a stridently anti-immigrant stance. Sonowal, a tribal, assumed the chief minister's role in 2016, leading to a significant number of tribal communities aligning themselves with nationalist sentiments.

The tribals also shared with the general Assamese population the burden of the demographic takeover of their land and culture. State action was minimal and tedious. As late as 2020, only 329 of the 1.43 lakh people declared foreigners by the Foreigners' Tribunal in the state had been deported to Bangladesh.

Clause 6 of the Assam Accord is the only barrier against that tide of immigration. It reads: 'Constitutional, legislative, and administrative safeguards, as may be appropriate, shall be provided to protect, preserve, and promote the cultural, social, linguistic identity, and heritage of the Assamese people.'

In 2021, the Assam government set up another panel, the fourth in thirty-six years, to push for its implementation. The safeguards that these panels have drawn up are robust. They recommend 80–100 per cent reservation in Assam's parliamentary, assembly, and local bodies for 'Assamese people'. Also, the same percentage in central and state government jobs. Besides, they propose watertight land rights and the use of the official language favouring the local population in Assam's mainland, Barak Valley, hill districts, and the Bodoland Territorial Area Districts. 'When?' is the question. Meanwhile, a ferocious territorial battle unfolds.

The birthplace of Srimanta Sankardev, the 15th-century ethno-religious leader and father of the Assamese identity, was once entirely encroached upon in Nagaon. Sarbananda Sonowal cleared these encroachments when he was the chief minister.

After Himanta Biswa Sarma became the chief minister in 2021, he evicted illegal Bangladeshi immigrants from the 180 bigha, or half-a-square-kilometre, of land surrounding the historic Dholpur Shiv mandir in Sipajhar, Darrang. This riverine stretch used to be swamped with settlers.

And then came the Garukhuti eviction, the forced removal of residents from the Garukhuti area driven by government efforts to clear land for development or other purposes, which led to significant controversy and opposition.

Major Avinash Upadhyay of the Indian Army, posted with the Territorial Army's 134 Ecological Task Force, was on duty on 23 September. The thirty-seven-year-old sinewy man from Ballia, the hometown of freedom hero Mangal Pandey, had joined the army in 2006.

On that September day, two people were killed and about ten injured in police action in Darrang. An armed mob had attacked the officials. A local photographer complicated matters by jumping on a man dying from police bullets. It made national and international headlines. Media and activists built a narrative of peaceful Muslim settlers being attacked by a bigoted administration.

But local accounts and credible, in-depth media reports suggest that the truth lies elsewhere. Upadhyay says that the river islands on the Brahmaputra from Dhubri to Darrang have been taken over by Bangladeshi immigrants. He further adds:

> When the flood comes, boats from Bangladesh start sneaking into Assam. The swelling waters make it extremely difficult for India's border security to monitor and check infiltration. They grow maize and use the kernel as fuel to cook during the floods. They build self-sufficient systems.

In Mangaldoi alone, 33,000 bighas, or 85 square kilometres, of land are under occupation. Gradual clearance under the Assam chief minister's Garukhuti Project has started. But evictions are not enough. The locals must learn how to make that land valuable and hold on to it.

Upadhyay says he trains ordinary farmers to become agri-soldiers—those who set up agricultural projects with the administration's help but also know how to fight for the land and defend it. Padma Hazarika, an All Assam Students Union strongman and leader from the 1980s, had also tried this approach.

But the problem has spread too deep and wide for such sporadic efforts. Reporting from the ground in Assam, Siddharth Singh, editor-at-large of *Open Magazine,* wrote about how both local Muslims and Hindus bore the brunt of immigration.

'Our land, like any other char, is fertile. Once the waters [of the river] recede, the land is ready for cultivation. No fertilisers are required. But now, many families have lost their land to the miyas [a term for Bengali Muslims],' says Islam.

The area has a long history of illegal migration, but it is now beyond a tipping point as the very survival of the community is at stake. 'We grew up with the Bhatias [Bengali-origin Muslims], but now they want our land. When we try to assert our identity, our language, and our mores, they turn to social media against us, claiming we display un-Islamic tendencies,' says Hafizur (name changed), a college graduate who works in the area.

According to Hafizur, the miyas are well-organised and have money and a network that helps them. 'Our ancestors were Koch people who lived freely on this land. They never thought about getting papers for the land. Now we are paying the price for that ignorance,' he says.

In Nagaon, land belonging to sattras or Vaishnavite monasteries has been usurped. Singh's report from December 2021 indicates that the lands of the Rampur sattra, as well as those at Norua, Bordowa, and Patekibori, have been taken away.

Besides encroachments along the river banks, outsiders acquire land through legal means. An entrenched nexus of politicians, bureaucrats, police, and forgers of legal and legacy documents facilitates illegal immigration. Bribery occurs openly. Local residents assert there is discrimination against the Hindu workforce. Assamese Muslims often secure work orders from the administration and delegate the work to their Bangladeshi counterparts. The direct economic loss to Assam and India due to illegal immigration amounts to billions of dollars.

Upadhyay says:

> The Brahmaputra banks have baandhs or dykes. Wherever there are evictions, one should construct baandhs to prevent the ingress of boats. By blocking access for boats coming from rivulets, and promoting fisheries and irrigation, Assam can become the food basket of Asia. We can create a vibrant economy from the ecology.

He envisions farming the robust Assamese variety of pigs and using cattle and pig excreta for fisheries. He suggests that ex-servicemen could train agri-soldiers in each district.

Local RSS shakhas have increased in number. Vidya Bharti operates 121 primary schools, 115 middle schools, and 341 secondary schools in the state, with nearly 2 lakh students enrolled. Additionally, there are 540 Ekal Vidyalayas or single-teacher schools. Other RSS affiliates such as the VKA, Seva Bharti, and VHP have been active in the region for decades.

Arunachal Pradesh

Similar to the Seng Khasi in Meghalaya and the Heraka in Nagaland, Donyi Polo, an ancient tribal faith, has resurfaced in a new avatar in Arunachal Pradesh, uniting the twenty-six major tribes and more than a hundred sub-tribes. Donyi and Polo signify the sun and the moon, respectively.

In 1968, the Adi and Galo tribes held a sombre meeting to resist the growing influence of Christian missionaries in the state. Talom Rukbo, a founding member of the Donyi Polo Yelam Kebang (DPYK), where yelam represents belief and kebang signifies a tribal council, served as the language officer before retiring to dedicate himself to full-time activism.

Rukbo and his friend Arek Megu transformed an orally transmitted faith into a fully structured institutional religion, yielding remarkable results. There are discussions about the development of a script for it. Donyi Polo Day was commemorated on 31 December 2019, with a bhoomi pujan or foundation worship, attended by RSS functionaries. Additionally, the local Rangfra faith, believed to be a variant of Vaishnavism, is gaining prominence.

The Congress party and some Church bodies are livid. They allege that the BJP and the RSS are driving their ghar wapsi or reconversion agenda in Arunachal, posing a threat to Christianity.

The underlying theme driving the rise of nationalism or the revival of indigeneity has been the apprehension of a demographic decline due to the assertive spread of evangelical Abrahamic religions. In Tripura, for instance, the BJP built social coalitions with various tribes, who had become a minority in the state and secured a landslide victory in the 2018 elections, ending the Left's rule of twenty-five years.

Back in Shillong, Pracharak Pratham Sambre offers insight into the new Indic resurgence in the Northeast:

> Around fifty years ago, there were doubts about the Northeast's allegiance to India. Now, it is certain that it won't go anywhere. Earlier, Independence Day on 15 August or Republic Day on 26 January had little impact here. Now, both are celebrated with a lot of fervour in most areas.

In the Garo Hills alone, which were once extremely hostile to nationalism, there are nine Vidya Bharti schools run by the RSS and nearly a hundred ekal vidyalayas. 'That is the kind of change the Sangh's extensive work has brought to the Northeast,' he says contentedly, scooping up tungrymbai, a local fermented soybean dish, with a piece of chapati.

CHAPTER 8

Bharat's Queer and Conservative

In popular perception, all LGBTQ+ people in India are Left-minded, anti-Hindutva, and bitterly opposed to Narendra Modi. At Pride events and on Instagram, images abound of angry non-binary youngsters mouthing Marxist tropes and carrying anti-Hindutva placards. Mainstream and social media amplify these images and stereotypes.

In reality, a vast and silent section of LGBTQ+ people exists beyond those small urban gatherings, feeling more comfortable within the Indic social fold than within Western constructs of gender and identity. Many among them are Hindutva and Modi supporters and avid nationalists. Quite a few have emerged as vocal spokespersons for that population.

They argue that much more has been done for same-sex and non-binary people during Modi's years in power than under so-called 'secular' and 'liberal' governments, such as the United Progressive Alliance led by the Congress or the United Front.

On 6 September 2018, for instance, the Supreme Court decriminalised homosexual acts under Section 377 of the Indian Penal Code. A five-judge Constitution bench overturned a 157-year-old British-era law which held anal or oral sex 'against the order of nature'.

According to Chief Justice Dipak Misra and Justice A.M. Khanwalkar:

> An examination of Section 377 IPC on the anvil of Article 19(1)(a) reveals that it amounts to an unreasonable restriction, for public decency and morality cannot be amplified beyond a rational or logical limit and cannot be accepted as reasonable grounds for curbing the fundamental rights of freedom of expression and choice of the LGBT community. Consensual carnal intercourse among adults, be it homosexual or heterosexual, in a private space, does not in any way harm public decency or morality.

While credit must go to the Supreme Court, Modi's government was the first to inform the court that it would not oppose petitions challenging Section 377. A supposedly 'ultra-conservative' government did what its 'liberal' and 'progressive' predecessors could not.

Additionally, the RSS publicly declared for the first time that while it did not encourage homosexuality, what happens between two consenting adults is a private matter that should not be criminalised. The statement by one of its senior-most functionaries, Dattatreya Hosabale, marked a radical departure from the Sangh's earlier standpoint. It signalled a generational rethink and demonstrated a level of flexibility and adaptation that RSS's adversaries would never credit it with, even in their most generous moment.

Following this, the Modi government introduced the Transgender Persons (Protection of Rights) Bill, 2019, in the Lok Sabha. The Rajya Sabha passed it on 26 November 2019.

The law defines a transgender person as someone whose gender does not match the gender assigned at birth. It includes trans men, trans women, persons with intersex variations[1], genderqueers, and persons with sociocultural identities such as kinnar and hijra. The law prohibits discrimination against a transgender person, including denial of service or unfair treatment in relation to: education; employment; healthcare; access to, or enjoyment of goods, facilities, opportunities available to the public; right to movement; right to reside, rent, or otherwise occupy property; opportunity to hold public or private office; and access to a government or private establishment in whose care or custody a transgender person remains.

In August 2020, the National Council for Transgender Persons (NCT) was established. It serves as an advisory body to the central government, guiding policies, programmes, legislation, and projects aimed at achieving equality and full participation of transgender people. NCT will also analyse and coordinate the activities of all government departments and NGOs. Its purpose includes resolving grievances faced by transgender people.

Adding symbolism to action, PM Modi participated in yoga sessions with LGBTQ+ individuals on World Yoga Day in 2022.

Abhijit Iyer-Mitra

One of the most prominent and controversial voices advocating for the Indic resurgence is Abhijit Iyer-Mitra, a security and strategic affairs expert. He is affiliated with the Institute of Peace and Conflict Studies, a security-focused think tank, where he focuses on nuclear and defence matters. He also contributes to the Observer Research Foundation, writing on security issues and speaking at conferences worldwide.

Both of his parents were bureaucrats. His Bengali father retired as an additional secretary (defence). His mother, V.S. Chandralekha, was Tamil Nadu's first woman collector and a close associate of Subramanian Swamy. She retired as a secretary in the Tamil Nadu government.

As he sits wearing a flowing cobalt blue cotton kurta and white pyjamas at a bookstore-cum-cafe in Delhi's Khan Market, the conversation flows alongside shots of espresso and tall iced teas.

> In those days, it was scandalous to have an inter-caste, inter-regional marriage, but I always enjoyed scandalising people, so, it was great fun. I was born in Madras. Then, there was a period in Kolkata that I don't remember at all. After that, we shifted to South Arcot, a district in the Madras Presidency of British India, covering the area of the present-day districts of Cuddalore, Kallakurichi, and Villupuram in Tamil Nadu. It was amazing because the collector's bungalow was my mom's residence. It was Robert Clive's own house, his personal estate. Imagine living in a historical house. Lots of memories out there. Then my parents divorced when I was around five or six, and they had an agreement that I would go wherever the education was better. My dad got posted to Moscow, so I went to the American School there, and then to Vienna to the American School. After that, my dad got posted to Srinagar.

Abhijit's father was posted there as the accountant general of Kashmir. He hated school because of its swimming pool. 'The water was completely untreated. It was just Jhelum water that would come in. Often, when you put your head down in the water, you would come up with a huge scorpion or a centipede or something on your face. It was scary as hell,' he explains.

He then moved to Delhi and enrolled in Delhi Public School, Mathura Road. From the tenth grade onwards, he attended Vidyamandir in Chennai.

> There were three different philosophies of learning. The American School encouraged individuality; it prioritised problem-solving and being yourself. I was always at the top of the class there. But, when I entered the Indian schooling system, I realised it aimed at completely squeezing the individuality out of you. It is not interested in your opinion or analysis; you basically are a walking, talking photocopy machine. And that wasn't me, so I was always at the bottom of the class. Then I came to Vidyamandir in Chennai. They were very clear that it wasn't about marks. It was a great school. I wanted to do my BA in economics or history. My mom was very clear: 'You're not going to get a job. You have to do your BCom.' So, I did my BCom from Vivekananda College, and again, I hated it. Bookkeeping was the most boring subject for me. But it helped me in the long run.

Then he spent two years at his mother's farm in Ooty. He smuggled in Hungarian pigs and chickens, and mated the foreign chickens with the local country ones.

> I managed to sell pork to the American embassy—really good quality pork. All the pork you eat today is post-war meat optimised. Before that, pork was mostly raised for its fat because in northern Europe, olive oil was not as prevalent, so pig fat served as the primary cooking medium and was

> much tastier. There were two best types: the Iberico pig in Spain and the Hungarian Mangalica pig. I acquired a pair of Mangalicas. There is also a very famous French chicken called poulet de Bresse. I smuggled their eggs via Italy. I was involved in animal husbandry until my mom received the bills. To fatten those pigs, you have to feed them nuts. Even with just five or six pigs, it took almost a hundred kilos of nuts … it was pretty damn expensive. My mother said, 'I don't care how much you're selling it for. The point is the input costs are too high.' I never did my BCom too well.

He enrolled at JNU but only lasted two months. He describes his experience with his supervisor, the Leftist academician Kamal Mitra Chenoy, as traumatising, 'He was so full of nonsense. He never made time for opposing viewpoints. His classes were nothing but propaganda. Once, I attended Jayati Ghosh's class, and that too was filled with propaganda.' His brief JNU stint made him run away to Australia to become a chef and join Le Cordon Bleu.

> I was out of money because my mom and I weren't talking anymore after I ran out on her. But I loved cooking so much that I didn't want to make it my profession because, you know, that's how you destroy your hobby. So, what I did was I converted it into a hotel management course. I did my internship in northern Australia at this beautiful hotel called the Sheraton Mirage Port Douglas. The main reason I went there was because I hated Sydney. I was in the Blue Mountains, which were beautiful, but they were too cold for me. I like warmer weather, a beach kind of environment. So, I ended up in Port Douglas, which is just 70 km north of Cairns, known for having the highest concentration of millionaires anywhere in Australia.

There, he even appeared as an extra in the 2008 movie *Fool's Gold*, starring Matthew McConaughey and Kate Hudson, Goldie Hawn's daughter.

> I realised that in Australia, they expect a lot of value addition from you. I realised the Indian view of work was all wrong because, in the Indian view of intelligence, if you can speak well, you are intelligent. That doesn't translate into intelligence because the hotel industry requires you to problem-solve. In India, when you talk to Zomato or Uber customer care, they say, 'Very sorry sir, very sorry sir', but they seldom solve your problem. There you are paid to solve the problem right away when somebody approaches you. So, it was great mental training. There, being smart wasn't about making smart comments; it was problem-solving. There you are actually encouraged to say 'no' to guests. If it is something you can't do, just say 'no', but immediately come up with three other options for guests. It was brilliant for training my mind for defence studies later on because that was what I wanted to do anyway. History and geography were always my best subjects. It is almost like training your mind in a military way. When you hit an obstacle, don't keep pushing at it. You will find ways of circumventing it. I learned a lot more in those five years in hospitality than I ever did in JNU and BCom combined because it gives you life skills.

After a while in the hospitality industry, he grew bored with the repetitive nature of customer complaints, problems, and solutions. He returned to his interest in international relations.

> I wrote a letter to Monash University expressing my interest in joining their international relations course. However, they

responded, 'Look, your marks aren't very good, so we can't offer you admission to the master's programme, but here is what we can do for you.' Once again, it was a case of 'No, but...' They proposed that I enrol in something called a graduate certificate in international relations, which spans one semester. Completing three of those semesters would lead to a master's degree. 'And if you score very well in that one semester, we can automatically upgrade it to a master's degree for you.' So, I closed shop, moved to Melbourne, and was admitted to Monash University. It was a great experience. I topped the class again. There seems to be a consistent pattern: whenever I am out of India, I consistently rank at the top of my class, whereas in India, I often find myself at the bottom. Within one semester, they offered me a teaching opportunity. Eager to accept, I began teaching a class on political Islam and strategic studies even before completing my master's degree. It was great fun.

Because he was teaching political Islam, the university wanted him to learn Arabic and sent him off for a course at the University of Damascus in 2006 to learn Arabic for six months. After Abhijit came back to Melbourne, he experienced a bitter break-up with his boyfriend. 'I decided to move back to India because I was going through an emotional crisis,' he says.

Once back in India, he joined a think tank, the Institute of Peace and Conflict Studies (IPCS).

There is virtually no primary research here, which was really shocking to me. On the other hand, the level of foreign, especially American, interest in India was enormous. That's when I started to focus on the human factor. For example, how do you maintain a strategically autonomous position when you don't have linguists in your foreign ministry? Everything for you has to be in English. You keep criticising the *New York Times* and *Washington Post*, yet those are your only sources of information because most of your people can't read *Der Spiegel* or *Paris Splash*. So, you are getting a completely Anglophile view that's controlled by these countries, which these countries themselves don't rely on. They train linguists who read local papers, who serve in those countries, even Vietnamese and Cambodians—they learn, go there, serve.

The first break Abhijit got after returning to India was at the *Pioneer*. Senior editor and nationalist ideologue Kanchan Gupta was known for giving young, bright individuals the opportunity to write. He said, 'You are good. You are kind of Right Wing.' Abhijit replied, 'I am not kind of Right Wing; I am quite Right Wing.' Kanchan Gupta then said, 'Very well, start writing.' He gave Abhijit a fortnightly column in the *Pioneer*, which he wrote for about three years.

Then he joined the Observer Research Foundation (ORF) and had its president, Samir Saran, as his mentor. 'He is a great boss because he pushes you into areas that you are uncomfortable with, and he has already planned your career out for you before you know it,' he says. After a while, he returned to IPCS.

Abhijit grew up as a hardcore communist. When his diplomat father was posted in Moscow, his greatest ambition was to be recruited by the KGB. He says he even went to the KGB office in Lubyanka, only to be politely shown the door.

There is a statue of Felix Dzerzhinsky, founder of the Soviet security service, out there. Because my American school bus used to pass by it, I made it a point to get out and salute the statue just to annoy the Americans. No other reason. I had read Marx. My father was quite Left-Wing, but he was getting worried about how far Left I was leaning. My mom was always Right-Wing. She was more pro-American and supportive of the free market.

Travelling from 1980s India to Moscow and St Petersburg, witnessing the great imperial palaces, imposing architecture, science, and opera had made him marvel at communism, although much of that was from a pre-communist era. But Tiananmen Square changed its views. His notion that communism is all about student power was shattered.

I was still a Leftist for quite some time until I came across, believe it or not, Ayn Rand. I was in the twelfth standard. It made me turn hard Right. But then what brought me back to a sort of centrist position was Albert Camus. When you start reading *The Plague* and *The Stranger*, they force you to be more humanist. You stop being theoretically hard Right. Until I was twenty-seven, I was Left-leaning. Even in Australia, for example, I remember hating John Howard when he went to war in Iraq. But when you sit down and talk to the Right out there, they are very clear about things. They are not ballistic or anything. I was slowly seeing how Right-Wing economics was helping on the ground. It's not subsidising failure but actually rewarding success.

What really pushed him over to the Right was when Barack Obama took over as the President of the US. 'I thought, this man is one of the worst peddlers of identity and subsidisers of victimhood. Everything that I hated about the Right—being identity-pushers, irresponsible greed—turned out to be far more true about Obama,' he says.

Abhijit says he is an atheist and still very uncomfortable with religion. He goes to temples to appreciate the architecture, he says, not for puja.

> As a kid, I used to be a Durga bhakt because I grew up in a Bengali household. But I have never needed spirituality to maintain moral composure. But I always identify as a Hindu because that is very important to me. My ideas of atheism come from Charvaka school of thought, not from Western literature.

Freedom fighter and Hindutva icon Vinayak Damodar Savarkar strongly influenced him. Abhijit read some of his essays and his book on the 1857 mutiny in his twenties. He connected instantly with Savarkar's atheism and his economically Right views.

But the most profound influence on him has been his parents'. Their openness has left a deep imprint on him as well.

Abhijit's father was a cartographer, as well as a diplomat, so he grew up surrounded by maps. He could pinpoint anything on a map, possibly giving him a foreign-policy thought orientation from a young age. Knowing six to seven languages made it easier for him to understand a broad spectrum of words.

They did not even have a beef with him having beef despite being a Hindu.

> Even though my mom was uncomfortable with me eating beef, she always insisted that I should try beef. If I didn't want to eat it, I would do it for myself and not because she forbade me to eat it. Even now you would see me on Twitter very open

about being gay, very open about eating beef. It doesn't take anything away from my Indianness, although I accept that different people's interpretations of Hinduness can vary. The point is, I don't push my Hinduism down your throat, and you don't shove your Hinduism down mine. Unfortunately, there is a very dangerous trend happening right now, which is the Abrahamisation of Hinduism.

Abhijit has been extremely vocal against intolerance, spirit of blasphemy and apostasy, and hard religious prescriptions creeping into a fluid faith like Sanatan Dharma.

In addition to being trolled by a section of the Hindu Right for posting on social media about his beef-eating, has the RSS also hounded him about eating beef?

> All the RSS pracharaks I have met have always been 'theek hain'. Surprisingly, the RSS has never hounded me. Some individuals who claim to be part of the Hindu Right, but are not associated with the RSS, get upset because they are recent converts. They are trying to be more Hindu than the Hindus. I have met the RSS sarsanghchalak [chief] once. I have met pracharaks several times, but they were perfectly accepting of it. They may not be pleased about it, but they never try to impose anything on you. They say, '*Bhaiya, khana hain toh khao, par kyun hamare naak mein ragadte ho* [Brother, eat if you want, but why do you have to rub it in)?' Which is fair enough. I respect that.

Abhijit ticks all the boxes for the elitist, Left-leaning liberal. He is the classic 'Lutyens elite': wealthy, with both parents as bureaucrats, drinks, eats beef, and is an atheist. He says:

> But what turned me against the Left was identity politics and the fake posturing and thought control that they have

always attempted. I never fit in. What used to irritate me was the sheer mediocrity on the Left. They were third-raters with very, very high opinions of themselves.

As he started getting introduced to other people on the Right, being invited to Right-Wing conferences, he began to find the people much more honest than Leftists, much less prone to posturing. He found his 'imagined community' online. He found half of his closest friends on Twitter.

> It doesn't mean that I don't have my disappointments with the Right. For example, there is a very loud but small group on the Right which says, 'We should only speak in Hindi.' For me, language serves a purpose; it is a means to an end, which is the transfer of information. The only reason nationalism suits a purpose for me is because it is better than the alternatives. I believe in nationalism, mostly because we are at a stage where we are not in the European stage of development. We are in an Asian pre-industrial stage of development where nationalism is necessary. The state needs to be stronger; it needs to take on the monopoly of violence, and societal violence needs to decrease.

He says he is economically hard Right, but he understands that in a country like India, one can't just allow people to starve to death because they don't work. He, however, is critical of what he perceives as Narendra Modi's socialist instincts, such as spending on large welfare programmes, subsidies, direct benefit transfers and suchlike.

> I am very clear about my Hindu identity. If you come up with a movement that suppresses identity equally, fine. But I am very clear about it: my identity is better than yours. Full stop.

There are no 'ifs' and 'buts'. I am unequivocal about it, which is why, culturally, I would say I am on the Right. In an area of competitive identity, I identify unambiguously as a Hindu. Economically, I am on the Right. I believe in nationalism in the Indian context. It is my criticism of Modi that he is a saffron communist, who is probably not even saffron.

In terms of strategic defence thinking, he is critical of the current government. He notes that most defence experts in India advocate for 100 per cent indigenisation. However, he argues that this approach does not align with modern industry practices, pointing out that even the US cannot afford total indigenisation.

He cites specific policy decisions, such as the continued focus on the Tejas (Indigenous Light Combat Aircraft), and expresses skepticism about HAL and DRDO despite ongoing funding. He suggests that, although ISRO is a great organisation, it could become much more efficient if it were restructured and its production activities were handed over to the private sector.

He says he might join politics at some stage. But in the same breath, he says he can't do mass mobilisation on the ground. 'I am the Rajya Sabha type. I am more the type who will sit and come out with policies. I can never be a mass leader. My whole life has been about pissing off people. You can't win an election by pissing off people,' he says.

He then talks about his encounters with the Indian Right on the issue of his sexuality. It has been a refrain of the Left that the Right is homophobic. Abhijit bluntly denies it.

This thing about multiple genders … this is the thing about Hinduism. It never stops you from exploring your sexuality.

> You are a man in love with a man. *Theek hain, kar lo.* You are a woman in love with a woman. *Theek hain, kar lo.* It has never been like, say, the Judeo–Christian genre, which was [stoning] to death. I have never actually faced homophobia on the Right at all. In fact, it has been quite the opposite.

Abhijit says that Left-Wing identity politics around LGBTQ+ issues often rest on a victimhood narrative. According to him, their identity is not built on being gay but on the victimhood associated with it. 'When I challenge them on this, I have never actually come across an genuine case of homophobia,' he says.

He adds that the Indian Right was actually welcoming and encouraging when he came out as gay.

> My Grindr and Tinder were full of messages saying we are glad you came out about being gay and being Right Wing and unapologetically Right Wing because we feel so constrained. If we come out with a Right-wing Hindu identity, the Left gets unsettled because all their social support structures are this pansy, free-Palestine, free-Kashmir kind of gay people who are all in the fashion or creative industry or some stuff like that. There are stories that I have been hearing on Grindr and Tinder. My Grindr is full of people trying to hook up with me these days; they are the ones also trying to talk to me about politics.

He says a lot of people write to him from Tier 2 cities like Pune who have not come out fearing they would be mocked at the workplace. They hide themselves at work but also conceal their political choices from the LGBTQ+ community.

> There are people from my old Monash University, which has apparently become a Leftist bastion, where people have to

hide who they are. Every narrative I hear out there is 'How do I find the courage to come out and say I am conservative, Right-Wing, and gay?' Similarly, people send me messages saying, 'How do I say I am Hindu and I am gay?' Now there are five or six of us on Twitter who are strong voices for those who are Right-Wing and gay.

He advises queer conservatives to come out. He says it is not as tough as it seems.

> Be financially independent first, then come out, because in India, nobody actually gives a damn about these things. In my case, I came out and everybody was okay with it. In a sense, my mother wasn't. She wanted me to see a shrink. The coolest thing was when we went up to the ancestral temple in Palakkad, the old head priest who never left those five villages, said, 'Love is between two souls; the body is immaterial to it.' And my mom was like, 'WTF, dude!'

Abhijit was jailed for forty-three days for making fun of the sexual figurines at Odisha's Konark Sun Temple in one of his signature prank videos, referring to it as 'humple'. It was one of the biggest challenges to his rebellious showmanship. His fellow inmates included Saradha chit-fund scamsters and a few serial killers. The jail toilet was sobering, as were the mosquitoes, the boredom, and the smell from the drain outside.

> Those mosquitoes were resistant to everything. It wasn't an airtight cell, so you could not get rid of them once and for all. The second issue was the odour because there was a big nullah outside the jail, constantly smelling of decomposition. I had stopped eating. If you don't eat for two or three days, both your olfactory and parietal senses become much more

acute. So, it was actually getting worse. The jailors were trying everything. Their wives cooked me idli-sambar one day, but I just wasn't eating. For me, the truly traumatic part was being away from Twitter and my phone, because the only source of entertainment there was TV, and I hate TV. I can't watch TV.

But he says even that suffering won't stop him from mocking religious places again.

I don't like religion. I only go to a religious place that has architectural value. Because I have been working in Central Asia and Muslim countries for the past two years, I ended up going to more Muslim countries than Hindu temples. I see more value in Hindu temples per se. I would say to anybody who was upset with what I did in Konark, that it is the Islamisation of India and the Abrahamisation of Hinduism that has led to this because outrage over it is not a Hindu thing. Will I stop doing it? Of course not, because if Hindus aren't going to mock their own religion, you cede that space to somebody else. And mockery of religion is an old tradition in India. They never frowned upon it.

The provocateur's latest run-in has been with none other than the Indian judiciary. He tweeted mocking how a sitting Supreme Court judge's son helped Alt News fact-checker Mohammed Zubair get bail in a case of hurting religious sentiments. After that, his Twitter account was suspended.

It does not seem that Abhijit will mellow his provocative thinking and brutal openness of expression anytime soon. His views and actions push the boundaries of the new Right in India, challenging and freeing it from the cloistered stereotypes that its opponents try to impose.

Mohit Gulati

One of the popular gay nationalistic handles on Twitter is @desimojito, run by thirty-seven-year-old event planner Mohit Gulati. He quit his job and left his boyfriend in the US to return to India in 2019 and do door-to-door campaigning for Narendra Modi. He visited Delhi's communal ghettos as a volunteer and has also been writing articles on the development India has witnessed since 2014.

The soft-spoken man with a Freddie Mercury moustache says:

> The best thing so far has been the infrastructure. I am amazed at the newly constructed highways. I travelled to Gujarat a few times for work and spoke with locals about how Gujarat changed under Modi. He is a self-made man trying to keep our culture and values alive. He is a great orator, and the Congress has always found him a threat to the dynasty. I don't have enough words to describe how Modiji influenced not only me but millions. He got us interested in politics. Those vibes on the thaali-taali day [when the PM exhorted Indians to stand at their doorstep and clap as a tribute to COVID-19 health workers during the first lockdown] were enough to prove how much the masses love him.

Mohit was born and raised in a middle-class family in Delhi with no political background. He started working in a BPO when he was eighteen. He graduated and completed his master's through distance learning, then finished his postgraduate diploma in advertising, PR, and events in 2010.

As an event planner, he executed major events such as Obama's dinner at the PM's house, the IIFA awards in various countries, and concerts for artists like Snoop Dogg and David Guetta. He also played cricket professionally for a club in Delhi, representing it in under-19 tournaments in South Africa.

Like many young men and women who later joined the new nationalism wave, his political involvement began with the India Against Corruption movement.

> I was never into politics but attended a few rallies of Kejriwal in 2011 for his anti-corruption stand. I later regretted it. I realised he was just another anarchist playing with people's emotions. As for the Congress, the biggest problem has been corruption. Being a part of the 2010 Commonwealth Games opening ceremony project, I realised how the Congress was looting us with all the scams. Moreover, their anti-Hindu approach destroyed them eventually.

His Twitter handle @desimojito ('mojito' the drink pronounced Mohit-o in Spanish), was created in 2016 for humour. 'But Leftists' and Islamists' hypocrisy converted me into a Right-Wing political person. I am proud of it,' he says.

It was challenging for Mohit to tell his parents about his sexual orientation, especially when they were looking for a girl for him to marry.

> But I didn't want to ruin anyone's life because of societal pressure. So, I came out to my parents in 2016. They asked me to leave the house the same day. But then they took their time and accepted me after a few days. I'm glad I showed courage that day. I am happy now. My parents have always voted for the BJP. They are liberals. But as they say, you support the LGBTQ community until the time you don't have one in your own house. It was not easy for them to accept the truth, but somehow they convinced themselves to accept me.

Mohit believes that a number of Hindu texts portray the homosexual experience as natural and joyful. *The Kama Sutra* affirms and recognises same-sex relations. Several Hindu temples, like Khajuraho, have carvings depicting both men and women engaging in homosexual acts.

> Hinduism is all about acceptance at the end of the day, unlike Islam, where homosexuals are punished by death. The problem with the LGBTQ+ community is that our movement has been hijacked by the communists, and it is high time that our community should rid itself of these hatemongers who defame Sanatan Dharma around the clock.

Mohit supports same-sex marriage but insists that it should be under the Special Marriage Act and not the Hindu Marriage Act. But he does not want people to convert to Hinduism and tarnish the reputations of Hindus.

> I receive many DMs on Twitter and Instagram from Right-Wing Hindus who are part of the LGBTQ+ community, but they are discreet. I always try to guide them in building a vision for the future and living an uncomplicated life. Yes, there are many Right-Wingers in the LGBTQ+ community who are out and proud. It is always good to connect with like-minded people and share views and opinions.

Mohit says Modi's path to 2024 may seem smooth now, but it won't be easy. 'Just like in 2019, I shall be volunteering to campaign for Modiji on the ground and on social media, with better strategies. Ab ki baar/350 paar [this time, BJP will cross 350]. Jai Shree Ram!' he concludes in his soft-spoken manner, which is deceptively different from his fierce online activist voice.

Deep Purakayastha

At Flury's, amidst Kolkata's winter morning mist mingling with the aroma of coffee, cakes, and bagels, Deep Purakayastha, one of the city's most prominent gender activists, discusses his work with men and boys, sexuality, and the growing influence of Hindutva.

His approach to gender issues diverges starkly from the mainstream Left LGBTQ+ narrative. Supported by years of grassroots experience in social work and extensive reading, he calmly articulates his points, devoid of drama.

> Terms like LGBTQ, pansexual, etc., come from Western political language. I find this strange. On one hand, they talk about gender fluidity, and on the other hand, they have these little boxes. How is it fluid, then? Yes, people are fluid; you can't really pin it down. But you want some certainty. If at 10 o'clock I feel I am a man and at 11 o'clock I am a woman, it will be very difficult for you to deal with me. Does it really happen like that? It doesn't.

Purakayastha explains that gender fluidity means the traits typically associated with masculinity or femininity aren't confined to fixed categories within an individual. There will always be a mix-and-match. Just being artistic or sensitive does not make you gay. The opposite might be true as well.

> The main issue with gender fluidity—even among individuals who identify as gay or lesbian—is that it often confines us to rigid categories. Somewhere, it creates a certainty, but the reality is not like that. Sexuality and desire are not one-to-one mappable things in one's life. Anyone interested in literature will tell you that. A character may appear distinct to different readers because there are numerous types of readers.

Purakayastha attended St Paul's, Kidderpore, for his schooling. He did not want to become a doctor or engineer in the customary sense. He studied economics at St Xavier's College in classes XI and XII and graduated from Jadavpur University. After completing his economics degree, he pursued an MBA. Then, he followed his calling and joined an NGO named Naz Foundation, one of the leading organisations working on men's sexual health. In 1997, he established Prajok to work with children on gender and sexuality, specifically focusing on boys.

> At that time, the stigma of being gay was much more. It was internalised by the individual because one wanted to fit in and be like others. Standing out was not always enjoyable. There were very few resources available to explain this to people. It wasn't even considered a significant issue here. Whatever information was available usually came from the West. Only those who had access to English and Western media had some understanding. If people made that extra effort, they would become convinced that it was a disease. Homosexuality was pathologised, suggesting culturally you were 'strange' and medically you were ill. Growing up, you also learned that it was illegal, making you a criminal. It was not easy to grow up under these circumstances.

People would not talk to their family about it, he says. You could only share if you met someone like yourself. Telling the family was often not even relevant or imaginable. Purakayastha explains that, at that time, people would not even share with their families that they were having sex with the opposite gender. So talking about same-sex relationships was out of the question. The idea of telling the family came much later, and even then, it was mostly in urban areas where people had limited space to bring friends over.

> My case was different because I was an avid reader. I used to read a lot, so I also came across positive things, such as in 1974, the American Psychiatric Association removed same-sex attraction from their list of psychological diseases, challenging many prevailing beliefs at the time. Strangely, many of my contemporaries were unaware of this. For me, it was not such a big internal challenge. I accepted that people are diverse, and society has always been evolving. They used to burn widows at one time, not allowing them to get remarried, but times have changed. So, I knew I needed to give it time. Attitudes developed over centuries do not change overnight.

There is another aspect to Deep's sexuality.

> My orientation was both ways. I had also become familiar with the term bisexual. It was very traumatic, but not something you would want to discuss with people. You did not want people to know about you. People might have noticed because I worked with gay men and effeminate homosexuals or trans women on HIV. They might also have been confused because of various stories circulating about me. However, no one ever confronted me directly or showed any obvious hostility. In the sector I have been working in, I faced no setbacks. So, I shouldn't complain.

After completing his MBA, Deep started working with an entrepreneurial software firm, where he held a position in customer relations. The company was introducing scanners into the Indian market. The owners trusted him a lot, and he enjoyed his job.

But then his calling for social work led him to join the Kolkata chapter of the Naz Foundation. It marked his entry into the social sector. 'Soon, we grew tired of the condom promotion programmes. We believed they would address deeper issues, but they didn't. Personally, I always wanted to work with children, right from the beginning,' he says.

As mentioned earlier, in 1997, he joined forces with three of his friends, took the risk, and established their own NGO, Prajok. Drawing from their experience, they began addressing gender justice issues with boys and men.

> We decided to work with boys in the most challenging areas, where no one else had ventured. This included government observation homes for juveniles in conflict with the law or those abandoned, as well as railway stations. Most of them have run away from homes, they sniff glue, they have no place to sleep, and are often abused or beaten up. That's where our work started ... at observation homes in Dakshineswar and Barasat. Our work at the stations started in Bandel. Later, we extended our reach to Palta, Asansol, Kharagpur, Siliguri, and Cooch Behar. Additionally, we collaborated with the government, working from Jalpaiguri to Balurghat to Midnapore.

Purakayastha is clear that Indian civilisation has been far more accommodating of gender fluidity and various sexualities than the West. It has provided a safe social and cultural space for differently oriented individuals for centuries.

> We were told that the Indian way of looking at things is not scientific. When I started social work, I subscribed to that view, although with a lot of discomfort. Personally, Indian philosophy gave me a lot of efficacy and rootedness. Later, I

realised that a lot of LGBTQ politics is an imposed cage on you. They tell bisexuals, 'You're sitting on the fence, you have to decide who you are.' Why do you have to decide which side you are on? There is no reason. So, the bisexual slogan is: 'I'm not sitting on the fence. Your fence is sitting on me.'

He says the rigidity comes from a Cartesian view of the world that only accepts dualism. The Indian cultural context does not make a big noise about it unless there are economic or social implications. There was this category in India called 'koti' or 'chhokra', referring to effeminate males who engage in role-play.

> I was talking to you about the 'chhokras' I was working with. They would engage in female impersonations as goddesses like Manasha or Shitala and tell a story. If you go to North Bengal among the Rajbonshi community, playacting itself is considered a puja or worship. The actor becomes a quasi-priest. If you want to look at the history of queer sexuality in India from a Western perspective, you won't find much social or historical information. But there is a wealth of spiritual and religious information. Just like among American Indians, these boundary-crossing experiences have always been considered spiritual in India. So, you have somebody like Swami Vivekananda saying that the aatma does not have a gender. It is neither a man nor a woman. In the Indian spiritual realm, such identities dissolve. Those who do not understand how Indian spirituality works have published books calling guru Ramakrishna Paramhans a homosexual.

He says there is a debate among those working on these issues within the Indian context about why gender fluidity should only exist in the spiritual realm and not in the social.

On that note, Swami Vivekananda aptly said, '*Moner Vedanta-ke ebar shomajey niye ashtey hobey* [Vedanta of the mind must now be brought into society].' Vedanta clearly states that potentially everyone is straight, gay, bisexual, transexual, and everything else. Because what exists in one human being is always dormant as a potential in another human being. Of course, we develop in different ways. But internally, we have all the possibilities; otherwise, we would not be able to communicate with one another. If what is within me does not reside or resonate even in a small way inside you, we would not even be able to understand what each of us is talking about.

He further explains that even if one uses a Western lens to examine the major Indian gods, none of them can be considered fully heteronormative. The fluidity present in Indian, Greek, or Roman gods and goddesses is absent in Abrahamic religions. A lot of our modern non-theological, sociological theories cannot deny that they come from an Abrahamic context, where you have to have this body-mind differentiation. That creates a lot of difficulty, he says, especially for people from traditional societies who are born into a particular view of what human beings are. Sometimes, it causes a very abrupt rupture.

Talking about our age-old traditions and literature, Deep says:

> Marxists and many others in academia have never engaged with living traditions in India. They have never done ethnographic work. There is a vast tradition, especially in the tantras, that they overlook. Their work has been limited to textual analysis, interpreting the Vedas and other texts from a Western perspective. Sometimes, they don't even consider the context. They don't regard oral tradition as important. There

is a vast amount of literature. One of my friends is writing about the travelogues of Ramakrishna Mission's Swami Achutananda—his visits to the twelve jyotirlingas, his trip to Kashi. My friend says that in Bengali travel literature, these accounts are goldmines. But many people will not consider this academic because he is a swami or sadhu, and it will automatically be classified as religious literature.

But this distinction never existed in India. It used to be read as Kavya or Darshan, poetry or philosophy. There is also a lot of literature all over India about sadhaks and sadhikas written by non-English-speaking sources, he says. Many of these traditions—tantric, Vaishnavite, Shaivic, Pashupata, Bajrayani—are quite open.

He adds:

> The Gaudiya Vaishnavs developed a strong theory on role play, believing that by assuming certain roles, they could approach God. This occurred long before Western theatre even evolved, dating back to the 16th century. I know scholars in Kolkata and elsewhere in the world who are using these darshanic [or philosophical] structures to reexamine social processes.

During COVID-19, Prajok conducted webinars on gender fluidity in the Indian context. Speakers discussed how Paramhans's wife Sharada Ma spoke about why women should not be forced into marriage, and also on menstrual taboos. Or how Ramakrishna told one of his disciples, Gauri Ma, to open schools for women. She founded the Mahakali Pathshala for women. This was even before Sister Nivedita had arrived in India. Ramakrishna was not an English-educated person. He had deep connections with traditional paramparas.

Purakayastha cites the example of Andhra Pradesh's Srikakulam, where women have been in the priesthood for more than 200 years. They would go out to earn, while their husbands stayed home to look after the children. Srikakulam is the lineage of tantra in Tamil Nadu, Kerala, and Andhra Pradesh, where worshippers venerate Shodashi, Sri Devi, and Tripurasundari.

> Modern Marxism and liberal feminism look down on motherhood, viewing it as an imposed role. Of course, not everybody becomes a mother. This is also expressed in Manu, who categorised women into two types: those who are Sadyovadhu, meaning those who marry, and others are Brahmavadini, who choose not to marry and pursue studies and other pursuits. Even now, women perform pujas at Ramakrishna and Sharada Matth. Anandamoyee Ma held a thread ceremony for her disciples in the 1930s. The pandits in Kashi told her that it was a tradition from long ago, though it does not happen now.

Purakayastha says that within Hindu philosophical structures, the liberation of human beings is possible with a balance between the individual and the collective. For instance, there are many forms of family in India. Sometimes, there is a single mother. Sometimes both parents are deceased, and the elder brothers and sisters are raising the children.

> When my aunt adopted a child, she gave him the example of Krishna and Yashoda. We don't celebrate Devaki's love for Krishna as much as Yashoda's love for him. In the Gaudiya Vaishnav tradition, there's Swakiya and Parakiya love. Swakiya means loving one's own mother, brother, wife because a strong self-interest is involved. Parakiya transcends

that, like Yashoda's love. Once we have the social and spiritual self together and engage in dialogue, we don't need Marxism or other such ideologies.

He rues the anti-Modi slogans raised at the Kolkata Pride parade and the deep division within the community. The 'ugra' or loud individualism is not something that many people, including LGBTQ+ persons, support in this country. Many of them identified with what was happening under the Modi government and approved of the re-emergence of the inclusive Hindu or Indic way of looking at things.

For somebody like me in the social sector, which is so dominated by the Left and so-called liberals, to be able to talk about the spiritual aspects that have emerged since 2014 is significant. Many of my Left-liberal friends, after hearing me talk, are saying, 'OK, can we know more about this?' They are asking me which version of the Bhagavad Gita should they read.

In Bengal, those like Purakayashtha are still a minority, but an increasing number of young people are writing about it. Prajok is informing people that they can find feminism and LGBTQ+ ideas in Indic traditions. They don't always have to look to the Suffragette Movement.

Deep further mentions that how his inspiration to do social work came from his mother reading to him from Bengali books about Ishwar Chandra Vidyasagar, Raja Ram Mohan Roy, Ramakrishna Paramhans, and Sharada Devi. 'It did not come from Marxist books. It came from a family rooted in Shakti worship. Nobody documents how tradition has been quietly passed on in the family by women who teach youngsters to touch elders' feet, pray to deities, and chant mantras,' he says.

Deep says there is an increasing number of people, both Hindu and Muslim, who are proud of their civilisational identities. These include Hindus and Muslims from Pakistan, Bangladesh, and Nepal. Some tolerant Sufis from Pakistan, like the 16th-century poet Madhoo Lal Hussain or Shah Hussain, actively embraced Hindu symbolism. Even today, many Pakistani hijras follow the Indic path.

Purakayastha says the arrival of Modi and the changes it has brought could be summarised in an image that played out in real life last year.

> When a transgender dancer receives a Padma Shree and uses her aanchal to bless the President of India, the Sovereign Head of the State, you know things are coming full circle. It's pure tradition. Once upon a time, transgenders used to bless the raja; now they bless the rashtrapati. And while she blesses the Indian Republic through the President, the Sovereign bends to accept her blessings. What could be a better visual representation of what is happening now?

CHAPTER 9

Our Minorities, Their Minorities

The most aggressive narrative that the Left and so-called liberal ecosystem has built against Hindutva is that it is inimical towards minorities, especially Muslims, painting Hindus as perpetual aggressors.

This Hindumisia (or Hinduphobia) has intensified manifold since Narendra Modi came to power. Even when he was the chief minister of Gujarat, the United States denied him a visa based on the plea of a handful of intellectuals citing the deaths of Muslims in the state in 2002. As mentioned earlier, while writing or reporting about the Gujarat riots, the media and academia relentlessly labelled it as a 'genocide', ignoring the fact that of the 1,044 dead, 790 were Muslim and 254 were Hindu. How can so many of the alleged perpetrators die in a genocide? Also, the riots were triggered after a Muslim mob in Godhra set fire to a train returning with Hindu pilgrims, killing fifty-nine of them.

The creators of this anti-India, anti-Hindu narrative have consistently downplayed, distorted, or denied the reality that this civilisation has borne the lethal wounds of Islamic invasions and European imperialism for nearly a thousand years. An estimated 80 million (according to historian K.S.

Lal's assessment) to 300 million Hindus were slaughtered during Islamic conquests, and another 100–200 million were killed during British rule by the sword, bullets, or man-made famines.

American historian Will Durant wrote:

> The Mohammedan conquest of India is probably the bloodiest story in history. It is a discouraging tale, for its evident moral is that civilisation is a precarious thing, whose delicate complex of order and liberty, culture and peace may at any time be overthrown by barbarians invading from without or multiplying within.

Three Islamic nations were carved out of Bharat because Islamic populations refused to coexist with Hindus, sensing their unbridled and undemocratic political power would end in an independent India. In spite of that, proponents of Hindutva argue that Hindus have never been vindictive and have only resorted to violence in self-defence and for survival.

But forces that seek to balkanise India focus on its fault lines. Their current campaign, into which they pour money and energy, aims to create disenchantment among Muslims regarding their treatment under Modi. They highlight sporadic incidents of lynching or beating of Muslims, amplifying them significantly. They lack data to support claims that such lynchings have increased. Moreover, they seldom report, let alone highlight, the numerous occasions when Muslims kill Hindus or Sikhs or Christians.

But facts and data tell a different story. Seven Islamic nations have awarded Prime Minister Modi their highest civilian honours. Modi is also the first Indian PM to visit Palestine and receive its highest civilian award. India's relations with some of the richest and most powerful Arab nations, such as Saudi Arabia, the United Arab Emirates, Jordan, and Bahrain, are at their best. The UAE and Saudi Arabia are India's third and fourth-largest trading partners, respectively. In Bahrain and Abu Dhabi in the UAE, the first Hindu temples were established due to Modi's diplomacy.

Internally, the Modi government has accomplished considerably more than its predecessor, the Congress-led UPA. A comparative analysis of expenditure incurred by the Ministry of Minority Affairs for eight years between 2006–07 to 2013–14 and 2014–15 to 2021–22 shows a two-and-a-half-fold increase in expenditure. During those eight years of the UPA, Rs 12,213 crore was spent, while under Modi, the figure has risen to Rs 30,616 crore.

In July 2019, Parliament scrapped instant triple talaq by adopting the Muslim Women (Protection of Rights on Marriage) Bill, fulfilling Modi's election promise. While mullahs and hardliners expressed anger, the change positively impacted thousands of women who previously risked losing their marriage over a phone call, WhatsApp text, or a domestic quarrel with their husbands.

A month before that, the Modi government announced scholarships for five crore students over five years, with 50 per cent of the endowments designated for girls. In the first six months of Modi 2.0, scholarships were sanctioned for more than 80 lakh Jain, Parsi, Buddhist, Christian, Sikh, and Muslim students, with 60 per cent being girls. Besides that, in 2019, 3 lakh poor and needy girls received the Begum Hazrat Mahal Scholarship.

The government has been making efforts to integrate madrassas into the mainstream, as many have been associated with Islamist fundamentalism. Over 750 madrassa teachers, including many women, have received training. Additionally, more than 650 school dropouts have been provided with bridge courses. Thus far, over 2.5 lakh minority youth have been imparted employable skill development schemes, such as Garib Nawaz Rozgar Yojana, Seekho Aur Kamao, Nai Manzil, Ustad, Nai Roshni, and Hunar Haat.

In India's most populous state, UP, led by saffron-clad BJP icon Yogi Adityanath and with a 19.33 per cent Muslim population, 39 per cent of beneficiaries of the Pradhan Mantri Awas Yojana (housing), 22 per cent of beneficiaries of Swachh Bharat (toilets), 37 per cent of beneficiaries of Ujjwala Yojna (cooking gas), and 30 per cent of beneficiaries of Mudra Yojana (loans) are Muslims. One of the state's signature schemes, One District One Product (ODOP), has disproportionately benefitted Muslims due to the sheer number of weavers and artisans from the community.

From Unani colleges and girls' hostels to a Haj portal and app, digitisation of Waqf records to the Kartarpur corridor, and rights to Sikh minorities after the abrogation of Article 370 in Jammu and Kashmir, the list of benefits to minorities under Modi is extensive, yet largely unacknowledged.

On 10 March 2020, the Indian Air Force's C-17 Globemaster touched down at the Hindon Airbase like a giant grey bird. It had flown back the first batch of fifty-eight Shia pilgrims to safety from Iran, then the world's third most severely coronavirus-hit country. The Modi government never showed any less alacrity in rescue efforts simply because the stranded individuals were Muslims.

Another instance was in 2014, when more than a hundred nurses from Kerala, many of them Muslims and Christians, were rescued from ISIS in Iraq. India tried its best to rescue thirty-nine Indians kidnapped by ISIS in Iraq in 2015, many of whom were minorities, but unfortunately, all efforts failed after three years of frantic diplomatic and underground outreach. The terrorists killed all of them, as later confirmed.

One of India's most remarkable overseas rescue operations was led by General V.K. Singh, then the minister of state for external affairs, from war-ravaged Yemen in 2015. Operation Raahat successfully evacuated more than 1,000 people from forty-one countries, including Indian citizens. Regardless of the religion of those stranded amidst the chaos of bombs and missiles, the operation prioritised their safety and welfare.

In 2018, the then foreign minister Sushma Swaraj facilitated the return of Hamid Ansari from a Pakistani jail. The young man, driven by love, had crossed over with a fake Pakistani identity card to meet a woman, only to find himself incarcerated. Meanwhile, Western media and India's self-proclaimed liberals, Leftists, and Islamists continued to propagate the narrative that the Modi establishment is virulently anti-minorities, especially targeting Muslims.

So, when the government passed the Citizenship Amendment Act (CAA), Islamist anger spilled onto the streets. Their above-ground inciters continued to press on the pretext that the law discriminates against one religion—Islam.

The fact that the CAA was a narrowly focused legislation intended solely for persecuted minorities of three neighbouring Islamic nations—Pakistan, Afghanistan, and Bangladesh—and did not affect Indian Muslims at all was deliberately suppressed. It was not mentioned that Muslims from abroad could still apply for naturalised Indian citizenship under the Citizenship Act of 1955. Moreover, it was carefully concealed that under the Liaquat–Nehru Agreement of 1950, following a bloody Partition, India upheld its end of the bargain by ensuring the safety of minorities. But minorities in these three nations have dwindled to near-extinction because of relentless persecution, including rapes, murders, land grabs, and forcible conversions.

The US media, for instance, continued to demonise the Modi government over CAA without once conceding that the US has a similar narrow-window legislation, the Lautenberg Amendment, which specially treats people from historically persecuted groups without requiring them to individually prove persecution. The amendment refers to 'Jews, Evangelical Christians, Ukrainian Catholics, or Ukrainian Orthodox' who are from the former Soviet Union, Estonia, Latvia, or Lithuania. The law was expanded in 2004 to include Jews, Christians, Baha'is, and other religious minorities from Iran.

Despite such widespread hypocrisy and narrative-setting, a number of bold and nationalistic minority voices are slowly emerging. They are challenging the agenda that seeks to exploit India's religious fault lines. They reject false victimhood and embrace the civilisational values of this land. In this chapter, we encounter a few of them.

Among Muslims, there are young politicians like Shazia Ilmi, Asma Khan Pathan, brothers Shehzad and Tehseen Poonawalla, Atif Rasheed, and Nighat Abbas, all of whom advocate for nationalist ideals. Anchor Rubika Liaquat, activists and columnists Amana Begum Ansari and Arshia Malik, Supreme Court lawyer Subuhi Khan, Nissar Guru, Sajid Yousuf, Suneem Khan, Wajahat Farooq, and handles such as @Zaffar_nama are among those who strongly reject hardline, divisive, and othering narratives within the community.

As *The Kashmir Files* made a nationwide impact by revealing the truth about the Pandit genocide in the 1990s, Kashmiri

Muslims like Khalid Baig (who runs a widely watched YouTube channel), Sualeh Keen, Emaad Makhdoomi, Yana Mir, Raja Muneeb, Javed Beigh, Sajid Yousuf Shah, and Shaikh Mohsin have been vocal critics of the jihad ecosystem.

In the government, Central Wakf Council member Rais Khan Pathan led the charge. Former renegade Kashmiri civil services topper Shah Faesal has rejoined the mainstream and boldly champions national interests.

While Kerala Governor Arif Mohammed Khan continues to be the intellectual torchbearer for Indian Muslim nationalism and a critic of Islamic orthodoxy, Judge Jaibunnisa Mohiuddin Khazi brushed aside arguments in court that a Muslim woman would cease to be Muslim without wearing a hijab and would face eternal damnation after death.

Indic voices are rising from other minority communities as well. Thus, while Savio Rodrigues breaks the stereotype of Christians opposing Hinduness, Puneet Sahani takes on Khalistani Sikh militancy fuelled from overseas.

From ideological collision and chaos, the seeds of a more unified and rooted India are slowly emerging, not just through Hindus but also through protagonists from other communities.

Amana Begum Ansari

One of the Modi government's strongest efforts to integrate Muslims into the national mainstream has been to recognise and give voice to Pasmanda Muslims, who draw their lineage and culture from this land. Their ancestors were mainly lower-caste Hindus who converted to Islam over the centuries. They comprise more than 85 per cent of Muslims in India.

India's new nationalism taps into the Pasmanda sentiment that upper-class and caste Ashrafis, who believe their ancestors came from a 'pure-blood' Islamic lineage from Arabia or Persia, have appropriated state benefits and community voice. While the Pasmandas remained poor and backward, the tiny Muslim elite of Ashrafis kept reinforcing aggressive (often separatist) stereotypes and worked against integration.

One of the most prominent young voices among Pasmanda Muslims is Amana Begum Ansari, the thirty-five-year-old political commentator:

> Muslims in India did not integrate themselves. Many felt that their personal interest lay in being part of the herd. They believed that the more they assimilated into a group, the more beneficial it would be for them. Then there is also a certain communal and tribal nature which comes from the interpretation of doctrine where you have to be treated like a community which is always under attack, where you should always protect yourself. The leadership of the Muslims could have changed things. But they saw that there was so much opportunity to exploit this mindset and never work on changing the narratives and reforming that mindset. You reform from the top down; it never goes down to the top. So, for the Ashrafi class at the top, it was very, very profitable. They focused on fighting against the Hindus, making Muslims a bloc.

She further states Ashrafis are Muslims whose ancestry is from outside of India or a few of them converted from the higher Hindu castes:

> Even Allama Iqbal or Muhammad Ali Jinnah's families were converted from upper-caste Hindus. They always had

power in the Muslim community, whether it was engaging in discussions or speaking on behalf of Muslims. For them, it was never profitable [to work on reforms]. Muslims have always been used as a vote bank. Even today, Mamata Banerjee does exactly the same thing, encouraging them to form more blocs, because, in the political calculation, it can be very profitable. Every community has reformer thinkers. But Muslims in India have found it difficult to accept one.

Amana draws a sharp line between Pasmanda and Ashrafi Muslims in terms of a significant disparity in opportunities and growth. She also exposes rampant casteism among Indian Muslims, despite Islam officially declaring itself as a classless, casteless, perfectly egalitarian society. 'There is a lot of casteism. There is even untouchability,' she adds.

She cites a first-of-its-kind survey, extensively covered by the BBC, conducted by researchers Prashant K. Trivedi, Srinivas Goli, Fahimuddin, and Surinder Kumar, which showed that untouchability was alive and well among Indian Muslims. They polled more than 7,000 households across fourteen districts in UP between October 2014 and April 2015.

A significant section of 'Dalit Muslims' reported that they do not receive invitations from non-Dalits for wedding feasts. They mentioned being seated separately in non-Dalit Muslim feasts. Almost a similar proportion of respondents stated that they ate after the upper castes had finished and were served food on different plates.

Around 8 per cent of 'Dalit Muslims' reported that their children were seated in separate rows in classes and during school lunches. A third of them stated that they were not allowed to bury their dead in upper-caste burial grounds.

About 20 per cent of respondents felt that upper-caste Muslims maintained a distance from them.

Amana says:

> There was even news from a Muslim village that a road was divided so that one side was reserved for the upper castes and the other for the lower castes. In my village, Mangalpur, which was mostly Muslim, it was divided through the middle so that Ansaris, who were the lower castes, were on one side and the upper castes on the other. There have been honour killings based on caste among Muslims. Swati Goel Sharma had reported those. The boys were from the lower caste, and the girls fell in love, but their families could not accept it and killed the lovers.

Amana laments that these incidents don't get reported in that manner. She points to a Deoband Darul Uloom fatwa which states that if a Syed girl (the highest caste, believed to belong to the bloodline of the Prophet) marries a boy from a lower caste, the girl's parents have the right to nullify the marriage. This fatwa was issued by the first Mufti of Darul Uloom Deoband, Azizur Rahman Usmani.

She explains:

> The writers don't have a source from the Quran, but they just write what they feel like. The famous maulvi Ashraf Ali Thanwi was very casteist and had written books priced at Rs 5 which are widely read in homes and contain casteist literature. Pasmanda activist Kahkashan Waqar told me that there is a book that says even if a boy from a lower caste is well-educated and rich, giving your daughter in marriage to him is like marrying her to a rich, disabled person. Even Yoginder Sikand, who is a Leftist writer, had written a beautiful book, *Islam, Caste and Dalit–Muslim Relations in India*. You don't

get it on Amazon these days, no matter how much you try. I don't know why. In that book, he recorded all the historical details. There was a fatwa which said that even if the lower castes or Pasmanda Muslims are educated, it is like putting a gold chain around the neck of a pig.

Amana's views are echoed by writer Abid Faheem in his essay, 'Elitism Among Indian Muslims: Caste, Power, Privilege and Inequality'. He writes:

> Maulana Ashraf Ali Thanwi shared the same mindset where he declared Syed, Sheikh, Mughals and Pathan noble castes and weavers, oil pressers razil [low caste]. He mocked weavers in many places. Once he said: 'The weaver prayed for three days only and considered himself a sacred person.'

He also criticises the father of the Two Nation Theory and founder of Aligarh Muslim University, Syed Ahmed Khan, for his casteism:

> Hailed as the father of Muslim India, [he] opposed the entry of so-called razil in legislatures and government employment, arguing that examinations for high government services [civil services] should not be held in India because that might lead to people from so-called razil castes entering government services and thereby ruling over the so-called Ashrafis [elites].

Faheem further states:

> In the 1946 elections, dubbed the consensus on Pakistan, in which the Muslim League won handsomely, there was a restricted electoral process where only the elite, i.e., Ashrafi Muslims got to vote. The votes of subordinated Muslim caste

groups were not even put to the test. After the Partition tragedy, the post-colonial states dominated by the Congress party preferred to work with the remaining Ashrafi sections as interlocutors for Muslims. This unstated policy resulted in an overrepresentation of high-caste Muslims [who constitute only 15 per cent of the Muslim population] in the power structure at the cost of subordinated castes. Since the 1990s, the Pasmanda movement—the movement of backward, Adivasi, and Dalit Muslims—has reactivated the intra-Muslim caste antagonism by contesting Ashrafi hegemony over Muslim politics.

Amana shares the same view regarding Pasmandas and Partition.

> Lower-caste Muslims were always against Partition. Abdul Qaiyum Ansari fought an electoral battle against the Muslim League in Bihar and won just six seats. But then, Pasmanda Muslims had no say. There was no adult franchise at that time. You had to be a zamindar or have a certain level of education. So, mostly the elites could vote. I don't remember if anybody voted at that time in my family. In partitioned India, initially, Pasmandas were given space, perhaps as a recognition for their support of India. However, slowly they receded into the background. I am not accusing all Ashrafis of being responsible for Partition. The percentage of votes that went to the Congress and not to Jinnah was not too much. But those were Ashrafis who did not want Partition.

Writing for the Pasmanda cause has begun to gain traction. As the Pasmanda movement expands, many Muslims have united to create a website called pasmandademocracy.com.

One such activist-doctor-writer, Faiyaz Ahmad Fyzie, conducts extensive research and regularly posts on Twitter. He manages a YouTube channel and makes appearances on television. He was once expelled from a WhatsApp group called Pasmanda Mahaz for opposing Sir Syed Ahmed Khan as an icon.

Another writer and professor, Masood Falahi, has written extensively about caste discrimination in Muslim society and in community institutions like the Aligarh Muslim University. He traced the precursor of this discrimination to the time of the Mughal durbar. You had to be a high-caste Muslim to sit in that durbar. If you were a lower-caste Muslim, even if you reached the durbar, you would be turned away if your caste got exposed. There were even fatwas that said 'teach them only five things' so that the lower-caste Muslims only know how to follow the basic Islamic tenets; there is no need for education.

Amana states:

> The voice of the Pasmanda Muslims can be heard because we gained access to education only after 1947. I am part of the second generation who have received an education. They started to realise after the second generation what was going on, why things were this messed up. History is replete with instances of Muslim casteism at various levels. In the Quran, there is nothing written about casteism. The point is that Islam was created by these people, so they created Sharia, they created everything and say that this is what Islam is all about. In the Prophet's last khutbah, he said a lot of good things against discrimination. But they have bypassed that and created the Kufu principles, which not only include casteism but also racism. They have created an entire hierarchy and

play a double game. Hierarchy is not officially there in Islam but at the same time, they have created laws which have it.

One such set of laws created by upper-caste mullahs in India is the Kufu or parity principles of marriage, which refers to equality between a prospective groom and wife in various aspects such as religion, lineage, social status, financial status and character. Amana explains that these laws uphold caste supremacy, adding that the Pasmanda movement is stronger than before:

> Lower-caste Hindus converted in large numbers to Islam, but high-caste Muslim girls were not able to marry them. They said, 'Why are we converting? We are still facing discrimination.' So, the scholars of that time brought in the Masawaat principle, which means everyone is equal. They succeeded in advancing their work of converting people and making the Muslims a more united community, but they never denounced the Kufu principles. A lot of people argue that Muslim casteism is borrowed from Hinduism. No. It has come from the Kufu principles. Sir Syed called us 'bajjat' castes because at that time we were fighting the British. Our occupation involved weaving sarees, and the tax policy of the British was very oppressive against the weavers. So, we were protesting as part of the Swadeshi movement.

Amana says whenever Pasmanda leadership rises, the community begins to realise that its culture is different. She asserts that Pasmanda Muslims don't marry four times. Most Indian Muslims don't marry four times.

Speaking in favour of the UCC, she says, 'It is better for us to have a Uniform Civil Code. You can see Ashrafi intellectuals talking against UCC, and I will show you a lot of Pasmanda intellectuals who don't see it as a bad thing.'

In the current Lok Sabha, Pasmandas have a representation of only approximately 0.08 per cent while their population constitutes 11 per cent of the country, according to RTI findings by journalist-cum-politician Ali Anwar Ansari. The population of Ashrafis is just 2 per cent, yet they hold a much larger representation in Parliament.

Amana was born in Ashwini Hospital, Mumbai. Her father was a chief engineer in the Indian Navy. The family lived in a quarter in Navy Nagar, Colaba. When she was one, her father left his job and started a fire-fighting business with his friends. But the startup failed to take off. After a search, he found a job in the UAE Air Force.

> In the UAE, they used to hire from other countries, but not at the higher levels of the military. When my father was hired, we moved to Abu Dhabi. One good thing that happened in my childhood was growing up in Dubai, which is a multicultural city. There were people from all around the world who did not look like you—whites, blacks, Arabs. The defence background also played a big role because I remember my mom and dad never told me that I couldn't have a friend who was a boy. A lot of Indians, leaving aside Muslims, felt I was very progressive. I was allowed to go out with my male friends, but I had to just tell my mom who I was with and where we were going. That used to come from a sense of parental concern. My dad said girls should have a proper education and a career before getting married. I believe that these things shaped me.

When the Gulf War broke out, Amana's family started to consider returning to India. Her mother, in particular, did not want to live under the clouds of war. The family returned to Banaras, the ancestral place of both her parents. They then moved to her father's village, Mangalpur, where she spent four years. In that small village with low literacy rates, less than 4,000 people and 500 houses, Amana began to perceive issues very differently.

> Life there was completely different. It gave me insight and empathy that people usually lack. For example, in the villages, people have a lot of kids. Muslims have more, but Hindus have a lot too. I used to ask, 'Why do you have so many kids if you can't even afford it? At least my family was able to afford kids.' They used to say that since law and order was not good in the villages, the more boys they had, the more protected they felt. There were more hands for the farms as well. Then you realise that they have ground realities of their own. Sitting in an AC room, it is very easy to judge them as jaahil or illiterate. But you are not living their lives.

One of her most profound influences is India's iconic defence scientist and former President, Dr A.P.J. Abdul Kalam.

> He showed that India is a land of opportunity, where your identity doesn't matter, and that Hindu society is very inclusive. It is up to you how much you integrate and how much you love your country. People say that Tarek Fatah was very one-sided and critical, but when I started watching his videos, they helped me. Though I had many disagreements, he presented a lot of new information. Then there are a few people, like Tabish Siddiqui, who write extensively about Islamic history.

She says while a section of Muslims are well-integrated, the majority still reside in ghettos. Venturing beyond these ghettos and integrating themselves into the mainstream is beneficial for their lives and livelihood.

I am openly a patriotic Indian Muslim, and I am deeply concerned about my country. It is essential for a nation's well-being that all communities stay integrated and intermingle. Muslims lag behind in this aspect the most. If they fail to integrate and if reforms are not implemented, it will ultimately burden the Indian nation. For example, during the polio eradication campaign, which occurred during the Congress regime, extensive additional efforts were required to persuade Muslims, as evidenced by government data. Additionally, there is the issue of violence. When the community becomes agitated, it disregards any leadership, and protests turn violent.

Why is it that only Muslims seem to feel alienated? This sentiment is not exclusive to India; it extends from the US to Europe to China and even within Islamic nations.
Amana says:

> Yes, we do observe a certain pattern, but every nation faces different issues. Take China, for example, there is not just one Muslim community. There are Han Muslims and Uighurs. You don't see issues among the Han [or Hui] Muslims, but you do observe problems among Uighur Muslims. Uighurs are of Turkish descent, so they have a slightly supremacist attitude. In France, for instance, the individuals rioting are not even recent immigrants. They belong to the second or third generation, those who came from Algeria and whom France had assimilated.

Muslims in India should reflect on why they are constantly in contradiction, suggests Amana. According to her, a significant issue, especially among South Asian Muslims, is their lack of understanding of Arabic.

She says:

> For us, what is Islam? For many of us, Islam is defined by what our pirs or maulvis say, as we lack the authority to read and understand it for ourselves. It's quite straightforward for Arabic Muslims, but we are excessively influenced by the teachings of our pirs and maulavis.

If anything goes against the interests of the clergy, they simply declare it as being against Islam, and nobody dares to question it.

> The influence of the clergy is significant, even though it is prescribed in Islam that the maulvi should wield considerable power. There have been incidents in which leaders who did not receive election tickets from their party rallied Muslims together and claimed that Islam was in danger. But, once they secured the ticket, the perceived danger vanished. Because they don't understand Arabic, it is easy for any mullah to manipulate them.

Amana predicts that there will be an 'Islam in danger' bogey over the UCC issue. Very few in the community will argue that Muslims follow the law in Western nations where UCC exist. Even in Turkey, most laws are secular. The Muslim elite, who see a threat to Islam in India, are desperate to send their children to America. Then they don't perceive a threat to Islam. In the UK, where she has been living for a while, men are not allowed to have four wives. But informal Sharia courts have been established in every corner.

In her posts, articles, and TV appearances, Amana emphasises the fact that the culture of Indian Muslims is Indian, not Arabic or Persian.

> When I went to stay in Dubai, I began to understand that their culture is vastly different. Despite being Muslim, I expected them to be similar to me, but that wasn't the case. It made me realise that our cultural practices are basically Hindu cultural practices. Thus, they came to see Indian Muslims are not adhering strictly to Islam and instead following Hindu customs. Even Wahhabism was concerned with this. The idea was to 'Islamise' Indian Muslims and make them more Arabic. Because the version of Islam we were following included basic Islamic principles along with many aspects of Hindu culture. I haven't seen my aunt or others in my family wearing hijab or niqab. They would wear sarees, dhotis. But the new generation has started adopting this type of dress. They [the Arabs] don't understand our needs or our cultural ways. They have nothing to gain by looking after our interests. They would benefit most by using us as a bloc.

She says it is a myth that the BJP does not receive even a single Muslim vote. It garners some votes in UP because Muslims in UP are not 'politically illiterate'.

> If someone tells me that Muslims in UP engage in bloc voting, I will never agree because I have seen in my family that some were supporters of BSP, some supported SP, and others were Congress supporters. But eventually, everybody stopped supporting Congress. Muslims don't vote for Congress in UP after the Babri incident. In the recent local body elections, out of the Pasmanda Muslims whom the BJP gave tickets in Muslim-majority areas, sixty candidates won. That indicates

Muslims are voting for BJP candidates. And I see in UP, Yogi has even run an admirable programme to reach out to the Pasmandas.

The French Revolution, which Amana read about in Class IX, left a lasting impression on her. Issues such as the shabby treatment of women in Europe at that time deeply affected her. She noted that while the rights of slaves were being discussed, women's rights were largely ignored. She realised that the relative equality she enjoys now is because someone in the past had fought for it. She sparked her interest in social justice. As she delved deeper into her reading, she began to wonder why Indian Muslims are different.

> For instance, most Muslim brides in the Middle East wear white suits during their marriage. But in India, they don't. They either wear red or green, reserving for occasions of grief. I now see that in China, too, wedding dresses are red. In the East, they symbolise culture, not religion. As a Pasmanda Muslim, I have seen women suffering terribly. They are not able to express their pain because doing so would be considered 'against Islam'. This made me think that someone has to speak up, someone has to do something.

Social media helped her start asking questions. It provided free-flowing debates and information, which helped her significantly, she says, and is also benefitting many other Muslim youth. 'Things were never perfect and they can be changed, but we have to consider if the life we are living right now is perfect and keep questioning that.'

Sinu Joseph

From her Keralite Christian roots to her engineering degree, and on to becoming an educator, writer, and expert on ancient Hindu knowledge concerning menstrual and reproductive health, Sinu Joseph's journey remarkably captures the civilisational awakening among the Indian 'minorities'. Step by unplanned step, she gravitated towards a completely unexpected and new life, answering her calling.

Joseph was born in 1982 in a Catholic family. She complemented her schooling and pre-university education at Christian institutions and holds a Bachelor of Engineering degree in Instrumentation Technology.

> I was largely cut off from Hindu thought processes until much later when I joined the NGO space in my late twenties. During school, there was mandatory Bible study and catechism classes, as it was a convent school. However, I always had a natural affinity for science, so I often wondered about the contradiction between the theory of human evolution from apes taught in science class and the creation story taught by our catechism teachers. I was generally good at studies and could memorise whatever was given to me, so I usually did well in both science and catechism. Once I was out of school, I felt relieved not to have to attend catechism classes, do forced confessions, and go to church sermons where I had to pretend to have faith. I became non-religious after school.

Sinu does not relate to being labelled an 'ex-Christian' since she had never been a practising Christian in the first place. With this religiously neutral attitude, she unknowingly entered the RSS ecosystem through an NGO she was volunteering for. It was there that her cultural and nationalistic grounding took place. 'Though I began with the lens of science, as I dug deeper, it naturally led me to Sanatan Dharma,' she says.

While she grew up as a Christian, her ideas and belief systems are solidly Indic. How does she reconcile these identities?

> There is nothing to reconcile. I am not a practising Christian; never have been. Christianity is based on inducing fear, guilt, and cultivating an attitude of not questioning anything. Where I come from, the elders in the Christian faith do their best to keep youngsters in fear-induced, low-frequency negative emotions so that it is easier to manipulate and control. Physical and emotional violence is a faith-justified part of the ecosystem I was raised in. However, that is the perfect recipe for one to turn rebellious if they have even an iota of intelligence and a little bit of courage. I did not go seeking any alternative religion because religion itself was not something I felt dependent upon. What interested me was science. Now, what can a person of science do when every inquiry that is dug deeper leads one to Sanatan Dharma?

Sinu Joseph was not seeking religion; she was searching for answers in science, which led her to the realm of Hindu concepts of religion and spirituality.

> The beauty of it is that in the Hindu way of life, the highest theories of quantum science are practically implemented in the form of cultural practices, allowing one to understand them through experience rather than as mere abstract theory. But if we fail to make the connection between Hindu cultural practices and advanced science, these practices may appear as superstition, leading to misconceptions and wrongly labelling them as taboos.

Sinu's area of work has been to decode the cultural practices and rules given in the shastras, using the language of science, encompassing both ancient/Indic and modern/Western perspectives. Within this broader framework, her focus has been primarily on women's menstrual and reproductive health. She entered Sanatan Dharma from a scientific perspective, which naturally evolved into spirituality for her, as she believes that in Hinduism, these two aspects are inseparable.

She bluntly challenges the Left-liberal narrative that religious minorities are in danger in Narendra Modi's BJP-ruled India.

> Having lived in the Christian ecosystem in my early years, I have experienced firsthand the animosity they direct towards RSS and Hindus. For them, loyalty to Christianity equals hostility towards all others. It is only an insecure religious identity that fosters hatred towards others, and Christianity today is an example of that. Even seemingly altruistic acts, such as those performed by Christian charitable organisations, often harbour hidden agendas of conversion or a façade of goodness to entice more people into embracing Christianity. In contrast, my decade-long experience with the RSS ecosystem, as well as with Hindus outside the RSS, has been completely different. Here, there is kindness for its own sake; there is truth because it is upheld as a high value. Unlike charity, where the doer is elevated to a pedestal, here there is Seva, where one expresses gratitude to those who provide opportunities to serve them.

Sinu says that in the RSS, there is respect for people of all faiths and belief systems, with the understanding that we are all part of a divine oneness. There is encouragement to question and seek answers, and there is profound humility derived from deep-seated spiritual wisdom.

While many perceive the RSS as a patriarchal setup with little consideration for women, Sinu describes the RSS ecosystem as a genuinely warm and paternal setup, in the sense of how they look out for others and assume the role of protectors.

> Senior pracharaks have been father figures in my life. I have learned so much from simply observing their personalities. Having grown up in an environment where physical violence against girls and women was considered normal by men, I was taken aback when I experienced the respect with which the RSS treats women, even young girls. Was it not Michelle Obama who said, 'The measure of a society is by the way it treats women and girls?' Well, if the RSS were a society, I would say that nowhere else are women treated with greater respect than within the RSS ecosystem. They take it seriously when they say '*yatra naryastu pujyante ramante tatra devata*', meaning 'where women are worshipped, the gods reside'.

According to Joseph, it is this compassionate consideration for women and girls that prompted a prime minister from the RSS ecosystem to address a global audience about the shameful reality of the lack of toilets and led the nation to embark on a mission to alleviate women from this hardship.

> Women of this nation, regardless of the religion they identify with, will never forget that. And this is just one of the many directly impactful projects that the Modi government has implemented. The developmental work undertaken by the Modi government has been unparalleled in the history of this nation since Independence. The ordinary people of the nation

know this from their direct experiences. The rest is merely a constructed narrative that does not hold sway beyond the virtual confines of social media.

Those who truly wish to understand the RSS and the type of men it nurtures should delve into Karma Yoga, urges Sinu. Apart from a few top leaders of the RSS, most people wouldn't even know the names of senior RSS members because they are Karma Yogis.

These men embody the principles of Karma Yoga by renouncing all material comforts and fame, taking only what is necessary for basic survival, and making Seva their full-time occupation, dedicating their lives to the revival of dharmic principles. Their lifestyle is not vastly different from that of monks, except that they do not pursue moksha by isolating themselves from people and worldly matters. Instead, they dedicate their lives to serving the nation. The pracharaks travel the length and breadth of the country with Bharat Mata in their heart and possess only basic items such as a notebook, a couple of worn and mended kurtas, a well-worn chappal, a jute bag, and an old HMT watch. With this 'wealth' the RSS men have protected and watched over our nation through times of crisis, adharmic acts, and political turmoil. We have never heard them complain or backtrack from their goals.

Sinu asserts that the dedication of RSS men to serving the nation cannot be understood solely through logical analysis by an outsider. It requires someone who is deeply rooted in the principles of Karma Yoga to truly grasp this.

We know Swami Vivekananda as a Karma Yogi, revered worldwide. But we are unaware of the many quieter versions of Swami Vivekananda who are the senior RSS pracharaks. As a nation, we find solace in the comfort of dharmic values and the freedom to express ourselves, even to rebel, thanks to them. As for Left-liberals, the venom they spew will eventually consume them, as hatred is the most unsustainable and self-defeating emotion.

Sinu Joseph worked actively in the NGO sector for a little more than a decade, from 2009–10 and 2019–20. During her time in the NGO sector, she extensively travelled across rural India, interacting with over 20,000 adolescent girls and women to gain a firsthand understanding of the practices and issues surrounding menstruation.

She co-founded the Mythri Speaks Trust in 2014, a grassroots voluntary organisation focused on women's health, rural development, and environmental issues. The trust emphasises developing realistic solutions and collaborating with communities. Prior to this, she worked with another NGO called Youth for Seva and volunteered with several organisations, including Vanavasi Kalyan Ashram, Hindu Seva Prathisthana, Vanita Sahayana Vani, and The Forward Foundation.

The extensive action-learning from firsthand interactions with rural women resulted in the book *Rtu Vidya*, which delved into the ancient science behind menstrual practices. This book, along with the talks surrounding it, marked a significant conclusion to her work on menstruation. Just before *Rtu Vidya*, she authored another book titled *Women and Sabarimala*, which explored how women's menstrual and reproductive health is impacted when they visit moksha dhams (pilgrimage sites) like Sabarimala. These books have had a direct positive influence on women's menstrual health and have helped dispel much negativity surrounding cultural practices. Although *Rtu Vidya* is grounded in Indian sciences, it is being referenced and recommended by gynaecologists as a means to prevent menstrual disorders.

> Yes, a significant portion of what I write pertains to Hindu temples and the science of how they impact human physiology. But that subject is so vast that merely mentioning it in passing here would not do justice to the depth of knowledge. When COVID-19 happened, gradually the fieldwork reduced, and that's when I began writing the books. Currently, I primarily focus on writing and sharing the science behind the cultural and religious aspects of Sanatan Dharma.

In 2016, she presented her third TEDx talk titled, 'The Super Science behind Menstrual Practices'. It provided an eighteen-minute overview of what she later published as *Rtu Vidya* in 2020. However, shortly after its public release in 2016, the talk unexpectedly went viral. Then, all of a sudden, it was banned. The primary TED organisers sent an email requesting the host to remove the talk because it was based on Ayurveda, which they did not consider a valid science.

> The local TEDx organiser faced the threat of losing their licence as a TEDx platform if they did not remove my talk. Can you imagine? Despite receiving at least another ten invitations for TEDx talks since then, I have turned them all down because of the way the narrative is manipulated to suppress native sciences. At that time, I keenly felt the absence of Indic platforms where we could showcase the knowledge of our native sciences. But look how far we have come now! It brings me immense joy that we have numerous Indic platforms actively promoting Indian knowledge systems,

without seeking approval from the West. The government has also initiated efforts to introduce Indian knowledge systems into the educational curriculum, signalling a revival on the horizon.

Sinu highlights that these changes did not occur because Narendra Modi personally instructed individuals to establish Indic platforms, arrange talks, or alter the narrative. It is simply that the atmosphere of this land has shifted, she says.

And in the radiance of that aura, we naturally came together, automatically establishing platforms, and witnessing the resurgence of Indic thought. Modiji's presence at the helm is all it took to shift the subtle energy dynamics, and we are all basking in it. The events, policies, etc., are merely external manifestations. Modiji is the Yug Purush this land has been waiting for. Fortunately, the ecosystem from which he emerged harbours many more silently luminous souls like him, ensuring that our future will be rooted in dharma for at least the next few hundred years. This marks just the beginning of our revival.

Zeba Zoariah

At only twenty-four, Zeba Zoariah stands out as one of the most prominent nationalistic Muslim voices in India's media and social media spheres. Currently in the final year of her law degree (LLB), she previously earned her bachelor's in international relations from OP Jindal University. She attended Delhi Public School for her earlier education.

Zeba was born and brought up in Dibrugarh. Her father is Muslim, and her mother is Hindu. She has a younger brother.

While her mother practises Hinduism, her father, a joint commissioner of income tax, is not particularly religious. Her grandfather, however, was a devout Muslim who went to Haj several times and prayed five times a day. He was highly respected within the community.

> But I was never forced to practise the tenets of Islam or to pray. Neither I nor my mother, nor even the younger grandchildren, were compelled. We were never forced to wear a burqa or hijab. We received a secular education. My grandmother was a feminist who wrote poetry and stories. She used to advocate for women to voice their opinions. Since childhood, I have been surrounded by an environment where reasoning and questioning were encouraged. We received a secular education. Since the age of three, I have been singing and dancing, which differs from some Muslim families.

When she had exams, her father, who was very keen on politics, would guide her on political matters and allow her the space to ask uncomfortable questions about community and religion. The family had a ritual of watching regional news over evening tea. Children were encouraged to read the newspaper.

While she has remained in touch with a portion of her mother's family and has accompanied her to temples, another part of her mother's relatives still do not maintain relations after her mother married a Muslim.

The state she hails from, Assam, has distinct politics concerning Muslims. Assamese or native Muslims resent Bengali-speaking ones who have illegally migrated from Bangladesh, and politicians like Badruddin Ajmal gain popularity through their support. Concerning the threat of linguistic and cultural dominance, Hindus and Muslims in Assam often find themselves on the same side.

> Not only do the Muslims of Assam have an issue with Bangladeshis, but even the Hindus do. It is a common problem. If you find a mosque, you will find slum areas nearby. The way of living and their behaviour.... And all the workers are from their community. Jobs are being taken. They are everywhere; you can't even distinguish them. They are utilising all our resources. They obtain ration cards and Aadhaar cards and such. Everything is politicised for vote banks.

She says there is very little conflict between local Hindus and Muslims across Assam.

Since her school days, she has been interested in debating and public speaking. She joined a writing society, where she met numerous professors who recommended books and materials for her to read. It was during this time that Zeba wrote her first article, focusing on mass, forcible conversions.

> In the South, you have Christians conducting mass conversions ... a lot of drama and rice-bag politics. Then I read about the forces aiming to break India. We formed a patriotic society [at Jindal University], comprising not only Right-leaning or Centrist individuals but also those leaning to the Left. We used to publish a magazine and wrote extensively about China, internal security, and the Kashmir issue. Then, one of my seniors mentioned they had a panel discussion and it might be perceived negatively if a Hindu girl spoke on the hijab controversy. 'Would you like to represent our university?' they asked. I said yes, why not? In March, I participated in the panel alongside Amana Ansari.

She encouraged me to speak more often. I was not sure if I was suitable for speaking on such significant platforms, but she insisted I meet new people. She also asked if she could share my video on Twitter. I agreed but expressed concern about potential backlash.

Zeba consulted her mother about whether the hijab was mandatory, and if so, why were women in Iran and Afghanistan protesting? She also sought the opinion of a close family member who had been to Haj regarding the hijab.

> She said, 'Why are you even speaking about it? It is mandatory. Don't you see that I adore it? It is written in the Quran.' I mentioned that my father's sister also went to Haj, but I don't see her wearing it, and there are many others, even from Pakistan, Turkey, and Lebanon, who don't follow this strict mandate. She broke relations with my family. It is not that I receive all the support for voicing such things, but if it helps give a lot of other people the same courage, I will still speak out.

Zeba points to a hypocrisy in Muslim society rooted in class. In the lower strata of Muslim society, weddings lack music and dancing, while the more affluent lead more liberal lives, she says.

As she started speaking out on these issues, she says she has silently and gradually started gaining support on social media.

> Initially, trolls would say, 'Just wait and watch, you will get a sweet taste of what you said.' But now, when I see so many young followers, both Muslims and Hindus, supporting me, I feel encouraged. There is always a civilised manner to engage

in discourse or question people. So now, on every issue I discuss in a civilised manner, I see around twelve people using the same kind of narrative, engaging in good discourse while countering others. I like it when people my age do it. My friends are somewhat apolitical, but when they listen to me, they are keen to know more. WhatsApp forwards or Insta forwards are not always true. You also need to consider the other side. Also, one has to shed personal biases. Just because a Left-leaning person has written a book, you shouldn't reject it. I always appreciate a good counterargument when it comes to me.

Zeba highlights the liberal hypocrisy of citing sedition against activists like Disha Ravi (who allegedly created and circulated a toolkit to stir trouble in India) and discussing the absence of freedom of expression in India but never mentioning the banning of Salman Rushdie's *The Satanic Verses*.

'All the Left-leaning professors hate me. There are Right-leaning professors, but they don't speak out as much. They have to protect their jobs,' she says.

With the sharp Hindu–Muslim polarisation in India right now, what is the way forward?

It is not the sole responsibility of the Hindu community to reform. The burden shouldn't fall solely on one community. Until now, the community [Muslims] has acted immaturely. It has not matured; it is ghettoised. Much of this has to do with Left-liberals and politicians who don't want them to break free from their victim mentality. What minority are we talking about? I am not a religious scholar, but Khan Abdul Ghaffar Khan said if you want to judge how civilised a society is, you have to see how it treats its women. People don't know about nikah halala; they are talking about hijab. The Rana

Ayyubs and Arfa Khanums won't wear hijab, won't send their kids to a madrasa, will benefit from a secular education, travel business class but advocate for hijab for ordinary Muslims.

One of Zeba's personal icons is Arif Mohammed Khan. She admires how vocal he is about religion and Islamic terrorism.

> Khan said that terrorism has been present in our community. It has been used as a political tool. And the label given to it is jihad. And you have to accept that terrorism has a religion ... you just can't deny it. They are deceiving people, and one must take their deception with a pinch of salt. You are in a country that supports you, offering many opportunities you can explore. Adopt secular education for yourself and your family. If the Islamist or extremist interpretation of Islam is the correct one, are you implying that people like Arif Mohammed Khan, Abdul Ghaffar Khan, or even myself are not true Muslims? That we are munafiq [hypocrites]?

Zeba believes that most fundamentalists do not interpret the Quran correctly. Otherwise, they wouldn't torment or kill others for the sake of violence.

> I am not considered Muslim enough because I don't wear the hijab. There was an incident I read about in J&K where terrorists asked passengers on a bus to recite Arabic verses to identify non-Muslims. There was a Hindu couple, and the husband recited a Sanskrit shloka in Arabic or Urdu. But the terrorists did not even realise that it was a Sanskrit shloka. They knew nothing.

She says that across Islamic countries, people have started voicing dissent at the risk of their lives, even in Pakistan.

And she says she can see a change around herself here in India as well. Every time Zeba appears on TV, her cousin watches and tells others. There are friends who are receptive to rational discussions and ideas.

> But those like Rana Ayyub keep saying that the burqa is a choice. Have you seen her wearing it? No, they won't. They will enjoy all the perks, fly business class, first class, go on vacations. This is their way of income. But other Muslims should realise that they can also travel first class by educating and skilling themselves. There are so many talented athletes, IPL stars, people like Nikhat Zareen who are Muslims. So, you can't say you are not given the opportunity.

Zeba says she has not received threats except for one or two online ones initially because hers is a very new voice.

> If somebody has to do something, they don't use a fake profile or a fake name. If you have to do something, come forward, and we will handle it in court. I don't say anything that is wrong. I speak based on facts and legal matters. If I say anything wrong, we'll deal with it in court. Courts are there for a reason. There are many people online whose location shows Kashmir or Pakistan. They don't have a name. They have a phone, they have the internet, and they have nothing to do in their lives; they are just keyboard warriors. If they have to harm me, they will one day, but I don't care. If I die for the country while doing something truly good, that would be great.

In the Nupur Sharma case, she asked the hawks in her community if the BJP spokesperson was wrong in quoting the Hadiths about Prophet Mohammed.

The way [Sharma] spoke may have been wrong, but what she said is a fact, isn't it? The other side provoked her, and she said what she said. A so-called fact-checker, who has been accused of inciting mobs against Sharma, is such a hate monger. He despises Hindus. People are not concerned about the truth. They pursue fame, name, money ... everything. That is miserable.

Zeba wants to complete her law degree. 'I am going to specialise in corporate law so that I have a reasonable amount of savings. I have an interest in energy laws and intellectual property rights. I will choose one.'

Her dad wants her to appear for the UPSC exam. Bureaucracy. Because it is his dream, she is going to give it a shot. But she jokingly asks him sometimes why he wants her to join the bureaucracy, where she won't be able to speak the blunt truth and express her opinions, which she enjoys so much.

Arshia Malik

One of the most cerebral and prominent nationalistic and reformist voices from Kashmir is that of Arshia Malik. Arshia's mother was the Shah Bano of Kashmir. She was served triple talaq by her husband. They remained separated for eighteen years and then reconciled. All this was happening when Arshia was in her teens.

Now forty-seven years old, Arhia was almost honour-killed by her family at the age of eighteen because she wanted to marry a Hindu man from Amritsar. Her parents and uncles colluded.

> It was a wake-up call for me that my family, who had raised me, would so easily decide to end my life. I had younger uncles closer to my age, and they discussed the logistical challenges of disposing of the body. Even though I mentioned the Constitution and my right to register under the Special Marriage Act as an eighteen-year-old, it was disregarded. I kept quiet because my uncles threatened to send militants after the boy. I had to save his life.

It was during this period that Arshia realised that ordinary Kashmiris were also in contact with militants, using them to settle property disputes, love affairs, and other longstanding enmities.

> For years, my wings were clipped. Then, I was locked up, and I had to take all my exams privately for the eleventh, twelfth, and first and second years of college. But I did not break; I started working. I haven't taken a rupee from my father since the age of nineteen. I have been teaching on my own since nineteen. I met Arshad because of my writing, and we bonded over our shared views. He was an atheist when we got married. I was bolder than him. He was a bit hesitant because he was an only child, and his parents and sister advised him not to speak out.

The 11 September attack on America was the event that pushed Arshia to speak out; she couldn't stay quiet anymore. She had directed Shakespeare's *Tempest* at Tagore Hall, Srinagar, in the morning. The news about 9/11 started coming in around 3 p.m.

> It was not just about me now; it was an entire civilisation against one barbaric culture. Planes are being flown into

buildings. The cheering around me [in Kashmir] ... I couldn't take it anymore. I saw these children cheering. I thought it was the success of the play. I asked what happened, and they said the planes had flown into the buildings. I was like 'People must have died, but you are cheering?' For me, it was like watching a Palestinian street with hijab and everything and cheering.

The first picture that hit her hard was the iconic one of a man falling from the World Trade Towers. She left her job teaching at school, joined an organisation for children affected by armed conflict, and travelled through some of the deadliest districts of Kashmir like Kupwara. She spoke to women, children, and militants, as well as young Indian Army soldiers posted there.

I asked the army boys, 'Why are there so many allegations against you about rapes and other things?' They said, 'What can we do, they call us there.' Rural women do not have inhibitions like city girls, so for them, it is okay to call these nineteen, twenty, twenty-one-year-old army boys—who are living dangerously and far away from their families—to the field. The army boys said they always get caught because the girl is bait. She lures them and then cries sexual assault. Immediately, a journalist is ready to take that story, and it travels to America. This is what is happening. Most cases are of entrapment.

Then she found a job with the *Kashmir Images* daily. Bashir Manzar was the editor.

I later came to know that he was a militant-turned-editor, and with the help of a top IB and R&AW officer, he got some funds to run his newspaper. He used to always go on tours to

Pakistan, PoK, and London. All these were atrocity circuits, atrocity tourism. They would talk about [army] massacres and not visit the Pandit houses. Bashir Manzar showed me some magnanimity. I said militants have also committed atrocities. I have four files with me from Kupwara; the girls are missing. Will you print it? He said yes. And he turned to a man behind and said, 'I haven't seen such people in my life.'

The man behind him turned out to be the one editing Arshia's articles. He was Arshad Malik, who would later become her husband. That was in 2002. That year, *Kashmir Images* took Arshia to a conference on truth and reconciliation in Jammu. A think tank from Washington was present.

I was amazed to see this tall, white American man apologising to Kashmiris for all the atrocities committed in the name of imperialism by white people. America didn't have anything to do with our colonialism, right? He was getting down on his knees. Arshad was there. I said, 'What the hell is happening?' I saw all these people who were part of the Intifada factory—Kashmir University doctors and professors, militant-turned-editors, militant-turned-writers—but no Kashmiri Pandit. I was the only one speaking up, and Bashir was trying to censor me. Then I left *Kashmir Images*. My job was taken away.

In Kashmir, Arshia could at most write for newspapers. There was no internet. She did not even have a phone until 2005. As her reputation as a very outspoken, pro-India journalist spread, work dried up. She even lost her job at Delhi Public School, Srinagar, which is owned by one of the most influential Pandit families, the Dhar family. Its original trustee, D.P. Dhar, was in the Indira Gandhi cabinet and was also the ambassador to Russia.

I should have been the most protected there. Instead, I was thrown out because of my vocal pro-India stance. This occurred in 2014, during the Kashmir floods when we lost a significant amount of assets, prompting my decision to leave. I responded to an ad in *TOI* and had to leave my husband and son there. I had intended to bring Arshad here; he would have found a job in *TOI*, but fate didn't afford him the opportunity. He passed away at the age of forty due to a heart attack. After years of censorship and stress … my son called me, panicked, informing me that his father was not breathing. He tried to revive him, while I counted, 1, 2, 3 … we called the ambulance, but he was pronounced dead on arrival. It has been traumatic for my son. He was thirteen when his father died in his arms. Since then, my focus has been solely on him. Now he is twenty.

The mother and son now live in Greater Noida.

Arshia fondly talks about Kashmir, which is opening up again today after the Centre ended its special status by revoking Article 370 and Article 35A from the state.

Many youngsters are now into sports, and the music scene is thriving again. The government has made significant investments in winter sports. Tourism is booming, of course, but people, especially those in the private sector, hesitate to invest due to terrorism. However, efforts are being made to tackle this issue, and there has been a notable improvement. This April saw a record influx of tourists in the last ten to eleven years. We have the largest tulip garden in Asia, which blooms in March and April. The Amarnath Yatra started a few days ago. The government is taking control. It brings children from various schools across India to show that the situation is not dire and that Muslims are not being oppressed.

Kashmir's traditional apple and carpet industries are also recovering. The state's immense knowledge of herbs is being utilised in sericulture and floriculture. The copper plates from King Harsha's time or the Jamawar shawls, which Napolean's wife Josephine used to have transported from here, are still famous.

Central Asian handicrafts arrived during the era of the sultans. The eighth sultan of the Shah Mir dynasty, Zain-ul-Abidin or Bud Shah, often regarded as the Emperor Akbar of the Valley, brought back the Pundits who had been chased away during Islamic invasions. It was a peaceful period during which handicrafts flourished. He also brought in many Central Asian artisans. Going further back in time, new research suggests that Neolithic Kashmir had a textile industry. After four decades of extensive excavations at Burzahom, 16 km northeast of Srinagar city, an Archaeological Survey of India report states that Kashmiris in ancient times were traditionally an artisan community, skilled in weaving and intricate craftsmanship. The report also links the Neolithic (or New Stone Age) site to the contemporary Indus Valley civilisation.

Thousands of years later, British missionaries would take over and run Kashmir's silk factories. The first silk factory revolt against the British occurred due to the working conditions.

> We were more famous for the Martand Sun Temple than for the Dal Lake, as many believe. The Martand Temple, like the Konark Temple, was one of the ancient temples—majestic and wonderfully maintained now. Unfortunately, it was featured in a song in the movie *Haider* for a devil dance.

Then, she goes on to speak with pride about Kashmiri scholars:

They say no manuscript was considered complete in the Indian subcontinent until it bore the seal of Kashmiri scholars. Abhinav Gupta is our Aristotle of the East, and his poetics are classic. As for the Kashmiri language, we used the Sharada script. Unfortunately, now we use the Persian script. It should revert to the Sharada script.

Arshia says Kashmir has endured a lot of misery—from Afghan governors, Botrajas, Mongol invaders like Dulcha, to the British. It is a long, ruthless history.

So, all Kashmiris want is comfort, and whichever party or group brings relief from the extremities of weather and harsh conditions, they will turn to that. If you go to remote areas like Gurez, which are still inaccessible, people will want to vote for the BJP because it is the only party bringing roads and water. The NC used to focus only on Srinagar and its affluent areas. The PDP had started making progress in Anantnag and Badgam districts. Today, senior citizens say they are receiving money in their accounts. 'Why should we not go support the BJP?' That's the narrative. Also, life has become easier with UPI transactions.

Kashmir's Hindu–Muslim problems have existed since her earliest memory. But it would be occasional, like India losing a match to Pakistan or Pandit houses being stoned during some festival. But there was some semblance of harmony. Many Muslims would visit the ancient Shankaracharya temple, and on Eid, Pandits would visit their Muslim neighbours' houses. Then 1989 happened—a meticulously planned pogrom. The Pandits refer to it as their seventh exodus.

> The social fabric was torn apart. Now, it's monochromatic— just Muslims and Muslims. No Hindus, no Christians,

no Buddhists. Non-Muslims are only present in gated communities. Jamaat has funding since the 1960s. There were exchange programmes with Palestinian students coming to Kashmir University. That's when the hijacking of Indian Airlines' Ganga occurred. All these ideas were coming from the Palestinians, including intifada-style stone-pelting.

While Arshia's boldness stands out, she says dissent against radical Islam is not new.

> Throughout history, during the golden period of Islam, there have been dissenters and critics much bolder than what you see today. Even during the Prophet's time. Even after his death, we had Caliph al-Mamoon, who built a House of Wisdom. He housed many manuscripts there. Asharites believe in texts over reasoning, while Mutazalites believe in reasoning over text and that the text could also be negated. The towering figures amongst Mutazalites were Ibn Sina and Ibn Rushd. Al-Ghazali was an Asharite.

Mutazalites took patronage from Khalif Mamoon and adopted manuscripts from all over the world since Baghdad had become the centre of the Islamic world, not Mecca, she explains.

> Shias are much more enlightened than Sunnis. Of course, Shias have historical resentment against Sunnis. Surprisingly, the Prophet is the only person, despite being the founder of Islam, who didn't receive funeral prayers. They were fighting over successor issues in the mosque that he made while Ali was tending to the body for hours in those desert conditions. These things are not taught here, but they are in Morocco, Egypt, etc. India is yet to catch up on that. It is stuck with Deoband, Aligarh, and Nizami.

New scholarship is emerging among Arabic and European Muslims that blasphemy must not be punished with death, for instance. But in the subcontinent, the clergy is unwilling to declare it as un-Islamic, she rues. The reason is that they follow Maulana Maududi, one of the most influential fundamentalist clerics in South Asia.

He is ours; we produced him. They won't reform; they won't talk about Ibn Rushd. They won't talk about the gay imam Daayiee Abdullah or Mustafa Akyol, who wrote three books on Muslim enlightenment, making a case for Islamic liberty and liberalism.

The Arab world, she says, has taken a turn for the better because the oil is running out, and the power centre is shifting. It is always going to be a struggle between Tehran and Riyadh for the custodianship of the faith.

> That the Arab world is beginning to accept the existence of Israel is a big development. It makes a huge difference that they have allowed women to drive without a male escort present and allowed Hindu temples to be built. I think the UAE and Saudi have got it.

Concurrently, cinema halls are opening in Kashmir after nearly four decades. 'They were protesting *The Kashmir Files* without having a single cinema hall. Completely illogical,' she says.

For Arshia, Sharia and Muslim personal laws have no role in Kashmir. She favours the UCC.

> One needs to first build consensus among Hindus. Anything that benefits Hindus will also benefit Muslims. Sharia is misogynistic, homophobic, and deeply discriminatory. Sharia law undermines women. It requires two female witnesses

> compared to one male witness. Even in cases of rape, male witnesses are needed. And if you bring those witnesses, it implies you are admitting to adultery. Do you see the Catch-22? Stoning is the punishment for adultery. The man will be punished only to the waist, but not the woman. She can't escape when they are stoning. Watch the 2009 movie, *The Stoning of Soraya M*, about Iran.

To underline the need for UCC, Arshia cites Turkey and Tunisia, where polygamy is banned. Instant triple talaq is also banned in Pakistan.

After relocating from Kashmir, Arshia taught at the NTPC school on its Dadri campus. She describes it as a mini-India with teachers from Kerala, Bengal, and Punjab, while she is the only Kashmiri.

> NTPC has its chimneys, but it's like an oasis. It's a wetland, so you get a lot of exotic birds and leopards coming in. My terrace has peacocks, monkeys, and egrets. It's a beautiful campus. I used to go around the villages where there are many Muslim women sarpanches. They keep talking about triple talaq, LPG cylinders, schemes for women entrepreneurs, healthcare. The Muslim women say they will vote for the BJP, but 'don't tell our husbands about it'.

Arshia says that in Uttar Pradesh, CM Yogi Adityanath has reined in Muslim boys on bikes who used to terrorise. Also, she believes that love jihad is a reality. The local Muslim women want polygamy banished.

Arshia admires the liberal Hindu outlook but points out that some liberal Hindus inadvertently aid radical Islam, doing a great disservice to Muslim women. They hinder critical inquiry and dissent.

They haven't lived under Sharia, and they haven't known our concerns. Many Muslim women live in homes where they can't be seen or heard. You can't question back. A brother can come and slap you, but you can't question back. This is not the case in Hindu culture. These useful idiots come and equate these cultural narratives, saying both cultures and religions are the same. Absolutely wrong. It's like comparing the sky and the earth. Hindus have embraced atheism, but we are not even allowed to think about it. They do not even know about the Mutazalite tradition. I do not understand these useful idiots. Frankly, I am beginning to understand how India was conquered.

Arshia says the 'useful idiots' wanted to co-opt Mughals and others into Indian culture without asking about their own culture. No one asked about the status of their women. She cites a video of a conference in Sydney where Muslims arrive, and the atheists start chanting, 'Where are your women?'

Is Arshia an atheist?

I am. I have believed in rational thinking right from childhood. Maulvi sir used to say whoever doesn't believe will go to hell, and I was very vocal. He would complain to my mom. Much later, I met Arshad, and we discovered Christopher Hitchens. Hitchens is uncompromising. For me, it's an ultimate slap for Muslims. British activist Maajid Nawaz, for instance, is an ally. I have read his book *Radical* in which he talks about Ukraine and Nazis. The only thing is he is still a believer. I do not understand why. Canadian writer Ali A. Rizvi and I follow each other, but we all got divided over Trump. Ali Rizvi was against him.

Arshia can be blunt even with ex-Muslims, whom most people with her political views would consider an ally.

Iranian–Canadian atheist activist Armin Navabi, for instance, started a campaign called 'Sexy Kali'.

> But I said I will like this picture if you do it with Prophet Mohammed as well. That wasn't done. That's the filter and the test. He failed to impress me. I said, 'This is why I don't support you people. You are living in liberal democracies where you have all the freedom but can't do this, while you dare to lecture us living in Third World countries.' I also said, 'Why shouldn't India be a Hindu nation if Muslims have fifty-six Islamic countries?'

Arshia says Muslims have made it impossible to even inquire if Prophet Mohammed existed, although Saudi Arabia and Israel have given permission to Arab scholars to conduct research on it.

Arshia believes that now there is greater hope for the integration of minorities in India. 'I am from Kashmir, and it is now clear to them that this is their nation. They don't say it out loud, but Pakistan's betrayal and the trauma of Partition have stayed with them. No child has ever been named after Jinnah,' she says.

She lists three defining events in the Islamic world that shaped the attitude of the community. First, the advent of the Islamic Republic in Iran. Second, the Egypt–Israel Peace Treaty, and third, the Soviet invasion of Afghanistan. 'Pakistan's export of jihad to Afghanistan was successful, but to Kashmir, it was unsuccessful solely because of the Indian Army,' she says. She has a lot of hope for Indian Muslims.

> We had leaders like Hamid Dalwai, who raised the triple talaq issue in the 1970s. We have Arif Mohammed Khan, we

had Dr A.P.J. Abdul Kalam. The only problem is the Owaisis. He may actually be giving the thumbs up to Pakistan, but as a Muslim, I know that he is Muslim 2.0. You have to understand those tricks which as a Hindu you can't. There is a similarity in the speeches of Jinnah and Asaduddin Owaisi. He can fool the masses, he can fool the Hindus, but he can't fool us.

Arshia says the Government of India will have to start thinking outside the box and not rely on its traditional advisers.

There are brilliant minds all over; we need to find and consult them. The Ulema also includes many progressive Muslims. The Barelvis and Deobandis have categorically separated themselves from the Taliban and have not issued fatwas. Indian Muslims accepted the Ayodhya verdict; they did not come out on the streets. Gyanvapi in Kashi is not disputed either. It is clear that it is a mandir, and they themselves are saying that they will give it back. It was only when Mohammed Zubair edited that clip that he mobilised mobs, which I am really angry about. Because when they hear something said about the Prophet, they believe it without realising it could be untrue.

Arshia is writing a book on unheard Muslim voices and these traditions which are not widely known in Islam.

'If you want to push back against Islamism, the Mutazalite tradition has to come back. I am not negating Islamic civilisation or culture or any belief system, but secularism is a must.'

CHAPTER 10

Bharat's Giant, Waking Diaspora

New York's Madison Square Garden thundered with chants of 'Bharat Mata ki Jai' and 'Modi, Modi' on 29 September 2014. India's Prime Minister Narendra Modi, sworn in just four months before the event, took the stage in a yellow kurta and saffron jacket. For the 18,000 people present there—mostly overseas Indians and dozens of top US politicians and business leaders—and the millions who watched the event live, it was undoubtedly a moment that would find its place in history.

A resurgent Bharat announced its arrival on the global stage. More importantly, the idea of Bharat beyond geographical boundaries seemed to awaken from its long slumber right there in the 1,000-megawatt rock concert atmosphere. Perhaps at no other time in history has India's gigantic diaspora been both organically enthused and purposefully awakened so widely and intensely.

Bharat's diaspora has a unique quality. Waves of immigrants went abroad, but an overwhelming majority never gave up on the Ramayana, Mahabharata, Gita, or Ramcharitmanas. Nor did they willingly abandon the social and family values they carried with them. Modi and the surge in nationalism seem to have simply reignited the Indian soul within that dispersed human mass.

The prime minister's visits to various countries are greeted with celebrations often bordering on hysteria. Yoga has become India's global currency of soft power, especially after the United Nations General Assembly adopted a unanimous resolution soon after Modi's election in 2014, declaring 21 June as the International Day of Yoga. Insults to Bharat and instances of Hinduphobia spark outrage across nations, and Hindu organisations are spreading to places that were unimaginable just a few years ago.

The RSS's overseas affiliate, Hindu Swayamsevak Sangh (HSS), has grown by 21 per cent, from 194 shakhas in the United States in 2018 to 235 shakhas across 164 cities and 34 states in 2022. It currently has 3,289 branches in 156 countries. HSS began its operations in Kenya and Myanmar in 1947. It mobilises the Hindu community to 'preserve, practise, and promote Hindu ideals and values'. HSS works closely with other Hindu organisations such as the Chinmaya and Ramakrishna missions. It also provides substantial aid during natural calamities such as the 1978 Andhra cyclone, the 2001 Gujarat earthquake, the December 2004 tsunami, and the 2015 Himalayan foothill floods.

Sri Sri Ravishankar's Art of Living Foundation has centres in 180 countries. As one of the largest volunteer-based organisations globally, its 30,000-plus teachers and over a million volunteers are engaged in service projects across 156 countries. It proudly claims to have impacted over 500 million lives, amassed over 12 million followers across social media platforms, and successfully transformed over 7,400 extremists. According to its website, Art of Living programmes have been attended by over 1,27,000 students on 101 university campuses worldwide.

Art of Living Foundation has provided training to over 5,000 women in Iraq in computer skills, tailoring, banking, and hospitality. During the 2022 crisis in Ukraine, it distributed 32,000 meals and provided accommodation for 5,875 refugees. Its trauma relief and resilience programmes have benefited 16,000 children and youngsters affected by the Syrian conflict in Lebanon and Jordan.

Sadhguru Jaggi Vasudev's Isha Foundation engages over 17 million volunteers worldwide through more than 300 centres. It has two major infrastructures in the US: the Isha Institute of Inner-sciences in Tennessee and the Isha Yoga Centre in Los Angeles.

The International Society for Krishna Consciousness (ISKCON) operates temples in eighty-two countries. In Europe alone, there are over 135 ISKCON-affiliated temples and cultural centres, with an additional thirty-one centres in Russia. The United States boasts fifty-six formally affiliated ISKCON centres, while Canada has twelve, including the self-sustaining Saranagati Eco Village in British Columbia. Mexico is home to five ISKCON centres. There are sixty affiliated ISKCON temples in South America, over eighty in Asia, sixty-nine in Africa, six in Australia, and four in New Zealand. ISKCON subsidiaries include the Bhaktivedanta Book Trust, the world's largest publisher of books concerning Krishna, with translations available in more than eighty languages.

Pandava Sena, a youth organisation based out of Bhaktivedanta Manor in Watford, UK, comprises professionals and university students. It has established Krishna Conscious Societies in thirty universities across the UK.

The Ramakrishna Matth and the Ramakrishna Mission currently operate 279 branch centres worldwide. Among these, 211 centres are located in India, while the remaining 68 are spread across twenty-four other countries. There are also 56 sub-centres, with 24 within India and 32 outside the country.

Another Hindu organisation, Sewa International, has global partners in twenty-two countries, supported by 11,180 dedicated volunteers.

The BAPS Swaminarayan Sanstha, which recently built the Middle East's largest Hindu temple in Abu Dhabi, inaugurated by Modi, boasts a network of more than 1,100 mandirs and 3,850 centres worldwide.

Hindu spiritual organisations overseas often operate under extremely challenging conditions. In China, for instance, where religion is proscribed under the threat of extreme punishment, a Hindu organisation quietly conducts underground satsang or congregations that are attended by more than 10,000 Han Chinese devotees.

Besides spiritual organisations, socio-cultural and political Hindu organisations have been emerging rapidly. The US now hosts the Coalition of Hindus in North America (CONA), which oversees the Hindu Parents Network (HPN). It has been established to ensure that the 'next-generation Hindus are raised with resilience and Dharmic values'. With 1,000 members worldwide, it has enrolled over 2,000 children in 10 training programmes.

The Hindu American Foundation (HAF), for instance, has emerged as a vocal platform for Hindus and against Hinduphobia. It has trained over 3,600 teachers to date, directly influencing more than 90,000 students, and developed almost fifty unique teaching materials and resources. Moreover, its Hindu American Internship has inspired over

50 emerging leaders and trained 2,200 dharma ambassadors and advocates.

It has highlighted Hindus suffering gross human rights abuses through twelve annual Hindu human rights reports and over thirty advocacy campaigns. It ensured that over 4,000 Pakistani Hindu refugees received vital medical services, and nearly 18,000 Bhutanese Hindu refugees were able to preserve their culture and integrate into American life.

Headquartered in Washington DC, HAF has collaborated with the US Congress and FBI to establish the anti-Hindu hate crime data category. It also engages with the Department of Justice on Hinduphobic hate crimes. HAF filed lawsuits against California's Board of Education, Department of Fair Employment and Housing, and the California State University system for violating Hindu American rights and attempting to institutionalise caste. California Governor Gavin Newsom ultimately vetoed the bill that aimed to add caste to a list of protected categories under the state's existing anti-discrimination laws.

Following HAF's advocacy efforts, the US Congress has recognised Diwali as a major festival. Other major issues it has taken up include fighting against the Dismantling Hindutva conference, which was widely accused of being openly bigoted and Hinduphobic. It also campaigns for displaced Kashmiri Pandits and against historians like Audrey Truschke, who glorify genocidal Islamist rulers of the past, such as Mughal Emperor Aurangzeb. HAF has also engaged in aggressive activism against Hinduphobia on campuses, addressing incidents directed at Indian students like Karan Kataria or Rashmi Samant.

Another organisation making significant strides in uniting Hindus globally is the VHP's overseas arm, the World Hindu

Foundation, led by Swami Vigyananand. WHF also hosts the World Hindu Congress, which serves as a vibrant platform for the exchange of Indic ideas and the gathering of influential individuals. An Indian working with artificial intelligence in the Bay Area connects with another teaching Vedic studies in Seoul. A yoga instructor in Dubai shares and exchanges notes with a rare earth entrepreneur in Mozambique. And a Bhojpuri-speaking politician in Mauritius discusses civilisational resurgence with an Indian Masterchef in London.

The diaspora is gradually uniting as an integral part of Bharat. In the words of historian David Frawley:

> We have also had this big Indian diaspora, which is largely a Hindu diaspora globally, where suddenly you have Hindu temples in America and even Arabia, where you have the Hindu–Americans as the most affluent and educated group in the country apart from the Jews. Overseas they compare the Hindus with the Jews. They don't compare Hindus with poor people. In the UK, it was very funny because they said recently, that the problem with the Hindus or the Indians in the UK is to have too much money. Before their problem was they were all poor, uneducated, and now suddenly they have too much money. So that narrative has also changed. Of course, you have had the spread of some of these Vedic teachings, Yoga, Ayurveda. That has helped a bit too.

Anuraag Saxena

'As an NRI, you can't help but compare how differently the world looks at issues of culture and identity,' says Anuraag Saxena, a Singapore resident. He is a chartered accountant from India and holds an MBA from the US. He also attended the LKY School of Public Policy at the National University of Singapore.

Anuraag grew up in Andhra Pradesh in a simple, middle-class home. His father worked for a steel mill, and his mother is a homemaker.

> My father, especially, is the bluntest, funniest, scariest man I know. Sounds like a contradiction, but that is what makes him a role model. My grandfather, a farmer who was clinically blind, ensured his children got a proper education. I strongly believe that education is the only ticket out of poverty. I have seen examples of lives changing course only because of the power of education. I'm not a fan of labels. I don't consider myself a 'Right-Winger' because I don't believe in the restrictive definitions we've borrowed from the West. They work for the small, homogenous societies they are, but not for large, diverse societies like ours with a rich and complicated history.

Anuraag is renowned for his unique form of 'ghar wapsi', that is, he helps Bharat reclaim its stolen heritage. His India Pride Project (IPP) facilitates the repatriation of murtis, statues, and artefacts that have been smuggled out of India over centuries. Anurag, who is in his late forties, says:

> Forts, museums, temples ... many Indians take these for granted, while the rest of the world reveres the same artefacts. Why do we find it acceptable to scribble on a thousand-year-old sacred wall, while a sixty-year-old building elsewhere is respectfully protected? The genesis of the India Pride Project was to instil pride in these civilisational symbols. In fact, pride is central not just to our name, but to our very existence.

In the first sixty-five years since independence, India brought back just thirteen heritage objects. But in the last nine years, 344 such artefacts have been returned. These include the murti of Ma Annapurna, brought back from Ottawa and restored at Kashi Viswanath, Vijayanagar-era Dwarapala recovered from Australia, Nataraja of the Punnainallur Arulmigu Mariamman temple, Kankalamurti and Nandikeshvaran of the Narasinganadar Swamy temple brought back from the US, four-armed Vishnu, Sridevi, Shiva, and Parvati from the US and Australia. Additionally, a 15th-century bronze statue of Ram, Sita, and Lakshman was brought back from London, while a Chola-period metal murti of Hanuman, stolen from a Vishnu temple in Tamil Nadu's Ariyalur, was recovered from Australia. The US recently promised to return 1,414 more antiquities and non-antiquities of spiritual value.

In the Antiquities and Art Treasures Act, 1972, antiquity is defined as:

> Any coin, sculpture, painting, epigraph or other work of art or craftsmanship; any article, object or thing detached from a building or cave; any article, object or thing illustrative of science, art, crafts, literature, religion, customs, morals or politics in bygone ages; any article, object or thing of historical interest which has been in existence for not less than 100 years.

The trade in Indian art is worth billions of dollars on the black market, particularly through stolen temple statues, Chola bronzes, and other items of spiritual significance.

'I agree with Shashi Tharoor; British Museums are essentially "chor bazaars" founded on a snatch-and-scoot mentality. Sadly, that colonial mindset still continues. The denial and whitewashing of colonial loot is as evil as colonisation itself,' says Saxena.

Anurag attributes the return flight of deities to a resurgence of civilisational understanding and pride among Indians.

> People on the street are discussing distortions in history, the national security aspects of the refugee crisis, the resurgence of vernacular languages, the pricing of defence procurements, and a whole bunch of topics that have been deemed irrelevant so far. Heck, even Yash Raj Films, after shooting movies in Switzerland for decades, just made a rural India-themed movie. We've now started to see a resurgence of civilisational pride. I'm proud people have stopped seeing khandahars [ruins] and see heritage as symbols of India's civilisation.

He speaks about the shift in people's perspective, especially related to our history and artefacts:

> Ten years ago, no politician wanted to touch issues like 'Bring Our Gods Home'. Today, even the AIADMK and the Congress are asking questions in Parliament about this. No media wanted to cover it. Today, you have Swarajya and IndiaFacts on one hand, and BBC and the *Washington Post* on the other, speaking about this positively. Earlier, researchers wrote blogs, published books, and gave speeches at posh conferences, all for their own glory. But no one engaged with the system to bring our gods home. Today, our gods are coming home.

Prosperous countries like the US and China have enacted heritage protection laws, as has Mexico. He laments that even Jordan, whose GDP is less than 2 per cent of India's, has an enforcement agency for heritage, but India doesn't.

Anuraag has been involved with the documentary *Blood Buddhas*, which addresses the issue of funding terrorism through heritage crimes.

> Now that the UN has declared that heritage crimes fund ISIS's terror operations, I'm certain governments will take notice. Smuggling narcotics, sex slavery, and similar crimes receive considerable attention. ISIS has turned to trafficking blood Buddhas because it's gone unnoticed. Dr Haroon Ullah, author of *Digital World War*, recounts a fascinating account of an ISIS terrorist utilising the dark web for these transactions, leaving no trace behind. It's no longer just a matter of national pride; it's a national security concern.

Anuraag does not see a problem with the current surge of Hindutva, but he is critical of a section within the Hindutvawadis.

> I see a self-anointed Hindutva brigade actually angry that not enough is being done. People are coming up with wish lists and demands that they want Modi to fulfil. Leaving their sense of entitlement aside, there are people who conveniently ignore bold moves on instant triple talaq and Kashmir, and instead focus on their one agenda that they want someone else to do something about. I was telling one of these Delhi-based, self-proclaimed Hindu 'thought leaders' recently: '*Modi ji ne apne aap ko pradhan sevak kya kaha, aapne toh unko apna personal butler maan liya* [Modi referred to himself as the prime servant, but you have taken him to be your personal butler].' So yeah, you will always have these paradoxical people. On the one hand, they won't do anything about their own cause. On the other hand, Modi is not good enough for them.

On the economic front, he praises the government's approach to empowering the bottom of the pyramid. He describes schemes like Ayushmann Bharat, Ujjwala, and electrification as great equalisers.

> Having said that, procedural reforms still have a long way to go. Tax terrorism remains a reality. The enforcement of contracts through judicial means is still a significant challenge. I'm glad that Sanjeev Sanyal is addressing these issues. That's what the government needs to do—bring in experts with a global perspective and allow them to develop solutions.

In twenty years, Anuraag envisions a country where people take pride in their civilisational identity and the global impact Indians have made.

> We know we invented zero and surgery. That India was once one of the richest countries. Or that Christopher Columbus was looking for India when he lost his way to America. But the narrative of lost glory and the sone-ki-chidiya [golden bird] is quite dangerous. It breeds lethargy. We need another revolution in our ambition. We need every Indian to reignite the fire within. We need creators, builders, innovators, and above all, doers.

Girish Alva

In 2014, a thirty-six-year-old e-commerce manager working in Singapore decided there was something more urgent than just pursuing a career. The man from Mangalore persuaded his company to transfer him back to India, fully aware that his professional growth would suffer, and returned to settle in Bengaluru.

The question is, why did the engineer with two master's degrees in design and management decide to return to India after living in Singapore for fifteen years and a few months in the US?

> I am not a celebrity, just an ordinary person. I don't align myself with Right or Left ideologies. My concern is for the country. I have travelled to ten to twelve countries and can speak about ten to twelve languages. I consider myself educated and well-travelled. What I observe in other countries is that caring for your nation is fundamental; it's not an optional extra. India requires substantial changes. We need structural development and a shift in mindset. We possess resources, but it's the mindset that needs altering. That's what I saw in Modi.

Alva closely observed Narendra Modi for ten years before 2014. His brother worked closely with Modi when he was the chief minister of Gujarat. What impressed him was Modi's straightforward approach to problem-solving. 'You don't need hi-end stuff; you just need the mindset to serve your country, and everything else follows,' he says. 'So, what did I do after coming back? I started working for the 2014 elections.'

Thousands of young Indians like Girish took a break from their jobs abroad and returned to India to work for Modi's victory. They worked quietly, away from the limelight. And then, after the elections, Alva decided to return from Singapore.

> Overseas, my career growth would have been better. And one doesn't face issues with daily necessities like water and electricity. It is so comfortable. Public transport is not an issue. But here, everything is chaotic. That is okay. When you are

working for your country, you have to be willing to sacrifice some comforts. When you are overseas and visit India once a year, you see the bigger picture. If you are here, you don't see it. It's a gradual change. That was my main motivation to come back and work.

Even while he was in Singapore, he began working for a Facebook page called 'NaMo4Karnataka'. Nearly 100 people from dozens of cities contributed to it. 'There was a lot of negative and fake news being spread about Modi. We immediately countered it with the correct narrative within minutes. This had a huge impact in 2014,' he says. NaMo4Karnataka was being managed by someone in Gandhinagar, but it was not funded by the BJP. Alva often paid from his own pocket.

> A lot of people had quit their jobs. I created a simple WhatsApp group to connect them with those who had companies and job opportunities to offer. I also included fresh graduates and people with little experience in the group. Over the last four years, we have grown from 25 people to about 700, and hundreds have found employment. Now, I have three admins, so I am a bit more hands-off. For 2019, we followed the same approach. There were teams working for Modi, so I simply connected them with people who had connections. Then, I started a group called Bharat Spandan on social media. We launched a hashtag #GiveUpAMeal.

Girish further explains the reasons for launching the hashtag and its impact. The initiative stemmed from an issue in a village near Male Mahadeshwara Betta, a pilgrim town in Karnataka. The impoverished villagers there rear desi cows.

When a drought hit the area, the cows began to perish due to water scarcity. The Swamiji at the local math or ashram reached out to him for assistance in supporting and saving thousands of cows.

'If the cows die, the farmer also dies. He will commit suicide. When the Swamiji came to me for help, I reached out to a few people, and together, we launched a campaign. Every Monday, we gave up a meal. We formed a small team of about sixteen people and campaigned on Twitter with the hashtag #GiveUpAMeal,' he says.

Alva and his team raised close to Rs 3 crore. They saved about 20,000 cows and assisted 150–200 farmers. The Karnataka CM and senior BJP leader B.S. Yeddyurappa presented them with a cheque for Rs 10 lakh. Newspapers hailed it as one of the most successful social media campaigns for a social cause.

Their next campaign focussed on 'panchagavya', highlighting the medicinal benefits of desi cows. It did not emphasise the spiritual connection of the cow as the mother but rather approached the topic from a purely scientific standpoint.

The third campaign was 'Save Rachel'. The ten-month-old daughter of his Christian friend from Manipur fell seriously ill with a lung problem and needed immediate surgery. The mother, who had come to Bengaluru to work after her divorce, didn't have the money for the treatment. The crowdfunding started Friday night, and by Saturday, there was enough money for the surgery. The girl was saved. The chief minister of Manipur also tweeted about it.

Bharat Spandan then mobilised funds and support for flood victims in Kerala and Karnataka. It also conducted an extensive India Votes campaign.

The majority community should vote. That is the key to any change. The UPA not only caters to its vote bank but also ensures their voting participation. They provide them with voter IDs and ensure they reach the polling booths. But, despite being 70 per cent of the population, only 50 per cent of us actually vote. That means only 35 per cent of the total population votes. In Bengaluru, of that 70 per cent, only 50 per cent possess voter IDs, and of those, only 50 per cent actually vote. That amounts to just 17–18 per cent of the majority. That's pathetic. That is why we have suffered for seventy years.

For Alva, the Communal Violence Bill of 2011 was a trigger point. He felt it sought to make Hindus second-class citizens in their own country. 'It was one of the major turning points in my decision to come back to India and take action. No country will develop if its majority is not supported. I started tracking down every top BJP leader's email and began writing to them,' he says.

Girish bluntly declares that he would not have worked for the BJP if Modi weren't there. 'I am very critical of the BJP, especially here in Karnataka. I have trended #WakeUpBJP here many times. We don't want anything. I have a job. I don't need the power or the money. I just want the country to, at least in my generation, attain a better place,' he says.

What good leadership immediately leads to, says Alva, is greater respect for Bharat internationally. 'Earlier, when I went to China, they would open my passport to check if it was fake. But now, whichever country we visit, we are respected a lot. I went to the US, and a taxi driver asked where I was from. When I replied India, he said, "Oh, Modi." Your passport carries a lot of value,' he explains.

Alva dreams of raising the quality of government schools to rival private schools. He wants to first address the fundamental issues of building and infrastructure. 'When I meet an MLA or MP, I tell them we have the social media power to reach a lot of people. Why do we always need money? If this road has one hundred potholes, you just need to make a call. This Sunday, one thousand people will come to fix it,' he says, adding government schools can be improved with the same model. 'Some money may be needed, but we can easily get the work done. The government itself offers many schemes and benefits.'

Alva is married, and his wife also has a good job in Singapore. He says he always has the option to go back there. 'I can still return to Singapore. But I don't think I will be going back. There are a lot of things to do here,' he says.

Yudhistir Govinda Dasa

ISKCON has long been one of the foremost ambassadors of Hinduism globally. Founded in New York by Bhaktivedanta Swami Prabhupada in 1966, the movement has spread across the world over the last six decades. In India, its director of communications, Yudhistir Govinda Dasa, a calm and articulate man in his mid-thirties, breaks down the Hindu resurgence into three levels and explains how ISKCON is a part of it.

> First is the foundational philosophical level. Then there is the social level: how you live, how you interact, what you wear, what your social identity and value system are. And the third is the application part—how you apply this value

system in your day-to-day life. ISKCON is contributing on all three levels because our founder, Srila Prabhupada, used to say, 'Religion without philosophy is sentiment, or sometimes fanaticism, while philosophy without religion is mental speculation.'

Yudhistir Govinda Dasa (his post-initiation name) narrates how a classmate in college once asked him the meaning of his name, Yudhistir.

And he was a practising Hindu. He had no idea at all who Yudhistir [the eldest of the Pandavas in the Mahabharata] was. Parents haven't invested their time and resources in educating their children about their rich culture, resulting in a generation with no understanding of their roots. Today, through ISKCON in Delhi alone, we have 10,000 congregations connected. At the all-India level, there are at least a few lakhs. They are now being taught these core philosophical texts.

At the second or social level, all ISKCON members practise a certain lifestyle and share it with their families and acquaintances. ISKCON's restaurants promote a sattvic vegetarian diet.

These restaurants attract a lot of people both in India and abroad. In his Stanford commencement speech, Steve Jobs said, 'I would go to the Hare Krishna temple for one full meal every week.' Even Paul Allen, one of the co-founders of Microsoft, was a regular visitor. So, it reached out to many people and gave them a glimpse of India.

Another way the message spreads is through festivals. For instance, rath yatras have traditionally been held in India.

But the first rath yatra in the Western world was organised by ISKCON in San Francisco. Since then, it has become an emblem of Indian culture in numerous parts of the world. 'We had a kirtan in Antarctica as well. Recently, our devotees went on an expedition there,' says Yudhistir, whose schedule typically involves travelling to ten to twelve nations.

His tryst with ISKCON started from birth. Both his parents joined the movement in their early twenties. His father joined in 1979 in Vrindavan, and his mother joined in early 1981 in Chennai. His father is from Prayagraj, and his mother is from Tirunelveli, near Madurai in Tamil Nadu. They met in ISKCON and had an arranged marriage.

His father's story of joining the movement is remarkable:

> My grandfather was in the Indian Army. Once, with all the family members, they decided to go to Vrindavan for a pilgrimage. My father could not make it because he was in college and had exams. Back then, ISKCON was known as the Angrez Mandir in Vrindavan because it was the only temple in Vrindavan which had foreigners. Then they went back to Prayagraj and said, 'We saw gore log [white folk] perform puja, sing bhajans.' My father was fascinated. After his exams, he asked my grandfather, 'Can I go to Vrindavan?' He said, 'No.' One night, he took whatever little money he had and snuck out of the house, went to the railway station, got himself a ticket, and came to Mathura. The money he had was just enough to get him a ticket to Mathura. He was practically penniless, and he asked people at the station, 'How do I go to the Angrez Mandir?' They told him to go to Barsana.
>
> He walked all the way from Mathura to Barsana, a 35–40 km walk. Then he had to ascend a hill. He reached what is known as the Maan Mandir. Barsana was the palace of

Radharani. The pujari told him, 'You have come to the wrong place. You need to go to Vrindavan.'

So, he walked again from Barsana to Vrindavan, another 25 km. By the time he arrived, it was 8 p.m., and the temple gates were just about to close. They welcomed him, and he stayed there for ten to fifteen days, beginning to learn philosophy and their practices. He decided to join ISKCON. My grandfather didn't take the decision well. He said, 'You have to make a choice: family or…' So, my father made his decision and joined ISKCON. It strained his connections with the family, but he felt, 'For dharma, if that's what I have to do, so be it.'

Yudhistir and his brother studied at the gurukul in Vrindavan. He pursued his undergraduate studies at the MassCoMedia Institute, operated by the Delhi Press, in Noida. He then completed a correspondence course in intellectual property from Bengaluru.

Yudhistir's mother's family belongs to Ramanujacharya's Sri Vaishnava lineage. His grandfather was a Vedic priest in one of the temples. During a visit to Chennai, his mother and her sister both joined the temple there.

Yudhistir explains the requirements for initiation into ISKCON through diksha. One must give up four things. First, intoxication of any form as it brings down one's control over the senses, hindering the ability to avoid vices. The whole idea of the viyoga system is to control the senses so that one can focus on the divine. Second, one must completely avoid all forms of non-vegetarian food because it reduces compassion. Third, no gambling is permitted. And fourth, avoiding illicit relationships is imperative.

These four, along with the 'naam jap' chanting process in the Bhakti tradition, are mandatory. One is expected to chant the Hare Krishna mahamantra sixteen times on the beads. One round comprises 108 beads, and it takes between one-and-a-half to two hours to complete. This practice continues for one year. At the end of that period, one is eligible for a written examination on philosophical understanding and basic questions on the Bhagavad Gita.

Yudhistir believes there has been a very visible and notable shift in how people perceive culture, religion, particularly Hinduism.

> Until 2014, there was a situation where many people felt uncomfortable identifying themselves as Hindus, both in India and abroad. First, a lot of babas turned out to be fraudsters. This built a perception that Hinduism is a religion of fraudsters. Second, there was the idea left behind by colonialists that everything native is bad, outdated, or regressive. But now this perception is changing and the Western world is beginning to embrace our practices. For the past two years, I have been compiling articles from Western media, for instance, how they now promote turmeric latte or doodh-haldi, claiming it to be very good for health. They are also attempting to patent certain Ayurvedic plants. Moreover, they now advocate for using water instead of tissues for personal hygiene, a practice traditionally followed for millennia.

Yudhistir notes that the Indian film industry also played a dubious role in its portrayal and the values it propagated.

> India is grappling with the menace of abuses against women. When you tell youngsters it's okay to pursue a girl even when she says no and you romanticise the whole concept, that's the value system you are passing down. All of these factors

> together created a perception that maybe Hinduism is not good for you. But post-2014, there has been a resurgence that asserts traditional values and teachings have their own place. Even in the West, now there is an emerging concept that the separation of Church and State is not really healthy because they have people emerging who are lost. They may have all the resources for a good life, but where do you go with that?

The Hindu resurgence is aiding ISKCON's work in the Northeast, an extremely challenging geography. Its tribal care programme is open to everyone regardless of caste, gender, or religion. Many of these families were converted 150 years ago.

> These places even today pose a big challenge for us. You have to first drive your car to some village, park it there, then go on a bike for another two hours, then get down and trek for another two hours. So even in 2019, if that's the challenge, you might think, back in the 1800s how the missionaries did that. That's something we are lacking—that spirit to go out and share. You don't need to convert anyone. At least share your practices, provide some services to the people.

Interestingly, there is a village in the remote jungles of Jharkhand where tribals, much like the Vaishnavas, avoid eating onion and garlic. They have been practising this for centuries. Another community, the Ram bhakts, still carry bows and arrows wherever they go because they believe Lord Ram passed through their jungles and their ancestors had met him. They don't consume meat. ISKCON provides them with social support.

> The biggest challenge is that in some places, if you are not a member of Christianity or Islam, you don't even get access

to social mechanisms. So, we provide them with microgrants and teach them skill sets to make shawls, sweaters, and jute bags. ISKCON buys and sells these products from temples, and the locals receive a percentage of the profit. We have also initiated free schools in all the districts where we operate. We are currently negotiating with IIT Kharagpur to train 1,000 tribal students. We will take care of their accommodation, lodging, and boarding.

The Tripura government asked ISKCON to take over 200 schools that were shut down because there were no students or teachers. 'But we felt that was too much for us to take on at once. We have taken on twenty, and as they develop, then we will take on the others as well,' he says.

ISKCON's operations abroad are often fraught with danger. In neighbouring Bangladesh, seemingly a friendly nation, it has paid the price of its rising popularity. Islamists have gone beyond hyperbole to label ISKCON as a 'terrorist organisation' despite its advocacy and actions against violence worldwide.

The reality is grim. ISKCON has faced a spate of violent crimes in Bangladesh. In 2022, as devotees prepared for the Gaur Purnima celebration, a 200-strong mob stormed the premises of Shri Radhakanta Temple in Dhaka and attacked them, leaving three injured. In October 2021, 500 Islamists raided the ISKCON temple in Noakhali, setting fire to the premises, assaulting devotees, and brutally killing devotee Pranta Chandra Das, tossing his body into a nearby pond. In 2016, a priest of Gaudiya Vaishnava ashram was beheaded by individuals associated with ISIS while preparing for the morning mangal aarti at 4 a.m.

Those working on the ground perceive the situation in Bangladesh as akin to what Gregory Stanton describes as the ten stages of genocide. Islamists are trying to build a public frenzy against Hindu organisations.

When a Muslim man was killed in a petty fight, the police arrested a young Hindu man as a suspect. They examined his Facebook profile and found that among the 250 pages that he had liked, one was ISKCON. Islamists immediately capitalised on the situation. They organised a large protest in downtown Dhaka, gathering 5,000–6,000 people. Mosques blared the message: 'ISKCON bhagao' (drive out ISKCON). The Sheikh Hasina government promptly deployed police across Bangladesh, especially around ISKCON temples.

The strong, underlying factor behind these attacks is that ISKCON attracts numerous Bangladeshis through its social work, food and education programmes, and festivals. And it is not only ISKCON's Rath Yatra or kirtan that draws people in. Yudhistir highlights that Bangladesh has a rich history of Krishna Consciousness dating back to the time of Chaitanya Mahaprabhu.

'Even Chaitanya Mahaprabhu's own grandfather hailed from what is now Bangladesh. All the major Gaudiya Vaishnava leaders—like Sanatan Swaroopa Goswami, who served as the finance minister of Nawab Hussain Shah—were based in Ramkeli, located in modern-day Bangladesh,' he explains.

Another significant flashpoint for ISKCON globally was a court case in Russia's Tomsk, which classified the Russian-language edition of *Bhagavad Gita as It Is,* written in 1968 by Swami Prabhupada, founder of ISKCON, as extremist material. Some scholars from Tomsk State University sought its ban, leading to the book being put on trial and sparking widespread outrage worldwide.

'A small wire service in Russia covered that news. Coincidentally, a journalist from Kolkata happened to be in Russia at the time and came across it. They published it in a local newspaper in Kolkata. A report from the *Times of India* saw the article and ran a story,' says Yudhistir.

The Indian Parliament was at a standstill. It marked one of those rare unanimous moments when leaders from across party lines voiced their support for the Bhagavad Gita. The Congress party was in power at the time, with S.M. Krishna serving as the foreign minister.

He says:

> In the evening, the foreign minister's office called. They requested all reports and updates, and we provided them with whatever information we had. The following day, S.M. Krishna and the parliamentary affairs minister addressed the issue. Sushma Swaraj, then the leader of the Opposition, delivered a fiery speech, and Lalu Prasad Yadav also spoke out against the Russian trial.

The strong India–Russia relationship was shaken. The then Russian ambassador to India, Alexander Kadakin, intervened. The next day, the prosecutor dropped the case. But it underscored the risk and hostility often faced in overseas endeavours for the Hindu cause.

Yudhistir emphasises that Bharat's path to the future will be decided by education. He strongly advocates for a transformation in the current education system, stressing the importance of incorporating the study of Sanskrit.

> Many Hindus, I am surprised, say that they don't want to engage with Sanskrit. But every language serves as

an expression of its culture, with certain nuances only understood within those cultural contexts. Sanskrit, besides being the most scientific language, also acts as a cultural ambassador of Indian heritage. Today, Bollywood is often seen as a representative of Indian culture, but where are the arts and philosophy? The Indian model of secularism is highly precarious. A healthier approach to secularism would entail offering all options on the table for learning. This way, at least children can establish some moral foundation.

He also stresses the need to replace India's jurisprudence system, which was borrowed from the British and is based on the Greek system. 'Where are our indigenous dharma-based laws?' he asks.

Yudhistir concludes with an episode from the Mahabharata. When Bheeshma lay on a bed of arrows, fatally wounded in the Kurukshetra war, Lord Krishna instructed the eldest Pandava, Yudhistir, to go to Bheeshma and learn as much as he could, because with Bheeshma's departure, an entire branch of knowledge will vanish forever. 'That is precisely what is happening. With each generation, we are losing valuable knowledge. We must redirect our focus and allocate our resources appropriately,' he says.

CHAPTER 11

Cow, Caste, Conflict, and Conversions

In 2021, former RSS pracharak Navin Puri (name changed for his security) received a call from a Muslim man in Bawana, a census town in the northwest extremes of Delhi, named after the Hindi word for the number 52, 'bawan', representing a cluster of fifty-two villages. He expressed that he and his four brothers had decided to return to the Sanatan Dharma fold, and twenty-five other family members joined them in this decision too. Since then, approximately 2,000 Muslims, from 400–450 families in that area, have undergone reconversion or 'ghar wapsi'.

One reason for the reconversion was that the Muslim families belonged to the dhobi or washer folk caste, which is eligible for reservation benefits if one is Hindu.

Puri says:

> Muslim dhobis realised that they couldn't benefit from reservation unless they returned to the Hindu scheduled caste umbrella. They had converted just two or three generations ago, so they did not have a strong aversion to returning to Sanatan Dharma. Some were given positions in the Dhobi Sabha, where they were shown respect.

Navin Puri, a fifty-year-old activist, is one of the thousands quietly fighting the demographic war that Bharat has been enduring for a millennium. This work is incredibly sensitive, time-consuming, and often dangerous. Puri and his associates, for instance, have been working in Bawana's dhobi community since 2018.

In Haryana's Sonepat, 2,500–3,000 Muslims, mostly from the 'dom' or scavenger community, have reverted to Hindu Dharma. In UP, the Randi Thakurs—descendants of the consorts that Thakurs kept—who had embraced Islam, have returned to Sanatan Dharma.

Several villages in the Northeast have entirely transitioned to Sanatan Dharma. For example, between 2015 and 2019, two villages in Meghalaya embraced the ISKCON perspective of Hinduness. Subsequently, other villages have followed suit.

ISKCON is active in Assam, Tripura, and now in Meghalaya. However, many areas where evangelical organisations are prevalent can be quite challenging. One must dress in pants and a shirt, rather than the usual ISKCON robes. A devotee who went to spread Krishna consciousness in Meghalaya villages was stabbed about four or five years ago.

To facilitate ghar wapsi, for instance, a massive project is underway in Rajasthan called 'Vanshabali Lekhan'. This initiative involves tracing the ancestral roots of lakhs of people who had left Hindu Dharma generations ago or more recently, and formally compiling the data. Vanshabali Lekhan has a pan-India scope.

In North India, a community known as Bhaat—referred to as Vahivancha Barot in Maharashtra and Gujarat—traditionally kept records. Additionally, millions of family trees are maintained at spiritual centres such as Kashi, Gaya, or Prayagraj, which Hindus have been visiting for centuries after a birth in the family or to perform the last rites of their kin.

Lists from this extensive database are then presented to Muslim and Christian families, showing them at which point their ancestors had converted. They are reminded of how age-old birth, marriage, and other customs have remained unchanged. For example, the Byavar Thakur community, purportedly descendants of Rana Pratap, converted to Islam, yet their rituals remained intact.

Among the Thakurs of Uttar Pradesh who converted to Islam, when the father dies, the eldest son wears a pagdi at the Rasm-e Pagdi ceremony to symbolise the transfer of legacy. Sadhus are invited, and Vedic mantras are recited. In 2020, at the pagdi ceremony of former MP Rasheed Masood's son, Shazam Masood, a maulavi left in a huff because several Hindu rituals were being performed. Shazam simply shrugged and said it had been like that for ages.

In Konkan villages, there is a tradition of carrying gods like Kal Bhairav or Devi from home to home. Muslims, many of whom even retain surnames like Joshi or Muzumdar, come out to pray to their kul devata or family deity.

There is an interesting anecdote. India's most wanted Islamist terrorist and criminal, Dawood Ibrahim Kaskar, comes from the Konkanasth Chitpawan Brahmin lineage. His ancestors hailed from Mumbake village. 'Kaskar' is derived from 'Kashikar', denoting those whose ancestors would journey to Kashi centuries ago and return alive, a pilgrimage that used to take three to four years on foot.

Such communities are then encouraged to return to the Sanatan fold. They can either adopt the caste of their ancestors, choose a caste of their preference, or opt not to pick a caste at all. A havan or ritual in front of the fire is performed, and those undergoing reconversion are given tulsi plants and photos of gods such as Ram, Vishnu, Shiv, Ganesh, or Lakshmi.

In many places, the reconverts face fierce social boycotts from the community they are leaving, so ghar wapsi is usually conducted in large groups of at least sixty to seventy families to provide a social cushion. Organisers often enlist the support of Hindu neighbours to assist with the adoption of new traditions.

But in many places, the assimilation of new converts into Hindu society is not easy. Many Hindus view the reconverts with stigma, refusing to eat with them or arrange marriages for their children. Organisers like Puri emphasise that the 'roti-beti ka sambandh' (relationships through food and marriage) is the most crucial aspect of ghar wapsi. Nonetheless, this stigma tends to fade within one or two generations.

Those involved in reconversions say that ghar wapsi has gained momentum, although there is no consolidated data available. Most of the work occurs quietly, without fanfare or spectacle. They believe that the Ayodhya Ram Mandir wave will certainly bolster these efforts.

'Muslims and Christians are beginning to tilt. If it is done in a positive way, discreetly without pomp and show, the ghar wapsi numbers in the coming months will be beyond expectation. Even weak-willed Hindus got coloured in the colour of Ram,' says a Sangh ghar wapsi organiser in Maharashtra, who requests anonymity.

He says that organisations like Chinmaya Mission, Narendra Maharaj in north Maharashtra, Baba Bageshwar Dham in Madhya Pradesh, some ashrams in Tamil Nadu, Agniveer, and many Hindu saints in Uttar Pradesh are silently but aggressively involved in the process. About 1,500–2,000 ashrams and organisations work at the local level. He notes that Vanvasi Kalyan Ashram plays a significant role in preventing Hindus from converting.

The head of an organisation working in Rajasthan, who prefers not to be named, confirms that ghar wapsi has gained momentum following the 'sthapana' (establishment) of the Ram Mandir. He also says:

> My involvement in ghar wapsi is through other organisations. My own organisation is not directly involved in it. We oversee approximately ten to twelve reconversions every month. But we don't openly discuss it because we are currently not in a position to make enemies. We provide indirect support to these projects.

Activists involved in ghar wapsi acknowledge that there are both advantages and disadvantages to sharing ghar wapsi figures. On the positive side, the figures inspire confidence among both those conducting the process and those returning to Hinduism. But they refrain from citing even approximate reconversion figures to avoid media attention and unnecessary controversy. Much more is accomplished through quiet, discreet work.

Surendra Kumar Jain

Whether it is ghar wapsi, cow protection, or the struggle against love jihad, the VHP has been at the forefront of addressing issues that the community needed to confront boldly. The Ram Mandir movement flourished under its leadership. It tackles issues that affect the civilisation, whether at the smallest, most local level like the use of a public park for namaz, or at a national or even global level, such as Hindumisia.

At the forefront of the VHP today is international joint general secretary, Surendra Kumar Jain. The retired principal of Hindu College, Rohtak, he also served as the third president and national convener of the more assertive Bajrang Dal.

Sitting over cups of tea in his modest Rohtak home, seventy-year-old Surendra Jain reminisces about his days at Delhi University.

> I have witnessed days when calling yourself a Hindu was considered embarrassing. It was 1971. I was a student at Delhi's Shriram College. Just in front of our college, a seminar was being held, and its participants were discussing two topics: 'India is a Doomed Nation' and 'We Should be Ashamed of Calling Ourselves Hindu'. There was no protest from any side. And then, three years ago at JNU, I saw 100–125 people raising slogans like '*Bharat tere tukde tukde, inshallah, inshallah*' [India, may you break into pieces, God willing, God willing]. The next day, 5,000 youth were on the streets of Delhi with the tricolour in their hands, singing 'Vande Mataram'. This indicates that over the past fifty years, one thing has changed—earlier, there used to be no protests, but now protests happen. Society protests, and so does the government. A government that opposes these actions could come to power because society felt there was a need for it. It was fed up with Muslim appeasement. Open challenges were being issued, copies of the Constitution were being torn. In the early 1970s, Bukhari, the shahi imam of Delhi, threatened to drag out MPs sitting in Parliament by their ankles, and the tricolour was burnt. But nobody protested.

Jain claims there was no action from the judiciary, politicians, or the opinion-making intellectual class. Hindu society was quietly observing this.

I remember at Delhi University too, Christian missionaries used to distribute literature that portrayed Draupadi as a prostitute. I have read it myself. It also used to be asked how Rama, who could not save his own wife, would be able to save you. So, seek shelter with Jesus. Cows were being slaughtered, and nobody had a problem. I asked India's prominent storyteller, orator, and preacher Morari Bapu one day if the change was evident. He said, 'Yes, earlier only the aged and women used to come to my sessions, now youths come too.' This was in the 1980s. His programme was here in Rohtak. The youths attending his sessions were educated. They were getting attracted to dharma, they wanted solutions, and they felt that it could be attained by embracing Hinduism.

Jain points out another change he noticed around that time. The most challenging pilgrimage in India is the Amarnath Yatra. Earlier, only 1,500–2,000 people, mostly the elderly, used to undertake this pilgrimage. But around 1985–86, young men and women started participating from Punjab, Gujarat, and Haryana, he says. The youth began to accept challenges for the sake of dharma. And terrorists, unnerved by these developments, started attacking the pilgrims.

Meanwhile, the Ram Janmabhoomi Andolan began in 1984. Jain was with the RSS at that time. He was interacting with the youth as a professor, observing the rapid changes.

In 1984, the Ram Janki Rath Yatra commenced in Ayodhya. Vir Bahadur Singh was the UP chief minister, so Ashok Singhal, the then president of the VHP, met him and informed him about a threat that Muslims would not allow the yatra. Singhal requested Singh to provide security. However, the CM refused.

So, saints called upon the power of the youth. From Ayodhya to Lucknow, almost 10,000 youngsters joined the yatra. Nobody dared to attack the entourage.

The same year, Bajrang Dal was formed. The saints felt that the Ram Janmabhoomi movement should extend throughout Bharat. The response was so resounding that during the shila pujan ceremony in 1989, held in 3 lakh villages, the youth came out in large numbers.

> Probably it was the world's biggest outreach programme. Society felt that this was a way to express our anger and also find a solution together. The youth were involved in such large numbers that Singhalji said people like me should now take up the reins of Bajrang Dal. Since the youth were coming in such large numbers, there was a need for a large number of organisers. I was taken into the all-India team. Vinay Katiyar was made the all-India president in 1992, and all-India bodies were formed in 1993. When the Muslims used to threaten us—Long March, Short March—our youth would stand up and respond. the Muslims did not dare to attack anywhere in the country. It was clear that Hindu society was starting to stand on its feet.

Jain reminisces about the turbulent, bloody days of 1990, when the then UP CM Mulayam Singh Yadav tried everything to stop kar sevaks. Bridges were pulled down to prevent people from other states from entering, but lakhs still came. Bullets were fired, and hundreds of kar sevaks were killed on 2 November 1990.

> At that time, my friend Koenraad Elst, a Flemish writer, wrote the book *Ayodhya and After*. He said nobody can stop the

progress of a nation whose youth are ready to make sacrifices for religion and society. He is a fantastic writer and a fantastic man. I call him an intellectual warrior. He does not demand anything for himself. There was a seminar in Mumbai that I attended as the main speaker. He was in the audience. I invited him to sit on the dais, but he refused. He said, 'No, I am okay here.' He did not even want recognition for himself.

Elst's PhD thesis, *Decolonizing the Hindu Mind*, was published in three volumes. Jain feels that his words are coming true today. The resurgence of nationalism and the revival of Hindu cultural are a testimony to that.

Earlier, kaanvar yatras used to have 1,000–5,000 participants, but now there are a crore. The Amarnath Yatra used to have 1,500–2,000 pilgrims, but now 1–2 lakh people go despite the challenges. Preachings of prominent gurus used to be attended by 5,000–10,000 people, but now 20,000–25,000 people, most of them youth, turn up. Why is this happening, Jain asks rhetorically.

> In every aspect of life, Hinduism has become the core. On campuses, if 150 activists protest, the next day 5,000 from our side take to the streets. In Bengal, I held a programme at the Calcutta University auditorium. I am not really a very popular figure. I expected the auditorium, which has a capacity of 2,000, to be vacant. But there were 5,000 youngsters there. People were sitting on the floor, and we had to install loudspeakers outside. They came to listen to a Hindu leader, not Dr Surendra Jain.

He cites the example of a young VHP–Bajrang Dal leader in Bengal, Sourish Mukherjee, who fights the aggression of the ruling TMC from the frontline, organises Hindutva events and rallies in frighteningly hostile political territory. As a consequence, he had to leave his home in Birbhum and stay in hiding for nearly three months after the 2021 post-election violence broke out in West Bengal. 'Sourish is a gem. He has become a youth icon there. He is fighting like anything. Even Mamata Banerjee has mentioned him without naming him. You must learn how to fight on social media from that person,' says Jain.

Jain considers Nehru as the main culprit for keeping Hindu society divided for voting and accepting partition for the sake of power. He states, 'When I delivered my speech at the Calcutta University auditorium, I mentioned that the people who ruled India after independence, like Jawaharlal Nehru, never came out of their colonial mindset. They subscribed to British-invented theories like the Aryan–Dravidian divide and the Aryan invasion.'

Jain quotes Mountbatten's press attaché Leonard Mosley, who wrote the book, *The Last Days of the British Raj*. He says that in the book, Mosley writes that Nehru, in an interview, told him that he accepted partition because otherwise, he would have had to fight even longer. Jain then narrates an anecdote to dispel the myth of the north-south divide.

> Three years ago, I went to Tirupur in Tamil Nadu. There, the Hindi language is not widely loved. My meeting was attended by almost 50,000 people. I was told it would be better if I spoke in English so the organisers could easily translate it into Tamil. I told them, 'You are informing me at such short notice. I can't speak in English and still make the impact you have called me to make.' I started speaking in Hindi, and they were translating it. The audience said, 'No translation!' I spoke for more than forty-eight minutes. I would have actually spoken for hardly

twenty-five minutes because there was constant clapping the rest of the time. That is our culture. The pujari who goes to Pashupatinath comes from Kerala. The pujari in Badrinath is from Gujarat. In Kedarnath, the pujari is from the south. Adi Shankaracharya, who was from Kerala, went into samadhi in Srinagar. He brought the entire country together. The kind of legitimacy he has in Kerala is the same as he has in Haryana or among Hindus in Jammu and Kashmir.

Jain says Gandhi had united people by conflating Ram Rajya with swarajya, which meant a ban on cow slaughter and religious conversions. But that did not stop the ethnic cleansing of Hindus in Kashmir.

Riots today happen only in places where there is Muslim appeasement. Why are riots not taking place in Uttar Pradesh [under Yogi] after the Muzaffarnagar riots when Akhilesh Yadav was the CM? Saharanpur riots happened in front of me. Shops of Sikhs were burnt down, and there were attempts to burn down gurdwaras. There is a park in Saharanpur called the Company Bagh. Outside, the park, there was a wooden kiosk where a Muslim provided haircuts. He had a broken chair and his razor. The wooden kiosk, chair, and razor were not worth more than Rs 5,000–6,000, but he received compensation of Rs 5 lakh after the riots. But a Sikh shopkeeper who had stocks worth Rs 2 crore received only Rs 10 lakh in compensation.

Jain says this kind of appeasement and injustice has led Hindus to rise.

People think that because of Modi, the Hindu uprising happened. But I believe that because of the Hindu uprising,

Modi could come to power. This was what B.R. Ambedkar said too—before a successful political revolution, it is important to have a successful social revolution. And the Ram Janmabhoomi movement can be called a successful social revolution.

Jain gives political examples of how the tide has turned. In 2021, Akhilesh Yadav said if he were the CM, he would have built a temple in a year. Rahul Gandhi, who used to say Hindus who go to temples harass women, is himself today going from one temple to another.

Jain says even Congress's own Anthony Committee report, after the election rout in 2014, clearly states that there has been a backlash because of the politics of opposing Hindus.

> That's why when people say that the Hindus are in danger, I tend to disagree. We have challenges, no doubt, but the Hindus are not in danger. Hinduism is immortal. Aurangzeb could not kill it, nor could Ghazni and Ghori. Will people like Tauqeer Raza end it? It is not possible. Or will some maulanas of Bengal be able to finish Hinduism with the backing of Mamata? It is not possible.

Jain cites K.S. Lal, who wrote that 80 million Hindus were killed during Islamic rule and invasions.[1] According to him, these people could not be converted. During Partition, the percentage of Muslims in undivided India was 24–25 per cent. Jain asserts:

> So, after a rule of 800 years, even after killing and converting so many, they could reach only 25 per cent. In other places they went, they converted 100 per cent of the population, whether it was Afghanistan, Iraq, or Iran. Even during those

dark times, Hindus could not be eliminated. How will they be eliminated now when RSS, VHP, Bajrang Dal, Modi, and Yogi are there, and there is such a massive awakening among the Hindus?. I have witnessed in Assam the time when Hindus lived in fear. Bangladeshis had the upper hand. Cows were slaughtered and Hindus could not retaliate. The land that belonged to Satras, centres established by the saint-scholar, Sankardev, for puja and performing arts, used to be encroached upon by the Bangladeshis. I have visited all those Satras. I have been to the Majuli Islands, the world's largest riverine island network. Today, if someone slaughters a cow there, society protests and may even kill those involved.

Jain says while the whole country believes that people in the Northeast eat beef, in Assam, the first Bihu is Gohu Bihu dedicated to the cow. Cow herders there are called gorakhiya, and they protect cows from slaughter.

He also discusses a recent change he has observed: not just cow slaughter, but today the Assamese have become extremely vigilant about infiltration.

> About four years ago, I visited a camp in Assam. It was set up in an entirely tribal area. I usually get up early in the morning and go for a walk. I walked a long distance from the camp. A woman about thirty-five years old came up and asked me who I was and where I was from. I told her that I was from the VHP. 'VHP? From where?' she asked. 'Delhi,' I said. 'VHP. Hindu? Okay,' she said. So, that woman was vigilant that no Bangladeshi infiltrated the village. This change was new to me.

Jain also recollects his conversation with then Sikkim CM Pawan Kumar Chamling. On seeing cows being slaughtered and beef sold in the open, he asked Chamling if the people of Sikkim eat beef. Chamling replied that only a handful of Sikkimese people ate beef.

> I asked, 'Why don't you ban it then?' He said he would. You will be surprised that Sikkim was the first northeastern state to officially ban beef and cow slaughter. In Tripura, I witnessed cow slaughter in a border village twelve or thirteen years ago. People said if they protested, they would be killed. Today, there can be no cow slaughter in Tripura. Recently, an order was passed in Dadra and Nagar Haveli that those slaughtering cows would face life imprisonment. It is a tribal area with a 40 per cent Christian population. In Bengal, it will take time. However, could we have ever thought that in Bengal on Ram Navami, 35 lakh people would be out on the streets? Although it is true that in some districts Hindus were killed by Muslims and TMC goons, how many such districts were there? What happened in the rest of the districts? There, the Hindus resisted. In Kerala, people are coming back in big numbers and becoming Hindus.

Elaborating on dharma jagaran or ghar wapsi, Jain says that worldwide, a movement called 'Back to the Roots' is underway. What were they before Christianity? What were they before Islam? People are attempting to reclaim their past and reconnect with it because they realise that their roots predate Islam or Christianity by a significant margin.

> India is not disconnected from that. That's why the ghar wapsi campaign is not about religious conversion but one that seeks to connect people with their roots. We are trying to reconnect those people whose ancestors were converted either by fraud, force, or allurement. The number of people coming

back is huge. The VHP did not start ghar wapsi. Before us, Dayanand Saraswati did it. Before Dayanand, Chhatrapati Shivaji Maharaj. Before him, Deval Rishi compiled the Deval Smriti (which prescribed the rules of reconversion) in Sindh. Deval Rishi lived in the time of Raja Dahir. The first Muslim to attack India, Mohammad bin Qasim, had killed King Dahir and undertook large-scale conversions. I am going so far back in history because it is the resolve of Hindu society that will bring back brothers and sisters who have been snatched away from their roots. These efforts have now gained momentum. Many Christian leaders say that you take back more people than we convert. But they must come back willingly. You may convert people by force, but you cannot bring them back by pressurising them.

Ghar wapsi is happening on a large scale in Gujarat, Rajasthan, Maharashtra, Tamil Nadu, Telangana, and Andhra Pradesh, says Jain. Both individually and in groups.

Hindu society is now changing and accepting those who are returning. Earlier, ghar wapsi used to happen, but there would be no roti–beti (commensality and marriage) relationship. So, they would go back. About five years ago in Rohtak, there was a sarva khap panchayat where it was decided that any Christian or Muslim—Muley Jats in particular, who had converted during Aurangzeb's time from the Parmar community—returning to the Hindu fold would be considered to have the same gotra as that of his/her ancestors. The roti–beti relationships would be governed according to that gotra.

And if one doesn't know the caste of one's ancestors? 'Everyone knows. Sheikh Abdullah knew. He has written in his autobiography *Aatish-e-Chinar*, "Three generations back I was a Kashmiri Brahman." Jinnah knew as well,' he explains. Jain mentions that one can become a Hindu without choosing a caste, like atheists, for instance. Many individuals follow the tradition of Gandharva Vivah, a consensual marriage between two people without rituals, witnesses, or family participation. 'In Bengal, there are many such cases,' he says.

Jain further states that besides the VHP, Arya Samaj is conducting ghar wapsi on a large scale. This practice is also carried out by Agniveer, Hindu Jagriti Sangathan, and an organisation called Dharma Jagran Manch, formed by some Sangh functionaries. He alleges that Swami Aseemanand was framed in the Ajmer blast, Mecca Masjid bombing, and the Samjhauta Express serial blasts due to his extensive ghar wapsi efforts in Gujarat and Madhya Pradesh.[2]

> A padri recently told me during a TV debate that if the VHP doesn't stop ghar wapsi, there will be a civil war. 'You take back more people than we turn into Christians,' he said. A few days ago, a German journalist asked me why there are atrocities against Christians in India. I asked the journalist, 'Can you give me even one example from any state where Christians have been prevented from going to church? Leave aside Kerala, can you name any BJP-ruled state?' 'The journalist said, 'In a few places in Haryana, Christians were stopped from holding changai sabha [prayer meeting].' I asked, 'What is a changai sabha?' It is a fraud, which says come to me, take the name of Jesus and you will be cured. If you can't walk, you will be able to. Your cancer will be cured. 'You call this atrocity because I am stopping you from doing what is illegal?' I asked.

Benny Hinn, an Israeli-born American Canadian televangelist, arrived in Bengaluru from the US via a private jet with the intention of converting people. He had a target of 1 lakh conversions as part of the Joshua Project to spread Christianity with business-like strategies in the Third World. However, despite support from the then Congress government, Jain claims he failed to convert even one person.

However, while acknowledging heightened conversion activities in Bengal, Jain states that some of the biggest missionary successes have occurred in Punjab.

A changai sabha was scheduled to take place in Moga, which the chief minister of Punjab, Charanjit Singh Channi, was supposed to attend. The CM had arrived in Moga, and actor Sonu Sood and his sister were also expected to come. However, due to protests by Hindus and Sikhs, neither Sonu Sood nor his sister, Malvika, attended. Channi also did not go. Channi is a crypto-Christian. He doesn't openly identify himself as one, but he practises Christianity. He wears the turban for political reasons, as wearing a cross would deter Sikh voters from supporting him.

Jain states that more Christians are returning to Sanatan Dharma than Muslims, as leaving Islam is considered the most severe crime and is punishable by death. Muslims had attacked the home of former Shia Waqf Board chairman Wasim Rizvi, who adopted the name Jitendra Narayan Tyagi. They tortured his wife, even though she had not renounced Islam.

In Kerala, an organisation of ex-Muslims held a press conference during which twelve or thirteen young men and women shared their experiences of living under Islam. They expressed that upon leaving Islam; they felt as if they had entered paradise.

When asked about the VHP's most important programme in the next four to five years, Jain responds:

> Our focus now is on preventing conversions [of Hindus] and conducting ghar wapsi campaigns. It will certainly happen. Love jihad is the most heinous form of conversion. Triple talaq, halala, mutah niqah, and sex jihad are internal predicaments faced by women in Islam. And what do they think about women from other religions? They are maal-e-ghanimat or war booty. They are treated as sex slaves. While you can do niqah with four women, there is no limit on the number of women you may have sexual relationships with or keep as mistresses. Muslim youths have been assigned targets to entrap non-Muslim girls. The entire world is fed up with this, and so is the Church in Kerala and Karnataka.

Even in Kashmir, the Sangh Parivar is highly active. It operates 350 ekal vidyalayas, or single-teacher schools, in the Valley. Requesting anonymity, a senior Hindu activist reveals that in many of these schools, the teachers are unaware of their affiliation but are provided with a nationalistic curriculum, which they adhere to. These vidyalayas are operated through NGOs with Kashmiri names, which are fronts of the RSS.

Jain and the VHP have also spearheaded a citizens' protest in Gurugram against the illegal blocking of parks and roads for offering namaz. This movement began in 2018. On Eid, the national highway was obstructed by nearly 10,000 Muslims from Mewat and other surrounding areas of Gurugram. Mewat, a Muslim-majority area, has seen repeated complaints from Hindus regarding harassment and even reports of women being abducted.

So, when Muslims blocked the national highway for namaz, many Hindus in Gurugram feared that one day the lifeline of Gurugram, its economic hub, could also be choked. They protested against this action and took the matter to court.

It was then decided at a meeting with the government that for the year 2019, Muslims would have the right to offer namaz only in thirty places in Gurugram. The court ruled that Muslims must not offer namaz in the open.

However, Muslims interpreted the permission for thirty places as a permanent measure. In 2020, instead of thirty places, they offered namaz at fifty locations. These included streets where even ambulances could not pass through. Parks where children used to play were occupied, and they even sat at crossroads inside residential areas, preventing girls from leaving their homes for fear of harassment. They began to claim certain areas as Waqf land where they intended to build mosques, but locals were aware of the history of those areas. Consequently, society rose in protest.

Did VHP help mobilise Hindus?

> Yes, we certainly did. There is a place called Palam Vihar in Gurugram. Outside Palam Vihar, there is a huge park. Almost eight years ago, about 500 Muslims suddenly started offering namaz. The number quickly increased to 1,000. They claimed it was Waqf land and they intended to build a masjid there. It was decided that 10,000 people would come from Mewat, offer namaz, and construct the masjid. Then the residents' welfare association and traders there rose in protest. They called me too. A large panchayat was held, but unfortunately, the then chief minister Bhupinder Hooda

agreed to the Muslims' claim. There was no revenue record of the Waqf Board, no historical evidence. And where were they coming from to offer namaz? From 50 km away. Their aim was very clear—to convert the entire Gurugram into Mewat.

A mahapanchayat was convened, attended by sarpanches from fifty villages. Jain was invited as well. Everyone declared their intention to perform aarti to Bharat Mata and organise a night-long jagran. People planned to arrive in tractors. Eventually, the government was forced to acknowledge that it was not Waqf land. The piece of land was barricaded.

> We asked who the Muslims were who offered namaz there. Were they all from Gurugram? There are a sufficient number of masjids in Gurugram. Some Muslims came from Nuh and other villages, while others came from Ferozpur Jhirka, which is 50 km away. Why did they come? It was a systematic takeover. In 1947, when the British were still there, namaz could be offered in the open at 130 places in Delhi. Today, in those 130 places, there are masjids or mazars. Gurugram has shown the way, and the ripples will reach the entire country. Open namaz is not aimed at propitiating Allah but at disturbing people and displaying strength.

VHP and Bajrang Dal have consistently been labelled a nuisance for their vandalism during Valentine's Day, targeting couples in parks. But such indignation does not bother Jain.

> When we stopped open namaz, the BBC called us a nuisance. When we stopped changai sabhas, the entire Christian world called it a nuisance. When we stopped cow slaughter somewhere, it was called a nuisance. When a camp was being

set up by some Muslim boys in Nagpur [outside the gate of Nagpur University] on how to catch Hindu girls on the occasion of Valentine's Day, parents came to complain at our Bajrang Dal office that the police were doing nothing. Our activists drove away the Muslim boys from there and it was called a nuisance. We don't have a problem being called a nuisance.

Devdutta Maji

One of Hindutva's bloodiest conflict zones is Bengal. In the last five years or so, there have been 168 documented cases of alleged political murders, 71 of which occurred after the 2021 state assembly elections. Additionally, there were eleven registered rape and assault cases, a number that is bound to increase significantly once oppression—as seen in Sandeshkhali where women protested against alleged atrocities committed by the ruling party—starts receiving public attention and being addressed. The Calcutta High Court has granted security cover to 303 victims of post-poll violence. Judges have recused themselves from hearing the cases due to the extent of the terror. In no other state is the violence so raw, palpable, and ever-present, akin to the scent of fish blood at the local bazaars.

Bengal has witnessed one of the bloodiest partitions in history, marked by a series of gruesome genocides starting from the Mymensingh riots of 1906, followed by the Dhaka riots of 1941, Direct Action Day in Kolkata, the Noakhali massacre of 1946, and culminating in the 1971 genocide and the Mukti Juddha, also known as the Liberation War of Bangladesh.

Bengal has been the nursery of Hindu nationalism, as documented by Bankim Chandra Chattopadhyay both as a journalist and in his novels such as *Anandamath*. From figures like Swami Vivekananda and Shri Aurobindo, Bipin Chandra Pal to Syama Prasad Mukherjee, and movements like Anushilan Samiti to Jugantar, Bengal has served as the fountainhead of Hindu nationalist thought.

Indian Census figures show that the Muslim population has increased from 5.1 million, constituting 19.85 per cent of the population in 1951, to 24.6 million, or 26.86 per cent, in 2011—an absolute growth of 19.5 million and a 7 per cent rise over the last six decades. According to some projections, the Muslim population is expected to reach or exceed the 30 per cent mark by 2031. The Hindu population has concurrently dropped by nearly 8 per cent, from 78.45 per cent in 1951 to 70.54 per cent in 2011.

Unchecked illegal immigration of Bangladeshi Muslims and, in recent years, Rohingyas from Myanmar, threatens to further skew the demography.

Devdutta Maji, forty-four-year-old founder and president of Singha Bahini, a group now both feared and admired for fighting on the ground against a possible Islamist takeover of West Bengal, explains:

> Demographically, we Hindus are being decimated. What I am observing is that, both in rural and urban areas, a majority of youth call themselves nationalists, but their nationalism stops at celebrating Independence Day and paying taxes. In UP, Bihar, or Rajasthan, youngsters want to take control of the steering by becoming IAS, IPS officers. But Bengal's youth want only to keep the car clean. We, the Hindutvawadis or so-called nationalists, have not been able

to pass on this message properly to the next generation. A gap has remained.

Maji believes that the lack of awareness and alertness among Hindus about the demographic war is self-destructive.

Maji is originally from Amta village in Howrah district, where electricity arrived only twelve years ago. The family's 'kaccha' or makeshift house is now 'pucca' or fully built. They also own farmlands and used to engage in fishing. Maji's father had come to Kolkata in 1970 and set up a lathe factory, which he sold about two years ago.

Maji used to run a brisk business until twelve or fourteen years ago. He worked in the Northeast, primarily involved in fencing border roads in Mizoram. He also spent time in Assam and Nagaland. He has stayed in ashrams for long periods as well.

Devdutta studied at Calcutta Boys School and was admitted to Bhowanipore College. But a tragedy occurred, and he dropped out of college.

> One of my friends, who used to stay on the floor above us, died in 1999. He fell from our terrace while playing cricket. It was a huge shock for me, and I started leaning towards spirituality. I used to go and stay in ashrams in different places, such as Assam. In a place called Chandrapur near Nagpur in Maharashtra, there is a temple of the Mother Goddess where I stayed for a few days. I also stayed in an ashram in Gujarat. From 2006 to 2007, I started working earnestly for Hindutva. I learned my lesson in Mizoram. There, since I used to perform pujas, apply tilaks, and engage in Hindutva activities, which I would upload on Facebook, my machines were set on fire by radical Christians. I suffered

massive losses. Then I met Tapanda [the late Tapan Ghosh of Hindu Samhati].

Tapan Ghosh had left the RSS by then, apparently because he found it too patient, too slow for his liking. In August 2009, Devdutta read a magazine published by Ghosh. He called up Tapanda, asked for his time, took a bike, and visited him at his residence near Sealdah-Bowbazar.

> We chatted for a long time. When I was about to leave, I asked him, 'Where did you see yourself five, ten, twenty years down the line?' Tapanda replied, 'I want to be like Teg Bahadur [the ninth Sikh Guru who was beheaded on the orders of Mughal Emperor Aurangzeb].' I got goosebumps. He then came to my factory on the bike. After that, he came to my house, looked around, and then told me, 'Join my organisation from today.'

Devdutta's journey with Hindu Samhati began. Maji did not have a Sangh Parivar or BJP background. He had never been a part of any political party in his early years. Although his father and he happened to be lifetime members of ISKCON, Hindu Samhati was his nursery of activism.

Exactly a year later, on 6–8 September 2010, the Deganga riots in North 24 Parganas occurred. Seven Hindu Samhati activists were arrested.

> We staged a major protest at Chapadali Mor. After three failed attempts by the legal team to secure their bail in court, Tapanda gave me the responsibility to get them free, whatever the cost. I managed to arrange bail within three to four days. Upon their release, all of them resigned from Hindu Samhati. Tapanda's secretary, joint secretary,

vice-president ... all resigned. Although Tapanda proposed making me the general secretary, I declined. I was running a business and was not sure how much time I could devote. Instead, I served as the vice president until 2018, during which time I handled all landmark issues, especially the Tuktuki Mondal case.

In 2015, Tuktuki Mondal, a Class X student from Magrahat in the South 24 Parganas district of West Bengal, was abducted while returning home from a nearby bank. Her father, Subhash Mondal, a daily wage-earner, claimed that three goons from a gang led by a hoodlum called Salim, who allegedly had the support of the ruling Trinamool Congress were responsible for her abduction.

Salim's men summoned Tuktuki's father for a meeting on the night of 7 March at the residence of a man named Babusona Gazi. Upon arrival, he discovered at least fifty armed men present. He was coerced into signing blank papers and withdrawing the police complaint. After initially refusing to sign, the helpless father eventually yielded. Tuktuki's mother later informed him that she had been raped repeatedly.

Hindu Samhati helped the family in filing a case, leading to the arrest of Babusona Gazi. Subsequently, the court ordered Tuktuki to be housed in Tapan Ghosh's house, to which her parents consented. Gazi would regularly visit her at Ghosh's house.

> Tapanda said nothing could be done, so Gazi should be allowed to meet Tuktuki. But one day, Babusona took Tuktuki away for the second time. A police report was filed. I scolded Tapanda the way a younger brother scolds an older brother. The police rebuked us, saying that although we had initially

rescued her, the girl was lured away from our own house by the boy, so they would not take any responsibility now.

Devdutta says he was too ashamed to take this case to the National Commission for the Protection of Child Rights. Meanwhile, Tuktuki and Gazi had a daughter. All seemed lost.

> I saw that there was nothing that could be done. I prayed to Ma Kali. Then Babusona Gazi died under mysterious circumstances. So Tuktuki had no other alternative; she came back to the pavilion. She returned to us, and more precisely, returned to me. Now she stays in her own home and comes to visit me from time to time. Today, her mother, sister, and daughter came to visit.

Tuktuki and her child were converted to Islam, but Maji reconverted them and changed their Aadhaar cards back again.

Maji was actively involved during the 2013 Canning riots between Hindus and Muslims, which erupted following the murder of a Muslim cleric by a group of men in South 24 Parganas' Nalekhali. 'I was involved in 99–100 per cent of Hindu Samhati's landmark movements, such as the effort to recover the kidnapped Hindu minor Tuktuki Mondal and the resistance against the perpetrators of the 2010 Deganga riots. My decision to support Israel against terrorism at the 2014 and 2018 rallies in central Kolkata was also a key initiative,' he says.

There was an attack on Maji in 2016 in Haroa. A YouTuber from Delhi named Ravijyot Singh had come for a survey, and Maji was accompanying him.

It was 16 August, the occasion of Direct Action Day of 1946. Hindu Samhati had organised a programme in Kolkata. Some Hindus had come from Haroa. When they returned, their houses were set on fire by Muslims, he says.

> They called us. There are elements like Shahjahan Sheikh [of Sandeshkhali notoriety] in that area. They had set a trap to kill Tapanda and me. They were calling us repeatedly, which forced me to think. I told Tapanda he need not go, but nobody should know that he is not going. We had alighted from our vehicles and were taking photos of the burnt-down houses. Suddenly, about a hundred Muslims came and attacked us with bamboo, rods, etc. A thick needle used for sewing blankets was stabbed into my ear, and I started bleeding. Then they began dragging us to the masjid. Their plan was to claim that we had come to break the masjid and were lynched to death by the public. Ravijyot managed to escape into a nearby bush and make a phone call. The police arrived in ten to fifteen minutes, prompting the assailants to flee. But they stole our watches, rings, necklace, camera, and other belongings. Since then, I have stopped wearing a necklace.

Maji says that four of those who carried out the attack are no longer alive. He adds that one of them is still in jail and has not applied for bail.

Another attack took place near Maji's house at a traffic signal on AJC Bose Road in Kolkata, between Park Circus and Maula Ali. He was in his car, sitting beside the driver, when an assailant appeared beside him, drew a pistol, and pulled the trigger. But providentially, the weapon got jammed. The entire incident was even caught on the CCTV camera of a nearby hotel.

Things were going well, but in 2016–17, the committee started to become somewhat pro-TMC. In 2018, Tapanda and Maji had a major difference of opinion over this. Maji left his mentor's Hindu Samhati that year.

Many of Devdutta Maji's admirers, especially on social media, call him the Gopal Patha of this generation. Gopal 'Patha' Mukherjee and his band of young men saved Hindus during Direct Action Day and the Great Calcutta Killings of 1946 by organising reprisals against jihadi mobs unleashed by Muslim League leader Mohammed Ali Jinnah and Bengal ruler Huseyn Shaheed Suhrawardy. Gopal ran a mutton shop, which is why the Bengali epithet 'patha' or goat was added to his name.

> What Gopal babu did for Bengal is tremendous. We pay tribute to him every year on 16 August. I am a fan of Gopal Mukherjee, and his house is near my factory. He lived a long life. I used to see him while going to and coming back from the factory. He would sunbathe in front of his house during the winters, sitting on a bench.

In January 2021, after the death of his mentor Tapan Ghosh the previous year, Maji joined the BJP. The main reason was to put to rest speculation about the growing closeness between the TMC and Tapan Ghosh's team. The BJP provided him with protection, and the Centre granted him CISF security. The BJP also gave him a ticket for the Chowringhee constituency in Kolkata in the 2021 elections. Chowringhee has 41–42 per cent Muslims and 7 per cent Christians. Despite polling the highest number of votes for the party from that seat, Maji lost.

A significant turning point in Maji's life was the Ram Mandir movement. He recounts:

I was quite young at that time, just thirteen. We kids used to play cricket on the road in front of our house whenever there was a bandh. The day after 6 December 1992, we were playing cricket on the street. Suddenly, we saw a big procession approaching us. They were carrying black and green flags. A Maruti van was passing by, and the Muslims intercepted the car. There were two people sitting inside. They were dragged out and chopped to pieces. The assailants were hitting them from all sides. I witnessed that firsthand. My friend's father, who was a Gujarati and lived on the floor above us in our building, pushed us kids inside the gate and locked it. Since then, I started to think about why these things were happening, why did they kill those two people.

Many years later, Devdutta was to witness and be part of far wider organised violence, especially the violence that broke out after the 2021 Bengal elections. Very few party leaders stood their ground in the face of the ruthless TMC-Islamist onslaught. Some leaders either switched off their phones or did not pick up calls. Some fled from their homes. Some candidates hurriedly took flights back to Delhi, abandoning the cadre that fought for them, while others fled in lorries.

> I fought the elections from Chowringhee. Some violence did take place there, but not much. Whatever happened, I was able to handle it. Not too far away from Chowringhee is Beleghata, where Abhijit Sarkar was beaten to death. Nine years ago, the same Abhijit and his brother Biswajit were beaten like this at night and thrown onto railway tracks so that they would be mowed down by a train. Their mother called me at 2 a.m. I took a taxi and reached their house at 2.30 a.m. I rescued the two brothers, put them in a taxi, and got them admitted to NRS Hospital. They were in NRS for

fifteen to sixteen days and were saved. This time on 2 May, he was lynched to death. At that time, even sparrows and pigeons would have been scared to fly to Beleghata. I went there immediately and brought his mother, brother, and three of their pet dogs—some of the dogs had also been beaten to death—to my home and kept them there. My mother said, 'You have filled the house with people; now you have brought in dogs as well!' Then this started to go viral. Naddaji [BJP president] came. I briefed him about what had happened.

Maji helped victims of the post-poll violence from Falta in Diamond Harbour, Mathurapur, some parts of Nadia, Birbhum, Nanur in Birbhum, and Udaynarayanpur in Howrah district.

News was coming in from all over, and I was rushing from one place to another ... Basanti, Charavidya. In Swarupnagar, Baduria, the BJP party office was shut down by the TMC. I went there on 8 or 10 May, stood there, and got the party office reopened. That office is still functioning. Around that time, I learned that in a village in Ushti, women had to row their boats for one-and-a-half kilometres to fetch drinking and cooking water. In that village, there has been no water supply line until now. The CPI(M), Congress, or the TMC had not provided it. I got a deep tubewell installed there out of my own money. Ushti is almost completely a Muslim-dominated area, and this is a small Hindu village. The women had to row boats to fetch water from Muslim neighbourhoods. I did the same in Udaynarayanpur and Srirampur as well. Every year during Durga puja, I gift new clothes to 2,000–3,000 Hindus, especially tribals, since the Christians try to influence them a lot.

Maji is also at the forefront of reconversions or ghar wapsi in Bengal. He claims this is the main reason he has been provided central security. 'A senior officer among them said that I have a threat from the Jamaat-ul-Mujahideen Bangladesh (JMB). According to the information they have, I have converted over a thousand Muslim women into Hindus,' says Maji.

Where do these reconversions take place?

> Everywhere, all over Bengal, I provide protection to Muslim girls who are involved with Hindu boys and wish to return to their mother faith. I help them and arrange their marriages. The officer also said I had brought back Hindu girls who had left Sanatan Dharma due to love jihad and made them Hindu again. A boy named Mohammad Zakiruddin lives near my home. His family consists of fourteen members. While his parents are old, all the others are below twenty-five years of age. So, out of fourteen, two are above fifty and the rest are below twenty-five. I successfully led the reconversion of this entire family. I facilitated their ghar wapsi. I have helped, for instance, one Syed Mirza Khan become Balaraman, a total Vaishnavite. He now worships Lord Krishna, reads the Gita, and engages in Gita discourses. Things are progressing, but the problem arises when I close my eyes and see that our struggle—and my struggle—is against a massive force.

Sanjeev Newar and Vashimant Sharma

Hardly anyone in India's Right ecosystem is unfamiliar with Agniveer. What started as a website founded by Sanjeev Newar, an almost six-and-a-half-foot-tall IIT graduate and IIM alum, evolved into an organisation, which, in turn, transformed into a movement. Such is its impact that today, several Agniveer branches exist across Bharat, with many of them not directly affiliated with the founding organisation. Newar says he does not mind as long as the work gets done and the objective gets fulfilled.

Agniveer's fame stems from its courage to venture into the most contentious arenas, making them its karmabhoomi: ghar wapsi, love jihad, caste equality, and cow protection.

It all started with Newar creating a website called Agniveer when he was in IIT. Fugitive Islamist preacher Zakir Naik was quite prominent at that time. Newar began uploading articles one after the other challenging Naik's fraudulent claims, which had captivated lakhs of Muslim youth and even facilitated the conversion of some Hindus and Christians to Islam.

One of Newar's early successes was reintegrating a fellow student into the Sanatan Dharma fold after they had converted to Islam under the influence of Naik's preachings. He worked tirelessly on his friend, using reasoning and exposing Naik's deceitful tactics.

Sanjeev was born and raised in Kolkata during the peak of the communist era under Jyoti Basu. He attended Hindi High School for his schooling and pursued his BTech in mechanical engineering from IIT Guwahati. In 2002, he completed his MBA from IIM Kolkata.

He started Agniveer in 2008 in response to conversion forces that were highly active on social media. Orkut, the most popular social media platform at the time, used to be the hunting ground for Zakir Naik and his team.

> Zakir used to be the darling of the UPA regime and journalists. He ran the Islamic Research Foundation and Peace TV, where he blatantly manipulated Hindu texts and scriptures

to argue that true adherence to Vedas required conversion to Islam. As absurd as it may sound, he had a dedicated team targeting Hindus, especially Hindu girls, who sought answers to philosophical and spiritual questions on his social media platforms in an effort to better understand Hinduism. He had readymade templates in place, which were then copy-pasted by his zombie-fied followers on social media. And then they began converting Hindus who were unaware of the profound roots of Sanatan Dharma.

Agniveer started as a counter to that conversion mechanism, especially after learning that Zakir Naik was an inspiration for many terrorists. Members wrote detailed rebuttals to his claims that Islam represented true Hinduness. These write-ups became very popular, and many of Zakir Naik's shows got cancelled.

As we went down this rabbit hole, we discovered that conversion was indeed a grim reality. Under the guise of peaceful Islam, Naik had orchestrated a whole nexus of conversion mafia across the country. We found that various 'flavours' of Islam were involved—from the more extreme Wahhabi Islam to the seemingly 'liberal' Sufi Islam. However, all of them shared the common agenda of converting Hindus, especially Hindu girls.

This was the inflection point at which Agniveer transformed from being a social media awareness site to becoming a counterforce against the conversion cartels across India.

While we were preoccupied with combating the fanatical version of Islam, which had previously claimed the lives of figures like Swami Shraddhanand [a Hindu guru and reconversion activist murdered in 1926 in Delhi], Mahashay Rajpal [the publisher of the supposedly 'blasphemous' book *Rangila Rasul*, who was stabbed to death by a fanatic in Lahore in 1929], and Pandit Lakh Ram [a social reformer and writer fatally stabbed in Lahore in 1987], they had a bloody history of killing anybody who opposed their views on how to deal with kafirs.

While confronting Islamic conversions, Agniveer also became aware of the 'soft conversion' tactics employed by Christian missionaries.

> It was also widespread. The modus operandi was different, but the foundation remained the same: if you desire a passport to the absurd notion of jannat, you must convert others. But this stupidity has a very sinister face, so we started campaigning against Christian conversions. Today, I am proud to accept the fact that we are among the foremost organisations working to counter conversions and conducting shuddhi or ghar wapsi.

Another issue that the organisation addresses is cow slaughter and the beef mafia. Newar feels it has less to do with the economy or profits and more with hurting Hindu sentiments. Agniveer has a team dedicated to countering cow smuggling and slaughter, working closely with the police and administrations of various states. The members primarily function as police informants.

Another area of Agniveer's operation involves combating drug cartels. 'Surprising, we found that in areas where conversions are rampant, there is also a booming drug mafia business,' he says.

Newar also founded an organisation called Gems of Bollywood in 2020, which highlights how cinema can be utilised as a tool for political and religious propaganda.

He states that this manipulation has persisted for decades, from the era of Dilip Kumar and Raj Kapoor to the current time of Shah Rukh Khan, Aamir Khan, and Akshay Kumar, aiming to deride Hindus and glorify Islam.

> It legitimises the illegal occupation of streets for offering namaz and depicts that without a noble Abdul chacha, no Hindu can be saved. Also, it portrays Brahmins and Thakurs as rapists and villains. It is a very systematic propaganda. Since then, we have witnessed a lot of positive changes.

A sister site called Gems of Books exposes how education has been used to promote anti-Hindu propaganda. Agniveer is also at the forefront of the fight against love jihad, deceitful marriage, conversion, and radicalisation.

Has ghar wapsi gathered pace after the Ram Mandir pran pratistha in Ayodhya?

> It is a mixed bag. There is a fanatical core among Muslims. But my assessment is that most Indian Muslims—if free from the influence of mullahs and social ostracisation, including punishments like nikah halala—want to integrate with the mainstream. They realise that generations ago they were Hindus. Many of them know their gotras. For them, the Ram Mandir pran pratistha has made it easier to embrace their Sanatan roots. Many of them are embracing Hindu dharma in its entirety. But the fanatical elements have also become very active. Unprovoked attacks have started. They are planning, they feel cornered ... so the opposition to ghar wapsi has also become very bitter in many areas.

Agniveer is experiencing significant success in ghar wapsi in Maharashtra and Gujarat. Despite a strong resurgence of

Hinduness in Uttar Pradesh, things often turn violent, says Newar. Rajasthan is very sensitive, and Bengal is among the most dangerous.

'During communist rule, Agniveer found it easier to conduct ghar wapsi. Currently, Bengal's demographics are rapidly changing, and the situation has become excessively violent,' he says. He says Agniveer has conducted over a lakh ghar wapsi so far, but that could just be the beginning.

While Sanjeev has branched out into other areas of Hindu activism, his friend Vashimant Sharma leads Agniveer from the front. The thirty-nine-year-old completed his PhD in energy sciences from IIT Bombay in 2014. He then joined NIT Jaipur as a faculty member and later moved to IIT Kanpur in 2017, teaching mechanical engineering. Vashimant met Sanjeev during his IIT days. However, his grounding in dharma was solid since childhood.

> I was fortunate to be born into a dharmic family. My parents taught us Ved mantras and Sandhyam havan when we were very young. From childhood, we were also told stories about Shivaji Maharaj, Maharana Pratap, and India's partition. Many of my family members migrated from Punjab. The mobs today do the same things that they did then.

An avid reader, Sharma was deeply influenced by the reformer Swami Dayanand Saraswati.

> If you look at Chapter 14 of his book *Satyarth Prakash*, he was the first person in India to analyse about 150–160 ayats and criticise Islam. You may have read Waseem Rizvi's book on Prophet Mohammad. In that too, he had written about Swami Dayanand, who was the first person to inspire people to criticise Islam.

When Vashimant was at IIT, he read Sanjeev Newar's articles and contacted him. They then met at the Delhi Book Fair, where there were three or four Islamic book stalls.

> They were trying to convert people right there. They claimed that Mohammad is mentioned in the Vedas. There is a Vedic mantra, '*Shatam adina shyam sharadah shatam*' ['A hundred autumns may we see/a hundred autumns may we live/a hundred autumns may we know/a hundred autumns may we grow'] from *Atharva Veda*. The Islamists at the stall claimed it as 'Shat Medina' and said, 'Look, our Mecca Medina is mentioned in your Vedas.' Also, they claimed that the word 'Narashamsa' in Atharva Veda is connected to Prophet Mohammed. I intervened and asked how this was possible. They said if you translate 'Narashamsa' into Arabic, it becomes Mohammed. I questioned them if names could be translated. Can you translate nouns? For example, let's say your name is Harilal, can I call you Hari-red?

During the argument, Vashimant found himself encircled by those running the stalls. It was at that moment that Sanjeev Newar appeared with his imposing stature. He pulled Vashimant away from the mob, but not before standing his ground and making his argument.

A long-lasting friendship began, and Vashimant started writing regularly for Agniveer.

> In Mumbai, we used to encounter cases where they would trap a Hindu girl and convert her. I had good connections with the VHP and Bajrang Dal, and by God's grace, we rescued many girls. I was adept at argumentation. So, they would invite me for shastrarth, or intellectual debates, with Muslims. Often, these shastrarth happened near or inside

masjids, with five to six maulavis present. On one side were representatives of the Muslim community, and on our side were Bajrang Dal activists and me.

With the rise of Zakir Naik, a new phenomenon emerged. They became more open and eager for debate. A trait of fools is that they don't know their limitations. Individuals who watch Zakir Naik's videos once or twice might assume they could easily win any debate, as he distorts Vedic mantras. They fail to realise that there are other segments of Hindus they have not encountered yet. Representatives from Zakir Naik's Islamic Research Foundation (IRF) were the ones who consistently participated in debates. They had an entire cadre of so-called intellectuals prepared for debate. There are also those who engaged in violence, followed by others who acted as their lawyers, and finally, those who would lament in the media about being victimised. These four groups collaborated seamlessly, unlike us.

Vashimant claims that through debate alone, his group was able to prevent many Hindu girls from converting to Islam between 2009 and 2011.

We used to tell the girls, 'If you want to leave, go ahead, but listen to the debate first.' Some girls would not agree; they were completely brainwashed. Yet, approximately forty-five we saved from love jihad. But I realised this approach wasn't sustainable. I believed conversion was necessary for our survival. That's when our shuddhi/ghar wapasi campaign started.

Vashimant performed his first reconversion, or 'shuddhi', in 2009. Initially, Agniveer targeted Muslims. Some individuals read his articles and subsequently interacted with him, resulting in conversions.

During that time, I realised that actually converting people is not that difficult, but Hindus don't have the ability to accept people easily. They would say, 'You have brought them in through conversion. Now, which jati will they be placed in? Which gotra will they belong to? Which mantra will they chant while performing havan? Where will they marry?' So, that is a big problem among Hindus.

Vashimant felt that the reconversion process was being hampered by caste issues. So, they started addressing the jati system, focusing on reconciling caste differences and fully integrating those reconverting to Hindu dharma into both the community and society.

Among the books that have deeply influenced Sharma is Vinayak Damodar Savarkar's *Mazi Janmathep* in Marathi. Savarkar writes that he witnessed a strange phenomenon in the Andaman prison. Hindus comprised political prisoners incarcerated in the Cellular Jail for fighting for the independence of their motherland, much like Savarkar himself. But the Muslims were hardcore criminals, charged with murder and rape.

In Savarkar's writings, he also found references to the Islamists' urge to convert non-Muslims by any means possible. Vashimant says Savarkar was inspired by Swami Dayanand Saraswati's *Satyarth Prakash* to start what he called 'shuddhi' or reconversion of Muslims.

> He taught that Vedic dharma was the best, and it does not matter if you have unknowingly done something, like eating a beef eater's leftover. And we are people who tell even beef-eaters, if you want to join, you have to promise not to eat beef from now on, and you are welcome. Trads [the orthodox on the Right] are foolish. They call Dalits 'Bhimta'. Around 75

per cent of all those who work in our gaushalas [cattle farms] are Dalits. Half of all our gau rakshaks [cow protectors] are Dalits. They would die fighting for the cows. You are talking about 25–30 per cent of the population.

Vashimant says even the much-maligned *Manusmriti* mentions that the Shudra, who cooks food at your house, along with his wife and children, should be fed first once the food is made. They must sit and eat. 'Then your family members eat from whatever is left. "Uchhistha" did not mean off the plate but the fresh part that is left. So first the Shudras ate, then you ate what remained. This was Manu's recommendation,' he says.

He cites one more shloka from *Manusmriti*:
Shudro Brahmanam eti Brahmanaschaiti Shudratam Kshatriyajjatam evam tu vidyadvaishyata thaivacha.
[This means Shudras can become Brahmans and vice versa. According to one's qualities [guna] and deeds [karma], one attains varnas.]

> These varnas are very flexible. Therefore, telling a sweeper's son that he must not study the Vedas makes no sense. Varna essentially means choice [of the category of work]. Lord Krishna says this in the Bhagavad Gita—*Shauryam tejo dhritirdakshya yuddhay chapyapalayanam*. Kshatriya is one who has physical might. One who has never fled from his foes, who is physically strong, who is gallant and is not meek is a Kshatriya. So, whether it is a child of a sweeper or anybody else, he can be called a Kshatriya if he has these qualities. To tell someone that he does not have the right to gain particular knowledge because he is not 'Sharmaji ka beta' [born of high caste] is nonsense. The Trads are beneficiaries of this. In the Vedas, the division between Brahman, Kshatriya, Vaishya, and

Shudra refers to the qualities of humans. There is a Purusha Suktam hymn in the tenth mandala of the Rig Veda, which deals with the make-up of human beings and of society. It says: 'Braahmanasya mukham aaseet, Baahoo raajanyoh Krithah, Ooroo thad asya yad Vaishyah, Padbhyaam Soodro ajaayatha', or the face of the cosmic being is Brahman, the arms are Kshatriya, the thighs are Vaishya, and the feet are Shudra. Those were gunas or qualities of every individual.

Swami Dayanand argued that if you take this Vedic mantra literally, the Brahman should have been like a football with no feet; the Kshatriya should have been like arms; Vaishya should have been like thighs; and the Shudra should have been like feet.

But is this the case? Do Brahmans not have feet or Shudras not have faces? 'This means that these four gunas are present in every human being. The hymn is called Purusha Sukta because every human is bound to have these four qualities. In what quantity is another matter? Our Vedas are clear,' he says.

While Maharishi Valmiki composed the Ramayana and enjoyed the highest respect—Ma Sita gave birth to her sons in his ashram—today, Valmikis are considered a backward sweeper caste, says Vashimant, arguing that narrow and rigid caste division appeared much later down the ages.

Tracing history downstream, Vashimant reaches Maharana Pratap. When his father turned him out of the house, he stayed with the Bhil tribe, eating and spending time with them. In the battle of Haldighati, while most Rajputs fought for Akbar, only a few Rajputs and mostly Bhils fought for Maharana Pratap.

Vashimant hits out at the Trads.

> Has anybody from the Trads invented a supersonic plane? Don't they claim to be Brahmans? How many of them have cracked the IIT exams? The people they call 'mlechchha' [foreigners] have manufactured cars for you, and yet you can't even make a wiper for those cars. So, what kind of Brahman are you? Does being a Brahman only mean that you will utter a mantra in four different ways? We are now preparing the Valmiki children to study the Vedas, and they will excel at it more than the Trads. So, we started organising sanskars and havans [Hindu religious rituals] conducted by Dalit Valimikis, and our programme takes place in several locations. We provide them with training. The Trads quarrel with us for giving them the janeu [the sacred thread]. Valmikis are more intelligent than the Trads, so we decided to give them the janeu.

He holds M.K. Gandhi responsible for coining the word 'Harijan' for Dalits.

> You should read Dr Ambedkar's views on Gandhi. Gandhi was the most casteist person alive. He used to be angry at Swami Dayanand because the latter said that the varna ashrama was not based on birth [janma] but on actions [karma]. Gandhi believed the jati system is based on birth. The Trads of today are essentially Gandhians. They refer to Arya Samajis as Arya Namazis and Agniveer as Hagniveer, simply because we don't believe in the jati system.

While Agniveer initially started with the reconversion of Muslims, it later shifted its focus to caste-related issues and expanded its activities. In tribal belts, it faced challenges posed by missionary conversions. He says even in Delhi–NCR or the southern cities today, there is a 50 per cent probability that housemaids, sweepers, and similar individuals are Muslims or Christians, even if they bear Hindu names.

Why is this happening?

> There is a vulnerable section of Hindus. Dalits and tribals are two such groups who can be easily marginalised because other Hindus never built any bond with them. I don't know how many children the sweeper woman in our house has, how her children celebrate Diwali, or if they celebrate Diwali at all. I will tell you the mentality of people in Delhi–NCR. When Diwali sweets go stale and nobody eats them, we say, 'Give them to the sweeper.' You have no connection with them. You consider them as lowly individuals who are not even allowed to sit with you or eat the same sweets you eat. You ensure that your kids don't play with their kids. Now, a person from New Zealand, Australia, or England comes and starts staying in their shanty. Then you wake up and cry conspiracy against the Hindus and talk about funding from outside. But it had to happen.

The 'outsiders' celebrate Christmas and Easter with him, feeding him chocolate and cakes every Sunday. Hindu Twitter warriors make 'rice bag' jokes about Christian converts.

> You fail to realise that 'rice bag' is not a joke on that person; it is a joke on you. If they change sides for one rice bag, who is stopping you from offering two rice bags and bringing them back? When your immunity is weak, you will be prone to diseases. The same goes for the girls going away as a result of love jihad. We bring back Muslim girls, so we know how much energy is spent on them.

In the past two or three years, Agniveer has 'brought back' more than 200 people. 'We had organised havans here,' he says.

> Even if they are in relationships with the boys, they are trying to convert the boys to Islam. Stopping this and bringing them here is a challenging task. When a Hindu girl is converted, sweets are distributed throughout the entire mohalla because a kafir girl has been acquired. They see this as a victory because they have acquired a womb. To them, it is like a new machine that has arrived.

While Shivaji Maharaj and Maharaja Ranjit Singh are believed to have brought back lakhs of those who had converted to Islam, ghar wapsi in modern India was started by Swami Dayanand Saraswati. Swami Dayanand emphasised that if your people are leaving, you must bring them back. His Arya Samaj started the Shuddhi movement. Swami Shraddhanand took it a step further. Agvineer estimates that during his time, 25–30 lakh Muslims returned to Sanatan Dharma.

> However, the Hindus did not have sufficient absorption capacity. In fact, they repelled those who wanted to return. They would cut off connections with those coming back and wouldn't marry their daughters to them. As a result, many of them returned to Islam. When someone goes back, they have to exhibit extra loyalty. Those people became the most orthodox. So, the Tablighi Jamaat was started in retaliation to the Shuddhi movement. In the Mewat region of Haryana and Alwar in Rajasthan, the highest number of shuddhi conversions happened. So, the Tablighi Jamaat started there.

It was then that a section of orthodox Hindus began promoting the narrative that Arya Samajis were not Hindus. As a result, there is a separate Arya Samaj Act for marriage.

You forced the Arya Samajis to such an extent that it obstructed their Shuddhi movement. So, the Arya Samajis were compelled to say that they had a separate belief system. They write 'Arya Samaj' and 'Vedic Hindu religion' in brackets on their certificates. Instead of supporting your protectors, you are saying that they are not a part of your society. Arya Samajis of today were Sardars (Sikhs) 200 years ago. The Sikh community was created for our protection. In Punjab, every Hindu mother raised her first-born son as a Sikh after Guru Gobind Singh. Every Hindu mother in Punjab vowed to make her first-born son a warrior. Sikh means warrior. Your fighting arm separated from you after 200 years. Arya Samaj was your fighting wing. Arya Samajis were not even 0.001 per cent of the total Hindus. But still, why is it that *Rangila Rasul* was written by an Arya Samaji? Because no one else had the gumption. The might of Dayanand ensured that if you attacked my religion, I would call your Prophet into question. I don't fear death.

Today's Sikh separatism and the Khalistan movement also have roots in such misconceptions, says Vashimant.

All Sikh heroes and gurus were Hindus. Khalistanis have successfully created propaganda that Guru Nanak refused to wear the janeu. I have written an article on this. No *Janamsakhi* [the biographies of Guru Nanak] proves that he refused. Guru Nanak conducted a havan during his marriage as well. He used to wear the janeu and tilak. Guru Gobind Singh wore a dhoti at his wedding. The Sikhs were not separate, but you let them become separate. You may have heard about Banda Singh Bahadur. There was no Singh, no Banda, no Bahadur in his original name. His name was Lakshman Das Bairagi. He was a Dogra Rajput warrior from Jammu and belonged to the Vaishnav sect. He became a Sikh general. In contemporary books, he is identified as a Sardar. Now, his name is written as Sikh Jarnail Sardar Banda Singh Bahadur. He was never a Sikh. And who said that? Historian Bhai Parmanand from Punjab, a direct descendant of Bhai Mati Das, who was a Sikh martyr. Bhai Parmanand wrote the book *Veer Bairagi*. He was also an Arya Samaji, though he had a Sikh ancestry. Like Bhagat Singh's grandfather, he was also a Sikh but an Arya Samaji. That is why Bhagat Singh fought this battle.

Vashimant says the VHP's Dharm Jagaran Manch, backed by the RSS, has done a commendable job on ghar wapsi. He also credits the VKA. Agniveer, which currently has 4,000–5,000 active members, works in coordination with these organisations in certain areas.

He speaks about Dang, an area in Gujarat, adding that nearly 5,000 people have been reconverted there:

> We had been focusing on Dang. Almost 80–90 per cent of the population there are Christians. We picked a district with 327 villages. Our Agniveer team works in all those 327 villages. Instead of diversifying our resources, we wanted to develop a proof of concept.

Unemployment is a significant problem in the tribal-dominated region of Dang. The tribal population has been kept so disconnected that they see anyone coming from outside as a messiah. Agniveer started job-generating activities there, such as making paper plates and cultivating crops that sell at a good price, like mushrooms and Ganoderma, a wood-decaying fungus with medicinal properties. A single set-up can support twelve to fifteen families.

> When a family achieves financial stability, they all attend our bhajan-kirtan programmes every Saturday. Through bhajan-kirtans, they have now embraced our path. The conversions there have a completely different character. These are not certified conversions. Missionaries claim that temples are places of Satan and encourage them to come to churches. They lure these people with chocolates for their children. They are easily swayed.

Vashimant says a lot of ghar wapsi is lined up in UP and Rajasthan. In these places, intensive work has already been done, and apparently, results are showing now. A fair amount of effort goes into reconverting Muslims to Hindu dharma. Some of them had been trapped by love or money, others by ideology. Agniveer workers try to convince them ideologically, explain the futility, and challenge them to debates. Vashminant narrates a personal experience.

> There was a nineteen-year-old boy from Bengaluru whom Zakir Naik had converted. This was in 2009–10. For one year, he practised Islam and underwent khatna or circumcision. I was tasked with working on him. I was in touch with him. He was very abusive in the first three months. He would tell me, 'So, you have come back to be abused?' Then slowly, he started to listen to what I had to say. One day during Diwali, I told him, 'Bring anybody whom you think can debate with me.' He brought someone and witnessed the debate. By then, I had softened them up, and he told those who had come to argue Islam's case, 'You are liars and frauds, and I am going back.' This was someone who was told that Islam was very good. This type of technique also works on girls who have embraced Islam, having been told that it is very good. We speak to them about women and

Islam. Many girls understand. The success rate is around 20 per cent.

Agniveer has compiled a database of 3,000 cases in which women had their throats slit for objecting to being forcefully fed beef or for refusing to give up idol worship. The list includes girls who were coerced into sleeping with their partners' brothers and uncles and were gang-raped by up to fifteen people.

> We present these instances to the girls and alert them that they could fall victim to similar crimes. They often argue that their lovers are not like that. We ask them to discuss Islam with them. We encourage them to ask questions about the Prophet, such as why Mohammed married a six-year-old girl? Our aim is to push them out of their comfort zone. Sometimes they ask and discover the truth for themselves. This is a long-drawn-out process. It is not resolved in a single session. Some people required counselling for six months before returning. Others did not.

Agniveer's next frontier is exceedingly ambitious. It has started work in the strongest bastion of Islamism, the origin of the philosophy that inspires a vast section of radical Muslims worldwide: Deoband.

> I happen to be in Deoband these days. In Deoband, there are three predominant castes: Jats, Gujjars, and Rajputs. Conversions occur within these three castes. They were aware of their Hindu roots. Now, in Deoband, there are hardly any Hindus left. A village identifies itself as a Muslim Gujjar village, knowing that their ancestors adopted Islam during the time of Aurangzeb or Akbar, hundreds of years ago.

Many Gujjars from both sides, Hindus and Muslims, are aware of their shared lineage. There exists a biological connection, which we leverage. We tell them, 'They are your brothers, or you are our maternal cousin.'

In rural areas, people are not very fanatical, says Vashimant. In west UP, Muslims are willing to come back. But the caste problem is a big hindrance. The caste panchayats of Rajputs, Tyagis, Gujjars, and Jats have witnessed entire villages coming forward in the past ten to fifteen years, requesting to be taken back. But the panchayats refuse, citing that they have changed sides and have been consuming beef.

But there are converted people who still abstain from eating beef, hoping that someday they will be accepted back. So, it is not a very one-sided issue. Hindus are not the only victims; they are also perpetrators. We have approached ten to fifteen cases. They agreed but asked us, 'Who will marry our daughters? Will they be accepted?' Last month, I went with some prominent Tyagis of this area to a Muslim Tyagi village. They know that there are relatives on either side. I had told the Hindus that all they have to say there is, 'We accept you.' But they did not say that. Instead, they said, 'We have just come to meet you. We have no agenda as such.' They promised me something else but changed their stance there.

Vashimant says wherever there are intelligent people, this strategy succeeds. 'We have done a lot of work on this in western UP. In the next two to three years, you will see a huge success in this, hopefully in lakhs, God willing. Work is ongoing to soften them up.'

Omendra Ratnu and Jay Ahuja

Away from the bustling pink parts of Jaipur, on the lawn outside a modest office on Shipra Path Road, friends Dr Omendra Ratnu and Jay Ahuja sip tea made from goat milk as the late morning sun intensifies.

This is the office of Nimittekam, an NGO primarily focused on assisting Hindu and Sikh refugees from Pakistan and integrating Dalits into the Hindu mainstream. Since its inception in 2016, Nimittekam has helped more than 12,000 people belonging to persecuted religious minorities such as Hindus and Sikhs from India's neighbouring countries. It has also facilitated long-term visas for every individual in need. And working behind the scenes without much fanfare, it lobbied and laid the groundwork for the passing of the Citizenship Amendment Act, leveraging concrete insights backed by official data.

Nimittekam has also initiated seven employment and basic skill development programmes for girls and women from impoverished families in Jaipur. This initiative has assisted more than 300 people in becoming economically productive and self-reliant. It also provides basic supplies and education to 120 orphaned children.

Jaipur-based ENT surgeon Dr Omendra Ratnu, who runs his own hospital, was engaged in social work when he met like-minded nationalist and businessman Jay Ahuja. Apart from conducting intensive groundwork and serving as the interface with the media, Ahuja provided the land on which the NGO operates today.

Dr Ratnu, who is also a singer, composer, writer, activist, and a Bhagavad Gita commentator, says:

> My friendship with Jay is purely ideological. Both of us agree that Hindus are in an existential conflict with forces aiming

to break India, and the Hindu samaj is lulled into inaction. So, our task is clear—to save as many Hindus as we can and awaken as many as possible.

His book *Maharanas: A Thousand-Year War for Dharma* is about the great kings of Mewar who fought Islamic invaders and refused to surrender even when their kingdom was encircled by enemies.

Dr Ratnu recently established the Dharmansh Foundation of India as a central fund for Hindu organisations working on the ground. It is his life's mission now.

> It is a platform for the economic consolidation of Hindus. As of today, there is no central core fund dedicated to the Hindu cause anywhere in the world. Dharmansh Foundation aims to fill that gap. A central, generic fund for Hindus everywhere. Rs 100 per Hindu per month, and we can fund Hindus on the ground. We will fight legal battles. We will fund those who build the dharmic narrative and combat the forces aiming to break India.

Nimittekam takes care of about 20,000 Hindus in Jodhpur and 10,000 in Jaipur. That includes their medical care, assistance with legal issues, police verification, visas, surrendering of documents to the relevant authorities, and eventually helping them acquire citizenship.

> We want to dismantle the evil death cults masquerading as religion because there can be no coexistence with mad dogs. Rape and murder are not religious activities. If any ideology, book, or mafia claims divine sanction for raping and murdering Hindus, then we must confront them. If you keep the wolf and the sheep in the same barn, inevitably the

sheep will suffer. Nimittekam envisions a free India, a free-market economy, and a liberal Bharat where every citizen is respected and protected.

How can greater Hindu unity be achieved? Dr Ratnu suggests that organisations like Nimittekam and Dharmansh Foundation are needed to awaken Hindus to action, either through donations and voluntary work or by building narratives through talks and seminars.

Greater Hindu unity will occur when the truth about cults masquerading as religion is spoken by the dharmaacharyas and mathadhishas [spiritual leaders]. Unfortunately, the Hindu opinion-makers of this nation are spreading lies of 'sarva dharma samabhav … vada pav'. It is a prescription for death. A significant portion of the Hindu leadership is either dull-headed or compromised. First, we must recognise the threat and articulate it properly. Today, Hindus fail to see the danger. '*Hum toh 8,000 saal se zinda hain, 8,000 saal aur zinda rahenge* [We have been alive for 8,000 years, and we will continue to live for another 8,000 years],' they say. How do you address this kind of inaction? A lot of assimilation work is needed.

Both of his parents were sanitation workers, or safai karmacharis, in Tamil Nadu. As the family's financial condition improved slightly, they started selling coconuts. Even during difficult times and while living in Chennai's Triplicane slum for a part of their lives, they ensured that their two daughters and two sons received an education. Today, one of their children, Ma Venkatesan, represents an estimated five million safai karmacharis across India. In 2021, he became the chairman of the National Commission for Safai Karmacharis.

This workforce broadly encompasses nine types of sanitary work, including cleaning sewers, latrines, faecal sludge handling, railway cleaning, work in waste treatment plants, community and public toilet cleaning, school toilet cleaning, sweeping and drain cleaning, and domestic work (according to a study by Dalberg Associates in 2018). Most of them come from the scheduled castes (SC) or Dalits.

Venkatesan, forty-three years old, is married with a daughter and a son. He started attending the local RSS shakha when he was just nine years old, studying in fourth grade. He earned his BA and MA in Philosophy from Vivekananda College, Mylapore, and joined the BJP in 2013. In 2016, he contested the Egmore elections and lost. He then became the state president of the BJP SC Morcha in Tamil Nadu.

Venkatesan has written eight books in Tamil on Dalit issues. One of these, *The Other Side of Periyar*, became popular. He also wrote *Hindutva Ambedkar*, in which he explains how, contrary to perception, B.R. Ambedkar was supportive of Hindutva.

One question that Venkatesan often faces is about the BJP's supposed anti-Dalit image. But elections in the last ten years have proven that the scheduled castes, scheduled tribes, and the entire spectrum of backward castes have solidly supported the BJP, joining its ranks in unprecedented numbers. This has derailed political attempts to forge a Meem–Bhim or Muslim–Dalit coalition. The BJP used to be seen as a Brahmin-Baniya party from North India. How did Dalits and tribals come to join its fold?

Ma Venkatesan says:

> After Modi became the CM in 2002, he did a lot for Dalits and tribals in Gujarat. I can recall two incidents. He took the

Indian Constitution on an elephant [the symbol of Dalits] for a yatra around the state. He also encouraged many Dalits to become priests in temples. Thanks to him, the lifestyle of SC and ST people improved. Every household has a tap water connection. During the Congress era, casteism was prevalent, and people faced many difficulties. They did not have access to water. After Modi gained power, things improved. During the 2014 elections, he garnered a lot of Dalit votes. He brought Dalit leaders from across the nation together in 2014, including Udit Raj in UP, Ramvilas Paswan in Bihar, and Ramdas Athawale in Maharashtra. He gave confidence to Dalit leaders that if they supported the BJP, the community would rise. He explained how he helped the Dalit community in Gujarat. After that, all these leaders teamed up with him.

Venkatesan then lists what Narendra Modi has done from 2014 to 2024 for the Dalit community:

- Modi celebrated the 125th birth anniversary of Ambedkar.
- There is a house of Ambedkar on Delhi's Alipur Road, where he had passed away. Modi allocated Rs 194 crore to restore that house, instilling confidence among Dalits that something was being done for them.
- He built the Dr Ambedkar International Centre at Janpath Road, featuring a unique statue of Ambedkar sitting cross-legged. This statue, not found elsewhere in India, serves as a source of pride for the Dalits.
- Ambedkar was cremated at Indu Mill in Maharashtra, where a large memorial is currently under construction.
- A memorial has been erected at the place in London where Ambedkar used to reside.

- Narendra Modi has significantly raised awareness about Ambedkar's contributions, particularly highlighting his role in establishing the Reserve Bank of India.
- He launched a dedicated website for Ambedkar, containing his writings, books, and comprehensive information, linked with the Ministry of External Affairs website.
- The Modi government amended the SC/ST Atrocities Act and declared 26 November as Constitution Day.
- Modi appointed a record number of Dalit ministries, with twelve SC ministers and eight ST ministers currently serving in the government.
- He expanded scholarships for MPhil and PhD candidates from the SC community.
- The BJP facilitated entrepreneurship among SC/ST individuals by creating hubs across the nation. Through Startup India, SC/ST entrepreneurs can access loans up to Rs 1 crore without collateral, with a new provision introduced specifically for SC/ST women.

Are Modi's efforts for the SC/ST community reaching the grassroots? Are people on the ground aware that their community is benefitting from them?

> North Indians are well aware, but people in the south are not. Because Tamil Nadu has been ruled by the Dravidian parties for almost sixty years, the dynamics here are different from those in the north. It is a political issue, but now people from the SC community are slowly becoming aware. This time there will be a change in Tamil Nadu. And not just in Tamil Nadu but also in Kerala, Telangana, and Andhra Pradesh.

He says there are three major sub-castes of SCs in Tamil Nadu: Paraiyar, Devendrakula Vellalar, and Arunthathiyar. Paraiyars comprise almost one crore (17–18 per cent) of the population, Devendrakula Vellalars make up about 50–60 lakh, and Arunthathiyars about 20 lakh.

PM Modi addressed a longstanding demand of the Pallar community to be renamed Devendrakula Vellalar. Ahead of the 2021 assembly elections in Tamil Nadu, the Lok Sabha passed the Constitution (Scheduled Castes) Order (Amendment) Bill, 2021.

Ma Venkatesan praises the tireless organisation-building efforts of Tamil Nadu BJP president K. Annamalai, who hails from the OBC Gounder caste. 'We need a powerful leader in the south from the SC community, and currently, we lack one. There are three or four emerging leaders from this community in Tamil Nadu. In another two years, we anticipate things will be better,' he says.

Venkatesan asserts that the RSS is quietly undertaking incredible efforts for the scheduled castes and tribes in Tamil Nadu, but it refrains from advertising them.

> I am from the SC community, and all campaigners have visited my house for meals. You may not be aware, but many SC girls have married RSS karyakartas. There have been numerous inter-caste marriages. Despite government reports indicating Maharashtra as having the highest number of intercaste marriages, it's actually Tamil Nadu. The RSS faces this issue; it refrains from highlighting the positive work it's engaged in. If there is any caste-related problem, the RSS is typically the first to intervene. They convene both parties peacefully and provide explanations. I remember one incident in Uthapuram where a wall was erected to stop Dalits from entering, leading

to a massive uproar. Communists demolished the wall, but the conflict persisted. Finally, the Sangh intervened, mediated between the parties, and restored peace. However, there was no publicity about this intervention.'

Venkatesan narrates another incident:

> There are usually different cups for SC and non-SC people at tea stalls in Tamil Nadu. Even when you visit someone's house, they don't serve SC people water in glasses; they just pour it into their hands. These practices still occur today. In some areas, you can't even enter with your slippers on; you have to enter barefoot. The RSS intervened in these issues as well. In Theni, they opened tea shops in SC areas and started drinking tea at those shops. As a result, shop owners who used to keep separate cups based on caste faced significant financial setbacks. They apologised for their behaviour and promised not to do it again.

The RSS, he says with a smile, did not publicise this either. He recalls how the Sangh brought major changes to the slums of Chennai, where he grew up.

> When I was in the fourth standard, they came to our area. Back then, no one there had studied beyond the tenth standard. Everyone used to smoke and drink. But the RSS folks started offering tuition classes in the area, and the situation changed. Now, many people from there have government jobs. The area around Parthasarasarathy Temple in Chennai is entirely populated by Brahmins. There is a Brahmin RSS karyakarta who lives there. He started offering tuition classes, which attracted many scheduled caste students to the area for their education.

In Kerala and Gujarat, RSS karyakartas train SC/ST people as priests. In many mandirs around the Tirupati Temple, the VHP has trained and appointed priests from backward castes, says Venkatesan. 'Such a wonderful practice has not come to Tamil Nadu because this is "Periyar bhoomi",' he says, breaking into a belly laugh. Venkatesan is confident that Hindutva will prevail in Tamil Nadu and overcome Periyar's ideology.

> Dravidian parties have ruled Tamil Nadu for sixty years but have not given a single SC or ST chief minister or deputy CM. Now, the BJP has Dalit deputy CMs in Madhya Pradesh and Rajasthan. There are many BJP MLAs and party presidents from scheduled castes. But in Tamil Nadu, there are none in the Dravidian parties. Here, you can't even nominate an SC candidate from a general constituency. But the BJP has done it in Tamil Nadu. The BJP has had two state presidents from the scheduled castes.

Venkatesan notes that the former party president from Tamil Nadu, L. Murugan, is from the Arunthathiyar community, the smallest among the scheduled castes. Additionally, two individuals from his community have been given Rajya Sabha seats.

In Tamil Nadu, most Dravidian leaders are devout Hindus, he says. But hypocritically, because of Periyarism, Sanatan Dharma is relentlessly attacked under the guise of opposing Brahmanism. Only 2 per cent of the population are Brahmins, while there are significantly more backward castes (BC) and other backward castes (OBC).

> The OBC–BC people have been passing diktats, such as saying Dalits should not go to temples or wear shoes. But they put the blame on Brahmins, and Brahmins have become

the villain. For instance, not a single zamindar is a Brahmin. There are hardly any Brahmins in politics too. J. Jayalalitha was a Brahmin, but she was protected because MGR was her mentor. MGR promoted her because of her knowledge and popular cinematic persona.

Venkatesan says the extent of conversions in Tamil Nadu is massive. In a village near Kanchipuram, for instance, fifty members of the Apostolic Christian Church recently faced resistance from residents and members of the Hindu Munnani as they went around a local temple asking people to convert.

In Madurthamalai, near Coimbatore, a student named Dinesh Kumar alleged that he was being coerced into converting to Christianity. He reported incidents of torture and physical assault for refusing to change his faith. Additionally, his educational documents were confiscated.

A television channel recently exposed instances where students were allegedly coerced into converting to Christianity. The National Commission for Protection of Child Rights (NCPCR) had to intervene and issue a notice to the Tamil Nadu Director General of Police. Parents of a Class VI girl in Kanyakumari released a video in April 2022 showing how a teacher forced students to recite Christian prayers and denounce Hindu deities.

Venkatesan feels that at the core of the conversion problem lies the societal failure to treat the scheduled castes humanely.

> Almost all SC leaders support conversions. They [missionaries] do a lot of brainwashing. If we create strong SC leaders, they can stand against conversions. In 2004, when Shankaracharya of Kanchi Kamakshi Peetham Jayendra Saraswathi was around, the RSS and BJP had started a conversation with the

community, but the initiative tapered off. People from within the community need to lead and persuade. Only then we will see a change.

Ma Venkatesan lists a slew of measures he has taken since he started heading the National Commission for Safai Karmacharis. These include clearing workers' dues up to Rs 10 lakh each.

People used to wait very long for payments. We started clearing dues in two to three days. The Supreme Court had instructed that sanitation workers receive Rs 25 lakh each, but we have disbursed Rs 30 lakh each. In every review meeting, we raise the issue of salary hikes, provident funds, and other benefits for sanitation workers. We have made insurance compulsory. We have also taken steps to make temporary contractual workers permanent staff.

Earlier, sanitation workers in only twelve states were using safety equipment. Within a year, this was extended to thirty-two states. Venkatesan travels for twenty days a month. He meets with the chief ministers, governors, chief secretaries, and collectors in the states to discuss the welfare of sanitation workers. 'People have started realising that there is a commission. A lot of complaints and grievances have started coming,' he says, smiling.

Abha Khanna

No region in Bharat has garnered more public attention than Kashmir. Until recently, it was primarily for the wrong reasons. Since the repeal of Article 370 in Article 35A, and the loss of its special status on 5 August 2019, the snow is melting. This time, from all evidence, for the right reasons.

These laws had stripped away the rights of the state's women, Pakistani Hindu refugees, LGBTQ+ individuals, Dalits, sanitation workers, and had served as the primary legal leverage for Pakistan-backed terrorism and separatism.

A plethora of development schemes have been implemented since then. Last year, the T-5 tunnel at Panthyal in Kashmir's Ramban district was inaugurated. The 870-m-long tunnel cost Rs 100 crore. This stretch of the strategic national highway (NH44) was previously notorious for landslides, turning it into a death trap. The year before last, the road had been closed down, resulting in a loss of Rs 1,500 crore for Kashmir's famed apple industry.

The 272-km Udhampur–Srinagar–Baramulla Rail Link (USBRL) is set to be completed by 2025. Featuring thirty-eight tunnels, it promises to be an engineering marvel. Additionally, the project includes the world's highest Chenab Bridge. PM Modi inaugurated the first electric train service in the Valley and launched the train service between Sangaldan and Baramulla stations. This year, the prime minister has initiated infrastructure projects for the state worth Rs 30,500 crore (approximately $3.65 billion).

Jammu and Kashmir welcomed approximately two crore (20 million) visitors in 2023, marking the highest influx in seventy-seven years. As the laughter of children echoed through Kashmir's idyllic gardens, the sounds of gunfire faded into the background. Terrorist incidents in J&K decreased to 44 in 2023 from 228 in 2018. In contrast, from 52 protests and 1,221 stone-pelting incidents in 2018, the number of organised protests dwindled to zero in 2023.

In the deeper background, significant civilisational changes have been quietly underway. Hindu organisations like the Art of Living have been engaged in deradicalising Kashmir's youth and reintegrating surrendered militants into the social mainstream.

The RSS and its affiliates have been quietly conducting their research, assessment, and actions. Rashtriya Sewa Bharati, affiliated with the Ekal Vidyalaya Abhiyan project, operates 1,250 schools in the Valley. Remarkably, more than 95 per cent of the students enrolled are Muslim. The schools are dispersed across ten districts, including extremely sensitive areas like Baramulla, which frequently witness sporadic terror attacks on civilians and security forces. Since 2022, there has been a 53 per cent increase in the number of ekal vidyalayas in Kashmir, rising from 800 to 1,250 in just two years.

The ekal vidyalaya project in Kashmir has persisted for years despite facing extreme hostility and endangerment to the lives of nationalistic social workers. Certain aspects of the school project were developed discreetly. Sometimes, even the teacher, tasked with delivering the nationalistic curriculum, might not have been aware that they were part of an RSS-supported education project.

Another RSS-supported project in the state is the Jammu and Kashmir Study Centre (JKSC), serving as a research organisation and think tank. Until recently, one of its most prominent faces was Abha Khanna, a fifty-two-year-old journalist with twenty-seven years of experience.

Abha Khanna was born and raised in Delhi. She attended a convent school and pursued her post-graduation in English literature. In 1997, she began her career at *Hindustan Times*, where she worked for twelve years. Following this, she had a short stint with *Sakal Times*, which shut shop within months. Khanna then worked as a freelancer for a long time before assuming the role of media director at the Jammu and Kashmir Study Centre (JKSC).

> I felt it was my calling. It was the most satisfying role I have ever had. It didn't feel like a job because I was volunteering my time there. A friend invited me to attend one of its seminars in Delhi. Since I was not feeling well, I intended to leave after an hour. But I found myself unable to do so. What struck me was that, despite being a journalist for so long and having Jammu and Kashmir as my favourite subject, the experts shared basic information that I was unaware of.

In 2002, just before the elections when Atal Bihari Vajpayee was the prime minister, Abha visited J&K. She was also in regular contact with J&K correspondents for updates on news from the state.

> An expert (whose name escapes me now) showed us a map of J&K. I was surprised to see how small Kashmir was in comparison to Ladakh, which constituted the largest landmass of the undivided state, and also Jammu. Kashmir accounted for just about 15 per cent of the erstwhile J&K. I was surprised by how much we talked about Kashmir in our reports and headlines, without ever addressing Jammu or Ladakh.

At the end of that meeting, Khanna approached the organisers and offered to work for them. They immediately welcomed her to JKSC.

> JKSC's team of volunteers was interesting. Some were researchers, others handled legal aspects, and some focussed

on raising awareness about issues. It was a diverse team, with some members being Kashmiris. They were all engaged in in-depth work. That was the first time I heard about Article 35A. Surprisingly, even some constitutional experts were unaware of it. Some judges on the constitutional bench of the Supreme Court were also not aware of Article 35A. Its insertion into the Indian Constitution was highly unconstitutional. It was a fraud.

Khanna and her team prepared a crisp but comprehensive note on Article 35A, outlining its social, legal, and national security implications. Article 35A was surreptitiously inserted at the insistence of then PM Jawaharlal Nehru via a presidential order, bypassing Parliament. It was directly inserted by the President into the appendix section of the Constitution, rather than being included in the main body. Article 35A derived its power from Article 370.

There were countless victims of Article 35A in J&K, but the mainstream media remained oblivious to it. These victims included Valmikis, women, and Pakistani refugees. Despite arriving after independence, the refugees continued to reside in temporary camps in Jammu even after seventy years. Human rights violations were rampant, but nobody, including the media, seemed willing to listen. When we raised these issues, it felt like we were speaking to a wall. It wasn't until we decided to challenge Article 35A in the Supreme Court that the media began to take interest and start covering it. Even then, JKSC conducted nationwide seminars and workshops to educate people about the truth, countering the narrative built by separatists and pro-Pakistan lobbies in the media. Before joining JKSC, I was naive. I was unaware of the media's deep biases.

Abha became actively involved when violence erupted at the National Institute of Technology (NIT), Srinagar, in 2016. The incident was triggered by India's loss in the T20 World Cup cricket match against the West Indies. Local Kashmiri students in Srinagar started celebrating, which upset students from outside Kashmir. The next day, the non-local students organised a march on the campus, holding the tricolour. But they were violently confronted by the local police simply because they had marched with the Indian national flag.

> I witnessed a brief scroll on a news channel. Upon inquiry, I discovered that several students had been severely beaten for holding the tricolour. Those who were bleeding received no first aid. Nobody listened to them. There was absolute silence from the media and politicians. This episode triggered something within me. It was the first I truly understood the power of social media. The incident occurred in the morning. By afternoon, we learned about it and started a campaign on social media. By evening, it had started trending. I spent the day on the phone and computer, urging people to take notes and provide coverage. Typically, TV channels swiftly pick up on a story, but in the Srinagar NIT case, it wasn't until 11.30 p.m. that one channel discussed the incident. And that was only because it had started trending on social media.

The Srinagar NIT case gained significant attention. Khanna remained in contact with the students at the campus.

> Can you believe that late at night, the students were asked to vacate the campus? There was no available transportation. It is not easy for a student in Srinagar to abruptly decide, 'I'm going home', especially if their home is outside the state.

Kashmir still wasn't a safe place. Our team intervened, and the situation was resolved. The students received justice.

Abha served as the director of JKSC for a couple of years before assuming the role of consulting editor with *Organiser Weekly*. She recounts how truth was manipulated in Kashmir. In 2002, towards the end of the bloodiest terror era of the nineties, she visited the state. Terrorism had not abated. 'The separatist media was amplifying the narrative that Kashmir would boycott the elections. But while speaking with common people, I sensed a completely different feeling. It seemed that people were actually looking forward to the elections,' she says.

Abha's assertions were eventually proved right, even though her journalist colleagues had initially trolled her. Her mentors at JKSC used to say that Kashmir was a matter of disinformation and misinformation, where both Kashmiris and the rest of India were being fed lies, ultimately fostering division between them. Then, on 5 August 2019, Article 370 and Article 35A were revoked, leading to the bifurcation of Jammu and Kashmir and the creation of Ladakh as separate union territories.

> It was one of the happiest, most jubilant days of my life. Things have changed remarkably in Kashmir now. I don't need to say it; it is for people to see how Republic Day and Independence Day are being celebrated there. Just the other day, somebody shared a photo showing the lights of Boulevard Road beside Dal Lake dressed in tricolour. There have been countless events indicating that the people of Kashmir have embraced the changes positively and are anticipating more changes. When things have been bad for so long, it takes time

to change. Nevertheless, the women of Kashmir are feeling much more relieved, terrorism has decreased, and daily killings are no longer happening.

Some of Khanna's friends recently visited Kashmir and were travelling in a local taxi. They asked the driver about the removal of Article 370. The driver mentioned that previously, his cab windows would often be broken due to stone-pelting, but such incidents ceased after 2019. Also, he noted that he was getting far more clients now.

These small pointers demonstrate how much things have changed. Abha suggests that we should shift the focus away from Kashmir and instead concentrate on liberating Pakistan-occupied Jammu and Kashmir (PoJK) and the areas of Ladakh occupied by China.

> The people of PoJK are extremely discontented. They look up to India, aware of the progress and democratic values prevalent on the Indian side, in stark contrast to their own stagnation. It's time we comprehend their issues and think about how to reintegrate them into India, while also devising strategies to remove the occupying forces. 'When we speak of PoJK, we are not only talking about the land but also about our people. Families have been separated since Pakistan's forcible occupation. Culturally, they are very similar. But PoJK feels left out because the rest of India has largely ignored their plight. It's imperative that we establish connections with the people of PoJK.'

Is a tornado of change going to blow across the Line of Control and end Pakistani occupation? Khanna's words certainly carry that whiff.

There are a thousand changes afoot in the new, resurgent Bharat. Some are evident, some are not easily apparent and some are emerging but still remain invisible. Whether the civilisation will draw inspiration from the best of its past to build a bridge to a creative and prosperous future, or succumb to darknesses from both external and internal sources, remains to be seen. This moment in Bharat's history will likely determine how strong that bridge will be.

Notes

Introduction: Civilisational Cyclone Alert
1. Prabhu Chawla, 'Modikaal Mantra for 1,000 years,' *The New Indian Express*, 11 February 2024, https://www.newindianexpress.com/opinions/2024/Feb/10/modikaal-mantra-for-1000-years
2. The Ministry of Information and Broadcasting tweet, 13 June 2023, https://x.com/MIB_India/status/1668593338243600384
3. Press Information Bureau, 'New India: Shedding the Vestiges of Colonial Past,' Ministry of Information and Broadcasting, 1 December 2022, https://pib.gov.in/FeaturesDeatils.aspx?NoteId=151220&ModuleId=2
4. Prime Minister Modi's reply to the motion of thanks on the President's address in the Rajya Sabha, Prime Minister's website, 7 February 2024, https://www.pmindia.gov.in/en/news_updates/pms-reply-to-the-motion-of-thanks-on-the-presidents-address-in-the-rajya-sabha-6/
5. Seshadri Chari, 'What Samjhauta blast acquittals mean for "saffron terror bogey" in election session,' ThePrint, 23 March 2019, https://theprint.in/opinion/what-samjhauta-blast-acquittals-mean-for-saffron-terror-bogey-in-election-season/210505/; Arun Anand, 'Bogey of Hindu terror,' *The Indian Express*, 6 April 2019, https://indianexpress.com/article/opinion/columns/bogey-of-hindu-terror-samjhauta-express-blast-verdict-acquittal-nia-5661310/

6 PTI, 'Minorities must have first claim on resources: PM,' *The Economic Times*, 9 December 2006, https://economictimes.indiatimes.com/news/politics-and-nation/minorities-must-have-first-claim-on-resources-pm/articleshow/754218.cms?from=mdr

Chapter 3: History: The New Kurukshetra

1 Sanghamitra, 'Krishna pointing the Eid moon, how the fake propaganda was busted,' OpIndia, 18 June 2018, https://www.opindia.com/2018/06/krishna-pointing-the-eid-moon-how-the-fake-propaganda-was-busted/; Jaya Bhattacharji Rose, 'Clarification on painting supposedly depicting "Eid ka Chand",' 17 June 2019, http://www.jayabhattacharjirose.com/clarification-on-painting-supposedly-depicting-eid-ka-chand/

2 My Ancient Aryavarta, '5 cases where true Indology exposed Audrey Truschke,' OpIndia, 18 April 2018, https://myvoice.opindia.com/2018/04/5-cases-where-true-indology-exposed-audrey-truschke/

3 https://jia.sipa.columbia.edu/online-articles/politics-demography-israeli-palestinian-conflict

Chapter 5: Narrative War: Mainstream Media vs Social Media

1 https://www.moneycontrol.com/elections/lok-sabha-election/indias-muslim-population-rose-over-43-from-1950-2015-eac-pm-working-paper-article-12716831.html

Chapter 8: Bharat's Queer and Conservative

1 Intersex variation refers to a person who, at birth, exhibits variations in their primary sexual characteristics, external genitalia, chromosomes, or hormones from the normative standard of the male or female body.

Chapter 11: Cow, Caste, Conflict, and Conversions

1. Aabhas Maldahiyar, 'Whitewashing genocides: Why KS Lal's claims of 80 million Hindus killed by Islamic barbarism hold water,' Firstpost, 13 November 2022, https://www.firstpost.com/opinion-news-expert-views-news-analysis-firstpost-viewpoint/whitewashing-genocides-and-history-phobia-why-ks-lals-claims-of-80-mn-hindus-killed-by-islamic-barbarism-hold-water-11618501.html
2. ET Online, 'Ajmer blast case: Assemanand acquitted by special NIA court; 3 other found guilty,' *The Economic Times*, 8 March 2017, https://economictimes.indiatimes.com/news/politics-and-nation/ajmer-blast-case-aseemanand-acquitted-by-special-nia-court-3-other-found-guilty/articleshow/57537022.cms?from=mdr

About the Author

Abhijit Majumder is a journalist, editor, and media entrepreneur with nearly 30 years of experience at India's topmost media houses. He is the co-founder and editor-in-chief of India's first Dolby Atmos–enabled audio, podcast, and video production platform Earshot. He is also the consulting editor of CNN-News18.

Abhijit was the editor of *Mid-Day, Mail Today,* and Asianet News (English and Hindi), and the resident editor of *Hindustan Times* (Delhi and NCR editions, and previously Bhopal and Indore editions).

Abhijit has interviewed leading politicians such as Amit Shah, Shivraj Singh Chouhan, Sachin Pilot, and Smriti Irani; spiritual leaders such as Sri Sri Ravi Shankar and Sister Shivani; film personalities such as Amitabh Bachchan, Salman Khan, and Aamir Khan; prominent mediapersons such as Tim Sebastian and Riz Khan; and former Chief of Defence Staff Bipin Rawat. He has also written columns and op-eds for a range of national and international media outlets. He writes on politics, social media, books, travel, and culture. He closely tracks and analyses political changes, especially the rise of the Right and nationalism in India and across the world.

www.ingramcontent.com/pod-product-compliance
Lightning Source LLC
Chambersburg PA
CBHW021807060426
42554CB00046B/683